REAL WORLD JUSTICE

STUDIES IN GLOBAL JUSTICE

VOLUME 1

Aims and scope
In today's world, national borders seem irrelevant when it comes to international crime and terrorism. Likewise, human rights, poverty, inequality, democracy, development, trade, bioethics, hunger, war and peace are all issues of global rather than national justice. The fact that mass demonstrations are organized whenever the world's governments and politicians gather to discuss such major international issues is testimony to a widespread appeal for justice around the world.

Discussions of global justice are not limited to the fields of political philosophy and political theory. In fact, research concerning global justice quite often requires an interdisciplinary approach. It involves aspects of ethics, law, human rights, international relations, sociology, economics, public health, and ecology. Springer's new series *Studies in Global Justice* takes up that interdisciplinary perspective. The series brings together outstanding monographs and anthologies that deal with both basic normative theorizing and its institutional applications. The volumes in the series discuss such aspects of global justice as the scope of social justice, the moral significance of borders, global inequality and poverty, the justification and content of human rights, the aims and methods of development, global environmental justice, global bioethics, the global institutional order and the justice of intervention and war.

Volumes in this series will prove of great relevance to researchers, educators and students, as well as politicians, policymakers and government officials.

Real World Justice

Grounds, Principles, Human Rights, and Social Institutions

Edited by

ANDREAS FOLLESDAL

University of Oslo, Norway

and

THOMAS POGGE

Centre for Applied Philosophy and Public Ethics,
Australian National University, Canberra, Australia,
Columbia University, New York, U.S.A., and
University of Oslo, Norway

 Springer

A C.I.P. Catalogue record for this book is available from the Library of Congress.

ISBN 1-4020-3149-1 (PB)
ISBN 978-1-4020-3149-6 (PB)
ISBN 1-4020-3141-6 (HB)
ISBN 978-1-4020-3141-0 (HB)
ISBN 1-4020-3142-4 (e-book)
ISBN 978-1-4020-3142-7 (e-book)

Published by Springer,
P.O. Box 17, 3300 AA Dordrecht, The Netherlands.

www.springeronline.com

Printed on acid-free paper

070918

Contents

Chapter 1

Introduction

Andreas Follesdal[1] and Thomas Pogge[2]

[1]The Norwegian Centre for Human Rights at the Faculty of Law and ARENA Centre for European Studies, University of Oslo; [2]Philosophy, Columbia University, New York, and Oslo University; Centre for Applied Philosophy and Public Ethics, Australian National University, Canberra

This volume discusses principles of global justice, their normative grounds, and the social institutions they require.

Over the last few decades an increasing number of philosophers and political theorists have attended to these morally urgent, politically confounding and philosophically challenging topics. Many of these scholars came together September 11–13, 2003, for an international symposium where first versions of most of the present chapters were discussed. A few additional chapters were solicited to provide a broad and critical range of perspectives on these issues.

The Oslo Symposium took Thomas Pogge's recent work in this area as its starting point, in recognition of his long-standing academic contributions to this topic and of the seminars on moral and political philosophy he has taught since 1991 under the auspices of the Norwegian Research Council. Pogge's opening remarks — "What is Global Justice?" — follow below, before brief synopses of the various contributions.

We are deeply grateful to all who made the conference possible, productive, and enjoyable: to Hilde Frafjord Johnson, Norway's Minister of International Development, whose opening speech is included in this volume; to Tom Eide of the Ethics Program of the University of Oslo, who conceived the idea and, in close collaboration with his colleagues Rolv Mikkel Blakar and Kristin Dobinson, secured the funding and organized the Symposium; to the Norwegian Research Council and its National Ethics Network which, on this and many other occasions, have done so much to strengthen moral and political philosophy in Norway; and to the participating scholars and students whose contributions coalesced to produce three days of engaging discussions as well as this volume. We also want to

A. Follesdal and T. Pogge, (eds.), Real World Justice, 1-19.

express our heartfelt thanks to Gillian O'Loghlin, Mike Bowern and Ling Tong who spent many long days helping us convert a bunch of unruly typescripts into the camera-ready copy required by the publisher.

The Symposium opened on the second anniversary of the destruction of the World Trade Center, and with the distressing news from Minister Johnson that her wonderful Swedish colleague Anna Lindh had not survived the stab wounds she had sustained the previous day. Deeply mindful of these realities, we sought to think clearly, critically, and concretely about how justice can be strengthened in a world so disfigured by violence and severe poverty.

What is global justice?

A literature search on "global justice" finds this to be a newly prominent expression — there are more books and essays on it in this millennium already than in the preceding one, at least as far as computers can tell. Of course, some of the broad topics currently debated under the heading of "global justice" have been discussed for centuries, back to the beginnings of civilization. But they were discussed under different labels, such as "international justice," "international ethics," and "the law of nations." This shift in terminology is significant.

Different users of a new expression may have diverse motives and ideas, and there may then be a personal element in the following account of the reflections that figured in its emergence.

We can begin with two distinctions. The first is between two different ways of looking at the events of our social world. On the one hand, we can see such events *interactionally*: as actions, and effects of actions performed by individual and collective agents. On the other hand, we can see them *institutionally*: as effects of how our social world is structured — of our laws and conventions, practices and social institutions. These two ways of viewing entail different descriptions and explanations of social phenomena, and they also lead to two different kinds of moral analysis or moral diagnostics.

Take some morally salient event, for example, the fact that some particular child suffers from malnutrition, that some woman is unemployed, or that a man was hurt in a traffic accident. We can causally trace such events back to the conduct of individual and collective agents, including the person who is suffering the harm. Doing so involves making counterfactual statements about how things would or might have gone differently if this or that agent had acted in some other way. We can then sort through these counterfactual statements in order to determine whether any of the causally relevant agents *ought* to have acted differently and thus is partly or wholly at fault for the regrettable event. This will involve us in examining whether any such agents could have *foreseen* that their conduct would lead to the regrettable event and could also reasonably have *averted* the harm without causing substantial costs to themselves or third parties. Inquiries of this kind might be referred to as *interactional moral analysis* or *interactional moral diagnostics* (Pogge 1995).

Regrettable events can also be traced back to standing features of the society or social system in which they occur: to its culture, for example, or to its institutional order. In this vein, one might causally trace child malnutrition back to high import duties on foodstuffs, unemployment to a restrictive monetary policy, and traffic accidents to the lack of regular motor vehicle safety inspections. Doing so involves making counterfactual statements about how things would or might have gone differently if this or that set of social rules had been different. We can then sort through these counterfactual statements in order to determine whether the causally relevant rules *ought* to have been different and whether anyone is responsible for defects in these rules that are partly or wholly to blame for the regrettable events. This will involve us in examining whether those responsible for the design of the relevant rules — for instance, members of the parliament — could have foreseen that they would lead to harm and could reasonably have reformulated the rules without causing substantial harm elsewhere. We might refer to inquiries of this kind as *institutional* moral analysis or *institutional* moral diagnostics.

The second distinction is that between *intra*national and *inter*national relations. These were traditionally seen as constituting distinct worlds, the former inhabited by persons, households, corporations and associations within one territorially bounded society, the latter inhabited by a small number of actors: sovereign states. National governments provided the link between these two worlds. On the inside such a government was a uniquely important actor within the state, interacting with persons, households, corporations and associations, and dominating these other actors by virtue of its special power and authority — its so-called *internal sovereignty*. On the outside, the government *was* the state, recognized as entitled to act in its name, to make binding agreements in its behalf, and so on — its so-called *external sovereignty*. Though linked in this way, the two worlds were seen as separate, and normative assessments unquestioningly took this separation for granted, sharply distinguishing two separate domains of moral theorizing: justice within a state, and international ethics.

Interactional moral analysis presumably emerged quite early in the evolution of moral thought. Institutional moral analysis is more demanding, presupposing an understanding of the conventional nature of social rules as well as of their, often statistical, comparative effects. Even a mere eighty years ago, the poor and unemployed were still often seen as lazy and delinquent merely on the grounds that others of equally humble birth had risen from dishwasher to millionaire. Many people then did not understand the *structural* constraints on social mobility: that the pathways to riches were limited and that the structure of prevailing markets for capital and labor unavoidably produced certain threshold rates of unemployment and poverty. Nor did they understand that existing rates of unemployment and poverty could be influenced through intelligent redesign of the rules. Today, after Keynes and after the US New Deal and various similar national transformations, these matters are quite well understood, and governments are held responsible for their decisions regarding institutional design and for the effects of such decisions on the fulfillment or frustration of human needs. This understanding has been — belatedly, yet very admirably — articulated in philosophy through John Rawls's classic *A Theory of Justice*. In this grand work, Rawls has firmly established social institutions as a separate domain of moral assessment and has marked this domain terminologically by associating it with the terms *justice* and *social justice*. This terminological innovation has taken hold, by and large, at least in Anglophone philosophy. So the term *justice* is now predominantly used in the moral assessment of social rules (laws, practices, social conventions and institutions) and only rarely in the moral assessment of the conduct and character of individual and collective agents. In the wake of Rawls, then, the distinction between *institutional* and *interactional* moral analysis has come to be marked as a distinction between *justice* and *ethics*.

We are quite familiar today with the focus of Rawls's book: with institutional moral analysis applied to the internal organization of one state. What is still missing, however, or just beginning to emerge in the last few years, is institutional moral analysis extended to the realm of international relations. This timelag is hardly surprising, seeing that the realm of international relations is traditionally conceived as so much smaller and more surveyable than the vast and highly complex inner workings of a modern national society. We do not need institutional moral analysis, it seems, for a world of a few dozen relevant actors in which, when bad things happen, it is usually pretty clear whose conduct is at fault.

The enduring grip of this traditional framework is nicely displayed by Rawls's late book on international relations — *The Law of Peoples* — which was published only five years ago and fully 28 years after *A Theory of Justice*. The earlier book exemplifies *institutional* moral analysis applied to the *intra*national realm: Rawls offers there a proposal for the comparative moral assessment of alternative ways in which a society's social order might be designed. The later book exemplifies *interactional* moral analysis applied to the *inter*national realm: Rawls offers there a proposal for what the rules governing state conduct should be. Institutional moral analysis — the idea of a comparative assessment of alternative such rule systems in light of the morally significant effects each would have — is absent from the later theory.

For Rawls buffs, let it be noted that the asymmetry is nicely apparent in the structure of the two theories. Rawls's international theory is *two*-tiered: it has an original-position thought experiment on one level and then a list of rules applying directly to the conduct of states on the other. His domestic theory is *three*-tiered: it has an original-position thought experiment on Level One, then the two principles of justice (Rawls's standard for assessing the comparative effects of alternative social institutions) on Level Two, and finally, on Level Three, concrete institutional arrangements which not only provide rules for the conduct of individual and collective agents, but importantly include so-called *constitutive* rules: rules that create and define certain agents, roles, and relationships rather than merely guide preexisting actors within a preexisting option space. Rawls thus complements his domestic theory of *justice* with an international theory (not of justice but) of *ethics*.

The concept of global justice breaks down the traditional separation of intranational and international relations and extends institutional moral analysis to the whole field. What motivates this dramatic reorientation? One important motive is the realization that the traditional conception of the world of international relations as inhabited only by states is untenable. We all know that this conception is rapidly losing its *explanatory* adequacy through the emergence and increasing stature of other agents on the international stage, such as multinational corporations, international organizations, regional associations, and NGOs. More important for our topic, however, is the realization that the *moral* adequacy of this traditional conception has always been lacking. It has never been plausible that the interests of states — that is, the interests of governments — should furnish the only considerations that are morally relevant in international relations.

Consider for example a long-term contract concerning the exportation of natural resources which the government of some African country concludes with a rich Western state or one of its corporations. Within the traditional philosophical framework, it is self-evident that such an agreement must be honored: "People are to observe treaties and undertakings" says Rawls's second principle of state conduct, and the third one adds: "Peoples are equal and are parties to the agreements that bind them" (Rawls 1999). But here is the reality. The African government is corrupt and oppressive, and its continuation in power depends largely on the military. The sales it conducts impose environmental harms and hazards on the indigenous population. Yet, most of these people do not benefit, because the revenues are partly siphoned off by the small political elite and partly spent on arms needed for military repression. (These arms are supplied by other rich Western states in accordance with other contracts executed, without coercion, between them and the African government.)

There is an obvious question here: by what right can a free and fair agreement between a military strongman in Africa and some foreign government or corporation entitle these two parties to deprive the inhabitants of that African country of their natural resources and to despoil their environment?

This question is invisible so long as we think of international relations as a separate realm in which each state is identified with its government. Conversely, once we see the question, the old philosophical framework becomes manifestly untenable. We cannot fail to recognize that it is a very substantial disadvantage of the existing international order that it recognizes rulers, merely because they exercise effective power within a state, as entitled to confer legally valid property rights in this state's resources and to borrow money in its name. Such recognition accords international borrowing and resource privileges to many governments that are unworthy of the name. These privileges are *impoverishing*, because their exercise often dispossesses a country's people who are excluded from political participation as well as from the benefits of their government's borrowing or resource sales. These privileges are moreover *oppressive* because they often give dictatorial rulers access to the funds they need to keep themselves in power even against near-universal popular opposition. And these privileges are *disruptive* because they provide strong incentives toward the undemocratic acquisition and exercise of political power, resulting in the kinds of coups and civil wars that are so common in the developing countries.

The concept of global justice thus breaks down the traditional separation of intranational and international relations and extends institutional moral analysis to the whole field. It makes visible how we citizens of affluent countries are potentially implicated in the horrors so many must endure in the so-called less developed countries, potentially implicated in the violence and hunger inflicted upon them.

The old framework was comfortable: we share responsibility for the institutional order of our own society and for any harms this order may inflict upon our fellow citizens. And we also share responsibility for our government's acting honorably abroad by complying with reasonable international laws and conventions, especially those relating to warfare, and by honoring its contracts and treaties. In this traditional framework, we generally bear no responsibility for the violence and poverty inflicted upon foreigners within the black box of their own state.

The new philosophical framework, associated with the expression "global justice," may not be so comfortable. Central to this framework is the causal impact of the design of the global institutional order upon the conditions under which human beings worldwide are living. Since the end of the Cold War, major components of this global order — such as the global trading system and the rules governing military interventions — have been substantially redesigned while other components — such as the international resource and borrowing privileges discussed earlier — have been left in place. There were many alternative ways in which the global institutional order could have been shaped and reshaped when, after the end of the Cold War, the North Atlantic powers found themselves in control. And the question is then: how would other paths of globalization have been different in their effects upon people worldwide, in their effects upon the incidence of violence, oppression, and extreme poverty, for example? And how, in light of such a comparative-impact assessment, is the existing global order to be judged in moral terms?

The global institutional order is causally related to the incidence of morally significant harms in two main ways. First, its rules may affect people quite directly. Consider, for example, the current WTO treaty system which permits the affluent countries to protect their markets against cheap imports (agricultural products, textiles, steel, and so on) through quotas, tariffs, anti-dumping duties, export credits, and subsidies to domestic producers. Such protectionist measures reduce the export opportunities of firms in the developing countries by constraining their exports into the affluent countries and also, in the case of subsidies, by allowing less efficient rich-country producers to undersell more efficient poor-country producers in world markets. In the absence of these constraints, the developing countries could realize an additional $700 billion annually in export revenues (UNCTAD 1999), which is over ten times the annual amount of all official development assistance worldwide. This particular aspect of the existing WTO treaty system may thus have a rather large impact on the incidence of severe poverty in the developing countries, understanding "impact" here in a counterfactually comparative way: if the WTO treaty system did not allow the protectionist measures in question, there would be a great deal less poverty in the world today. This example illustrates the more direct impact of the global institutional order on the living conditions of people worldwide.

The rules of the global institutional order may also affect people indirectly, by co-shaping the national institutional order under which they live. The international resource and borrowing privileges accorded to despotic rulers provide an obvious example. By enabling tyrannical rulers and juntas to entrench themselves in power and by giving potential such oppressors a strong incentive to try to take power by force, these privileges facilitate and foster oppressive and corrupt government in many developing countries where the resource sector is a large part of the national economy and where ordinary citizens have few means to resist their oppression.

Much more could and should be said about these two examples. But the point here is not to demonstrate injustice, but merely to illustrate what institutional moral analysis applied to the global institutional order would look like.

Now, insofar as the current global institutional order does turn out to entail substantially more violence and severe poverty than would exist under a better designed alternative order, we might go on to ask who bears responsibility for this order having been shaped the way it was shaped and whether these responsible parties could have foreseen and could reasonably have avoided that excess in violence and severe poverty.

The dominant role in shaping the post-Cold-War global institutional order was played by the governments of the more powerful developed countries, the so-called G-7 in particular. In shaping that order, these governments have given much weight to the interests of their domestic business elites and rather little weight to the interests of the poor and vulnerable populations of the poor countries. The resulting global institutional order is arguably unjust insofar as the incidence of violence and severe poverty occurring under it is much greater than would have been the case under an alternative order whose design would have given greater weight to the interests of the poor and vulnerable. Insofar as the G-7 countries are reasonably democratic, their citizens share responsibility for the global order their governments have wrought as well as for the comparative impact of this order upon human lives. At least this is the kind of moral diagnosis that would move center-stage if normative debates about international relations were to shift from the *international ethics* to the *global justice* paradigm, if institutional moral analysis were extended beyond the state.

To conclude, consider two objections that someone still heavily invested in the old international-ethics framework might want to put forward against the new philosophical paradigm.

Objection One holds that the global institutional order is immune from moral criticism insofar as it has been freely consented to also by the poorer and less powerful states. The objector would allow that, in some cases, the consent given to the WTO treaty system, for example, was perhaps problematic. He would be willing to entertain the possibility that some weak states were negotiating under considerable duress and also lacked the expertise to work out whether the asymmetrical market access rules they were being offered were better or worse for them than remaining outside the

WTO. Our objector might even be willing to consider that perhaps the bargaining power of states entering the negotiations was inappropriately affected by historical crimes, such as colonialism. Still, the objector would insist, *insofar* as states have freely and competently consented to common rules, these rules are morally acceptable. *Volenti non fit iniuria.*

The proponent of the new global-justice framework could reject this reasoning on three mutually independent grounds. First, the consent in question was given *by governments.* Such government consent cannot be considered consent *by the governed* unless the government in question is minimally representative of the interests of those it rules. Many governments in the poor countries lack such minimal representativeness. And their consent to the WTO treaty system or, more generally, to the present global institutional order cannot then shield this order from moral criticism on behalf of those they governed. The consent of the Mobutos, Sani Abachas, Mugabes, Suhartos, and SLORCs of the developing world, however freely and competently given, could not have given away the rights of their badly oppressed subjects.

Second, the proponent of global justice could point out that a government, even if it is minimally representative of the people it rules, cannot through its freely and competently given consent give away the *inalienable* rights of its subjects. What these inalienable rights are is controversial to some extent. But it is widely accepted that persons cannot give up their rights not to be tortured or enslaved and their rights to the most basic necessities of human survival. Insofar as the current global institutional order foreseeably causes such inalienable rights to be more widely unfulfilled than would be reasonably avoidable, this order cannot be defended by appeal to the direct or indirect consent of those whose inalienable rights are now unfulfilled.

Third, even if persons could give up even their most fundamental rights and could authorize their government to give up these rights on their behalf, such persons would have to be of some minimal age. Severe poverty and violence in our world disproportionately affect children. Neither children, nor their parents or governments can validly consent to the imposition upon these children of an institutional order under which their most fundamental rights are foreseeably and avoidably unfulfilled.

Objection One therefore fails. A global institutional order that — foreseeably and avoidably — produces a large excess of violence and severe poverty, such an order cannot be justified by even the unanimous consent of *all* governments.

Objection Two holds that it is the very point and purpose of governments to represent and promote the interests of their people. It is therefore entirely appropriate and permissible for rich countries' governments to do their utmost to shape the global institutional order in the best interest of their citizens.

There is evidently some truth in this objection. Surely a government is not required to give equal weight to the interests of all human beings worldwide, but rather is permitted to be partial by showing special concern for the interests of its own people, present and future. But such permissible partiality has its limits.

There are obvious ethical or interactional limits to a government's partiality: insofar as it is impermissible for us citizens to kill innocent people in order to advance our own interests, it is likewise impermissible for our government to do the same on our behalf.

The limits on permissible government partiality with regard to the shaping of the global institutional order are less familiar but no less indisputable (Follesdal 1991, 1997). Quite generally, partiality is legitimate only in the context of a "level playing field," broadly conceived as including fair rules impartially administered. This idea is familiar and widely accepted in many contexts: it is perfectly all right for persons to concentrate on promoting the interests of themselves or of their group, sports team, or relatives, provided they do so in the context of a fair competition. Because such a fair setting is a moral precondition for permissible partiality, such partiality cannot permissibly extend to the subversion of the level playing field. To the contrary, those who are *partial* in favor of their own group must, as a condition of the permissibility of such partiality, also be *im*partially concerned for preserving the fairness of the larger social setting. In a domestic setting, for example, it is entirely permissible for you to concentrate your time and money on securing a good education for your own children, at the expense of other children whose education you might also promote. Yet it would be morally wrong for you to seek to promote your children's prospects by using your political influence to oppose equal access to education for children whose gender, color, or class differs from that of your own children. In short: partiality of concern is alright within a minimally fair setting, but not alright when it seeks to undermine the minimal fairness of this setting itself. The minimal fairness of the terms of the competition must not itself become an object of this competition. And the justice limit, the institutional limit, to a government's partiality in favor of its own citizens is then that its partial conduct must not undermine the minimal fairness of the global institutional order. An appeal to permissible partiality cannot justify the imposition, by the most powerful governments on the rest of the world, of an unjust global institutional order under which a majority of humankind are foreseeably and avoidably deprived of anything resembling a fair start in life.

This concludes the sketch of the philosophical framework associated with the increasingly prominent expression "global justice." Distinctive of this framework is the focus on the causal and moral analysis of the global institutional order against the background of its feasible alternatives. Within this general global-justice approach, distinct conceptions of global justice will differ in the specific criteria of global justice they propose. But such criteria will coincide in their emphasis on the question of how well our global institutional order is doing, compared to its feasible alternatives, in regard to the fundamental human interests that matter from a moral point of view. Extending institutional moral analysis beyond the state, this question focuses attention on how the massive incidence of extreme poverty and violence in the world today might be reduced not merely through better government behavior, internally and internationally, but also, and much more effectively, through global institutional reforms that would, among other things, elevate such government behavior by modifying the options governments have and the incentives they face.

The importance of this global-justice approach reaches well beyond philosophy. It is crucial for enabling ordinary citizens — in the developed countries especially — to come to an adequate understanding of their moral situation and responsibilities. And it is very helpful also for pushing social scientists, and development economists especially, to overcome their bias toward explanatory nationalism, their tendency to explain poverty and hunger in terms of causal factors that are domestic to the societies in which they occur. However valid and useful, such nationalist explanations must be complemented by substantial inquiries into the comparative effects of global institutional factors upon the incidence of severe poverty worldwide. It is very satisfying that the development of the global-justice approach for once shows the owl of Minerva spreading its wings well *before* the falling of dusk, that philosophy can give an important conceptual impulse to economics, political science, and politics. What effect this impulse will have, however, remains to be seen.

Synopses

The volume addresses four main topics regarding global justice: the *grounds* for moral claims about the global institutional order, substantive normative *principles* for a legitimate such order, the role of legal *human rights* standards, and ideas for reshaping global *social institutions* so as to render them less unjust.

Grounds

Rainer Forst lays the challenge of providing sound arguments about global justice. Certain moral approaches to the problems of severe poverty and underdevelopment miss the real normative issues. They ignore the economic-political institutional reality of past and present injustice, thereby veiling rather than exposing the situation of global injustice. Humanitarian arguments of duties of the able to assist the deprived ignore the pervasive issues of economic exploitation and political powerlessness. Humanist arguments for securing a minimum of basic needs also miss the political and institutional root causes of poverty. A human rights focus recognizes the impact of institutions, though it tends to hold the domestic government responsible rather than addressing the global basic structure underlying the plight of the poor. Justice would seem to require more fundamental changes, beyond alleviating poverty and securing human rights. The global poor suffer not only from lack of means of subsistence, but from institutional injustice in the form of multiple domination and powerlessness.

Alison M. Jaggar hones the challenge further, insisting that issues of global justice must also inform our understanding of the injustice suffered by poor women in poor countries. It is not only their local culture that constrains their autonomy and makes them vulnerable to violence and exploitation. The global basic structure — the international political economy and strategies of global politics — also contributes significantly to the poverty and abuses suffered by poor women. Indeed, insofar as democratically elected Western powers bear responsibility for enforcing an unjust global order, it remains an open question whether the West is best for poor women in poor countries.

The challenge of global justice is thus before us. If there is a transnational order correctly regarded as a basic structure of justice it must be adequately justified to those subject to that order. The current system is very much in need of justification and should strive for the establishment of relations in which such justifications can really take place, among persons treated as agents, not to be subjected to structures of power they cannot influence. Which claims by the global poor must be met, what principles of justice do these claims support, and how might the institutions of a global basic structure satisfy these requirements?

The contributors of this volume explore and address this challenge in several ways.

Geert Demuijnck holds that insofar as people accept even minimal positive duties towards their unlucky compatriots, they should accept similar duties towards unlucky foreigners. There are plausible arguments in favor of implementing social justice by means of social security systems and the like at the national level. However, he argues that there are no convincing arguments for giving compatriots preference that would stop such institutions of social and economic rights at state borders.

Thomas Mertens lays out central features of three competing theories of international or global justice: Kant, Rawls and Pogge. They differ profoundly in how they distinguish among territorial layers of justice, especially between justice on the domestic, national level and justice on the international and global scale. Kant and Rawls, in different ways, argue that what justice requires differs across these layers, domestic requirements being stronger and more demanding than international requirements. Pogge agrees with Rawls's claim that the primary object of justice should be the "basic structure of society," but holds that a global basic structure exists and should be regulated by standards of justice. Mertens addresses a variety of objections to such cosmopolitanism, including empirical, conceptual and moral concerns. Regarding the latter, he argues that improved understanding of the causes of poverty under conditions of economic and political globalization may help bring us close enough to the faraway poor as to consider their lives as our moral responsibilities.

When, then, are we responsible for addressing the acute deprivations of others beyond state borders? One widely held view is that we are responsible for addressing or preventing acute deprivations insofar as we have contributed to them or are contributing to bringing them about. *Christian Barry* refers to this principle as the 'contribution principle,' and examines its plausibility and practical significance. Barry notes that while this principle is commonly invoked in global policy debates, the basis for the distinction between contributing to acute deprivations rather than merely failing to prevent them (or being altogether irrelevant to them) is rarely defined. He shows that, surprisingly, the idea of contribution cannot plausibly be interpreted in terms of purely empirical concepts of causation or in terms of a contrast between what happens through someone's agency as opposed to what would occur "in the course of nature." Determinations of whether an agent has contributed to another persons' deprivation depends, he argues, on prior evaluation of her conduct — such as whether her causal relevance to it results from her discontinuing assistance to that person or involves the failure to discharge a debt.

Barry argues that while it is not the only principle that can plausibly seen as relevant for identifying responsible agents, the contribution principle has many features that recommend it. He further supports this claim by examining and rejecting two common objections to the contribution principle — that it is a principle of "corrective" justice which does not help agents who are working out what to do in the future, and that it would absolve all but a few well-off agents from taking action to remedy acute deprivation because conclusive evidence of their contribution to it is lacking. He concludes that, to the contrary, a conscientious application of the contribution principle would likely call for changes in conduct, policies, and in the structure of global institutional arrangements — changes that would significantly advance the cause of alleviating acute deprivation.

Ser-Min Shei argues that the persistence of world poverty is a failure for which humankind as a whole is morally responsible, by having had full control over the ongoing global order which engenders world poverty. Each of us, the global poor included, bears this responsibility by simply being a member of humankind. In addition to our positive duty of mutual aid, we therefore share a negative duty to eradicate world poverty and to compensate the global poor for their loss and suffering. But because of their difficult situation, he points out, the current global poor must bear much less of this burden than the rich and powerful. On the basis of a detailed account of 'harm' involving collectivities and groups, he agrees with Pogge that the global poor are harmed by the ongoing unjust global order imposed by the relatively affluent. He disputes Pogge's further claim that the relatively affluent individuals have *harmed*, and are harming, the global poor *unduly*, in virtue of supporting and/or participating in the ongoing global economic order.

Principles

What principles of justice should the global basic structure satisfy?

Stefan Gosepath considers, only to discount, the "Principle of Subsidiarity" as a fundamental principle for political order. Subsidiarity is often thought to guarantee a plurality and hierarchy of state and sub-state institutions or entities against an overly powerful supra-national political union. The principle appears to hold that authority should preferably be placed with smaller social institutions or entities rather than with larger ones — thus reducing the need for global transfers and other distributive arrangements. Gosepath argues that while subsidiarity is an essential and often neglected principle of justice, it does not deserve as prominent a status as Catholic social teaching and the European Union treaties would have us believe. The Principle of Subsidiarity is subordinate to more general principles of justice, such as those of distributive justice. In particular, it is unjustified to place obligations of social and economic assistance with smaller institutions, such as the family — or with poor states in a global basic structure.

Alessandro Pinzani insists that citizens should be able to demand a justification of economic power as well as of legal and political power — especially since all three can devastate individuals' lives. We should not separate power in different spheres of human action, each with their own rules and principles, but instead consider the complex network of power that provides some with the capacity to determine other people's actions and behavior in a broad sense. Important power is wielded when manipulating others' opportunity spaces. All exercises of such power require justification. In particular, he argues that the problem of world poverty requires a double solution: we should first eradicate the immediate consequences of poverty, namely, death and suffering. Then, secondly, we should address the main causes of poverty by reducing the power gap between rich and poor, internationally and domestically.

Véronique Zanetti contrasts and discusses two distinct kinds of principles for global justice. The claim can either be to a minimal standard for each individual, or to equality regarding some index — be it chances, opportunities or resources. She argues, against both Rawls and Pogge, that a minimal standard is insufficient to realize global justice. A "pragmatic" renunciation of the "ideal" standard of global equality is at best an attempt at accommodating those who reject Rawlsian premises. Defending international redistribution on the basis of rich individuals' responsibility for unjust institutions may be sound. Yet this argument from "corrective justice" undermines the premises of the normative theory itself, leading to charges of double moral standards. The question Pogge addresses to Rawls must be answered by all contending theories: can we justify to the global poor to require the difference principle for the national level, while abandoning it for pragmatic reasons on the global level?

Alexander Cappelen provides an answer to Zanetti's challenge. He considers how a liberal egalitarian theory of international justice in principle can take account of national autonomy, and how legitimate claims to national autonomy might justify some international inequalities. Nations may be held responsible to some extent for the inequalities that result from factors under their control. However well such arguments hold in theory, they do not support present practice. Cappelen argues that the most important inequalities in the world today — those suffered by the poor of the poorest countries — can only to a very limited extent be attributed to differences in national preferences. Furthermore, the poorest countries in the world do not satisfy the minimal conditions for holding citizens responsible for national polices. Allowing some national responsibility for economic policies in principle does thus not allow us to hold these countries responsible for their own poverty. Even though certain types of international inequalities might be justifiable, the present global inequalities are not.

Human rights

International legal human rights are often regarded as central and plausible principles of global justice. Several contributors address the role and justification of human rights standards.

Henrik Syse presents and discusses the natural-law tradition from which the more recent human rights theories emerged. They share a critical potential against unjust aspects of existing social orders, and both insist that human relationships must rest on moral commitments rather than self-interest alone. He argues that human rights doctrines secularize the natural-law idea, seeking to avoid controversial premises concerning the harmonious order of the cosmos as created by God. The method of avoidance has come at a cost, holds Syse. Important for the topic of global justice, the natural-law tradition has long addressed other duty bearers than government officials, and offers more in the way of sources of motivational support than theories of human rights that strive to avoid metaphysical commitments.

Regina Kreide and Andreas Follesdal both respond to these challenges to human rights stemming from alleged global normative pluralism. *Regina Kreide* rejects the skeptical assumption that the fact of incommensurable interpretations of human rights and power struggles implies that there is no normative standard for judging the legitimacy of legal human rights. On the other hand, Kreide rebuts the "moralistic" claim that human rights can be directly deduced from moral principles. She discusses two procedural models of right justification, the "Deliberative Model" and the "Model of Fair Bargaining" which, despite certain similarities, differ in a major aspect. The Deliberative Model presupposes a "hierarchy of reasons" where Kantian moral arguments always trump non-moral arguments and moral and legal human rights are identical. Kreide argues that this approach universalizes human rights at the cost of narrowing the support for an agreement, excluding competing moral theories as well as arguments that appeal to specific cultural practices. Moreover, making a direct link between moral and legal human rights threatens to delegitimize the genuine idea of moral rights by making them seem too like instruments of political power. The "Model of Fair Bargaining" she lays out overcomes these problems as it is based on fair procedures that do not presuppose further inherent standards of moral evaluation. Nevertheless, it does not give up the idea of agreement about moral human rights: they can possess "performativity" in political negotiations; the author illustrates this idea by examining the process that led to the *Universal Declaration of Human Rights*.

Andreas Follesdal addresses the issue of whether human rights are "Western" in ways that undermine their use as standards for global and domestic justice. In what has come to be known as the "Asian Values" debate, he identifies several objections of this sort in the *Bangkok Declaration*. Drawing on Confucian, Hindu, and Islamic sources, he argues that very many theories of human rights and moral traditions condemn the behavior which human rights serve to protect against. Most of the objections fail to hold against a wide range of human rights theories spelling out their basis and content. The remaining objections do not repudiate human rights norms — at most they support some accounts and specifications of rights over others. Human rights can hardly be dismissed as an objectionable exercise in Western ideological imperialism.

Leif Wenar offers a practical conception of human rights that specifies the ways in which state officials must and must not act toward their own citizens. Violations of these human rights can morally permit — and in some cases morally require — interference by the international community. Historically, this conception of human rights only emerged after World War II. Before then state officials violated, coerced, and neglected those within their territories with almost total impunity, appealing to the Westphalian ideal of state sovereignty to immunize themselves from external criticism and intervention. For Wenar the theorist's task is to develop a theory that rationalizes, corrects, and extends the accounts of human rights in the various declarations and conventions — to extrapolate from what political leaders have actually accepted to what all individuals could reasonably accept. Such corrections must adjust the biases in these texts owing to their political genesis, seeking a unified account across competing human rights claims and other rights; and expanding the perspective to further agents than state governments. Wenar submits that the guiding question about human rights, practically conceived, is this: what are the considerations that state officials must and must not take into account, such that failures count as failure of legitimate state action permitting or requiring outside intervention? When their government fails to secure their human rights, individuals have a right that outside agents act to remedy the breach and prevent further infractions.

Wilfried Hinsch and Markus Stepanians attempt to spell out the conceptual commitments involved in speaking of a "right" not to suffer severe poverty. According to what they call the "classical" theory of rights as it is exemplified in the work of Wesley N. Hohfeld, for A to have a right is to stand in an interpersonal relation with at least one other person B. If so, a complete specification of a right not to suffer severe poverty requires the identification of the relevant duty-bearers. However, since such a right could not reasonably be conceived as a right everybody holds against everybody else but only against some others, the problem arises as how to identify the relevant group of duty-bearers. That is, the proposal to regard severe poverty as a human rights violation gives rise to what Hinsch and Stepanians call

"the allocation problem." To solve it is to say who the potential violators are. The authors suggest that doing so is a prerequisite of giving the idea of severe poverty as a human rights violation any substance beyond mere rhetoric.

Social institutions

The final set of contributions address some of the institutional changes required by global justice.

Thomas Pogge advances four critical reflections in regard to the first and most prominent of the widely celebrated UN Millennium Development Goals. Though retaining the idea of "halving extreme poverty by 2015," MDG-1 in fact sets a much less ambitious target than had been agreed to at the 1996 World Food Summit in Rome: that the number of poor should be reduced by 19 percent, rather than 50 percent. Tracking the $1/day poverty headcount, the World Bank uses a method that is internally unreliable and may paint far too rosy a picture of the evolution of extreme poverty. Shrinking the problem of extreme poverty, which now causes some 18 million deaths annually, by 19 percent over 15 years is grotesquely under-ambitious in view of resources available and the magnitude of the catastrophe. And this go-slow approach is, finally, rendered even more appalling by the contributions made to the persistence of severe poverty by the affluent countries and the global economic order they impose. An apparently generous gesture toward the global poor helps conceal these contributions.

Jean-Christophe Merle opposes two paradigms of global justice: just exchange and distributive justice, correlated with two different accounts of the causes of world poverty. The first paradigm is exemplified by John Rawls's *The Law of Peoples*, the second by Thomas Pogge's "An egalitarian law of peoples." Pogge presents his proposal of a Global Resources Dividend (GRD), proportioned to resource consumption, as modest (the levy amounts to only 1 percent of the global social product), expressing the hope that it can avoid the need for a powerful world government and thus be acceptable to Rawls and other opponents of global distributive justice. Tracing some of the massive institutional implications of global distributive justice, Merle argues that such modesty is ultimately incompatible with global distributive justice, which may be conceivable in the absence of a world government but cannot be implemented without one. In particular, he argues that corruption, which Pogge presents as a crucial cause of persistent poverty, cannot be stamped out without international interventions in domestic political and social affairs. And if, on account of such encroachments upon national sovereignty, the distributive-justice paradigm is in any case unacceptable to its opponents, then, Merle argues, it might as well set forth stronger distributive demands than Pogge's GRD envisions.

Andrew Kuper argues that normative political theory regarding international business must go beyond ethical or legal codes that can be adopted by corporations. Corporate agency and moral psychology must be taken seriously not merely as aspects of a kind of applied ethics but as a central problem of political philosophy and development theory. Theorists are still prone to understanding political authority in terms of territorially defined units. Instead, he argues that we must understand the empirical capabilities and opportunities of non-state actors, so as to allocate obligations that states cannot meet or that these actors are better at meeting. In particular, Kuper suggests that other actors than states should be given standing before the International Court of Justice, such as NGOs like Amnesty International and Human Rights Watch that may in a certain sense "represent" some basic interests against state governments. He also presents and discusses the UN Global Compact, an attempt at enticing multinational companies to voluntary subscribe to certain principles concerning human rights and environmental protection. The very inclusive strategy pursued by the UN has unfortunately served to water down the principles of the Compact when compared to initiatives to combat illegitimately traded diamonds and Transparency International, which targeted key corporations.

Chapter 2

Poverty and Global Justice: Some Challenges Ahead

Hilde F. Johnson
Minister of International Development (Christian Democrat), Government of Norway

Let me start by quoting a man from Ghana, testifying about an everyday incident: "Take the death of this small boy this morning. The boy died of measles. We all know that he could have been cured at the hospital. But the parents had no money and so the boy died a slow and painful death — not of measles but of poverty."

Poverty is the scourge of our time. It means human suffering, untimely deaths and disease. It implies an enormous waste of human lives — a cost we cannot accept in the 21st century.

Who are we — if we don't do anything to change the map of global poverty?

Does it suffice to say that because I pay my share in taxes — some of my money goes to development aid — I do my part? With your permission I will spend a few minutes to answer this question — but if you wish I could make it brief; the answer is no.

To me, it is intuitively unacceptable not to mobilize our political, financial and technological skills to combat poverty; to fight global injustice. Some might do this from a motive of enlightened self-interest — in a world without walls. My approach is different. Intuition has cultural roots, and when I reflect on my convictions it should be said that my intuition is rooted in Christian/Humanistic culture. The human value of the individual is one and undivided; all people are part of the unique creation.

My human dignity is violated if I threaten yours — or refuse to oppose those who do — even if you are a small boy in Ghana, and not my neighbor. We have but one world and one measure of the value of human dignity. Extreme poverty is a violation of human dignity.

My conviction is not only based on intuition, it is based on an understanding of rights, human rights. There is much debate about the relevance and importance of the different categories of human rights. In my

A. Follesdal and T. Pogge, (eds.), Real World Justice, 21-26.

opinion, we should not engage in a discussion about whether political and civil rights take precedence or not over civil and political rights. All human rights are interrelated and interdependent. No set of rights stands above the other. They are mutually reinforcing. Article 25 of the *Universal Declaration of Human Rights* is clear — everyone has the right to a standard of living adequate for the health and well-being of herself and her family.

Extreme poverty is a violation of rights, usually a violation of a number of rights at the same time, and not least — in too many instances — to the right to life itself. Development is also a question of rights: of the progressive realization of rights, whether social and economic rights or political and civil rights.

If a child is born into circumstances which are such that she has very slim chances of being properly fed, getting basic health care, getting an education, then it is our responsibility, to do something about it — if we can.

And we can. We are therefore obliged to study what kind of measures are useful and necessary in order to combat poverty. And we should also examine whether our behavior affects poverty in a positive or negative way.

Let me try to give you my understanding of the challenges ahead and an outline of where I understand the international consensus is heading.

The UN millennium development goals are the roadmap we use in the fight against poverty. You will remember that the UN millennium goals were adopted unanimously by heads of states and governments at the UN General Assembly at the turn of the millennium. The millennium goals constitute a concrete agenda for the fight against global poverty until 2015. Through the millennium development goals we are committed to halving the proportion of people living in extreme poverty and halving the occurrence of hunger, to halting the spread of HIV/AIDS, to reducing by half child mortality and to securing for all children primary education by 2015. There are seven concrete goals with the deadline 2015. And they are ambitious. They are ambitious regardless of useful disagreement over calculation and methodology.

There is no mention in the seven concrete goals of where the primary responsibility to reach the goals lies — no methodology so to speak. But in goal 8 the expression of partnership between the developing and the developed countries is clearly stated. Here we have, and I quote, "a commitment to good governance, development and poverty reduction — nationally and internationally."

Our common roadmap for the fight against poverty entails an explicit acknowledgement of the need to focus on the international framework conditions, as well as on the policies conducted by each individual state.

For most developing countries it is commonly understood that international framework conditions influence the prospects for growth at least as much as, if not more than, the flow of international development aid. Trade is paramount. But the difficulties developing nations have in entering the markets that matter with the goods they can produce are well known. Protectionism in rich countries costs developing countries between US$100–150 billion per year, at least twice the amount they receive through development assistance. Rich countries spend many times more on subsidies to their own farmers than on development aid. If we allow ourselves to be flippant about a serious matter for a second — it is 2 1/2 times more lucrative to be a cow in Europe than to be a farmer in Africa. Subsidies and export credits in rich countries depress incomes in rural areas in poor countries.

"The Doha (trade) negotiations are a central pillar of the global strategy to achieve the Millennium Development Goals: a strategy to reduce poverty by giving poor people the opportunity to help themselves.

We need a decisive break with trade policies that hurt economic development. Donors cannot provide aid to create development opportunities with one hand and then use trade restrictions to take these opportunities away with the other and expect that their development dollars will be effective." These past two paragraphs are taken from a communiqué given by Horst Köhler, Jim Wolfensohn and Donald J. Johnston in the wake of the Cancun meeting. The aim of the communiqué is to persuade governments to agree to reform.

Reform in international framework conditions is necessary. Reform of official development aid is necessary — particularly for the poorest countries. It is normally assumed that we need to double OECD development aid in order to arrive at poverty reduction on a level prescribed by the millennium goals. Both US and the EU countries have promised increased funds: we are steering towards a 30-percent increase in 2004. We are on our way — but lagging behind; we are far from the goal of 0.7 percent of GNI we adopted decades ago. We need more development aid — and we need better development aid. We are talking about development aid reform, a topic I will not develop further here today.

Trade, debt and development aid — these are areas in which OECD countries need to do more. But it is my firm conviction that the governance issue must be included at the national level as well. "Good governance is perhaps the single most important factor in eradicating poverty and promoting development" is a much-used quote of UN Secretary General Kofi Annan. Developing countries need to put their own house in order, improve their policies and governance. Reforms are needed. Speaking frankly, I think the governance issue on the national level is an area where we on our side for too long have been reluctant to speak up.

But good governance is not only an issue of stable macro-economic policies. Good governance must include anti-corruption policies, democracy building and respect for human rights. Poverty reduction and sustainable development is the aim.

When poor people are systematically discriminated against, through laws, lawlessness and a fence of rich-people privileges, they have little opportunity to make use even of their limited resources.

A rights-based understanding of the problem of poverty is important — also on the national level.

Where does the responsibility to eradicate global poverty lie? Among international decision-makers there has been in the past years a move towards convergence of opinion between those who have advocated that the way out of poverty is to be found solely in the international framework conditions and those who pointed to ill-judged national policies as the root of poverty. It is essential to focus on both.

Are there links between the nature of national governments and international society?

Yes, there are and there have always been, several.

One problematic link between the two levels is corruption. Corruption comes in many shapes and forms — from the underpaid policeman who cannot feed his family unless he takes payment for services rendered to the large-scale setting aside of the nation's resources for private or semi-private interests. For all cases the bottom-line is the same — corruption is stealing from the poor. There is a fine line, or should we say continuum, from corruption to the usurpation of national resources for the conduct of wars. Recent studies, amongst others by the World Bank, point to the relationship between abundance of natural resources and competition over their control on the one hand, and internal strife and conflict on the other.

Is this merely an issue to be addressed by developing countries themselves?

No longer — at least not only by developing countries. We have, albeit reluctantly, started to say aloud that when we deal with corruption on a large scale there is more often than not an agent, directly or indirectly, from a developed nation on one side of the equation.

And, perhaps most importantly, the issue of corruption is being perceived as a more fundamental ill of a political as well as economic nature. There is more interest in the issue of how the possibilities for private enrichment through politics shape decision-making. The days when private as well as state-owned companies from OECD countries could deduct bribes as expenses in their balance sheet are over. But the problem has not evaporated — and more determined action is needed.

There are several initiatives internationally. I would like to mention here the *Extractive Industries Transparency Initiative*. Based on the declaration by the G-8 countries, and following an initiative by Tony Blair, it focuses on extractive industries and the importance for transparency in finance flows from natural resources. Reporting from the industries, as well as from the host countries, about financial flows resulting from extractive industries is aimed at greater transparency.

There is a growing awareness that as buyers or lenders we should not be totally indifferent to the effects of money flows originating from us.

Transparency is not a new issue. The new situation is — in my opinion — that these issues now land at the table of governments and international development institutions and are seen as bona fide development challenges. Too little has been done — but I sense a change of heart. I would not be totally surprised if the current interest in transparency and legitimate use of resources would lead this work into other realms of international exchange as well.

Last March, the Center for Global Development, a research institute based in Washington, launched the "Commitment to Development Index." It attempts to index OECD countries according to a number of specific policy criteria, with the aim of measuring the comprehensive impact of the given state's policies towards poor countries. The key word here is coherence, coherence in all aspects of policies with an effect on poor countries.

OECD countries need to be monitored on their comprehensive policy towards poor countries.

But positive coherence is extremely difficult to achieve. It takes more than average courage for a government to set aside perceived, concrete material interests of voters in order to implement policies which may benefit the global poor who live in distant lands, and who may see the benefit very slowly (although the zero-sum image is — on an aggregate level — wrong). Poor people in Africa do not vote in OECD country general elections.

International cooperation in this field is important in order to nudge one another forward. International agreements are necessary in order to avoid freeriders and underbidding. And poor countries need sponsors and lobbyists. They have too few friends — and sometimes the wrong kind.

Which leads me to the reason why I wanted to come here today. We need change. But I am extremely concerned that unless our general awareness about global issues becomes stronger, unless the public debate about poverty becomes more pervasive and more sophisticated, we have only a small chance of bringing about change on a level sufficient to combat global poverty. And to focus on ourselves: in complex democracies, consensus on a certain level is needed if change is to be implemented. My question to you is: is it conceivable that the research community could be more visible in the work to combat global poverty?

I wish that you understand my question also as an expression of gratitude towards the University and the Ethics Program and the Norwegian Ethics Network. This conference is important; the issues you raise are crucial. We need insight, we need arguments, we need debate. But we also need your engagement in public debate.

Why does global extreme poverty persist? I often ask myself this naïve question: when we can put a man on the moon, why can we not eradicate poverty? The answer is — we can. We can, but we must do more, we must want more. We need to build a resolve to act on a global level. Towards global justice.

I wish you a fruitful and interesting conference and look forward to hearing more from you all.

Chapter 3

Justice, Morality and Power in the Global Context

Rainer Forst
Political Science and Philosophy, Johann Wolfgang Goethe Universität, Frankfurt

1. It goes without saying that philosophical discourses about global justice have to start from and respond to the reality of global *injustice*. But it is worth stressing that this holds true for the levels of both description and evaluation. We can go wrong in our assessment of the global situation (and its local consequences), and we can go wrong in providing normative theories about it *because of* the first error. Theories of "explanatory nationalism" (Pogge 2002a: 143–5) which locate the main causes for underdevelopment within poor and badly organized states are a case in point, though it is also important to see that in such theories descriptive and normative considerations are interwoven in a complex way.

To be sure, the time when there was a critical social theory at hand that was considered to provide a historical-scientific, materialist account of capitalist relations of production and domination that at the same time entailed a normative story about exploitation as well as (the necessary steps towards) emancipation is gone. And yet, the project of a critical theory of global injustice and justice must not be given up, insofar as in our normative considerations we have to find a "reflective equilibrium" (to use Rawls's term in a different context) between an adequate, critical assessment of the existing economic and political transnational relations and our well-considered general theories of justice and morality. Only in this way can we construct a *critical and realistic theory of global injustice as well as justice* (see Forst 2001). "Realistic" does not mean here: within the reach of practical politics; rather, it means: in touch with reality.

2. In my following brief argument, I want to contribute to the normative "groundwork" of such a realistic and critical theory. For I believe it is essential to see that with respect to theories of global justice, there is the danger of a *dialectic of morality*: certain moral approaches to the problems

A. Follesdal and T. Pogge, (eds.), Real World Justice, 27-36.

of severe poverty and underdevelopment miss the real normative issue that they needed to address because they fail to take into account the economic-political, especially institutional reality of past and present injustice in the global context and therefore turn into *false* theories that — against their intention — veil rather than expose the situation of global injustice. Most importantly, such theories turn an injustice into a morally "bad" situation, a wrongdoing into a "state" of badness.

3. To begin with, I ask the reader to undertake a thought experiment. There is a picture by Sebastião Salgado that shows Serra Pelada goldmine in Brazil (the picture is reprinted on the cover of Thomas Pogge's *World Poverty and Human Rights*), where you see a huge number of workers, very poorly dressed, who carry heavy sacks of mud on their shoulders uphill using primitive and steep ladders of wood. From looking at the picture — the stooped bodies of the workers, the dirt, the crowdedness of the situation — you get an idea of what it must be like to work there — a vague idea, of course, far from knowing or experiencing what it is really like. Of all the workers, almost no one looks straight into the camera, with the exception of one person, on the right side of the picture.

Try to imagine now you are this worker, and since I do not know anything about Serra Pelada goldmine in particular, imagine you are working in a goldmine like that one: your working day is twelve hours of extremely hard and dangerous work; you have, given your poor education and your obligations to others in your family who depend on your salary, no choice but to work there. You are being poorly paid, so that you can hardly buy enough food and clothing for yourself and your family. You have no social insurance. The company is owned by a consortium, some capital comes from people and companies in your own country, the most comes from other, wealthier countries. If one were to write the history of the mine, it would have to go back to early colonial times and show in what way the structures of the current economic situation still reflect hierarchies of power established back then. The profits of the mine, such a story would show, are distributed in a complex way — benefiting the owners, partners, the state (taxes), local elites (bribes), etc. But you yourself are as far away from a "just" return for your work as you can be.

Now imagine you get a letter from the recently established "Global Court of Distributive Justice;" you are asked to make your case for justice in that court, and the court will see to it that justice will be realized. You are stunned and hardly believe your luck, especially because the letter of the court says that not just your own situation, but that of people like you generally will be improved given the demands of justice. Many others will be heard, therefore, and the result will potentially be a new international system.

You are worried, of course, whether you will have the means — especially all the knowledge you need — to make your case in a proper and convincing way, since those whom you will possibly charge with being responsible for the injustice being done will probably have much more efficient means to present their story. But the court reassures you: it will give you a number of the best social and moral theorists to make your case.

The social scientists are the ones to start, and they make their best effort to reconstruct the economic and political situation that is relevant for you; they include the historical dimension and the current relations of power, from the situation in your home country to the international sphere, including the actual terms of trade, the gold market, and so on. The rest of the work is being done by the justice experts who will argue your case and with whom you had some consultations.

The day of the court proceedings comes. The global judge opens the hearings, you are being introduced, and then your justice attorneys start.[1]

(a) The first one presents your case in a *humanitarian* way. He argues that it is an undeniable moral duty that every human being who has the relevant resources (to a sufficient degree) helps others who are in severe need, i.e., who lack the goods necessary for the fulfillment of basic human needs: food, housing, health, but also minimal education. He points out that there is some disagreement about such lists of basic goods, but if one defined them in a very minimal way, a generally acceptable list could be formulated. And he also stresses that making sure that all human beings on earth are rescued from bad living conditions as defined by the lack of these goods is a demand of human solidarity and mutual help — not so much a matter of rights, for example.

But somehow, even if you think that the attorney has said a number of important things about what is bad about being in a bad situation, you have the impression that his way of presenting your case is very much beside the point. Normatively, he has not even used the word "justice" or, for that matter, "injustice," and institutionally, he has not even begun to address the issues that really define your situation: economic exploitation and political powerlessness, for example. So you thank the attorney and relieve him of the duty to represent you.

---

[1] For the sake of a brief and nuanced characterization of the positions of the attorneys, I have refrained from connecting them to current theorists advocating similar approaches.

(b) The second attorney thinks she knows what was wrong with the first one and presents your case in a *humanist* way, as she prefers to say. She does use the rhetoric of justice, yet she argues that justice is not about comparing the goods that one person has with those of another; rather, she believes, justice is about each person having "enough" of the goods necessary for a decent and good life, as defined by a list of basic needs and capabilities — by "absolute" standards. According to her, basic moral respect for each and every human being demands a distribution or redistribution of goods: a moral concern for a human life "in dignity."

Again, you may wonder about the use of the term "justice" here, and, in fact, a few of the colleagues of the attorney who also call themselves "humanists" do not believe that this is an argument about justice but one of a different moral nature. Anyway, you still think, as in the first, humanitarian case, that this argument on your behalf is beside the point. For, first, the injustice of your situation, both historically and actually, the reality of exploitation and domination, is not really addressed, and, second, the redistribution policies that are being suggested certainly try to improve your situation — yet they do not try to fundamentally change the very political and economic structure that lead to your situation. In fact, alternative institutions will probably be established in which those who are in power remain in power, though they now also have certain humanitarian tasks. You still are dependent upon them, but now as a recipient of basic goods. And, as you see it, this is very far away from being treated with respect for your dignity. So you turn to the third attorney, who seems to understand.

(c) And indeed, this one has a clear understanding of the difference between the normative realm of justice or *human rights* on the one hand and the realm of humanitarian aid on the other, and he is clear that your case has to be understood in terms of the first category. Thus no appeal to human solidarity or some vague notion of dignity is made, but rather to strict duties of justice and to rights obligations. Universal human rights, the moral lawyer says, are grounded in basic interests of human beings, and among them is the right to subsistence, founded in an undeniable fact of "natural" human neediness. Any further claims to distributive justice he only thinks possible in closer national contexts, and he also believes that the fulfillment of subsistence rights is a matter of subsidiarity. Therefore, he says that the main addressee of your claims is your own government. Here is the most important locus of failure and of injustice.

With that last point you partly agree, for your social scientists have indeed explained to you how your government and local elites benefit from the way the goldmine works, and yet you think that this story is insufficient both on empirical and on normative grounds. For it lacks other parts of the empirical picture, such as the role of foreign companies, governments, international agreements, and so on — and the way in which foreign powers support your government and its power over you. And more than that, you disagree with the way justice is truncated in this story and reduced to either minimal human rights or to issues internal to societies. For justice, you may think, generally is about establishing justified structures of social relations, and then the contexts of justice cannot be separated in the proposed way. Who owes what to whom has to be explained in a larger, more complex framework. So you thank this attorney and turn to another one.

(d) This fourth attorney stresses the point you had in mind and disagrees with the way justice has been bifurcated between thin international and thicker national justice. He believes that justice is called for wherever grave inequalities of power and of the distribution of goods appear, and he clearly thinks that they do appear on a global level; further, he argues for a broader understanding of the "minimum standard of living" as a core criterion of justice, as well as for a universal duty of establishing institutions for the realization of such minimal justice.

Well, the argument for global justice because of certain responsibilities of Western societies especially for having created and for continuing a situation of global injustice sounds right to you, and such a universal "thin core notion of human flourishing" is attractive, given your bad situation. But still, you would flourish much more if your *basic desire for justice* were fulfilled first, not just by receiving certain goods that improve your life but by knowing that the current system of injustice will be institutionally and structurally changed — changed into a system in which you are no longer a mere recipient of goods. Whether the result of a more just system would then be the minimal list of goods that has been proposed you do not know — but given what your social scientists told you about the material wealth on earth, you hope that it would be more than minimal. But be that as it may: the first thing is to become an *agent of justice*, not just a *recipient of justice*.

The judge of the court raises his eyebrows as he hears this, for this could also be an offense against the authority of the court, yet he gives you another, last chance for picking an appropriate attorney.

(e) The fifth attorney belongs to an *egalitarian* law firm. He argues for the principle that every distribution of goods is to be mutually and generally justified to all those affected, and he sees no significant differences between national contexts and the global context of justice. On the basis of a "presumption in favor of equality," all goods have to be distributed equally, at least as long as no other arguments (property rights, for example, or notions of desert based on individual effort) call for a different distribution.

This makes the plea of the attorney a bit difficult to understand, for it is not quite clear what kind of equality remains once the priority of the other considerations is heeded. But the egalitarian is quite convinced that henceforth your situation will be much improved.

You may trust the egalitarian in that, and yet you still may have qualms. For in his statement the attorney did not once mention the facts of past injustice and, more than that, he did not talk about the institutional structure of the redistributive machinery that is to follow from his argument. For your worry again is that you will be treated as a mere recipient of goods, not as an agent of justice, i.e., as an agent who is an autonomous and equal, cooperating subject in the production of goods and in the political institutions which oversee the way goods are produced and distributed. Again, you fear that neither the concrete injustice of your situation is addressed nor the institutional means to structurally change it.

4. Let us leave the court proceedings here. For if this thought experiment is of some value, it may help us in gaining important insights into the demands of justice in the current global context.

Justice, to be sure, is to be understood as a part of morality, but as a special part. In a context of justice like the one at hand, replacing it by other parts or aspects of morality — humanitarian aid based on human solidarity, consequentialist reasoning, teleological considerations, etc. — or by a truncated notion of justice is a mistake. It is wrong, for example, to turn a claim of justice into an appeal for "help" based on benevolence or a general, "imperfect" moral duty. It blinds us to the real situation, both empirically and normatively: its causes, its effects, the responsibilities for it, the resulting obligations, the necessary institutional consequences of a structural change. It is here where I find myself in agreement with one of the central insights of Thomas Pogge, who writes:

> As it is, the moral debate is largely focused on the extent to which affluent societies and persons have obligations to help others worse off than themselves. Some deny all such obligations, others claim them to be quite demanding. Both sides easily take for granted that it is as potential helpers that we are morally related to the starving abroad. This is true, of course. But the debate ignores that we are also and more significantly related to them as supporters of, and beneficiaries from, a global institutional order that substantially contributes to their destitution (Pogge 2002a: 117).

What Pogge criticizes here is an instance of what I call a "dialectic of morality": a good moral argument at the wrong place can turn into its opposite, into a veiling of the injustice it tries to alleviate or overcome. I believe, however, that in this light some of Pogge's own arguments about a "thin conception of human flourishing" as a "core criterion of basic justice" (Pogge 2002a: 36f) which I alluded to in my thought experiment appear problematic. They make it seem that granting such a minimum standard is what justice essentially demands. To be sure, justice also of course demands this, but in another way, as part of a larger picture, not as a substitute for it.

Such a larger picture must start from an empirical theory of the global context of political and economic relations — a critical theory of the status quo of injustice, so to speak. It has to address the history of the current situation and the factors responsible for it as best as it can, and it needs to connect this history to an adequate representation of the actual situation which is to be described as a situation of injustice rather than as poverty (which it is, too). It is not just that poor people *lack* necessary means of subsistence, it is that they are *deprived of* such means in situations of *multiple domination*. In a complex network of powers several agencies influence the actions of others so that a number of them profit, whereas others — collectives or persons — profit very little or not at all. Transnational companies dominate the national elites in a developing country, whereas those elites — again in multiple situations of rivalry — dominate parts of their citizenry who may then be forced to work under conditions like the ones depicted on the photograph of the goldmine.

Furthermore, a critical account of injustice/justice like that must connect the analysis of economic exploitation and political domination with claims for changing this situation: with claims for economic equity and the just distribution of profits, and with claims for democratic institutions exercising legitimate power locally, nationally as well as transnationally. This is what justice demands: not a more or less extensive machinery of *re*distribution but a lasting structural change in the institutions of production, distribution and political decision-making. To alleviate injustice by policies of redistribution is a good thing, but it is not good enough. It does not sufficiently change the situation of injustice for, normatively speaking, the recipients of redistributed goods remain "mere" recipients, which still is a sign of being passive, second-order citizens, and institutionally speaking, such measures do not go deep enough. They leave the dominant power structure intact. Redistribution policies, whether humanitarian or egalitarian, begin at the wrong end: at the "output" end of an unjust system, but by altering the output they do not change the system. To overturn a complex system of injustice, one needs to start with the *first question of justice*: the question of the distribution of *power*. Power, then, is the most basic of all goods: a meta-good of political and social justice. If you do not change the power system, you do not really change a situation of injustice.

5. Yet here one may quite plausibly object that we actually lack what I seem to presuppose in my argument, namely (1) a reliable and noncontroversial theory of the global status quo, since such theories are themselves contested, in part also normatively: there seems no "neutral" description. And one could also reply that (2) in order to critically describe a situation as one of "injustice," we need to have a noncontroversial notion of justice first. But this again seems not to be in place. More than that, in order to find one it seems that we have to start from one of the five approaches I have just criticized.

To a certain extent, I grant both points: we do not have a non-contested theory of the current world system, and in order to have a theory of global injustice, we need a conception of justice that can claim universal validity. And that does not seem to be in sight.

But to a certain extent, I also disagree with both points: for the purposes of an analysis of the current "world order," we do not need a neutral theory from a God's eyes' view, and we also do not need a very specific conception of justice. To mark the most important inequalities of power, be it political or economic, one only needs to look at the way things are: who has most power in transnational institutions like the WTO, who determines the terms of trade and decides where and which investments are being made, etc.? What is the current distribution of resources, and who uses and profits from them, and so on? One can also start with local "stories" — like the one of the goldmine in my example. To understand how such a local system works and how it is embedded in the international framework one does not need a fully unified background theory: you only need to know the way things have developed and work.

But what about the notion of justice I have been using? Is this maybe too broad and demanding? The answer is that it may be demanding in its consequences, but in its conceptual core it is quite slim. For its main principle is a *principle of justification*: justice demands that every political and social basic structure is to be justified with reciprocally and generally non-rejectable arguments to all those to whom it applies; hence, if we can properly speak of the transnational order as a basic structure of justice — or at least one that is in need of justice — even if a thinner one as compared to national contexts, the transnational basic structure has to be adequately justified to those who are subject to that order (for the following see Forst 2001).

This first claim of justice, or *fundamental justice*, therefore, calls for a proper *basic structure of justification* — in order to (ideally) achieve *maximal justice*: a *fully justified basic structure*. Such a fundamental structure of justification first and foremost is to be established as the primary task of justice. Here again the question of *power* appears as the first question of justice. For the first thing is to inquire how such a fair structure of justification could be established, on the national levels as well as on the transnational one. And from that angle, the question of the necessary capabilities and functionings for participation in such discourses reappears, though now in a very specific perspective, internally linked with the problem of institutionalizing a structure of fair and equal justification. So none of the (reasonably) disputed normative or empirical questions of the greater picture of justice or injustice is answered by authority or apriori reasoning: rather, everything that is not implied as a presupposition of a fair structure of justification is to be discussed within the institutions that have to be established in order to realize fair terms of national and transnational discourse and bargaining. Hence this "fundamental" or "minimal justice" is not so minimal after all; but still it is not a notion of justice that paternalistically says what maximal justice would mean.

Its main ideas are, first, that even though we do not (and, given the unavoidable connection between empirical and normative perspectives, cannot) have a non-contested social theory of transnational relations, we know that the current system is very much in need of justification and we should strive for the establishment of relations in which such justifications can really take place. And secondly, this does not only do justice to past and present injustice done to those who live and work under conditions such as in the goldmine I mentioned, it also draws our attention to the real roots of injustice and to the institutional means to change it. Fundamentally just institutions serve to realize the *force towards the better argument*: they force those who benefit from the current global situation to explain why this should be so. It is important that such force is exercised by those who suffer(ed) from economic exploitation and political powerlessness: they have, so to speak, a discursive veto-right in such debates. Their story, properly told, will be decisive in finding out what justice demands. Third, normatively speaking, this is an approach that plausibly claims to start from the dignity of human beings as agents, as persons who are not to be subjected to unjustifiable structures of power they cannot influence. Such an approach respects the dignity of autonomous beings who no longer are seen as objects of injustice *or* of certain redistributive policies of justice. They are seen as moral persons with a basic *right to justification* that has a real, institutional meaning in this context (see Forst 1999a).

6. To come back to my thought experiment, this means that the authority of norms of justice rests neither with the perspective of one of the moral theorists I mentioned, nor simply with that of our worker (as I partly assumed for the sake of argument), nor with a global judge (as I also assumed provisionally): every claim to justice that goes beyond

fundamental/minimal justice — which is not so minimal, as I stressed, since it establishes an efficient and fair system of justification and provides persons (and collectives) with the necessary means for that purpose — towards maximal justice (which is a regulative idea) has to stand the test of empirical and normative reasoning, also in a diachronic dimension. This calls for a complex arrangement of discursive institutions and procedures, to be sure; yet if a "minimally" fair basic structure of justification were in place instead of the current power asymmetries, the most important progress would already have been made.

Obviously, given the fact of "multiple domination," as I called it, to talk of a single "structure of justification" (fundamental justice) or of a single "justified basic structure" (maximal justice) is misleading, for local, national and global structures and contexts are interwoven as contexts of injustice as well as, accordingly, of justice. There can be no global justice without internal justice, and vice versa. This complex connection, among other factors, makes the achievement of justice so difficult. So the struggle for justice has to take place at many fronts and can take many forms; yet the idea of justice always remains the same and needs to be kept free from other moral considerations: to establish truly justifiable basic social structures among persons who are autonomous agents in various contexts of justice.

Chapter 4

"Saving Amina": Global Justice for Women and Intercultural Dialogue[*]

Alison M. Jaggar
Philosophy, University of Colorado at Boulder

This paper is dedicated to the memory of Susan Moller Okin, whose
work and friendship have been inspirational for me. Susan's dedication
to justice for all women was unfailing both in her theoretical writings
and in her life commitments. Before her death, Susan read this paper
and graciously addressed its challenges.

One of the innumerable electronic petitions flashing across the Internet in
the early months of 2003 held special interest for feminists. Carrying the
name and logo in Spanish of Amnesty International, the petition asked
recipients to "sign" electronically an appeal against the sentence of stoning
to death declared against Amina Lawal, a divorced Nigerian woman, who
had had a baby outside marriage. In August 2002, an Islamic court in
Katsina state in northern Nigeria had convicted Lawal of adultery under
Sharia law. The "save Amina" petition collected many thousands of
electronic signatures from around the world but in May 2003 it was followed
by another e-communication with the subject line, "Please Stop the
International Amina Lawal Protest Letter Campaigns." The second e-

---

[*] This essay was initially written for a conference sponsored by the Carnegie Council on
"Global Justice and Intercultural Dialogue," held in Shanghai, January 2004, and a slightly
different version of it will appear in *Ethics & International Affairs*. The quotation in my
title is taken from an article appearing in *Essence* magazine, although the *Essence* article
portrays Lawal's Nigerian woman lawyer, Hauwa Ibrahim, rather than Western feminists,
as "saving Amina" (Sansoni 2003). The present article develops arguments made in Jaggar
1998, 1999, 2001, 2002a, 2002b, 2002c, and 2004. I would like to thank Abigail Gosselin
for her assistance in preparing the paper and participants in the "Global Justice and
Intercultural Dialogue" conference, especially Thomas Pogge, for their helpful comments.

A. Follesdal and T. Pogge, (eds.), Real World Justice, 37-63.
© 2005 *Springer. Printed in the Netherlands.*

message was signed by Ayesha Iman and Sindi Medar-Gould, representing two Nigerian human rights organizations supporting Lawal. Iman and Medar-Gould asserted that the "save Amina" petition in fact endangered Lawal and made the task of her Nigerian supporters more difficult, in part because the petition contained a number of factual errors, including a false assertion that execution of the sentence was imminent. They also observed, "There is an unbecoming arrogance in assuming that international human rights organizations or others always know better than those directly involved, and therefore can take actions that fly in the face of their express wishes" (Imam and Medar-Gould 2003).

Electronic petitions have become a popular means by which Western feminists endeavor to "save" women in other countries. A 1998 e-petition on behalf of women in Afghanistan, begun by a student at Brandeis University, garnered so many responses that Brandeis was forced to close the student's mailbox. The petitions often use sensational language to denounce some non-Western culture for its inhumane treatment of women and girls. Worries about non-Western cultural practices are not limited to those in the West who identify as feminists. The popular press regularly runs stories about non-Western practices it finds disturbing, especially when these concern women's sexuality and/or are noticed occurring among immigrant groups. Recent news stories have raised the alarm about arranged marriage, "sexual slavery," dowry murder ("bride-burning"), "honor" killings, genital cutting ("circumcision," "mutilation"), sex-selective abortion, and female infanticide. Newspapers in the United States have also questioned whether female US soldiers, stationed in Saudi Arabia, should be required when off-base to conform to Saudi laws mandating covering their bodies and forbidding them to drive.

The perceived victimization of women by non-Western cultures has now also become a topic within Western philosophy. In this paper, I draw on the work of other feminist scholars to argue that conceiving injustice to poor women in poor countries primarily in terms of their oppression by "illiberal" cultures provides an understanding of the women's situations that is crucially incomplete. This incomplete understanding distorts Western philosophers' comprehension of our moral relationship to women elsewhere in the world and so of our philosophical task. It also impoverishes our assumptions about the intercultural dialogue necessary to promote global justice for women.[1]

---

[1] A note on my terminology: In this paper, "we" refers to philosophers sympathetic to political feminism who work in North America or the European Union. I have in mind primarily citizens but also, to a lesser extent, permanent residents. In speaking of countries' geo-political and geo-economic locations, feminist scholars have used a variety of terminologies — all problematic in some respects. From the 1970s through the mid-

1. Philosophers saving Amina: Two influential philosophical treatments of injustice to women in poor countries

1.1 The debate in women's studies

The interdisciplinary literature in women's or feminist studies has discussed the perceived victimization of women in non-Western cultures for at least thirty years. In this academic context, two main positions have been opposed to each other. The first is global radical feminism, a perspective that made its appearance in the early years of second-wave Western feminism. The radical feminists wished to establish that women were a group subjected to a distinct form of oppression and their earliest writings postulated a worldwide women's culture, existing "beneath the surface" of all national, ethnic and racial cultures and colonized by these "male" cultures (Burris 1973). Global radical feminism asserts the universality of "patriarchal" violence against women and sometimes advocates an ideal of global sisterhood (Morgan 1984).[2] Opposed to this position is postcolonial feminism, which asserts the diversity of women's oppression across the world and emphasizes that this oppression is shaped by many factors, among which past colonialism and continuing neo-colonialism are especially important. Postcolonial feminism charges that global feminist criticisms of

---

1990s, feminists usually spoke of First, Second and Third Worlds but, by the mid-1990s, the collapse of the Soviet bloc, followed by the expansion of the global market and the establishment of the World Trade Organization, made this tripartite division seem less apt. Nevertheless, some theorists continue to use the term "Third World" as a political designation that also sometimes includes communities of color in North America and the European Union. Other scholars speak of the developed and developing worlds, but this terminology is open to the objection that it suggests a linear and Western-oriented model of development. Since the mid-1990s, my own preference usually has been to speak in terms of the global North and the global South, since this language suggests several contrasts that I find important in the present global political economy. Although I often find the terminology of global North and South provides a useful shorthand, in the present paper I speak mostly of countries that are poor and rich because this terminology is less theory-laden. All the available terminologies have different implications and all suggest binary oppositions that are in various ways objectionable.

[2]   Mary Daly, for example, contends that women worldwide are subjected to male violence, through such practices as witch-burning, *sati*, footbinding, and "female genital mutilation" (Daly 1978: 109–12). Daly is not isolated in her views. In November 2003, the controversial film "Warrior Marks: Female Genital Mutilation," was shown at the University of Colorado at Boulder as part of a week-long series of events billed as "Breaking the Global Silence: Exposing Violence Against Women." Volpp provides a good overview of the feminist controversy surrounding "Warrior Marks" (Volpp 2001: 1208–09).

cultural practices outside the West frequently are forms of "imperial feminism" or "feminist orientalism," often exoticizing and sensationalizing non-Western cultural practices by focusing on their sexual aspects (Amos and Parmar 1984; Apffel-Marglin and Simon 1994). The polarized debate in women's studies has sometimes seemed to suggest that Western feminists who are concerned about the well-being of women across the world are confronted with a choice between colonial interference and callous indifference (Jaggar 2004).

Central to the women's studies debates has been the question of "essentialism," especially as this pertains to many Western feminist representations of "women."[3] Postcolonial feminists argue that universal generalizations about women are essentialist, because they reify gender by treating it as separable from class, ethnicity, race, age and nationality in ways that the postcolonial critics regard as incoherent and mystifying. "Essentialist" generalizations are always sweeping and treat groups as internally homogeneous but they are not always universal. For instance, an influential article by Chandra Mohanty challenges the essentialist contrasts between Western women and "the average Third World woman," which she finds implicit in much Western feminist writing. Mohanty argues that this writing represents Western women "as educated, as modern, as having control over their own bodies and sexualities, and the freedom to make their own decisions," while depicting non-Western women as victimized and lacking in agency. She criticizes patronizing Western representations of "the typical Third World woman" that portray this woman as leading "an essentially truncated life based on her feminine gender (read: sexually constrained) and her being 'third world' (read: ignorant, poor, uneducated, tradition-bound, family-oriented, victimized, etc.)" (Mohanty 1991: 56).

---

[3] This debate arose out of concern that the supposedly universal "woman" invoked in much Western feminist writing in fact was a woman privileged along a number of dimensions. For instance, many theorists implicitly imagined her as white, middle-class, heterosexual, able-bodied, and so on. The feminist literature on essentialism discusses how the relationships among various aspects of women's diverse "identities" should be conceptualized (are they additive or multiplicative, analytically separable or not?) and problematizes the whole idea of a universal woman; for example, Carby 1982; Fuss 1989; Spelman 1988; Spivak 1988. The critique of essentialism is now widely accepted within the discipline of women's studies, where the term "essentialist" has become exclusively pejorative. The critique has been extremely valuable in revealing the biases lurking in many Western feminist generalizations about "women," although some theorists worry that denying that any essential characteristics can be attributed to women pulls the theoretical rug from under feminist activism (Martin 1994).

1.2 The debate in philosophy

In the 1990s, academic debate about the gendered aspects of non-Western cultural practices moved out of the feminist fringe and into the mainstream of Western philosophy. This occurred primarily as a result of bold work by Martha Nussbaum and Susan Okin (Nussbaum 1988, 1990, 1992, 1993, 1995, 1998, 1999, 2000, 2002; Okin 1994, 1995, 1998, 1999, 2002). The recent work of Nussbaum and of Okin diverges in important respects but the present paper focuses on some parallels between them.[4] In their discussions of poor women in poor countries (and of cultural minority women in rich countries), Nussbaum and Okin both turn away from earlier debates about the universality or otherwise of "patriarchy." They reframe the issues in terms of ongoing philosophical debates between liberalism and communitarianism, on the one hand, and liberalism and multiculturalism, on the other. Both take as their problem the question of how Western philosophers should respond to non-Western cultural practices perceived as unjust to women and both believe that answering this question requires addressing several current philosophical controversies. These include: moral universalism and cultural relativism; the possibility of "external" as opposed to "internal" social criticism; and the question of whether liberal societies can tolerate illiberal cultural practices within their borders.

Nussbaum and Okin both identify themselves as liberal feminists but both follow the radical feminists in staunchly opposing what they see as the oppression of women in non-Western cultures. They provide new arguments against postcolonial feminists, casting them as relativists who seek to avoid forthright condemnation of injustice to women in developing or Third World countries. They also charge that the anti-essentialism advocated by postcolonial feminists rationalizes a disingenuous refusal to acknowledge forms of injustice that are distinctively gendered. Finally, Nussbaum and Okin suggest that women who seem content with unjust cultural practices suffer from adaptive preferences or learned desires for things that are harmful, a phenomenon called "false consciousness" by Western feminists influenced by the Marxist critique of ideology.

Nussbaum's work on this topic draws on Amartya Sen's concept of capabilities, which was developed originally as an alternative to welfarism for measuring international levels of development. Nussbaum has modified the concept of capabilities and uses it to counter "cultural relativism," which she thinks often serves as a pretext for excusing outrageous injustice to women in poor countries. In a spate of books and articles published

---

[4]   Philosophical disagreements between Nussbaum and Okin have recently become more explicit (Okin 2003; Nussbaum forthcoming).

throughout the 1990s, Nussbaum defends the universal values that she believes are embodied in the capabilities, appealing to these values to condemn cultural practices that subordinate women. An early article provocatively defends "Aristotelian essentialism" against what Nussbaum regards as a "politically correct" anti-essentialism that rationalizes "ancient religious taboos, the luxury of the pampered husband, ill health, ignorance, and death" (Nussbaum 1992: 204). In responding to the challenge that many people, including many poor women in poor countries, do not accept the capabilities as universal values, Nussbaum invokes the concept of adaptive preferences.[5] She argues that existing desires and preferences may be corrupted or mistaken when they are adapted to unjust social circumstances; for example, women may sometimes fail to recognize that they are oppressed.[6]

Susan Okin has also been concerned to address the situation of poor women in poor countries. Her analysis draws on her own earlier critique of Western practices of marriage and family, in which she argues persuasively that the traditional division of labor in marriage unjustly disadvantages Western women economically and in other ways (Okin 1989). Okin's analysis of the situation of poor women in poor countries is parallel to her analysis of the situation of Western women: in her view "the problems of other women are 'similar to ours but more so'" (Okin 1994: 8). Like Nussbaum, Okin challenges feminist anti-essentialism, quoting Nussbaum approvingly on this topic.[7] Also like Nussbaum, she worries that "false consciousness" arising from adaptive preferences and internalized oppression limits the usefulness of "interactive" or "dialogic" approaches to justice and advocates an alternative Rawlsian method of hypothetical dialogue in the original position (Okin 1994: 18f).

---

[5] Sen's concept of capabilities was designed in part to address the problem of adaptive preferences; he illustrated this problem by reference to Indian widows, who had learned to disregard their deprivation and bad health (Sen 1995 and elsewhere).

[6] More generally, Nussbaum contends that, because preferences may be adaptive, existing desires provide an unreliable guide to justice and the good life, subverting intercultural agreement on universal values. In defending the universality of the capabilities, Nussbaum's earlier work appealed to the Aristotelian method of critically refining the *eudoxa* or reliable beliefs (Nussbaum 1998: 768). More recently, Nussbaum has developed a "non-platonist substantive good" approach that allows her to postulate the capabilities as universal values even in the absence of expressed consensus (Nussbaum 2000). For critical discussion of this method, see Jaggar forthcoming.

[7] Unlike Nussbaum, however, Okin does not limit herself to rhetorical gestures against anti-essentialism. Instead, she argues against the essentialists that sexism can indeed be separated analytically from other categories of oppression, using empirical data to show that attention to gender is comparatively new to justice theories and development studies — and that it matters.

Okin's concern about cultural injustice to women emerges again in her contributions to the multiculturalism debate. In the discipline of philosophy, this debate focuses on the question whether cultural minorities within liberal cultures should enjoy special group rights (Kymlicka 1995). Okin argues that the rights claimed by minority groups may conflict with liberalism's commitment to women's equality, so that a tension exists between multiculturalism and feminism (Okin 1998, 1999). In Okin's view, supporters of multiculturalism have failed to appreciate that illiberal cultural practices are often especially burdensome to women. In addition, she believes that some feminists have paid so much attention to differences among women that they have fallen into cultural relativism, ignoring the fact that "most cultures have as one of their principal aims the control of women by men" (Okin 1999: 13). Okin asks rhetorically, "When a woman from a more patriarchal culture comes to the United States (or some other Western, basically liberal, state), why should she be less protected from male violence than other women are?" (Okin 1999: 20).

1.3 Some non-logical implications of Nussbaum's and Okin's work

Okin and Nussbaum deserve great credit for drawing the attention of mainstream Western philosophers to issues previously neglected by what Thomas Pogge has called the academic justice industry (Pogge 2002a: 145). Like all groundbreaking scholarship, Nussbaum's and Okin's work has shaped the subsequent literature in distinctive ways, highlighting some concerns and obscuring others. Specifically, their work has encouraged Western philosophers to understand injustice to non-Western women as a matter of oppression by local cultural traditions. The issues that Nussbaum and Okin raise are crucial to understanding the injustices suffered by non-Western women but the present paper focuses on the issues they have *not* raised, on their omissions and their silences. In other words, I am concerned here with what Cheshire Calhoun would call the non-logical implications of Nussbaum's and Okin's work in this area, including the moral and political significance of their emphases and their *lacunae* (Calhoun 1988).

In discussing the contributions that care ethics makes to moral theory, Calhoun argues that Western moral philosophy has produced a lopsided ideology of moral life and thought that reflects the moral preoccupations of propertied males and obscures the moral concerns of (among others) many women.[8] Analogously, I argue that Nussbaum's and Okin's representations

---

[8] For instance, focusing exclusively on people's shared humanity and equal membership in the moral community diverts attention from the ways in which people's basic interests and

of the injustices suffered by poor women in poor countries are lopsided, reflecting some preoccupations while obscuring others. Calhoun suggests that the ethics of care, construed as a focus on hitherto neglected aspects of moral life and thought, can help to redress the gendered bias of moral theory. Similarly, I suggest that a focus on certain aspects of the global political economy, hitherto neglected by Western philosophers, can help to present a fuller and fairer understanding of the situations of poor women in poor countries.

My concern is not that Nussbaum and Okin pay excessive attention to the sensationalized sexual issues that preoccupy the popular press. On the contrary, they take the poverty of many non-Western women extremely seriously, recognizing that poverty constrains women's autonomy and makes them vulnerable to a range of other abuses, such as violence, sexual exploitation and overwork. However, Nussbaum's and Okin's discussions give the impression that female poverty is attributable primarily to local cultural traditions, especially traditions of female seclusion.[9] For example, both treat as exemplary a study by Marty Chen, which explains that many women in India, especially female heads of households, are left destitute because the system of secluding women denies them the right to gainful employment outside the home (Chen 1995).[10]

Nussbaum's and Okin's focus on the injustice of non-Western cultural traditions reinforces several assumptions commonly made in popular Western discussions of the situation of poor women in poor countries. These assumptions are as follows:

1) A major, perhaps the major, cause of suffering among women in poor countries is unjust treatment in accordance with local cultural traditions — traditions whose injustice is not necessarily recognized by the women involved. Call this the "injustice by culture" thesis.

---

empirical desires may differ, depending on their social locations. Focusing exclusively on the adult capacity for consistent and universalizable moral reflection diverts attention from the indispensability of moral motivation, education and the social availability of morally relevant information. Focusing exclusively on the dangers of egoism and partiality to one's own diverts attention from the dangers of self-sacrifice and devalues the moral significance of special relations (Calhoun 1988).

[9] Both Nussbaum and Okin identify their topics as philosophical problems about culture, specifically, cultural relativism and multiculturalism. The term "culture" is also prominent in the titles of their writings about poor women in poor countries; one of Nussbaum's books is titled, *Women, culture and development*, and Okin's article analyzing the problems of poor women in poor countries is titled, "Gender Inequality and Cultural Differences."

[10] Nussbaum (1995: 62) regards Chen's study as evidence of the need for her universal capabilities approach. Okin (1994: 15) refers to Chen's work as evidence for her claims about cultural injustice to women.

2) The unjust local traditions in question may resemble some Western practices but they are causally independent of them. Call this the "autonomy of culture" thesis.

3) Non-Western cultures are typically more unjust to women than is Western culture. Call this the "West is best for women" thesis.

I doubt that either Nussbaum or Okin would assent to these theses in anything like the simple terms in which I have stated them. Nevertheless, I worry that both philosophers' preoccupation with opposing the perceived injustice of non-Western cultures encourages many Western readers to derive such non-logical implications from their work. In addition, I worry that Nussbaum's and Okin's work in this area promotes too narrow a view of the task of those Western philosophers who seek to explain injustice to poor women in poor countries. In other words, I am afraid it promotes the view that:

4) Western philosophy's task is to expose the injustices imposed on women by their local cultures and to challenge philosophical rationalizations of those injustices, many of which rest on mistaken views about essentialism and relativism.

Thesis Four is the philosopher's version of "saving Amina." In the next section of this paper, I critically discuss Theses One to Three; in the following section, I discuss Thesis Four.

2. Non-Western culture and injustice to poor women in poor countries

Assessing claims about cultural injustice requires having some sense of what is meant by the term "culture," which Raymond Williams describes as "one of the two or three most complicated words in the English language" (Williams 1983: 160. Cited by Tomlinson 1991: 6). The 1982 report of a UNESCO conference on cultural policy stated that, in the view of some delegates, "culture permeated the whole social fabric and its role was so preeminent and determining that it might indeed be confused with life itself" (Tomlinson 1991: 5). In most contexts, however, the term "culture" is useful only if it is marked off against other areas of social life, so culture is often distinguished from politics and the economy (Tomlinson 1991: 5). Contemporary philosophical discussions of culture typically accept some version of this distinction. For example, Nancy Fraser contrasts concerns about cultural recognition with concerns about economic redistribution (Fraser 1997). The items on Bikhu Parekh's list of minority cultural practices in Britain all concern marriage, sexuality, dress, diet, education, body marking and funeral customs (Parekh 2000: 264f). In Okin's view, "the sphere of personal, sexual, and reproductive life provides a central focus of most cultures ... Religious or cultural groups are often particularly concerned with 'personal law' — the laws of marriage, divorce, child custody, division and control of family property, and inheritance" (Okin 1999: 12f).

When culture is equated with dress, diet, sex, and family, it becomes an area of life that has special significance for women. Most of the practices on Parekh's list apply mainly or even exclusively to women and girls and his last item is simply, "Subordinate status of women and all it entails including denial of opportunities for their personal development in some minority communities" (Parekh 2000: 265). Thus, Okin's observation is uncontroversial:

> As a rule, then, the defense of "cultural practices" is likely to have much greater impact on the lives of women and girls than those of men and boys, since far more of women's time and energy goes into preserving and maintaining the personal, familial, and reproductive side of life. Obviously, culture is not only about domestic arrangements, but they do provide a major focus of most contemporary cultures. Home is, after all, where much of culture is practiced, preserved, and transmitted to the young (Okin 1999: 13).

Benhabib writes, "Women and their bodies are the symbolic-cultural site upon which human societies inscript their moral order" (Benhabib 2002: 84). Because women are typically seen as the symbols or bearers of culture, conflicts among cultural groups often are fought on the terrain of women's bodies, sometimes literally in the form of systematic rape.

2.1 The limits of injustice by culture

The thesis of injustice by culture asserts that local cultural traditions are a major, perhaps the major, source of the injustices suffered by women in poor countries. Is this thesis correct? Certainly it is undeniable that many non-Western cultures are unjust to women. Striking evidence is provided by Amartya Sen's famous calculation that up to a hundred million women are "missing" as a result of Asian cultural practices, including both direct violence and systematic neglect (Sen 1990). It also seems indisputable that women in legally multicultural societies tend to suffer disproportionately from religious/cultural law (Shachar 1999, 2000a, 2000b). That injustice to women is inherent in many cultural traditions confirms second wave feminist arguments that the personal is political and Okin's work on Western marriage and family has made a valuable contribution in drawing mainstream philosophers' attention to such injustices. However, the poverty and associated abuses suffered by poor women in poor countries cannot be understood exclusively in terms of unjust local traditions. To understand such poverty and abuse more fully, it is also necessary to situate these traditions in a broader geopolitical and geo-economic context.

Contemporary processes of economic globalization, regulated by the Western-inspired and Western-imposed principles and policies of neo-liberalism, have dramatically increased inequality both among and within countries.[11] Applying neo-liberal principles across the world has produced a windfall for some people and a catastrophe for others. Those who have reaped the rewards of neo-liberal globalization have belonged mostly to the more privileged classes in the global North or to elite classes in the global South. Those who have been injured by it are mostly people who were already poor and marginalized, in both the developing and the developed worlds.[12] Since women are represented disproportionately among the world's poor and marginalized, neo-liberal globalization has been harmful especially to women — although not to all or only women. Women comprise 70 percent of the world's poor and 64 percent of the world's 876 million illiterate people (UNDP 1999b). In what follows, I offer a few examples of the impact of neo-liberal globalization on poor women in poor countries.

Most poor women in poor countries traditionally made a living in small-scale and subsistence agriculture; even quite recently, 70 percent of the world's farmers were said to be women. However, the impact of neo-liberal globalization has made small-scale and subsistence agriculture increasingly

---

[11]   The principles of neo-liberalism include commitments to: free trade (except for the flow of labor); government withdrawal from the social welfare responsibilities assumed over the twentieth century; deregulation of such aspects of social life as wages, working conditions and environmental protections; bringing all economically exploitable resources into private ownership. Policies justified by these principles have been imposed as conditions of borrowing on poor countries across the world by Western-dominated international financial institutions, such as the World Bank and the International Monetary Fund.

[12]   In 1960, the countries with the wealthiest fifth of the world's people had per capita incomes 30 times that of the poorest fifth; by 1990, the ratio had doubled to 60 to one; by 1997, it stood at 74 to one. By 1997, the richest 20 percent had captured 86 percent of the world's income, while the poorest 20 percent captured a mere 1 percent. For many — perhaps most — poor people in the world, neo-liberal globalization has resulted in their material conditions of life deteriorating not only relative to the more affluent but also even absolutely. In more than 80 countries, per capita incomes are lower than they were a decade ago; in sub-Saharan Africa and some other least developed countries, per capita incomes are lower than they were in 1970. In developing countries, nearly 1.3 billion people do not have access to clean water, 1 in 7 primary age schoolchildren are not in school, 840 million people are malnourished, and an estimated 1.3 billion people live on incomes of less than $2 per day. Meanwhile, the assets of the 200 richest people in 1998 were more than the total income of 41 percent of all the world's people.

unviable. One reason for this is the expansion of export agriculture, typically mandated by programs of structural adjustment, especially in South America and South East Asia. Another reason is the refusal on the part of the wealthiest countries to conform to their own neo-liberal principles. The United States and the European Union currently spend $350 billion a year on farm subsidies, six times what they spend on aid. As neo-liberalism compels poor countries to open their markets, locally grown agricultural products are unable to compete with the heavily subsidized foods dumped by richer countries.

The decline of small-scale and subsistence agriculture has driven many women off the land and into the shanty towns that encircle most major Third World cities. Here the women struggle to survive in the informal economy, which is characterized by low wages or incomes, uncertain employment and poor working conditions.[13] Many become street vendors or domestic servants. Those who remain landless in the countryside are often forced to work as seasonal, casual and temporary laborers at lower wages than their male counterparts. Many women are driven into prostitution, accelerating the AIDS epidemic, which ravages the poorest women in the poorest countries.[14]

Neo-liberal globalization has also destroyed many traditional industries on which poor women in poor countries once depended.[15] More fortunate women may obtain jobs in newer industries, especially the garment industry, which produces the developing world's main manufactured exports and in which women are the majority of workers. However, conditions in the garment industry are notoriously bad because poor countries, lacking capital, can compete in the global market only by implementing sweatshop

---

[13] The informal economy is a shadow economy whose operations are not reflected in official records, whose workers typically do not pay taxes, and whose jobs are unregulated by health and safety standards. It covers a wide range of income-generating activities, including declining handicrafts, small-scale retail trade, petty food production, street vending, domestic work, and prostitution, as well as home-based putting-out systems and contract work. Women predominate in the informal economy.

[14] The worst devastation from AIDS occurs in the developing countries, where 93 percent of people with HIV/AIDS lived by the end of 1997, and especially in sub-Saharan Africa, where 80 percent of all deaths occur (UNIFEM 2000). The higher incidence of HIV among people living in the developing world has special significance for women's health, because women comprise a higher percentage of adults living with HIV/AIDS in these areas than they do in the wealthy countries. In sub-Saharan Africa, women account for 55 percent of all new cases of HIV (Nierenberg 2002).

[15] The United Nations reports, "Small women-run businesses often can't compete with cheap imported products brought in by trade liberalization. In Africa, many of women's traditional industries such as food processing and basket making are being wiped out" (www.unifem.undp.org/ec_pov.htm).

conditions. The situation for garment workers in poor countries is worsened by continuing protectionism in the garment industry on the part of the United States and the European Union.

The most obviously gendered consequences of neo-liberal globalization are the worldwide cutbacks in social services, also often mandated by programs of structural adjustment. These cutbacks have affected women's economic status even more adversely than men's, because women's responsibility for caring for children and other family members makes them more reliant on such programs. Reductions in social services have forced women to create survival strategies for their families by absorbing these reductions with their own unpaid labor, and more work for women has resulted in higher school drop-out rates for girls. In addition, the introduction of school fees in many Southern countries has made education unavailable, especially to girls. Less education and longer hours of domestic work contribute to women's impoverishment by making it harder for them to attain well-paid jobs.[16]

The above examples are not intended to suggest that the poverty and poverty-related abuses that afflict many women in poor countries are caused exclusively by neo-liberal globalization. Obviously, these problems result from interaction between factors that are both macro and micro, global and local. It is impossible to explain why women suffer disproportionately from the deleterious consequences of neo-liberal globalization without referring to local cultural traditions. For example, if women were not assigned the primary responsibility of caring for children, the sick and the old, the cutbacks in social services would not affect them disproportionately nor would they find it harder than men to move to the locations of new industries. Only the injustice of cultural tradition seems to account for the fact that, within male-headed families, women and girls frequently receive less of such available resources as food and medical care.[17] Nevertheless, the above examples do show that the poverty of poor women in poor countries cannot be attributed exclusively to the injustice of their local cultures. To suggest this would be to promote a one-sided analysis that ignored the ways

---

[16] Since women are primarily responsible for caring for children, women's poverty is reflected in disturbing statistics on children's nutritional status, mortality and health. In many Southern countries the number of children who die before the age of one or five has risen sharply after decades of falling numbers. A new report by the United Nations Children's Fund (UNICEF), the first to measure child poverty scientifically, states that globalized trade and cuts to aid budgets keep a billion children in poverty (Frith 2003). Child poverty is a good indicator of women's poverty.

[17] This implies that poverty may be understated even by the United Nations report that women comprise 70 percent of the world's poor, because this report is based on studies of consumption in female-headed compared with male-headed households.

in which neo-liberal globalization is, among other things, a gendered process that frequently exacerbates inequalities between men and women.[18]

2.2 The limits of the autonomy of culture

Faced with the evidence of the previous section, Nussbaum and Okin would certainly acknowledge that neo-liberal globalization bears considerable responsibility for women's poverty in poor countries and they would surely condemn its injustices. However, they might also observe that injustice in the global economic order simply has not been the focus of their work thus far.[19] Surely, they might say, an author cannot be faulted for choosing to address one topic rather than another, especially if the topic chosen is important and unduly neglected; moreover, if anyone is to be faulted for philosophy's failure to deal with the gendered aspects of the global political economy, why should Nussbaum and Okin be singled out? I agree that it is reasonable for philosophers wishing to address injustice to poor women in poor countries to focus sometimes on local rather than global problems and on cultural rather than economic injustices. However, when discussing issues involving the seeming injustice of non-Western cultures, it is problematic to write as though these cultures are self-contained or autonomous without also noting the ways in which their traditions have been and continue to be shaped by Western interventions.

Theorists of the second wave of Western feminism sometimes inquired whether male dominance had existed in all societies or whether it was introduced to some societies by European colonizers.[20] Whatever the answer to this once hotly debated question, it is indisputable that many supposed cultural traditions in Asia, Latin America and Africa have been shaped by encounters with Western colonialism. For instance, Veena Oldenburg argues that the practice of dowry murder in India had imperial origins (Oldenburg 2002). Non-Western cultural practices especially affecting women often gain new life as symbols of resistance to Western dominance. In Kenya, for

---

[18] Treating the poverty and economic dependence of non-Western women primarily as a matter of cultural constraint disturbingly echoes old Marxist analyses of women's issues as "superstructural" rather than part of the basic economic structure. It also encourages imaging non-Western women as "outside history," stuck in the backwaters of pre-modernity. (For extended criticism of this view, see Jaggar 1983.) This image continues to affect calculations of the economic contributions of women "at home," which are notoriously undercounted (Dixon-Mueller 1991).

[19] In fact, Okin's latest work turns toward issues of political economy (Okin 2003).

[20] Somewhat similarly, critics of recent Western-planned development projects have argued that these projects have often reinforced the subordination of women (Boserup 1970; Kabeer 1994; Visvanathan 1997).

example, "clitoridectomy became a political issue between the Kikuyu and Kenya's white settlers and missionaries, as well as a symbol of the struggle between African nationalists and British colonial power" (Brown 1991: 262). Uma Narayan describes how the supposed "Indian tradition" of *sati* (immolation of widows) was likely "an *effect* of the extensive and prolonged debate that took place over the very issue of its status as tradition. As a result of this debate, *sati* came to acquire, for both British and Indians, and for its supporters as well as its opponents, an "emblematic status," becoming a larger-than-life symbol of "Hindu" and "Indian" culture ..." (Narayan 1997: 65). Today, "marginalized by exposure to an onslaught of conditions of modernity, the market economy, and imperialistic transnational enterprises, distinct cultural groups tend to view themselves as being under pressure to demonstrate their ritual purity and allegiance to traditional high culture" (Obiora 1997, cited in Volpp 2001: 1198n78). This sense of being economically and culturally beleaguered may help to explain the current worldwide flourishing of religious fundamentalisms, defined by Volpp as modern political movements that use religion as a basis for their attempts to win or consolidate power and extend social control (Volpp 2001: 1205n108). Contemporary fundamentalisms all "support the patriarchal family as a central agent of control and see women as embodying the moral and traditional values of the family and the whole community" (Volpp 2001: 1205n108).

Western culture is not only a passive stimulus for gender-conservative reactions by those who have the authority to define "authentic" cultural traditions. In addition, Western powers may reinforce or even impose gender-conservative cultures on non-Western societies by supporting conservative factions of their populations. For most of the twentieth century, for example, British and US governments have supported a Saudi Arabian regime that practices gender apartheid. The Taliban government of Afghanistan, which also practiced gender apartheid, was installed after the US provided extensive training and aid to various mujaheddin forces opposing the then-communist but secular government. President Reagan described the mujaheddin as the moral equivalent of the founding fathers of the United States. Following its overthrow of the Taliban, the United States has installed a weak government in Afghanistan under which women's lives in many ways are even more precarious. The burkha is no longer legally required but most women are still afraid to remove it and they are not safe on the streets. Girls' schools are burned, families threatened for sending girls to school, and three girls recently have been poisoned, apparently for attending school (Bearup 2004). Women are banned from singing on radio and television, and there has been an unprecedented increase in the number of suicides and self-burnings among women. At present, the United States is trying to build an Iraqi government to succeed the Ba'athist regime it has overthrown. Under the Ba'athist regime, whatever its other faults, the conditions of Iraqi women were much better than those of women elsewhere in the region. Today, women are afraid to leave their homes (Sandler 2003) and news media report that the US is seeking political leadership for Iraq among its tribal and religious leaders — few of whom are women or whose priorities include improving the status of women.

Sharp contrasts between Western and non-Western cultures cannot ultimately be sustained. They rely characteristically on what Uma Narayan calls cultural essentialist generalizations, which offer totalizing characterizations of whole cultures, treated as internally homogenous and externally sealed. Typically, such generalizations are quite inconsistent with empirical realities (Narayan 1998). In the Western philosophical literature, it is becoming more common to observe that cultures are internally diverse and often conflict-ridden and that they are not autonomous relative to one another, but it is still unusual to note that they are only partially autonomous relative to political and economic structures. Yet, as the global political economy becomes more integrated, so too do its cultural manifestations. Thus, when multinational corporations exploit women in export-processing zones located in poor countries, it is impossible to say that this practice exclusively reflects either Western or non-Western culture. When Asian governments tempt multinational corporate investment with stereotypes of women workers as tractable, hardworking, dexterous and sexy, it seems meaningless to ask whether these stereotypes are Western or non-Western or whether the super-exploitation and sexual harassment of these women represents Western or non-Western cultural traditions. It seems equally meaningless to attribute the increasing sexualization of women worldwide to either Western or non-Western culture. Many women around the world have been drawn into some aspect of sex work. This includes a multi-billion dollar pornography industry and a worldwide traffic in women, in which the sex workers participate with varying degrees of willingness and coercion. It also includes servicing male workers in large plantations, servicing representatives of transnational corporations, servicing troops around military bases, and servicing United Nations troops and workers. In some parts of Asia and the Caribbean, sex tourism is a mainstay of local economies. Prostitution has become a transnational phenomenon, shaped by global norms of feminine beauty and masculine virility.[21]

---

[21] Media in Europe and North America still portray brown or black women as tantalizing erotic subjects, while in non-European countries white women are exoticized and eroticized (Kempadoo and Doezema 1998). Connell documents the emergence of a hegemonic transnational business masculinity, institutionally based in multinational corporations and global finance markets (Connell 1998).

In the new global order, local cultures interact and interpenetrate to the point where they often fuse. Some patterns seem discernible, for example, worldwide preferences for women as factory workers, sexual playthings and domestic servants (Anderson 2000), but these patterns shift and merge in an unending variety of particular combinations. Poor women in poor countries certainly are oppressed by local men whose power is rooted in local cultures, but they are also oppressed by global forces, including the forces of so-called development, which have reshaped local gender and class relations in varying and contradictory ways, simultaneously undermining and reinforcing them (Sen and Grown 1987; Moser 1991; Kabeer 1994). A new but still male-dominant global culture may be emerging, relying on the labor of a new transnational labor force that is feminized, racialized and sexualized (Kang 2004).

2.3 Is the West best for women?

Much of the Western philosophical debate over multiculturalism discusses the relative situations of women in "liberal" and "illiberal" cultures. It tends to equate Western with liberal culture and non-Western with illiberal culture and it usually takes for granted that Western culture is more advanced than non-Western culture. Okin writes, "Many Third World families, it seems, are even worse schools of justice and more successful inculcators of the inequality of the sexes as natural and appropriate than are their developed world equivalents" (Okin 1994: 13). In her view, "the situation of some poor women in poor countries is different from — as well as distinctly worse than — that of most Western women today. It is more like the situation of the latter in the nineteenth century" (Okin 1994: 15).

As intercultural interactions accelerate, we have seen that it becomes increasingly problematic to contrast whole cultures with each other. The idealized and unrealistic images of cultures constructed by essentialist generalizations are typically designed to promote political agendas. What Narayan calls the colonialist stance presents Western cultures as dynamic, progressive and egalitarian, while portraying non-Western cultures as backward, barbaric and patriarchal. Colonialist representations characteristically engage in "culture-blaming," for instance, by treating discrimination and violence against women as intrinsic parts of non-Western but not of Western cultures. While the West historically has blamed non-Western cultures for their backwardness, it has portrayed its own culture as staunchly committed to values like liberty and equality, a "self-perception ... untroubled by the fact that Western powers were engaged in slavery and colonization, or that they had resisted granting political and civil rights even to large numbers of Western subjects, including women" (Narayan 1997:

15). Today, as Narayan notes, violence abounds in the United States, yet cross burnings, burnings of black churches, domestic violence murders and gun deaths are not usually treated as manifestations of United States culture (Narayan 1997: 85). When cultural explanations are offered only for violence against poor women in poor countries, Narayan notes that the effect is to suggest that these women suffer "death by culture," a fate from which Western women seem curiously exempt (Narayan 1997: 84f). Many philosophers continue to write as though Western culture is unambiguously liberal, ignoring Christian fundamentalism's influence on the present United States government, as well as its growth in several former Soviet bloc countries (Grewal and Kaplan 1994: 24). For instance, Parekh treats polygamy as an exclusively Muslim practice, ignoring its existence among Christian groups in the United States. It is true that what Parekh calls the public values of Western societies are mostly liberal (2000: 268–70) but Western cultures certainly are not liberal all the way down — and illiberal values frequently rear above their surfaces.[22]

Although the superiority of Western culture appears self-evident to most Westerners, non-Western women do not all agree. For instance, Western feminists have long criticized non-Western practices of veiling and female seclusion but Leila Ahmed argues that the social separation of women from men on the Arabian Peninsula creates a space within which women may interact freely with one another and where they resist men's efforts to impose on them an ideology of inferiority and subservience (Ahmed 1982: 530f). Nussbaum and Okin suggest that non-Western women's acceptance of seemingly unjust cultural practices may be due to adaptive preferences or false consciousness. In Okin's view, not only do "many cultures oppress some of their members, in particular women ... they are (also) often able to socialize these oppressed members so that they accept without question their designated cultural status" (Okin 1999: 117). To someone like myself, brought up in the British class system, this assertion seems indisputably true. However, raising questions of false consciousness only with respect to non-Western women who defend their cultures could be read as suggesting that these women's moral perceptions are less reliable than the perceptions of Western women whose consciousness is supposedly higher or truer. Such a suggestion reflects a second aspect of the colonialist stance, namely, the "missionary position," which supposes that "only Westerners are capable of naming and challenging patriarchal atrocities committed against Third-

---

[22] Earlier this year, Lieutenant General William G. Boykin said of his Muslim opponent, "I knew that my god was bigger than his. I knew that my god was a real god and his was an idol" (Carroll 2003). This remark, offensive to Muslims across the world, including in the United States, suggested that the war on Iraq was after all a religious war or, as President Bush expressed it earlier, a "crusade."

World women" (Narayan 1997: 57, 59f). Nussbaum and Okin both recognize explicitly that non-Western women are perfectly capable of criticizing unjust cultural traditions and frequently do precisely that, but their practice of raising questions about adaptive preferences and false consciousness only when confronted by views that oppose their own encourages dismissing those views without considering them seriously. In fact, the question of the superiority of Western culture for women, especially poor women, is not as straightforward as Westerners often assume.

The thesis that the West is best for the poor women of the world is not necessarily true. Even if we set aside deep philosophical questions about how to measure welfare, development or the quality of life and agree to assess cultures according to their success in preserving poor women's human rights, at least three sets of concerns cast doubt on the West is best thesis.

1) First, it is of course true by definition that liberal cultures give a higher priority than illiberal cultures to protecting civil and political liberties. However, the ability to exercise these "first generation" human rights can be enjoyed only in a context where "second generation" social and economic rights are also guaranteed. As noted earlier, poverty makes women vulnerable to violations of their civil and political liberties, including assaults on their bodily integrity, and Western societies are very uneven in their willingness to address women's poverty. The feminization of poverty is especially conspicuous in the United States, where women continue to suffer extensive violence. Thus, it must be recognized that the human rights especially of poor women are routinely violated even in liberal Western societies.[23]

2) Second, and turning to poor women in poor countries, it is hard to deny that Western powers are disproportionately responsible for designing, imposing and enforcing a global economic order that continues to widen the staggering gap between rich and poor countries. Since gender inequality is strongly correlated with poverty, Western countries are disproportionately responsible for creating the conditions that make non-

---

[23] On some accounts, for much of the twentieth century women fared better in the erstwhile Second World than in the First World. After the collapse of so-called communism, elites benefited from the privatization and exploitation of hitherto publicly owned resources, but the dismantling of welfare states meant cuts and deterioration in services in health, education and childcare, contributing to deteriorating quality of life for most people. In 7 out of 18 East European countries, life expectancy was lower in 1995 than in 1989 (falling as much as five years since 1987) and enrolment in kindergarten declined dramatically. Women suffered disproportionately from the massive unemployment which followed the collapse of the socialist economies and the decline of social services. They were pushed especially out of high-income and comparatively high-status positions in areas such as public management or universities, and many highly educated women were forced to turn to prostitution, street-vending or begging.

Western women vulnerable to local violations of their rights. It is especially disturbing to wonder how far the prosperity that undergirds Western feminism is causally dependent on non-Western poverty.

3) Third, it must be acknowledged that some of the same Western powers that trumpet democracy and liberalism at home support undemocratic and gender-conservative regimes abroad, fomenting coups, dictatorships and civil wars (Pogge 2002a: 153). Poor women are disproportionately affected by these interventions. They suffer most from the absence of social programs cut to fund military spending and they also suffer most from social chaos. They constitute the majority of war's casualties and 80 percent of the refugees dislocated by war.[24]

These three sets of concerns raise serious questions for the thesis that the West is best for women, especially for the vast majority of the world's poor women.

2.4 Conclusion

I do not wish to romanticize non-Western cultures and traditions or to assert that Western culture is intrinsically violent and racist. Such reverse colonialist representations would be as essentialist and distorting as the claim that the West is best for women. In addition, suggesting that neo-colonial domination is the cause of all the problems in poor countries would portray the citizens of those countries simply as passive victims, denying their agency and responsibility. My goal has been to challenge the images of both Western and non-Western cultures that are implicit in much of the most influential philosophical discussion on these topics. I do not dispute that non-Western cultures often treat women unjustly but I have argued that global forces help to shape those cultures, as well as creating the larger political and economic contexts in which poor women find themselves.[25] Western powers play a disproportionate role in enforcing an unjust global order, so bringing into question the assumption that, overall, the West is best for poor women in poor countries.

Expanding our understanding of the causes of women's poverty in poor countries requires that Western philosophers also expand our conception of

---

[24] During the twentieth century, civilians rather than soldiers constituted an ever-increasing proportion of the casualties of war. In World War I, 20 percent of the casualties were civilians, but in World War II, 50 percent were civilians. Some 80 percent of the casualties in the Vietnam War were civilians and about 90 percent of the casualties of today's wars are estimated to be civilians.

[25] Although women almost everywhere suffer from cultural injustice, this does not mean that we are all are victims of a universal patriarchy. Our respective situations, histories and powers all vary widely and for this reason our responsibilities also differ.

our responsibility towards such women. No longer can we be satisfied to assume that our responsibility as philosophers is limited to employing the tools of our trade to analyze the injustices perpetrated on poor women in the name of non-Western cultural traditions. Once we acknowledge that we share past, present and future connections with poor women in poor countries, we see that we inhabit with them a shared context of justice. We do not look at their problems as outsiders, from an Archimedean standpoint external to their social world. Our involvement gives us a firmer moral standing for criticizing non-Western cultural practices, provided our criticisms are well informed and, in O'Neill's words, "followable by" members of the society in question (O'Neill 1996). However, it also requires us to investigate how much moral responsibility should be attributed to the citizens of Western countries for the continuation of these practices as well as for the unjust global order that traps many women in poor countries in grinding poverty.

3. Rethinking global justice for women: What is on the agenda of intercultural dialogue?

In Western philosophy classrooms, "cultural abuses" of women have become staple and sometimes titillating examples used to enliven discussion of issues such as moral relativism and the possibility of cross-cultural social criticism. Some Western philosophers address perceived cultural injustice to women by recommending an aggressive cosmopolitanism; others promote a "culturally sensitive" relativism. Increasingly, however, Western philosophers recognize that cultures are neither static nor hermetically sealed and they advocate intercultural dialogue (Parekh 2000; Benhabib 2002).[26] I certainly agree that intercultural dialogues are indispensable and I have previously explored some of their difficulties (Jaggar 1998, 1999). In this section, I wish to suggest some items for inclusion on the agendas of intercultural dialogues among philosophers concerned about global justice, especially justice for poor women in poor countries.

Most obviously, Western philosophers should not regard intercultural dialogues as opportunities for "saving Amina" by proselytizing supposedly Western values or raising consciousness about the injustice of non-Western practices. It is always more pleasant to discuss other people's blind spots and

---

[26] Fifteen years ago, Nussbaum and Sen already challenged sharp dichotomies between "internal" and "external" social criticism, noting the existence of extensive cross-cultural linkages (Nussbaum and Sen 1989).

faults than our own but we need to think more carefully who is Amina and from what or whom does she need saving.

High on the agenda of intercultural dialogue about global justice for poor women in poor countries must be questions about the global basic structure, as well as the justice of those Western government policies that directly affect poor women's lives. Important questions of economic justice include: how to understand "natural" resources, when things like fossil fuels, sunny climates, coral beaches or strategic locations become resources only within larger systems of production and meaning; how to determine a country's "own" resources, when every country's boundaries have been drawn by force; what is the meaning of "fair" trade, and can trade be free in any meaningful sense when poor nations have no alternative to participating in an economic system in which they become ever poorer. Important topics of political justice include reexamining the Westphalian conception of sovereignty, at a time when the sovereignty of most countries is limited by the rules of world trade and the sovereignty of poor countries is rendered almost meaningless because of their domination by international financial institutions and trade organizations.[27] Although superficially ungendered, these topics in fact are all deeply gendered, most obviously because women suffer disproportionately from economic inequality and political marginalization.

Intercultural dialogue about global justice must also address the problem of militarism. Following and despite the end of the Cold War, arms expenditures rose and wars continued in many non-Western countries, exacerbating and exacerbated by the poverty associated with global neo-liberalism. In the late 1990s, "over half the nations of the world still provide higher budgets for the military than for their countries' health needs; 25 countries spend more on defense than on education; and 15 countries devote more funds to military programs than to education and health combined"

---

[27] The institutions that govern the global economy are formally democratic but in practice they are heavily influenced by a small group of wealthy countries. At both the World Bank and IMF, the number of votes a country receives is based on how much capital it gives the institution, so rich countries have disproportionate voting power. Each has about 150 members with a Board of Executive Directors with 24 members. Five of these directors are appointed by five powerful countries: US, UK, France, Germany and Japan. The President of the World Bank is elected by the Board and traditionally nominated by the US representative, while the managing director of the IMF is traditionally European. The World Trade Organization is also formally democratic in that each of its member countries has one representative who participates in negotiations over trade rules but democracy within the WTO is limited in practice in many ways. Wealthy countries have far more influence than poor ones, and numerous meetings are restricted to the G-7 group, the most powerful member countries, excluding the less powerful even when decisions directly affect them.

(Peterson and Runyan 1999: 120). Since 9/11, 2001, arms expenditures have skyrocketed. In today's world, the top arms exporters are the USA, Russia, France, UK, Germany, Netherlands, with the United States accounting for more than 50 percent of sales.[28] The United States also maintains over 200 permanent bases across the world, distorting local economies and employing many thousands of women as prostitutes (Sturdevant 2001). As noted earlier, poor women and their children suffer disproportionately from war and militarism and the expansion of these raises deep philosophical questions about the meanings of war, peace and security — especially security for women.[29]

Another set of topics for intercultural dialogue about global justice for women concerns remedial justice, reparation or compensation for past and continuing wrongs. Do countries that have expropriated resources or fought proxy wars in other countries owe reparations to those countries and, if so, how should these be determined? Should wealthy countries compensate poor countries for the environmental destruction to which they have made a disproportionate contribution not only through militarism, which is the single largest cause of environmental destruction, but also through other destructive practices, including the careless extraction of resources from poor countries, the establishment of factories in poor countries with weak environmental standards, and extravagant patterns of consumption, especially the profligate burning of fossil fuels. The last produces carbon dioxide that causes acid rain and global warming, accompanied by devastating floods and hurricanes and a rise in sea levels that may cause some Southern countries to disappear entirely. Since poor women in poor countries suffer disproportionately from poverty, social chaos and environmental destruction, they would benefit the most from any system of remedial justice that might be established.

Most of the above topics concern issues of justice among countries. Since such justice is likely to be slow in coming, intercultural dialogue about global justice might also address the question of how in the meantime individual citizens can directly assist Amina Lawal and other poor women in

---

[28] India and Pakistan are among the poorest of all countries but India is now the fifth largest importer of major conventional weapons while Pakistan is the twelfth largest. Farrukh Saleem points out that, "When the poverty-ridden East fills (the) West's craving for drugs, there is talk of 'supply control.' (However), (t)he West remains ... the largest seller of arms to the East" (Saleem 2003).

[29] In addition to the considerations mentioned earlier, women suffer most from militarism's environmental destruction and its promotion of a sexist and violent culture in which men are glorified as warriors while women are either degraded or portrayed as national resources. Rape is a traditional weapon of war and military activity is usually associated with organized and sometimes forced prostitution.

poor countries. Imam and Medar-Gould note that not all victims of human rights violations can become international *causes célèbres* or subjects for letter-writing protests. They suggest that Western feminists who wish to help Lawal contribute to BAOBAB for Women's Human Rights or WRAPA, Women's Rights Advancement and Protection Agency, organizations that they respectively represent. Because money always comes with strings attached, promoting civil society initiatives in poor countries raises questions about the subversion of local democracies. Some critics argue that Northern-funded NGOs are a new form of colonialism, despite using the language of inclusion, empowerment, accountability and grassroots democracy, because they create dependence on non-elected overseas funders and their locally appointed officials, undermining the development of social programs administered by elected officials accountable to local people.[30] In an integrated global economy, however, nonintervention is no longer an option; our inevitable interventions are only more or less overt and more or less morally informed. Although the foreign funding of women's NGOs has dangers, it is not necessarily imperialistic. Nira Yuval-Davis reports that many NGOs in the global South have been able to survive and resist local pressures through the aid provided from overseas, "as well as the more personal support and solidarity of feminist organizations in other countries." She observes, "it would be a westocentric stereotype to view women associated with NGOs in the South as puppets of western feminism" (Yuval-Davis 1997: 120f).[31]

4. "Saving Amina"

The images of Amina Lawal that flashed around the world earlier this year show a beautiful African woman, holding a beautiful baby, looking at first sight like an African madonna. However her head is covered, her eyes downcast, she looks submissive, sad and scared. Portrayed in bare feet and described as illiterate, she epitomizes the image of the oppressed Third World woman described by Chandra Mohanty. Her image has also been widely regarded as epitomizing the barbarity of Islamic fundamentalism. Such images encourage Western feminists to take up the supposed white

---

[30] Kalpana Mehta observes that, in India, "NGOs could be said to be running a parallel government in the country, with priorities determined abroad and with no accountability to the people" (quoted in Silliman 1999: 147).

[31] Western feminists may also support transnational feminist networks opposing violence against women and promoting their rights, such as the Latin American and Caribbean Women's Health Network, Women Living Under Muslim Laws and ABANTU for Development (Keck and Sikkink 1998a; Ewig 1999: 83; Yuval-Davis 1997: 121).

man's burden of "saving brown women from brown men" (Spivak 1988: 296).

Challenging the "save Amina" petition and letter-writing campaign, Imam and Medar-Gould write:

> Dominant colonialist discourses and the mainstream international media have presented Islam (and Africa) as the barbaric and savage Other. Please do not buy into this. Accepting stereotypes that present Islam as incompatible with human rights not only perpetuates racism but also confirms the claims of right-wing politico-religious extremists in all of our contexts (Imam and Medar-Gould 2003).

They explain that when protest letters represent negative stereotypes of Islam and Muslims, they inflame local sentiments and may put victims of human rights abuses and their supporters in further danger.

Sensationalized criticisms of non-Western cultures reinforce Western as well as non-Western prejudices, promoting the impression that Western democracies are locked into a life and death "clash of cultures" with militant Islam (Barber 1992; Huntington 1996). Even philosophical criticisms sometimes have consequences outside the academy. Philosophy is often portrayed as an esoteric discipline practiced exclusively in ivory towers, but many moral and political philosophers intend also to influence the "real" world.[32] Philosophical criticism may be a political intervention and may be taken up outside academia in ways that its authors do not necessarily intend (Alcoff 1992). *Nation* columnist, Katha Pollitt, upset that militant Islamists had forced the Miss World pageant out of Nigeria, commented, "Not a good week for cultural relativism, on the whole" (Pollitt 2002). Western criticism of non-Western cultural practices is not in principle patronizing or xenophobic but critics should be aware that our colonial history and current geopolitical situation influence the interpretation and consequences of such criticisms; for instance, opponents of immigration cite non-Western cultural practices as reasons for closing the borders of the United States to immigrants from poor countries.[33] Given this context, Western philosophers need to consider how their criticisms of non-Western cultural practices may be used politically. Amos and Parmar contend that racist British immigration

---

[32] Nussbaum is one philosopher who is explicit about this (Nussbaum 2000 and elsewhere). That academic writing does indeed have an influence outside academia is shown by politically motivated attacks on ethnic and feminist studies, as well as more recent attacks on postcolonial and Middle Eastern studies.

[33] A recent letter to the *Colorado Daily* stated, "First, we need a five year moratorium on all immigration into this country to give us a 'collective break' from the onslaught of foreign languages, diseases being imported, female genital mutilation practiced by Middle Eastern and African muslim immigrants that is barbaric … " (Woolridge 2003).

policies were justified partly by invoking feminist opposition to arranged marriage (Amos and Parmar 1984: 11). President G. W. Bush and his wife Laura both rationalized the bombing of Afghanistan by the United States as necessary to save Afghan women from the oppression of the burkha (Bush, G. W. 2002; Bush, L. 2002, cited in Young 2003a: 17f).

Philosophers wishing to save Amina and similarly situated women certainly are at liberty to criticize cultural traditions in Nigeria and other countries and such criticisms are often well deserved. However, it behooves us also to ask why these practices have become ensconced as cultural traditions. Nigeria is a country that enjoys huge oil revenues, yet its real per capita GDP declined by 22 percent between 1977 and 1998 (UNDP 2000: 185, cited in Pogge 2002a: 235). As we have seen, gender inequality is correlated with poverty and, according to Thomas Pogge, the poverty suffered by most Nigerians is causally linked with the "resource privilege" that the existing international system accords to the de facto rulers of all countries. This encourages military coups, authoritarianism and corruption in resource-rich countries such as Nigeria, which has been ruled by military strongmen for almost three decades and is listed near the bottom of Transparency International's chart of international corruption. In Pogge's view, "corruption in Nigeria is not just a local phenomenon rooted in tribal culture and traditions, but encouraged and sustained by the international resource privilege" (112f). In such circumstances, for philosophers to focus exclusively on the injustice of Nigerian cultural practices is to engage in a form of culture blaming that depoliticizes social problems and diverts attention from structural violence against poor populations (Volpp 2000).[34]

In addition to bearing in mind the larger context that sustains many unjust cultural practices in the global South, Western philosophers who criticize those practices should also remember that Southern women are not simply passive victims of their cultures — notwithstanding the images of Amina Lawal. On the contrary, many countries in the global South, including Nigeria, have long-standing women's movements and Nigerian feminists remain active in struggles to democratize their cultures and to protect women's human rights (Abdullah 1995; Basu 1995). Nigerian women are also active in struggles for justice against Western corporations; for instance, women from Itsekiri, Ijaw, Ilaje and Urhobos are also currently challenging the activities of Shell Petroleum Development Company in the Niger Delta (Adebayo 2002). These women activists may have a better

---

[34] Briggs and Mantini-Briggs describe Venezuelan public health officials blaming cultural practices for high morbidity and mortality from cholera, thereby deflecting charges of institutional corruption, inefficiency, indifference, and genocide (Briggs and Mantini-Briggs 2000, cited in Volpp 2001: 1192n47).

understanding of their own situation than that possessed by many of the Western philosophers who want to "save" them.

Western philosophers concerned about the plight of poor women in poor countries should not focus exclusively, and perhaps not primarily, on the cultural traditions of those countries. Since gender inequality is correlated so strongly with poverty, perhaps we should begin by asking why so many countries are so poor. To do so would encourage us to reflect on our own contribution to Amina Lawal's plight and this would be a more genuinely liberal approach because it would show more respect for non-Western women's ability to look after their own affairs according to their values and priorities.[35] As citizens and residents of countries that exert disproportionate control over the global order, philosophers in the United States and the European Union bear direct responsibility for how that order affects women elsewhere in the world. Rather than simply blaming Amina Lawal's culture, Western philosophers should begin by taking our own feet off her neck.

---

[35] "We demand the right to choose and struggle around the issue of family oppression ourselves, within our communities ... without white feminists making judgments as to the oppressive nature of arranged marriages" (Amos and Parmar 1984: 15).

Chapter 5

Poverty as a Human Rights Violation and the Limits of Nationalism[*]

Geert Demuijnck
Philosophy, Université Catholique de Lille

1. Introduction

According to Albert Einstein, nationalism is an infantile sickness, it is the measles of the human race. Notwithstanding, many people go on, in an almost ridiculous way, being proud of their country. But beyond these, admittedly to some extent innocuous patriotic sentiments, the most elaborate forms of *social justice* are situated on the level of the nation-state. The notion of social justice implies, according to the most current conceptions, a considerable redistribution of wealth or income, implemented nationally. Rich countries have elaborated generous solidarity systems which redistribute wealth to people who are badly off through no fault of their own, that is, to unfortunate fellow citizens. To most people, this redistribution seems legitimate on the basis of economic and social claim-rights attributed to the citizens of a particular nation.[1]

---

[*] A previous version of this paper has been presented at a UNESCO workshop on "Poverty as a Violation of Human Rights" held in Paris on April 29, 2003. I am grateful to the participants of this workshop as well as to Thomas Pogge and Andreas Follesdal for helpful comments.

[1] However, such claim-rights do not seem legitimate to libertarians. The latter only accept that we have a negative duty not to harm other people, but no positive duty to contribute to the effectiveness of social and economic claim-rights. Thomas Pogge's argumentative strategy is based on the demonstration that people of rich countries, by their implicit support for the current international institutional arrangements, definitely harm the poorest people on the planet. From this demonstration, it follows that even the most radical libertarianism, and a fortiori all other people, should admit that the institutional scheme should be modified. In this paper I leave aside the rather theoretical position of strict

A. Follesdal and T. Pogge, (eds.), Real World Justice, 65-83.
© 2005 *Springer. Printed in the Netherlands.*

This paper explores merely one question: whether or not it is acceptable, from a moral point of view, to limit the attribution of such claim-rights to fellow citizens. My point is that *insofar* as people accept even minimal positive duties towards their unlucky compatriots, they should accept similar duties towards unlucky foreigners. More particularly, it will be defended that, although there are plausible pragmatic arguments in favor of the implementation of social justice (by means of social security systems or other forms of social policy) at the national level, there is not one single convincing moral argument for excluding non-citizens from elementary social and economic rights. The paper aims to show that even the most plausible arguments in favor of "national preference" do not stand serious scrutiny.[2]

When using the term "right," we should distinguish between positive rights, i.e., the obligations imposed de facto by public authorities ("enforceable rights") and moral rights, which *should* be imposed by an ideal, currently non-existent international political order.[3] We use the term "right" here in the second sense, that is, in the sense of a moral right, or, to use a more Rawlsian wording, as a legitimate expectation (Rawls 1971: 311).

Paradoxically, the philosophical debate seems very important and completely futile at the same time. It is important, given the scale of the problems related to poverty, and futile for the following two reasons: first, complicated philosophical discussions are barely necessary on that topic. A little common sense is largely sufficient to perceive the injustice of the current situation. A quick look at the figures quoted by Thomas Pogge (2002a) or others should suffice. What is equally obvious is that although many privileged people understand that the current situation is intolerable and, over time, probably untenable, even admitting that it is unjust, these people are not ready to give up their privileges any more that the French

---

libertarianism. This position is theoretical in the sense that there are no societies without any form of institutionally organized solidarity. Therefore, as Hilary Putnam puts it, theories like Robert Nozick's libertarianism "prove too much" (cf. Putnam 1990). Admittedly, it is also for non-libertarians important to know whether they are merely helping too little or also harming too much. Still, I focus here on justifications of the limitation of claim-rights to co-nationals.

[2] This text was initially written in French. In this language the expression "la préférence nationale" is highly polemical since it is a slogan much used by Jean-Marie Le Pen and his Front National.

[3] It should be noted that the term "moral right" is not used here, as it is quite commonly used, in a weak sense to indicate (moral) rights that do not demand any legal enforcement. According to my definition, people living under a dictatorial rule, in which there is no right to vote, have a moral right to vote: any morally defensible system should include such rights.

nobility were willing in 1789. In other words, the problem is not a genuine lack of philosophical perspicacity in the first place.

Secondly, if the topic of global justice is discussed in the framework of non ideal theory, (i.e., in the framework of a theory which takes the current situation and the constraints of political feasibility into account), most authors largely agree: global egalitarianism seems utopian nowadays but the satisfaction of basic needs should be guaranteed as a claim-right. Most people at least agree on the direction reforms should take.

However, despite the relative futility of the philosophical debate as such, some philosophical questions still need to be clarified. In this paper I focus on a single topic: giving priority to fellow citizens in distributive justice. Section 2 sketches how global justice has become a major topic in the egalitarianism debate. Section 3 discusses the associativist argument in favor of national preference, i.e., the idea that we do not need a further justification for giving priority to compatriots beyond the mere fact of shared citizenship. Section 4 examines some indirect arguments in favor of national preference.

2. Is "egalitarianism" necessarily global?

2.1 The moral arbitrariness of nationality

It is astonishing that those political philosophers who put social justice high on the agenda, notably John Rawls and the authors who contributed to the post-Rawlsian discussion, implicitly or, in Rawls's case, explicitly assume that social justice is specifically a national issue. Until a few years ago, one *obviously* established solidarity with one's compatriots.[4] However, this is quite amazing since the Rawlsian framework *demands* an extension to global justice for two reasons. This section briefly presents these reasons. The first reason is straightforward; the second relies on a contradiction in Rawls's theory.

The straightforward argument goes like this. First, our opportunities in life are largely determined by our nationality, i.e., mostly by the country in

---

[4] The issue of global distributive justice is relatively new. Discussions about poverty and solidarity with people in developing countries are much older. For example, Peter Singer (1972) argued in terms of moral obligations, but not in terms of an unjust international institutional context.

which we are born.[5] Secondly, birthplace and the nationality of one's parents are clearly "morally arbitrary" in the Rawlsian sense:[6] we cannot see how someone could be held responsible for her nationality nor for its negative consequences. Three, consequently, the current international order is a kind of feudal state: some are imprisoned within the borders of territories without many resources, whereas others benefit from a particular "liberty": not being disturbed by the worst-off on the planet (see Carens 1992: 26).

Faced with this situation, two positions seem coherent. First libertarianism, which rejects claim-rights in general, be they from co-nationals or from foreigners. The second position consists of generalizing the scope of claim-rights globally. Most problematic is the most popular nationalist position which holds that we have only minimal Samaritan duties to foreigners and more substantial obligations towards compatriots.

2.2 Does Rawlsianism imply economic patriotism?

The second argument which shows that the Rawlsian framework demands to be extended globally is that, assuming a globalized economy, the scope of weakly egalitarian concepts of social justice, i.e., concepts partially based on principles of equality, can only be limited to the nation-state at the price of accepting strange and incoherent moral motivations of that nation's citizens. This argument draws on G. A. Cohen's criticism of Rawls's acceptance of so-called incentive-inequalities. Although Cohen's criticism of Rawls is not fully convincing, and has indeed been the object of different meta-criticisms, it nevertheless points to a difficulty of Rawlsian arguments in a context of international mobility of people and capital.

In order to spell out this point, let us start from the difficulty in Rawls's theory pointed out by G. A. Cohen.[7] The moral foundation of (weak) egalitarianism is the notion of equal respect — mostly related to concepts such as *common humanity*.[8] Equal respect remains an empty and somehow hypocritical notion if it is not implemented in formal institutions. That means practically such things as that your basic rights should be respected,

---

[5] Herbert Simon argues that "any causal analysis explaining why American GDP is about $25,000 per capita would show that at least 2/3 is due to the happy accident that the income recipient was born in the U.S." (Letter to the organizers of 7th Basic Income European Network Conference published in *Basic Income* 28, quoted by Van Parijs 2002: 131).

[6] See Rawls 1971: 141 and Pogge 1989: 247.

[7] In different writings, but my reconstruction is mainly based on Cohen 1995. See Pogge 2000a for further references.

[8] To the extent that social life is organized in a closed self-sufficient nation-state, this comes practically down to a concept of common citizenship.

which in turn leads to more practical questions like access to essential services such as health care, education, etc. Weak egalitarians who argue for a more equal distribution of these essential goods admit that strict equality of condition is not the ultimate goal. Pareto-superior allocations, especially such allocations that improve everyone's situation (and in which the worst-off are better off than under a strict egalitarian regime) are morally acceptable.

However, this egalitarian argument à la Rawls which seems prima facie so easily acceptable contains a major difficulty: taking its assumption seriously implies rather an argument in favor of strict equality. Why is that? Let us start from a contradiction between two elements in Rawls's reasoning.[9] The first of these elements is that Rawls considers that any inequality which results from natural or social inequalities is unjust: "[t]he existing distribution of income and wealth, say, is the cumulative effect of the prior distributions of natural assets ... and their use favored or disfavored over time by social circumstances ... . Intuitively, the most obvious injustice of the system of natural liberty is that it permits distributive shares to be improperly influenced by these factors so arbitrary from a moral point of view" (Rawls 1971: 72). It is obvious that, if the influence of these arbitrary factors is systematically removed, we will end up with equal resources (Cf. Barry 1989). Nevertheless, Rawls believes that some deviation from this strict equality is permissible if it improves the situation of the worst-off. This necessity is linked to the role of those *incentives* which motivate the talented. In short, even if there is no *cause* justifying inequality, the beneficial *consequences* to which it sometimes gives rise may in themselves provide a form of justification.

The second element is that, according to Rawls, in a just society all the citizens agree with the principles behind the institutions and consider them legitimate. The principles of justice in a society are *stable* when people who are educated within those institutions which embody these basic principles develop accordingly a corresponding sense of what is just and manage to quash any egoistic tendency to move towards injustice (Rawls 1971: 454). In other words, they are motivated by the idea of fraternity which is embodied by the difference principle: "the idea of not wanting to have greater advantages unless this is to the benefit of others who are less well off" (Rawls 1971: 105).

The question is, then, why people who are firmly convinced that the situation of the worst-off should be improved as far as possible and who are disposed to abstain from the exploitation of natural or social circumstances

---

[9]   This argument draws on G. A. Cohen 1995.

should need incentives.[10] Indeed, if the talented adhere coherently to the principles which form the basis of the difference principle, they will agree to work for a normal reward for their effort. Of course, an exceptional reward which would recompense an exceptional effort merely respects the principle of equality.[11] What is at stake here are those incentive-based forms of reward which lead to inequality. In other words, inequality creating Pareto-improvements could also be made in ways that preserve the initial equality (Cohen 1995). Therefore, the conclusion is that those who seriously give priority to the worst-off should defend a much more egalitarian position. In fact they should defend strict equality.

One could reply to this criticism by distinguishing radically between private and public values. A person may admit that public institutions should be so conceived so as to "maximin" the relevant *distribuendum*, and yet as an individual act to further his own interests without any further concern for solidarity. For example, he may work less hard if tax thresholds are such as to make any extra effort hardly worthwhile. This radical separation between public and private values makes intellectual assent to the maximin and the selfish logic behind the incentives entirely compatible.

The separation of public and private values dovetails with the idea that justice is to be applied to the basic structure of society, in other words, that we have to apply other principles to judge behavior and decisions of individual persons or institutions with a specific objective, such as firms. If this dualism, as Liam Murphy has dubbed the claim "that the two practical problems of institutional design and personal conduct require, at the fundamental level, two different kinds of practical principle" (1999: 254), is accepted, then we may indeed conclude that, from a moral point of view, priority to the worst-off, and not strict equality, is the better ideal.[12]

An important point to stress here is that social justice then becomes possible on the basis of a weak motivational assumption, i.e., justice does not demand that one should fully refrain from the pursuit of individual well-being. It relies on a *double* reciprocity: one between the needy and the better-off and one for the better-off amongst themselves. The first can be interpreted as a hypothetical or actual insurance mechanism: I could have been born handicapped too, or I could lose my job too. Reciprocity among

---

[10] "For by arranging inequalities for reciprocal advantage and by abstaining from the exploitation of the contingencies of nature and social circumstance within the framework of equal liberty, persons express their respect for one another in the very constitution of their society" (Rawls 1971: 179).

[11] Notice that this egalitarianism does not imply equality of income. Cohen admits that hard work should be compensated, but simply for the sake of justice and not for incentive reasons.

[12] Note that Murphy (1999) defends monism, i.e., the denial of dualism.

the better-off means that each person individually agrees to pay his contribution if he is sure that the others will pay as well. Any mutual distrust which would undermine this reciprocity is overcome by legal enforcement. This makes justice not only a desirable but also a feasible ideal.

People like G. A. Cohen may advance the following objection to this "dualist" vision: why should people, as citizens, adhere to Rawlsian principles when their personal choices are based on principles which conflict with Rawlsianism? In other words, it seems impossible to separate completely the normative background of personal choices and of interpersonal behavior (the social *ethos*) from the normative background of the basic structure of society. Personal choices, social ethos and basic structure should be grounded in one and the same normative argument.

However, Cohen's position has been criticized from different perspectives. An internal criticism is based on the fact that G. A. Cohen himself admits some incentive inequalities, from which a slippery slope argument shows how difficult is to distinguish "justified" from "unjustified" incentive inequalities (Williams 1998, Pogge 2000a, Joshua Cohen, forthcoming). Further, it has been argued that G. A. Cohen's representation of Rawls's theory is somewhat misleading: Rawls does not neglect the importance of the social ethos favorable to egalitarianism (and the reciprocal influence of that ethos and the basic structure (Joshua Cohen, forthcoming). More fundamentally, it has been argued that "monism" would lead to a tyrannical system in contradiction with Rawls's first principle of justice, which says that basic liberties should be maximized (Pogge 2000a). Finally, it is shown that a weaker version of egalitarianism, in terms of basic human rights, is not subject to the tension revealed by G. A. Cohen (Pogge 2000a).

These arguments have clearly shown the limited scope of G. A. Cohen's criticism. However, Cohen's point has, indirectly, some relevance for our issue of national preference: the contradiction between private and public values reappears, even more sharply, if one considers an international, integrated economy in which a talented person can maximize his income or, more generally, his well-being, by leaving his country.[13] In this case, the emigration of the talented is fully opposed to improving the situation of the worst-off. In this case the somewhat schizophrenic compatibility between the logic of incentives (and private egoism) and the logic of maximin (and generosity by means of a political institution) disappears. It follows logically that sincere acceptance of the difference principle should necessarily be combined with some degree of patriotism, defined as the refusal to leave one's community in order to improve one's own economic situation elsewhere. A patriot consciously limits the exploitation of his talents for

---

[13] Van Parijs (1993) explores the contradiction from this angle.

reasons of solidarity with the worst-off in his own community.[14] However, this requires mixing public and private preferences in such a way that social justice now demands more than the weak motivation based on a guaranteed reciprocity: how can I, as a talented person disposed to stay despite financial advantages abroad, be sure that other talented citizens will display the same disposition?

If some degree of globalization is a fact, the conclusion of this discussion is a trilemma: you should either accept that giving priority to the worst-off implies inequalities resulting from incentives that are unacceptable (thereby dropping the tension between personal interests and impartiality in favor of the latter), and become a strict egalitarian, or you should argue for an extension of your principles of justice at a global level (and bite the bullet of the absence or at least the weakness of international enforcement mechanisms), or you have to suppose that people have a very strange motivation structure: people are motivated by both personal interest and impartiality, with the border of their country as the horizon of their impartial view. Beyond these borders things become strangely complicated: their activities over there are constrained on the one hand by very limited obligations towards the local people (to respect their basic rights, to restrain from brutal exploitation) and not by any further form of solidarity, but on the other hand their obligations towards their own compatriots become at once very strong: the most obvious reason to cross the border, i.e., to make more money than one earns in his own country, is morally unacceptable, whereas this very logic of incentives is fully acceptable at home. Moreover the nationalistic motivation is supposed to be very strong, because a state enforcement not to flee, i.e., Hobbesian logic of public enforcement to overcome the Prisoners' Dilemma, comes down to begging the question.

3. The moral value of nationality

Why should nationality be the right level for social justice? And why should global justice not prevail over national social justice? In this section, I shall discuss two variants of the "associativist" argument in favor of giving priority to one's compatriots. In a nutshell, this argument says that we have

---

[14] The requirement of patriotism is a pragmatic answer to this problem. If, on the one hand, one is ready to decline foreign incentives for reasons of solidarity with one's compatriots, why should one accept domestic incentives? On the other hand, someone who accepts the difference principle accepts the principles it is based on: inequalities resulting from morally arbitrary characteristics are unjust, and nationality is clearly one of these. And the question then arises why we should limit considerations of justice at the border of a country (cf. Van Parijs 1995: 228ff).

special obligations to our compatriots and, correspondingly, special claims on them, just because we are compatriots. In other words, belonging to the same nation creates a particular relationship which, in itself, has moral significance. Although we do not choose our nationality, according to this vision it constitutes a kind of extended (similarly not chosen) kinship: just as we have special obligations towards our parents or our children, we have particular, though different obligations towards our compatriots (cf. Singer 2002: 167). It is obvious that this vision may be qualified as "communitarian." Alasdair MacIntyre, communitarian *par excellence*, is very explicit: "I am a citizen of this or that city ... I belong to this tribe, that clan, this nation. Hence what is good for me has to be what is good for one who inhabits these roles. As such, I inherit from the past of my family, my city, my tribe, my nation, a variety of debts, inheritances, rightful expectations and obligations. These constitute the given of life, my moral starting point" (MacIntyre 1984: 220).

It is indeed obvious that we indeed have at least a spontaneous feeling of having special obligations towards some categories of people. However, we should not accept these feelings at face value. First, we should in general be wary of these particular relationships and ask whether they are legitimate, that is, whether or not they can be justified in a universalizable way. If they can not, they are merely questionable forms of favoritism. After all, a particular obligation towards people of the same ethnic background on the basis of spontaneous sympathy is what we call racism.[15] Historically, it has been proven that people are able to overcome tribal reflexes.[16]

Secondly, particular links, even when they are legitimate as defined above, do not *as such* trump obligations of justice. It is, for example, unacceptable for a public servant to favor some member of his or her family in the context of his professional activities.[17] Similarly, if the arguments we are now analyzing turn out to be unconvincing, respecting norms of justice implies, a priori, not favoring compatriots to the detriment of foreigners. Finally, a fundamental distinction has to be made, I think, between

---

[15] Cf. Singer 2002: 161ff. Singer mentions the partial relation between parents and children as a form of partiality which can be justified impartially "given the unavoidable constraints of human nature" (162). To illustrate how strong this constraint is, Singer mentions the difficulties encountered in collective education projects in kibbutzim communities, where mothers felt frustrated not to be allowed to take particular care of their own children.

[16] See again Singer (2002: 163) for examples. The shocking remarks of, e.g., Hume and Kant on race illustrate how recent the general agreement on the moral rejection of racism is. Cf. Eze 1997.

[17] Cf. Pogge 2002a: 120–1. Swift (2004) develops a compelling argument limiting parents' rights to excessively favor their own children, i.e., at the expense of the basic claims of other children.

obligations which are based on face-to-face relationships (kinship, long-standing intimacy, etc.) and institutionally based, i.e., anonymous relationships. Unlike intimate relationships such as the mother-child link which seems particular in a perhaps genetically determined way, the adequate level of institutional relationships among people, such as, for example, participating at a pension fund, is certainly neither genetically constrained nor based on particular feelings. For example, if French people living in Paris are able to attribute claim-rights to people living on La Réunion (in the Indian Ocean) whom they will probably never meet, because that island happens to be French, there is no reason to suppose that they could not attribute the same rights to the people from Madagascar.

The idea that sharing the same nationality is nevertheless a special morally significant relationship quite similar to kinship is sometimes spelled out in related terms such as identity or culture. I briefly present these variants in order to show how unconvincing they seem.

3.1 Identity and justice

The first variant of associativism often advanced is that, although nationality is not something you have chosen, it is part of our identity. The people who make up a nation share this identity, and have thus a legitimate desire to determine their collective future and, so the argument goes, also specific mutual obligations and rights.

First of all, it is not obvious that people's identities are above all national. Within a nation there may be groups of people who define themselves in the first place on the basis of their ethnicity, religion, region, or language.

But more fundamentally, even if the people of a particular nation really share a national identity, this is not a sufficient reason for saying that social justice is above all a national matter. The link between national identity (or any other identity) and social justice is highly questionable.

Admittedly, one should not deny that morally arbitrary factors such as the color of one's skin, the place where one was born, one's nationality or one's mother tongue are definitely essential aspects of their identity. There is no point in altering or denying them as some people like, for example, Michael Jackson would like to. However, one should strictly separate identity, on the one hand, and particular forms of justice and solidarity, on the other. Clearly, arguing for the opposite implies that since I am white, I owe more to fellow white needy people than to similarly needy blacks. Since, as a matter of fact, people currently mix up identity and justice, we have to conclude that national feelings nowadays are much more related to racism than to a defensible form of solidarity.

Consider the following evidence. As everyone who happens to lecture at some university in sub-Saharan Africa will confirm,[18] many African students try to get a visa for Europe and dream of obtaining a European passport. I am quite confident that we could find more people in Africa, Asia and South America who want to be Europeans than there are actually inhabitants of the countries of the European Union. Of course their desire has nothing to do with European identity. If there were no relationship between opportunities and basic rights on the one hand, and national identity on the other, there would simply be no point in "wanting" to be European. People would be allowed to be what they are, which is the very meaning of identity. People who argue that identity is important, should therefore not merely conclude that justice should better not be based on collective identity, but rather that global justice is a necessary condition for preserving these intrinsically valuable identities. Global injustice is what causes some people to deny their own identity. As a consequence, in this matter there need not necessarily be a contradiction between cosmopolitan justice on the one hand and patriotism (or, similarly, the will to preserve a particular cultural identity) on the other.[19]

The same argument holds with respect to the argument for rejecting the priority of global justice, and, accordingly, for limiting immigration, based on the desire to preserve a particular cultural identity. Again I cannot see here a decisive normative reason why an entity characterized by a particular culture should be the ultimate level for achieving "social justice." Consider the example of Belgium, a nation with two different culturally defined entities: there is no *moral* reason why autonomous cultural policies in Flanders and Wallonia should imply a separate Welfare State. The recent Flemish claim for a separate Welfare State is clearly not based on a distinguished deep commitment to a particular conception of social justice in Flanders and Wallonia but, more down to earth, on the fact that there is a regular transfer from the North (Flanders) and the South (Wallonia) because of demographic and economic reasons.

---

[18] I have taught a couple of times at the University of Yaoundé, but I am quite confident that the aspirations of other African students are very similar as those of the Cameroonian students.

[19] Patriotism, understood as "love of one's country" may be understood in a "republican," i.e., a non-chauvinist, way. Republican patriots desire their people to be respected by other people and, as a consequence, adhere to cosmopolitan justice. Cf. White 2002 and Appiah 1996.

3.2 Shared values

The second associativist variant for rejecting the theory that global justice should prevail over national social justice is also communitarian: the concept of social justice is a culturally determined "thick" concept, which means one thing on this side of the Pyrenees and something else on the other side. Moreover, the meaning of "goods" (i.e., products, benefits or assets) would be dependent on a person's particular background. Therefore, it would be impossible to conceive a universal conception of distributive justice.[20]

This second variant has been developed by Michael Walzer (1983) and has often been repeated since. But I think that, as an argument in favor of national preference, it is absolutely unconvincing. We may admit that the relative value of some particular goods depends on a particular cultural background, which determines their meaning: this is certainly true of bottles of whisky, CDs with rap music, headscarves, etc. But it is totally wrong for the most common benefits. The real significance of safe drinking water is the same for Americans as for Nigerians (and even its meaning for non-human animals must be quite similar). The same holds for electric lamps, antibiotics, bread or petrol, etc.

Moreover, even if in some countries there exist specific lifestyles for which particular things have special significance and value, it is far from sure that this meaning is shared by all the citizens of the country.[21] Yet, despite different cultural or religious backgrounds people can very easily identify with their multicultural nation and subscribe to its concept of social justice (see Miller 1999a). Finally, specific significance may also be shared across borders. Intellectuals from different countries share with one another their appreciation of the value of intellectual life, literature and books, more than with other social groups in their respective countries.

Some have even argued from the opposite point of view that sharing the same values does not necessarily imply sharing your solidarity mechanism. "Shared values" with someone is different from feeling solidarity with them. Will Kymlicka remarks that the Quebecois have roughly the same value system as other Canadians, but yet wish to have their own solidarity system

---

[20] Notice that both variants of communitarian associativism are very different from and actually conflict with each other. The first variant merely says that communitarian identity is a very important value, and this implies a communitarian shared future, mutual obligations and rights. The second variant says that all values are grounded in particular communities. As a consequence, the value of communitarian identity is not absolute (as the first variant claims) but depends on how a particular community values it.

[21] Weinstock (2002: 277) gives some examples of contrasting views on traditional lifestyles in Canada.

(Kymlicka 2001: 261f). Although I have doubts about the relevance of "particular feelings" as motivation for sharing a solidarity mechanism, this argument again illustrates the arbitrariness of the link between shared values and social justice.

4. Indirect arguments for giving priority to one's compatriots

Let us now consider some arguments in favor of giving priority to compatriots which are not based on "special relationships" or on such considerations as identity. After all, there might be more down-to-earth ethical arguments for rejecting the primacy of global justice over national distributive justice.

4.1 The nation as a cooperative venture

The first argument to consider social justice at the national level is that nations are cooperative ventures for mutual advantage. This expression is originally Rawls's.[22] Mutual advantage means that everyone concerned with gaining benefits for himself is better able to do so within a system of social cooperation than in one where this is absent. Of course, this cooperation is made possible by institutions and principles with which each individual can agree. Therefore, the idea of a cooperative venture embodies a combination of interdependence, mutual benefit (reciprocity) and mutual consent. In such a situation, rules of justice concern the way in which the cooperative surplus, i.e., what is jointly produced minus what each could have produced on his own, and jointly provoked harms should be shared. More precisely, justice is about the relationship among the partners in the venture. Relationships with other people fall beyond the pale of justice. If a nation is indeed a cooperative venture, and there is no cooperative venture on the international level, then, as a consequence, our obligations to people from other nations do not belong to the realm of justice. The rich nations have at most a duty of assistance (Rawls 1999: 116).

The idea of a nation as *and only as* a cooperative venture has some serious drawbacks. For one thing, it is highly questionable from an ethical

---

[22] "Although a society is a cooperative venture for mutual advantage, it is typically marked by a conflict as well as an identity of interests. There is an identity of interests since social cooperation makes possible a better life for all than any would have if each were to try to live solely by his own efforts. There is a conflict of interests since men are not indifferent as to how the greater benefits produced by their collaboration are distributed" (Rawls 1971: 126).

viewpoint: it implies that people with whom mutually advantageous arrangements are impossible, for example, because they are seriously disabled, should be excluded from the solidarity system. For another, this vision implicitly assumes that a nation is a self-contained unit. However, this idea no longer fits in with reality. Globalization means that interdependence and mutually advantageous relations exist all over the planet nowadays.[23] Therefore, insofar as there is a *global* cooperative venture, the scope of justice should be increased to include the whole globe. It could be objected here that our moral obligations should be smaller to some nations to the extent that their economies do not participate in globalization. However, economic interdependence no longer merely concerns trade: it may as well be related to climate change.[24] Finally, the notion of mutual consent seems equally wrongheaded from a historical viewpoint. Nations are not *voluntary* cooperative ventures at all. Current immigration policies show that the opposite is true.

4.2 Efficiency, effectiveness and general question-begging arguments

Sometimes it is argued that only nations are able to implement justice, because nations are the only entities that can levy taxes and require policemen and soldiers to obey orders.[25] Similarly, only nations have the legitimacy to impose formal solidarity systems which incorporate those ideas about social justice which are largely shared by the population. Of course these are question-begging arguments which do not need much comment. Darrel Moellendorf calls them forms of "justice-positivism," analogous to legal positivism: "One stands under a duty of justice only if the institutions have been developed to hold us accountable" (2002: 39).

However, some have advanced more subtle variants. One of these comes from Robert Goodin's (1988) argument which is based on efficiency. Roughly, Goodin says that if nations are not particularly responsible for implementing justice among their citizens, then justice might not be implemented at all. Just like someone who has broken down by the side of the road may wait a long time for a lift or for help when there is a lot of traffic because no passing driver feels a particular duty to help. When almost no cars come along, the first driver who does is more likely to stop. This

---

[23] Singer (2002) explores the different dimensions globalization has taken as well as their ethical implications.

[24] See again Singer 2002 for an overview.

[25] This argument is often repeated in replies to Martha Nussbaum's essay *For Love of Country*, notably by Nathan Glazer and Gertrude Himmelfarb.

argument may have some value, but only from an instrumental viewpoint and, moreover, only when resources are more or less equally divided among the different nations.[26] Otherwise, the obligations incumbent on the better-off from poor countries could be excessively high: if he has not stolen his money, why should a rich African have to pay for all his poor fellow citizens (and thus sacrifice his wealth) if all these rich Western people do not have the same obligation? At most, one could argue that both should contribute, and that both may refuse to carry the burden alone.

A second variant is formulated in terms of the link between egalitarianism and democracy. People would have a stronger obligation to reduce inequality within a nation than among different nations, because profound inequalities within a country constitute a danger for a democratic political community: formal rights such as the right to be elected would be ineffective, made unrealistic by huge economic inequalities. Moreover, profound inequalities could possibly lead to oppressive relationships. This undermines democratic equality, i.e., the fact that people relate to one another as equals (despite some moderate social and economic inequalities) and, as a consequence, can consider one another as belonging to the same political community.

However, although these arguments make sense, it is not obvious that they imply that our obligation to reduce inequality within our own society overrides our obligations towards the world's poorest people. For one thing, these obligations are not necessarily mutually exclusive.[27] For another, if it is important for democracy that inequalities should be limited, by transferring money to poor people in the poorest nations, rich people from rich countries can make a greater contribution to reducing inequality within the poorer nations than to reducing inequality in their own nation (cf. Singer 2002: 175). Finally, it is sufficient to have a quick look at the social audit reports of the sweatshops in Asia which supply Western companies to know how oppressive relations between citizens of different countries can be.

4.3 The social nature of consumption

Another often heard argument in favor of giving priority to one's compatriots is that perception of one's own poverty is relative to the wealth of the environment in which one lives. "Poverty" would be a culturally and

---

[26] David Miller defends the same idea, not only in an instrumental but also in a substantial perspective: "positive obligations to protect basic rights fall in the first place on co-nationals" (Miller 1995: 79).

[27] Note that precisely these countries with limited internal inequality are often the most generous donors of development aid (Denmark, Sweden, Norway and the Netherlands).

socially determined notion. A person who lives poorly in a wealthy country would suffer much more than a poor person among other poor people. It all depends on the pattern of consumer behavior in one's immediate environment (Wellman 2000: 547f).

This is simply wrong. Authors who advance this point of view clearly show by their statement that they have never traveled in developing countries. People all over the world, even in the poorest regions, often have the opportunity to watch television. For instance, in countries of sub-Saharan Africa, people almost exclusively watch European or American television programs. In French-speaking Africa in particular, people have more information about the traffic jams around Paris and about the French soccer league than about a *coup d'état* in a neighboring country. It is impossible for them not to compare their standard of living with the standard of living of the people in the TV series they are watching. Similarly, when a European cooperates with African colleagues, it seems impossible for the latter not to compare their working conditions with those in Europe. It is certainly not the case that people in developing countries are unaware of their relative poverty. The opposite is true: people in rich countries have no idea of what happens in poor areas of the globe. The argument about "the social nature of consumption" is just a case in point.

4.4 Examples of egalitarian systems

An argument that is not often heard is the following one advanced by Darrel Moellendorf (2002: 66). Moellendorf says that one reason for not letting global justice take precedence over egalitarian national justice is that it is important, especially for unequal nations, to have *examples* of more egalitarian systems. The "loss of an egalitarian model of wealth distribution" (Moellendorf 2002: 66) would indeed be a pity, but this seems a purely theoretical danger: we can hardly imagine that humanity will quickly forget about the social and economic rights which are currently in force in Western European countries (and it would definitely be progress if the whole world population had similar rights).

4.5 Political culture and immigration

The last of the arguments I want to discuss is a mixture of the associativist argument described in section 3.1 and the question-begging argument in section 4.2. It has been argued, and notably by David Miller (2000), that it is justified to subordinate global justice to national solidarity if this is necessary to preserve a particular *political* culture with a specific conception of social justice. Miller rejects the predominance of global justice because, in the conflict between self-determination and global justice, those nations deprived of self-determination (because of the obligations of global justice) would be prevented from practicing social justice. In other words, Miller's most important reason why self-determination "trumps" global justice is not, as one might expect, the preservation of a national culture, but the possibility of realizing a particular form of social justice.[28] One implication of this position is that it is legitimate to restrict immigration as well as emigration if these would undermine that possibility.

We can recall the general point I advanced earlier: justice is always a moral constraint on several different levels at the same time. My obligation to behave justly to my children or my colleagues, etc. do not weaken my obligations to behave justly on a wider level, e.g., to pay my taxes and other contributions to the social security system. Similarly, the requirement that governments should establish social justice through some form of social policy does not exempt them from their obligations towards other people.

For the question of migration, it is important to stress that movement into and out of a country should be considered in a coherent way. On the one hand, it is a moral obligation — also according to Miller who is perfectly coherent in this respect — not to leave your nation merely for the sake of financial advantage (2000: 293). One might think, for example, of British academics who could command bigger salaries in the United States. It is an obligation, not to people in the country that is likely to provide this financial advantage, but to your compatriots with whom you live in one cohesive community. Solidarity with your fellow countrymen does indeed imply the obligation not to flee if your emigration, although personally advantageous, penalizes them. The flip side of the moral obligation not to leave your country for the sake of financial advantage is the much more popular right of a community to refuse economic immigrants.

However, both points, i.e., the argument to limit emigration *for reasons of social justice* and its flip side, the moral right to restrict immigration, seem questionable. First, what if people emigrate not for their own well-being, but precisely for the well-being of their compatriots, that is, if they are motivated by solidarity? Consider the following situation: a few million African people feel a strong moral obligation to feed their families. There is no serious way to achieve this aim in their own country. In the eyes of these people the world must appear as a very unjust place. So they prefer to go to France and to become good French citizens. Can they be blamed? Not according to Miller's argument, it seems.

The moral right to limit immigration in the name of social justice suffers from a similar weakness. Again, let us focus on the African economic

---

[28] Miller also advances other reasons, some of which are discussed earlier in this paper.

refugees moved by solidarity and not on, for instance, French engineers who emigrate to California for tax reasons. Of course the French will refuse these African people. Is this refusal legitimate? The justification cannot be that they threaten the particularity of French national identity, since the latter is not ethnically based. We may suppose that these Africans speak French very well, and they are perfectly able, despite their different cultural background, to adhere to this thin concept of nationality and to the principles which underlie the Sécurité Sociale (The French Welfare State). Low-skilled Africans are not less able to become good French citizens, and to sing the Marseillaise, than the talented football players with mostly African roots who won the World Cup.

The legitimate reason to turn them back cannot be either that the principles of solidarity that underlie the Welfare State presuppose the current standard of living of the industrialized nations. If an important inflow of immigrants led to a decrease in the average income, the legitimacy of these principles would not be weakened. After all, the current Welfare State was created in 1948, at a moment when the GNP/capita was not even half as great as it is now, and it functioned very well. Thus the normatively valid reason for the French refusal can be neither the intrinsic nor the instrumental value of nationality, i.e., the implementation of social justice. The crucial explanation — which is not a justification — for refusing these economic refugees is that even immigration on a small scale might slightly diminish the welfare prospects of current French citizens (whether or not they have French or foreign ethnic roots), i.e., the prospects of a group of individuals, who are, I think wrongly, convinced that they have a legitimate claim to their current welfare level. After all, foreign investors are not rejected for reasons of nationality.

5. Conclusion: oculi habent sed non videbunt

The position which seems defensible to me and to many other people is that states, communities, or even individuals may organize their own lives as long as they respect the rules of justice determined at a wider level. This wider level may be the state level, but it may also be the global level: national self-determination should be exercised within the limits imposed by our principles of global justice as personal and group autonomy is limited by the requirements of national justice.

I discussed briefly some arguments that several authors have advanced to defend the opposite position, i.e., to justify the facts that rich Western people have established to justify "national preference," thereby denying, in reality, the rights of the poorest people on the planet. From a philosophical viewpoint, my arguments are not complex. They are almost blatantly simple. Of course this may be due to my limited philosophical competence, but one cannot exclude the possibility that it may also be related to the weakness of the arguments I had to combat.

Let us, for the sake of argument, consider the latter possibility. In this case, one major question crops up: if the weakness of moral justifications for discrimination according to nationality is so obvious, why are people still convinced by them?

A first possible explanation is that people's moral judgment is swayed by their self-interest. People think, wrongly, that if they recognize that the poorest people have some rights, this will require them to make enormous sacrifices. Secondly, it might be the case that a lot of people on the planet are convinced that the current situation is unjust, but that these people are simply heard less often because the richest people dominate the mass media. Thirdly, a major explanation is undoubtedly what Thomas Pogge calls "explanatory nationalism," i.e., the fact that economic data are presented as "national" data and the fact that policies are discussed as "national" policies creates the illusionary perception that the causes of poverty are also national. This way of presenting economic phenomena makes people blind to the violation of basic human rights imposed by the current international economic order. Sometimes, for example, when Italian Ferrari-freaks wave Italian flags while hearing the German national anthem, we see funny breaches in this way of representing all kinds of events from a nationalistic perspective.

However, whatever the exact explanation, as long as people are convinced of the legitimacy of the current and even growing inequality of the global distribution of resources, serious transfers of purchasing power are simply politically not feasible. Yet morally, they remain an unquestionable obligation.

Chapter 6

International or Global Justice? Evaluating the Cosmopolitan Approach[*]

Thomas Mertens
Law School, Radboud Universiteit Nijmegen, the Netherlands

1. Introduction

It is commonly argued that philosophers take moral theory too seriously. Were they but to leave their studies and head out into the real world, they would quickly realize that they had been pursuing empty ideals. Philosophers' dreams may sound good, but are of no practical validity, and thus a politician, interested in the art of the practical, rightfully looks down on the theorist as a mere academic (Kant, 1793: 62, 1795: 93). Kant, however, in both "On the Common Saying: 'This may be true in theory, but it does not apply in practice'" (1793) and in "Perpetual Peace: A philosophical sketch" (1795), challenges the view that moral theory is of little value for ordinary practical life, and his writings aim at convincing his audience that what is right in theory, not only ought to, but also can be applied in practice, in both the private and the public life of men.

Despite Kant's efforts in this regard, the problem of how to transform sound moral theory into political practice has haunted authors ever since. Because of it, many recent authors have downplayed the level of the moral ambitions of their theories, and argued, like Walzer for example, in favor of an account of morality which seeks to stay close to practical life. Pogge's recent "cosmopolitan" contribution to the Global Justice debate takes a more Kantian line however. His *World Poverty and Human Rights* (Pogge 2002a) argues in favor of a radical, yet in his eyes feasible, transformation of the prevailing international "basic structure" which he considers to be in flagrant

[*] Many thanks to the editors of this volume and to Morag Goodwin and Thomas Kraniotis.

A. Follesdal and T. Pogge, (eds.), Real World Justice, 85-102.
© 2005 *Springer. Printed in the Netherlands.*

contravention of the requirements of justice. The gap between what is commonly acknowledged as requirements of morality and the actual conduct of citizens of the rich and wealthy countries must be bridged, according to Pogge, and he confronts these moral requirements with a vast collection of empirical data concerning the massive underfulfillment of basic social and economic rights worldwide.

It is fair to suggest that Pogge's moral argumentation is strongly influenced by and indebted to the moral philosophies of Kant and Rawls, but that it also departs profoundly from the positions they take. The demand for an institutionalization of a truly international global order does not seem reconcilable with the work of either. This then sets the agenda for this contribution. It will explore the different approaches to the concern of global justice among these three philosophers: Pogge, Kant and Rawls. Although Rawls in his writings criticizes Kant because of his adherence to a "comprehensive," metaphysical viewpoint, he nonetheless sides with Kant in distinguishing among several layers of justice, especially between justice on the domestic, national level and justice on the international, global scale (adding local justice as a third layer). What justice requires differs between these layers, domestic requirements being stronger and more demanding than international requirements. In comparison with both Kantian and Rawlsian views, the kind of transformation of the "law of peoples" proposed by Pogge is thus a quite revolutionary and utopian rejection of the "statist" approach defended by Kant and Rawls. Here, I intend to bring the main arguments together by confronting pleas for "international" justice with arguments in favor of "global" justice. By doing so, I hope to contribute to answering the question as to whether the cosmopolitan approach of Pogge and others represents an unjustifiably "moral theory," unfit for the highly complex practical life of the international society of societies, or whether it can be understood as a utopian, but nonetheless viable alternative for the vanishing Westphalian world of nation-states whose sovereign independence is no longer assured. First, I will present the Kantian and Rawlsian arguments in favor of a layered approach to justice. Secondly, the cosmopolitan's arguments in favor of "global" justice will be presented. Contrasting these views will enable me to then raise the Kantian question: if the requirements of global justice are true in theory, why are they so difficult to apply in practice? Does this difficulty point to the nature of morality itself?

2. Kant's rejection of world government

In modern philosophy, Kant was among the first to emphasize the moral obligation to establish legal relations not only with our co-nationals, but with all humans. Since the earth is a globe in which interaction cannot be avoided, no human being can be excluded from this legal constitution. It is thus a moral duty to leave the state of nature and to unite oneself with all others, subjecting oneself to external coercion in accordance with public laws (Kant 1797: 137f). The need to establish legal relations with all, however, does not imply equal legal relations. With the people of my nation I have to establish a republican constitution; as a member of such a republic I must contribute to the realization of a federation of free states; finally, foreigners and foreign communities ought to be treated with respect. In Kant's "ius cosmopoliticum" (Kant 1795: 99n), however, the distinction between same and other is not denied, nor is patriotism ruled out.[1]

For what reasons did Kant adopt such a layered legal structure? First of all, Kant rejects the world-republic as being contradictory: if a number of nations were to form one state, it would constitute a single nation and it would cease to be an "international" state. This is not a strong argument. If the establishment of peaceful legal relations among all humans as the "highest political good" (Kant 1797: 175) can only be reached by establishing a world-republic, why would the historical plurality of political communities then count as a counterargument to cosmopolitical government (Gerhardt 1995: 95)? Secondly, Kant (1795: 102, 105) argues that the concept of a world-republic is true "in thesi," but not "in hypothesi," since it does not correspond to the will of states. This argument is not particularly strong either: in his ethical writings, Kant does not seem to take into account that humans often do not want what they ought to do. The moral law has nonetheless an unconditional validity. Why would morality be applied differently where the moral actors are states instead of individuals? States are indeed more powerful than individuals and thus more reluctant to give up their arbitrary will, read: sovereignty, but that is a pragmatic argument, not a moral one.

Kant's (1795: 104) third argument is of a more serious nature: "While natural right allows us to say of men living in the lawless condition that they ought to abandon it, the right of nations does not allow us to say the same of states. For as states, they have already a lawful internal constitution, and

---

[1] The distinction between despotism and republicanism (Kant 1795: 101) is preceded by the distinction between despotism and patriotism. In despotism the entire freedom of the subject is suspended. Therefore it makes a patriotic attitude impossible, because nobody is able to regard the commonwealth as a maternal womb or the fatherland as a treasured pledge (Kant 1793: 74); see also Riedel (1993: 6, 12–13).

have thus outgrown the coercive right of others to subject them to a wider legal constitution in accordance with their conception of right." The analogy between individuals in a lawless state of nature and states in the international realm is not complete. The establishment of legal relations among states has to take into account their internal legal development. While individuals have nothing to lose when leaving the state of nature, states run a considerable risk when establishing international law. They might end up losing their internal lawful condition when choosing inappropriate legal means to escape from the state of war among them. If, for example, they were to opt to fuse the separate nations into a world republic, they could end up in the despotism of a "universal monarchy." Such "global justice" is, according to Kant, incompatible with respect for the diversity of different nations and a world-republic can only be created by negating those differences.

Fortunately, Kant concludes, in the long run no nation will be able to impose its will on all other nations and establish "universal monarchy." He mentions two reasons: first, laws progressively lose their impact if the government increases its range. This is the classical argument that a stable government is incompatible with too large a territory; second, differences among nations are too strong to be annihilated. According to Kant (1795: 113f), the intermingling of nations in a world-republic is prevented by nature itself, which intentionally divided mankind according to linguistic and religious differences. These differences among nations cannot and should not be overcome by legal arrangements on a world scale. The amalgamation of nations and gradual extinguishment of their characteristics is not beneficial to the human race (Kant 1798a: 320; Laberge 1995: 166f). Mankind is not only threatened by the differences among nations, but also benefits from the rivalry among them (Kant 1795: 114).

This picture of a peaceful system of nevertheless conflicting nations is deeply rooted in Kant's philosophy (Brandt 1995: 141; Laberge 1995: 160). In his philosophy of nature, Kant conceptualizes matter as a dynamic entity held together by the conflicting forces of attraction and repulsion. The structure of human society is not perceived much differently: the human race is characterized by unsocial sociability. Men tend to come together in society, but they also resist this tendency and threaten to break society up (Kant 1784: 44). All efforts to establish one single world republic with equal membership for all humans fail to acknowledge the unsocial element of human nature. A "realistically utopian" view on international law therefore aims at a decent antagonism, i.e., an antagonism among nations regulated by principles of external freedom (Kant 1797: 168f).

This third reason for rejecting "global justice" is not very convincing either, as it is based on a metaphysical conception of (human) nature irrelevant in a post-metaphysical era. Here, however, hasty conclusions should be avoided. One might also argue that Kant refers here to common sense. Everybody seems to accept that human beings, in order to develop their identity, always need to form part of a particular family, a particular language and a particular culture. Only within those particular backgrounds do human beings learn ethical and moral rules. Accepting this fact does not imply the exclusion of other particularities or the denial of universality, but may well explain the moral significance of borders (see Höffe 1995b, 264f). Many human beings tend to go beyond these linguistic, cultural and national borders by traveling or migrating. The risk that some people may seclude themselves in their own particular nation should not lead us to deny the significance of particularities. Without acknowledging such natural facts, moral knowledge becomes a moralistic, rigid ideology. Kant tries to avoid this rigidity and rejects the despotic boundaries of a world republic and advocates instead a cosmopolis of homelands (Riedel 1993: 17).

3. Rawls's theory of (domestic) justice

In the context of 20th century philosophy, Rawls's *A Theory of Justice* (1971) aims at reformulating and at bringing to a higher level of abstraction the familiar theory of the social contract as found in Locke, Rousseau and Kant (Rawls 1971: 10). Like these writers, Rawls holds that the principles of justice for the basic structure of society should be the object of an original contract. This he calls "justice as fairness": principles for a society are just when chosen by representative citizens placed within "fair" conditions.[2] When studying Rawls's text, it becomes evident that this theory of justice is meant to apply to the basic structure of a well-ordered society, the boundaries of which are supposed to coincide with a self-containing national, autarkical community. He admits that this presumption may need to be adjusted in the light of principles for the law of peoples, but he does not give much attention to formulating those principles (Rawls 1971: 457, 4). Despite its more abstract level, Rawls's theory thus seems in line with Kant's layered structure of justice.

This, of course, is not self-evident. Since the 18th century, it has become clear that a national state is not enough to guarantee natural rights, as supposed in social contract theory. Since these rights precede any political community, they need to be embedded and defended not only nationally, but also internationally. Their very nature requires a global legal order, as formulated in Article 28 of the 1948 *Universal Declaration of Human Rights*: "Everyone is entitled to a social and international order in which the

---

[2] Using the idea of pure procedural justice, see Rawls 1971: 85.

rights and freedoms set forth in this Declaration can be fully realized." This article aims not at adding yet another individual human right, but formulates the necessary legal precondition for the realization of basic rights, namely a global legal order. Human rights are not only important claims of individuals on other individuals and on their states, but also on the institutional order in which individuals and states are to function (Pogge 2002b). Furthermore, this seems to be fully in accordance with Rawls's moral intuition, namely that a person's prospects and possibilities in life should depend on choices that she makes for herself and on the responsibilities she accepts, but not — at least not to a large extent — on the natural and social structures into which she is born. Individuals should start with equal rights, and their societies should not give an undeserved advantage to some and an equally undeserved disadvantage to others. In our present world, the prospects of individuals are undeniably not only determined by their "social" place of birth within the national society, but also by the placing of their national society within the global order.

This then would suggest that Rawls would be in favor of a cosmopolitan interpretation of the social contract. The basic elements of Rawls's thought experiment, the initial position and the veil of ignorance, do not compel us to apply its outcome, i.e., the famous two principles of justice, to a national community only. Above that, such an interpretation seems confirmed by Rawls's statement that the relation among peoples should also be guided by some principles of justice, to be derived from an initial position as well, in what he calls "a second round" aiming at formulating the "law of peoples" (Rawls 1971, §58). According to many, the outcome of this second round is disappointing in that Rawls's principles of international justice replicate the conservative, state-oriented principles generally recognized in public international law: nations have the mutual right of self-determination and the right to self-defense; they should observe international agreements, including the laws of war (Rawls 1971: 378f). Such an outcome is easily understandable when noting that Rawls's negotiating parties in this second round are state representatives who make decisions based on the interests of those collective entities. But another understanding is surely possible. Why not see those negotiators as representing the relevant social positions that exist within these states and as reflecting the diversity of social positions in the world as a whole (Pogge 1994)? If the latter interpretation is followed, these representatives would not differ very much from their counterparts in the first initial position. In this (second) initial position they would similarly argue in favor for principles of justice that would ensure for each the largest possible share of primary goods. In the second, international round, the same two principles would be accepted and the distinction between the first and the second initial position would collapse. In both, representatives would opt for a division of basic goods in accordance with the two principles of justice and Rawls's theory of justice would then indeed be a theory of justice for the only "self-contained society" imaginable: the world community. The existence of a diversity of peoples and nations would fully depend upon whether this would aid realization of the two principles or not. The existence of "peoples" would be a matter of pragmatics, rather than a matter of principle.

Clearly, such an interpretation is not what Rawls defends. Firstly, an interpretation in which "basic rights and liberties" are understood globally does not fit the framework within which Rawls asks for the principles for the law of peoples. In *Theory of Justice*, these principles are developed in connection with the issue of obligation and the citizen's duty of obedience. International law is developed from the "internal" perspective of a question raised in society. Rawls argues that even within a (nearly) just society, serious questions may arise as to whether and when disobedience is permitted. In a society regulated by the two principles, citizens might nevertheless feel compelled to oppose certain parts of the law. After all, determining the principles of justice is important, but not enough for a "just" society. A society needs to pass through the more concrete stages of drafting the constitution and creating further legislation. Furthermore, laws and rules need to be applied by citizens in concrete situations and interpreted by judges and public bodies in particular cases (Rawls 1971, §31). If citizens think that specific legislation or the application of the law violates the higher principles of the legal order, on the level of the constitution or on that of its principles, they will consider the legal order as in contradiction with itself, and as a result they might feel compelled to violate the lower norm in order to obey the higher norm. But when is so-called "civil disobedience" justified and when not? An important case in this regard concerns military obligations. A theory of justice must provide an answer to the question as to when conscientious objectors are justified in resisting the use of military means by their society. Therefore, then, it is necessary to know what justice among states means. Representatives of the second initial position have the duty to determine these principles. *Theory of Justice* then gives the following answer (Rawls 1971, §58). A citizen can refuse his military obligations if he has good reasons to believe that his state is or will soon be involved in an unjust war. If the criteria of a just war are not met, citizens have the right, or even the obligation to refuse to participate in that war. The principles of international justice agreed upon in the second initial position are thus not designed for a cosmopolitan order. *Theory of Justice* rather departs from the world as it exists, namely, as an aggregate of independent unities.

A cosmopolitan interpretation of Rawls's *Theory of Justice* must also be rejected on the basis of his priority rule. In short, this rule states that breaches of liberties are justified only with regard to the scheme of those liberties itself, but never in pursuance of expanding the socioeconomic welfare of the society as a whole if a situation of moderate scarcity is reached. In connection with this, Rawls suggests that the two principles of justice in combination with the priority rule only suit a society that has already attained a certain level of economic development and living standards. It is said, therefore, that the two principles cannot be read as an abbreviation of universally applicable (civil, political and social) human rights. Now, this point should of course be dealt with carefully. This priority has been the subject of an extensive discussion, induced by H. L. A. Hart's provocative article (1973). On this issue, I can only be brief. Hart drew attention to the fact that Rawls's two principles with their "priority rule" form a specification of the more general conception of justice, according to which all social values, including liberties, must be "distributed equally unless an unequal distribution of any, or all, of these values is to everyone's advantage" (Rawls 1971: 62, 303). According to this *general* conception, it would be unjust to restrict liberties unequally, but it would not seem unjust to restrict liberties equally if this would lead to an increase of society's welfare as a whole. However, the priority rule excludes this limiting of liberties for the sake of social welfare and is thus a more *specific* conception of justice. In the initial position, representatives will only accept the priority rule if they know that their society satisfies certain favorable social and economic conditions. Only if these conditions are met will they exclude the possibility of restricting (certain) civil liberties for the sake of enhancing other social values (Rawls 1971: 152). Under circumstances of improving conditions of civilization, it will not be rational to accept a lower level of liberty in exchange for an increase of material well-being. The marginal significance of extra welfare will decrease in comparison with the appreciation of liberty (Rawls 1971: 542).

Hart criticized Rawls on this point: the increasing significance given to "liberty" by the representatives in the initial position of a relatively advanced society can only be based on the ideal of "liberty" not accounted for within *Theory of Justice*. In answer, Rawls (1993a: 289–371) was quick to declare that Hart's interpretation made him adjust his theory and that he indeed expressed himself wrongly: the priority rule was not based on some "comprehensive" preference for "liberty." Accordingly, Rawls (1993a: 371n, 1999: 44f) seriously revised *Theory of Justice*, paragraph 82, and no longer assigns priority to liberty as such, but to "a fully adequate scheme of equal basic liberties" compatible with an equal scheme for all, as the necessary condition for a society of free and equal persons.

This adjustment, however, does not change the argument against a universalistic interpretation of the priority rule concerning the two principles. Scattered remarks both in *Justice as Fairness* (Rawls 2001: 47) and in *The Law of Peoples* emphasize that the priority of basic rights and liberties depends on whether reasonably favorable conditions occur. It is even difficult to avoid the impression that *Justice as Fairness* consists of a hermeneutical "description" of what it means for a particular society to interpret itself as a fair system of cooperation among free and equal persons (Rawls 2001: 5), with the initial position being a heuristic device rather than an abstract thought experiment, applicable universally. If such a reading is correct, the two principles have no universal validity and the distinction between domestic and global justice is rightfully upheld by Rawls (1999: 11).[3]

4. Rawls's theory of international justice

For Rawls (2001: 11, 13f), global justice is the most encompassing layer of justice, to be distinguished from local justice applicable to institutions and associations within a domestic society, and from domestic justice formulating principles for the basic structure of a society. Rawls discusses global justice most extensively in *The Law of Peoples*.

Here, Rawls (1999: 10, 22) follows Kant's lead and explicitly defends the idea of a double contract. He holds that a realistic utopia departs from where we are, here and now, namely, in a situation in which we find a plurality of political communities (Rawls 1999: 30, 32, 83). The "law of peoples" results from a second original position, in which the parties are representatives of those peoples whose basic institutions satisfy the principles of justice selected at the first level (Rawls, 1993b: 48, 1971: 64). Rawls explicitly rejects the suggestion of Beitz (1979) and Pogge (1994: 205f6) to define principles of global justice by imagining only one all-embracing original position, in which the parties are not representing peoples, but persons holding various social positions and offices worldwide (see, e.g., Pogge 1994: 205f). This position is referred to as "cosmopolitanism." According to Rawls, a realistic utopia cannot ignore the existence of a diversity among peoples with different cultures and traditions of thought (Rawls 1999: 11). Contemporary cosmopolitanism represents a non-realistic utopia of establishing world government.

Like Kant, Rawls sees liberal democratic societies as the focal point of a federation of peoples. Because such liberal societies are internally structured by the rule of law and have a certain moral character (Rawls 1999: 8, 25),

---

[3] "Justice as fairness" is only characteristic of the most egalitarian form of liberalism. See also Rawls 1993b: 51.

they are prepared to offer fair terms of cooperation to other societies. Statistical evidence confirms this: liberal societies are inherently peaceful.[4] Societies that are structured differently, for example, hierarchically, might accept the fair terms offered by their liberal counterparts, but will not themselves take the initiative to develop the law of peoples. Key elements of the law of peoples are the right to self-determination, the right to self-defense, basic "politically neutral," "not politically parochial" (Rawls, 1993b: 69, 1999: 65) human rights, such as the right to seek and enjoy asylum from persecution in other countries,[5] and the humanitarian law of war in line with Kant's sixth preliminary article.[6]

In following the institutional form of Kant's "international justice" so closely, Rawls also appears to follow Kant's conception of nature and the concept of the "social unsociability." He argues that the "law of peoples" is in line with deep tendencies and inclinations of the social world. Its principles and precepts are workable and applicable to the political and social arrangements of the world we inhabit (Rawls 1999: 128, 12f). Of course, Rawls no longer subscribes to Kant's belief that the great artist "Nature" would guarantee the end of war. Yet he defends that establishing the "law of peoples" is possible and he denies that the political world of states and communities is an irreducible Hobbesian pluriversum. Without denying the unsocial tendencies, Rawls, like Kant, holds that man's "sociability" will prevail. In this respect, he adds two elements: first, public reason and publicity will have a beneficial role in overcoming unsociability and in convincing political leadership of what the real interests of society are (Rawls 1999: 97); second, world commerce will have a beneficial effect in this direction too. This follows from Rawls's concept of so-called burdened societies. Societies that are burdened by unfavorable circumstances do not refute the thesis that world commerce in general has beneficial effects. Generally they are burdened more by the lack of political and cultural traditions than by economic monopolies and trade barriers invented by well-off peoples (Rawls 1999: 106).[7] Such societies will make progress as soon as

---

[4] This is sometimes referred to as Doyle's law, see Doyle 1983. However, see also Cavallar 2001.

[5] I ignore the differences here between the two versions of "the law of peoples." Rawls incorporates the right to emigration into the list of basic human rights, see Rawls 1993b: 68. In the extended version, Rawls (1999: 8–9, 38n) puts more emphasis on a people's qualified right to limit immigration. See also *Universal Declaration*, Article 14.1.

[6] The main difference between Kant and Rawls is the latter's acceptance of what he calls the "supreme emergency exemption," which allows combatants to set aside the strict non-combatant status of civilians under certain special circumstances, see Rawls 1999: 98. According to Kant (1795: 97), however, this sixth article is of the strictest sort and allows of no exception.

[7] Pogge (2002a: 15, 143–5) calls this explanatory nationalism.

they have developed a decent internal political culture. Therefore there is no need for a more egalitarian oriented "law of peoples," in which an element of distributive justice, like the difference principle, is included. The difference principle is valid only for a liberal society with strong egalitarian features (Rawls 1993b: 51). The crucial element, according to Rawls (1999: 117), in how a country fares is its political culture, and not the level of its resources.[8]

Although Kant's and Rawls's versions of "international justice" have much in common, there are however a number of important differences. The situation in which they wrote differs substantially. Kant wrote in a time of transition from monarchical to republican rule. The units from which "Perpetual Peace" was to be created had still to be developed. A concrete society of societies regulated by the rule of law seemed hardly imaginable. Almost two centuries later, Rawls had the experience of international law and international organizations on which to build. With this in mind, the "law of peoples" is considerably less utopian than Kant's in his day. The reason for this is clear: Rawls does not share Kant's metaphysical belief in human history as guided by an immanent teleology, nor does he share Kant's metaphysical, comprehensive liberal view. Within the frame of Kant's liberalism, it was evident that any institutional design for a lasting peace should start from the institutions as they were developing "then and there." When Kant drafted his proposal, the political world consisted of no more than a few states, which only very roughly approximated his ideal of the republican state. The emergence of such a constitution in France, Kant's prime example, was filled with misery and atrocities (Kant 1798b: 182). Kant's starting position "there and then" did not keep him from sketching a bold proposal of an entire world consisting of such republican states, since he considered mankind to be embedded within a reasonable course of history. Rawls, however, defends a political liberalism.[9] Just like "justice as fairness," the "law of peoples" must thus be a freestanding view, i.e., a mere defense of the modest claim that the actual laws of nature and society (and its present institutions) admit of the possibility of establishing a worldwide and stable loyalty based on international principles. If indeed the Enlightenment project of "a perfect civil union of mankind" (Kant 1784: 51) really lacks metaphysical underpinning, it has to create its own support and

---

[8] This statement in general and the absence of anything like an international difference principle in the 1993 version of "the law of peoples" has provoked fierce criticism. But Rawls did not change his position in 1999.

[9] He locates the historical origins of political liberalism in the Reformation and its aftermath of the religious civil wars of the 16th and 17th centuries. The theory tries to answer the question of how a stable social order can be established, given a plurality of conflicting, but reasonably comprehensive doctrines (Rawls 1993a, xli).

should minimize its utopian elements. Rawls feels thus compelled to take his starting position in the institutional situation in which we live, here and now. But is that indeed the case? Could not the argument be reversed? If no metaphysical guarantee exists and the historical perspective and the moral argument are no longer harmonized in some transcendent "reason," why would one feel compelled to consider the present political world, apparently neatly separated into distinct closed societies[10] as the necessary starting point of utopian reflection (Rawls 1999: 121, 128)? Are Rawls's reasons convincing when he insists on a domestic original position first, to be followed by a second round among representatives of those domestic societies?

5. The cosmopolitan approach to justice

The so-called cosmopolitans are not convinced. In the sometimes heated debate with the so-called statists, who accept and endorse (praise!)[11] states as the main agents of international justice, they emphasize the need to take persons as the primary focus of global justice.[12] Without doing full justice to the well-elaborated and empirically underpinned positions taken by several cosmopolitan authors, I concentrate on Pogge's work.[13]

Taking Rawls seriously long before he wrote *The Law of Peoples*, Pogge (1988a: 241) stated: "Rawls's principles for domestic institutions would be sufficient, if modern states were indeed closed schemes. ... But since modern societies are not closed, we must at some point go beyond Rawls's first approximation and ask how the theory might be best adapted to the complexities of the real world. ... I will argue for viewing the parties as immediately addressing the world at large, and as dealing with the organization of national societies only within the context so provided: Taken seriously, Rawls's conception of justice will make the life prospects of the globally least advantaged the primary standard for assessing our social institutions." In much the same vein, he then criticizes Rawls's mature view on international justice for lacking a principle that assesses the global economic order in terms of its distributive effects in the way that Rawls's own difference principle judges the domestic economic order (Pogge, 2001c, see also 1994).

---

[10] E.g., Rawls 1999: 26, 1993a: 18. Of course, this is a fiction, see Hoffmann 1995.
[11] "Lob des Nationalstaats" (Kersting, 1998: 544–8, 552, 1997a: 274–312, 1996: 191–206).
[12] This opposition is summarized in Forst 2001.
[13] For a more extensive review, see Besson 2003.

Thus, Rawls's thesis that the primary object of justice should be the basic structure of society and not, for example, personal attitudes of citizens is fully accepted by Pogge. However, Rawls's idea that such a basic structure is only to be found in particular national societies is rejected. It is argued that a global basic structure exists (e.g., Buchanan 2000) and that it is clearly in need of moral improvement. The principles of justice chosen behind the veil of ignorance need not so much be applied domestically, but should be applied globally. If indeed the life prospect of human beings (depending on their share in primary social goods) is largely determined by this global basic structure, Rawls's two-level bottom-up approach is no longer acceptable. The question of domestic justice no longer has any priority, since in a globalized world the basic structure of any domestic society depends on this overarching basic structure. It is maintained, however, that this has no major implications for the political autonomy of domestic societies. Global justice does not ask for a world government as a super-sovereign, whose task would consist of imposing the principles of global justice. But even if it did, this would not change much in comparison with the present situation. A presently existing global basic structure empowers the rich and privileged at the cost of the poor and unprivileged. There is no real opposition between the alleged current situation of mutually independent domestic societies on the one hand and a world government trying to implement despotic principles of global justice on the other. The real opposition is rather between an unjust global structure and attempts to reach a more just structure. Domestic societies now already fully depend on the existing global structure, which is advantageous to some and disadvantageous to many others. Taking global justice seriously aims, in the long run, at taking away the existing injustice and thus at fulfilling our negative duty not to impose on others an unjust institutional order.

The adjustment of that basic structure to principles of justice in which the interests of all human beings are taken into account can be reached with relatively little cost to those who benefit from the present situation. Rather modest (re)distributive rearrangements like the introduction of a Global Resources Dividend of a Tobin Tax, aiming not at global economic equality but merely at fairer distribution, would suffice. Pogge additionally argues that the present global basic structure would improve enormously its moral standing if certain key principles of international economic life were redesigned. In particular, he argues in favor of the abolition of what is called the International Borrowing Privilege and the International Resource Privilege (Pogge 2002a: 113–15). Of course, such arrangements would, some argue, significantly reduce the political autonomy of domestic societies as we understand it, but it is argued that the contrary is the case. With respect to democratic accountability, these rearrangements would only be helpful. It is as a consequence of these two privileges that in poor countries kleptocrats are stimulated to seize state power and that they, once in power, are not interested in winning local support. The present unjust global structure undermines democracy by stimulating warlords to take control of a nation's resources, and by afterwards making the transition from dictatorship to democracy very difficult. These institutional facts contradict, according to Pogge, Rawls's conjecture that poor societies are burdened more by their internal structure and the lack of political and cultural traditions than by the present global structure in which the well-off created economic monopolies and invented trade barriers. "Explanatory nationalism" does not explain much. The sources of the present global inequality are not primarily domestic, although internal factors may not be unimportant, but they result from the present unjust global basic structure actively supported by the rich states, according to Pogge. A present-day theory of justice should thus concentrate on what really matters: not the well-being of affluent political communities, but the ways in which the global basic structure affects the well-being of all individuals, irrespective of their nationality.

6. "Global justice" contested

The description of the ever growing global inequality of resources and goods, of extreme poverty and world hunger by Pogge and others is striking and an explanation in terms of causal relations between these facts and the global economic system seems convincing.[14] Prima facie, this would make any feasible alternative to change this inequality morally compelling to most. Yet, fierce opposition to schemes for "global justice" exist and the Rawlsian two-level bottom-up approach is strongly defended. Opposition ranges from the empirical level to the conceptual and to the moral.

Empirically, it is argued that principles of justice can only apply to contexts in which certain degrees of stable institutional cooperation exist. While indeed transnational bonds among domestic societies exist, the primary unit of institutional cooperation is still the national state, and not the international, cosmopolitan world. We ought to start indeed with the world as it is, and thus with the *Faktum* of the plurality of states. A law of peoples should not aim at more than merely regulating their peaceful coexistence, it is argued. The problem of distribution of primary social goods should be regulated within these units according to their domestic standards, and these standards do not necessarily coincide, as Rawls rightly noted, with the egalitarian standards as formulated in, for example, *A Theory of Justice*. The

---

[14] I cannot go into detail here. See, e.g., Pogge 2000b, 2001b.

kind of liberalism Rawls defended reflects the understanding of "his" society as a cooperative enterprise of free and equal citizens. Other societies have different self-understandings. Moreover, as it is already extremely difficult to compare individual levels of well-being within egalitarian societies, this problem can surely not be resolved on a global scale.

Conceptually, the globalist's proposals for a global dispersal of sovereignty (Pogge 2002a: 178) rather than its concentration by means of a transfer from domestic sovereignty to world government are met with skepticism and the distinctions between moral and legal cosmopolitanism, or between weak and strong cosmopolitanism (Pogge 2002a: 169) are not taken too seriously. Redistributive arrangements or the abolition of the two Privileges can only be achieved by means of global institutional bodies. These bodies will have to adjudicate on questions such as which domestic community has to pay what taxes, or which community is democratic enough to decide on its resources and on its borrowing policy. "Global justice" can only function if the question of the "who decides" is solved. The institutional bodies necessary to take such decisions will either tremble before the pressure of domestic communities or will evolve into an independent world government. Although the proposals for improving the global structure are presented as feasible and merely modest reforms, in fact they appear to imply structures of the kind Kant feared even more than international anarchy, namely those belonging to a "universal monarchy." Echoing Kant's words that such a situation would bring about the end of freedom, Kersting (1997a: 297) defends the "statist" position by arguing that the life of human beings in such a global impersonal distributive arrangement would be reduced to that of production slaves. This vision may be deemed far-fetched, but it reflects to some degree Kant's "naturalist" and "pluralist" argument: nature intentionally keeps mankind divided into a plurality of domestic societies because of religious and linguistic differences, so as to prevent mankind from "indulging in pleasure rather than into taking pains in enlarging and improving" its natural capacities (Kant 1785: 423). Global justice would endanger valuable differences among human beings and human communities.

Finally, the cosmopolitan approach is accused of neglecting some fundamental features of morality. Pogge presents us with a situation in which there is a wide gap between what are commonly acknowledged as requirements of universal morality on the one hand and the practical conduct of citizens of the rich and privileged countries on the other. By allowing the problem of world hunger to continue, these citizens do not adhere to what they themselves regard as their deep-seated moral convictions. This represents, according to Pogge, a great contrast to the progress made in the last centuries toward universal moral norms and practical conduct. What is accepted in theory regarding moral universalism and human rights is not applied in practice.

Pogge tries to explain this blindness by listing the common excuses given for ignoring world poverty: fighting poverty just makes the problem worse; the problem is too immense to be solved; the problem of poverty is gradually disappearing anyway, etc. However he takes the position that ignoring world hunger is not a rational, let alone a moral option. By indicating the causal links between world hunger and the existing global structure, he urges us to improve on our practical conduct in order to put it in line with our moral convictions. What is true in moral theory must be applied in practice! When acting, at least in the context of maintaining, changing or establishing institutions, we should take the fundamental interests of all human beings into consideration, not only those with whom we form a domestic society.

In order to get a better understanding of this difference between universal moral convictions and practical conduct, it is necessary to take a further step and to look back, first, at Rawls again. His "law of peoples" is strongly aware of global pluralism, a pluralism even more encompassing than within a liberal society. The diversity of cultures and traditions among peoples accounts for the existence of what Rawls, following Mill, calls "common sympathies," so that some peoples are more willing to cooperate with one another than with other peoples and put a greater emphasis on their common interests than on the interests of outsiders. When establishing international law, peoples, according to Rawls, do not so much aim at getting the largest possible share of a global set of primary goods for each of its members, but rather at the preservation of their common life. Because of their *amour-propre*, they want their common lives to be respected and recognized by other peoples (Rawls 1999: 11, 18, 23, 34). Since people care primarily about what is common and close to them, Rawls (1999: 39n) quotes Walzer with approval: "To tear down the walls of the state is not ... to create a world without walls but rather to create a thousand petty fortresses." This step, however, seems not to bring much: moral universalism does not deny that people care more about their relatives and less about foreigners. It only stresses that such local preferences should take place within a fair global framework, which does not exist at present.

A second step in grasping the disjuncture builds on the analogy suggested by Pogge and others between the situation of ordinary citizens of the rich countries with regard to starvation and world hunger and the situation of ordinary Germans in Nazi Germany with regard to the Holocaust. The analogy would then consist in the fact that people then and now simply do not wish to see the problem, or that they simply do not understand the problem as their moral problem once confronted with it. Arendt describes as one of the most frightening remarks made by Eichmann during his trial in

Jerusalem that "he could see no one who was actually against the Final Solution." This was the most potent factor in soothing his conscience. This determined what Arendt (1992: 116, 287) characterized as the most striking elements of Eichmann's personality, "thoughtlessness," a concept used by Pogge when he (2002a: 145) compares the attitude both of ordinary German citizens during the Nazi era and of citizens of the rich and privileged countries at present. Now I would suggest that understanding how the Holocaust was possible may enable us to understand widespread indifference to world hunger. Bauman holds that the following lesson can be learned from studying the Holocaust, namely, that morality is apparently unable "to bridge too long distances" and that a connection exists between morality and proximity such that "morality tends to stay at home and in the present" (Bauman 1989; Vetlesen 1993: 373f). Primarily, morality teaches me to take responsibility for people who are close to me, both in the territorial and in the emotional sense of the word (see Chatterjee 2003 for discussion). In cases in which the lives of others are removed out of our sight, either because they are deliberately removed and sealed off from our lives by a series of wicked administrative measures or because they literally live at so far a distance that it seems almost impossible to imagine ourselves in their position, the voice of morality can be silenced.

The importance of the spatial element for morality is acknowledged by Pogge (2002a: 4): most rich people live in extreme isolation from severe poverty and are not familiar with people who are extremely poor, and "if we had such people as friends or neighbors," many of us would feel compelled to help to eradicate this problem. However, since rich people live far removed from lethal poverty, they tend to ignore the relevance of the (unjust) global basic structure and to resort to "explanatory nationalism," not only as an exonerating mechanism, but also as the result of morality's inability to follow an overlong causal chain. Along similar lines, Bittner has linked morality with (physical) proximity as an answer to the question of why morality does not cause people to combat world hunger. This link, he argues (Bittner 2001: 27), does not entail a denial of moral universalism, but it does imply an important distinction: cosmopolitanism with regard to the principles of moral action does not entail cosmopolitanism with regard to moral action: "moral agents should act on principles that could receive approval of all human beings, but these principles do no require a certain conduct towards all human beings." Universal moral principles do not necessarily imply structures of global justice.

The important question now is: what follows from morality's limited imaginative force? If morality is unable to bring us close enough to the faraway poor to consider their lives to be our moral responsibility, do we then have to dismiss all pleas for global justice as originating in what Hegel calls "abstract morality"? Should we confine ourselves to Rawls's realistic "law of peoples," at least utopian enough to reconcile us with the world we live in (Rawls 2001: 3)? To a certain extent, this would not be so bad: his "law of peoples" includes the international "duty to assistance" and if it were acted upon the lives of the global poor would improve significantly. A conclusion along such lines would, however, give too much credit to "international justice" and too little to the cosmopolitan, global approach. The global approach may indeed at the moment be too weak to address the problem of world hunger, but it is much more developed in other areas. This follows from a second feature of morality that Bittner adds to "closeness," namely "imputability." Morality concerns those states and events that can be ascribed to a specific agent or a specific group of agents. In the case of world hunger, it is difficult, if not impossible, to ascribe or impute this misery to any such identifiable agent or group of agents. World hunger results from a long series of actions, interactions and institutions and "we do not have a clear understanding of who brought it about, or who is bringing it about" (Bittner 2001: 33). The connection between closeness and imputability is evident: if it were possible to translate the causal connection between the victims of world poverty and our wealth into an "imputable" relation between those victims and "us" as perpetrators, the moral imperative would not lack sufficient motivational force for us to act in order to improve the situation of the global poor. Where clearly "imputable" instances of global injustice do exist, morality does not lack sufficient motivation to act. In recent years, important steps have been made to develop a system of international criminal law ranging from the acceptance of universal jurisdiction, as in the Eichmann case, to the adoption of the *Genocide Convention* in 1948 and to the acceptance of the Rome Statute creating a permanent International Criminal Court. Institutionalizing "criminal global justice" is, I admit, very different from bringing about "economic global justice," but the one may clear the way to the other in two ways: first, since in the field of international criminal law the problem of how to establish global institutions with universal jurisdiction is at least tentatively being resolved, these procedures might aid our understanding of how to develop more encompassing global institutions. Second, understanding the nature of international criminality will make clear that global justice should not aim at punishing international criminals only, but also at preventing criminality, requiring a careful description and understanding of the globalized world we are increasingly inhabiting. Thus, we can remain faithful to Rawls, who (1999: 7) rightly held that the "great evils of human history follow from political injustice and that eliminating them would make those great evils eventually disappear."

Chapter 7

Understanding and Evaluating the Contribution Principle[*]

Christian Barry

Editor, Ethics & International Affairs, Carnegie Council, New York

This essay examines a principle that is often given substantial (and sometimes decisive) weight in most people's assessments regarding what (if anything) is owed, and by whom, to those who suffer from acute deprivations. This principle, which I shall refer to as the "contribution principle," asserts that *agents are responsible for addressing acute deprivations when they have contributed, or are contributing, to bringing them about.*

Three sets of interconnected questions can be asked about the contribution principle:

- *Meaning*: How should the distinction upon which the principle rests — between contributing to acute deprivations rather than merely failing to prevent them — be understood? What is the status of the distinction: is it purely empirical, so that we can classify conduct as having contributed to or having merely failed to prevent some acute deprivation without recourse to evaluative judgments; or does the correct application of the concept, like democracy, liberty, and (perhaps) coercion, depend on evaluative judgments? Can any such distinction be stated clearly?
- *Application*: What allocation of responsibilities would the contribution principle entail in our world? What policies and institutional arrangements would it forbid, permit, and require? Would it, as many have suggested, serve to justify the present neglect of acute deprivation amongst most well-off agents?

---

[*] I owe thanks to Sanjay Reddy, Katja Vogt, and Jeremy Waldron for their helpful critical feedback on an earlier presentation of some of the ideas in this essay and especially to Thomas Pogge for his extensive written comments on an earlier draft.

A. Follesdal and T. Pogge, (eds.), *Real World Justice*, 103-138.

- *Plausibility:* If the distinction upon which the contribution principle relies can be clearly stated, does this principle retain its plausibility? If so, then what weight should be given to this principle in practical deliberation about responsibilities in relation to other (potentially competing) principles?

These are very large questions, and this essay will not attempt to address even one of them exhaustively. It will, however, draw some conclusions that are relevant to answering each:

(1) It concludes that there is no plausible account of the distinction between contributing to and failing to prevent (or being altogether uninvolved in) some deprivation that interprets it as a purely empirical distinction.

(2) It evaluates several claims that might be made on behalf of the contribution principle: that an contribution to acute deprivation is (C1) the *only* normative factor that is relevant for determining whether and to what extent agents are responsible for addressing it; (C2) a normative factor of special significance for determining whether and to what extent agents are responsible for addressing it; (C3) a normative factor that is relevant, though no more significant (and perhaps less significant) than other factors for determining whether and to what extent agents are responsible for addressing it. It concludes that, while (C1) and (C3) lack plausibility, some versions of (C2) have features that strongly recommend them.

(3) It shows that two objections to the contribution principle — that it is impractical, and that it would yield wildly counterintuitive assignments of responsibilities and institutional proposals for enforcing them — are unconvincing.

1. The problem of determining responsibilities

That our world is characterized by acute and widespread human deprivation is generally held to be not merely unfortunate or regrettable, but morally unacceptable. Indeed, when confronted with facts — such as that 34,000 children under the age of five die daily from hunger and preventable diseases, that some 880 million people lack access to basic health services, or that in Africa less than 2 percent of the people in need receive antiretroviral therapy, the only life-prolonging treatment available for those who suffer from HIV/AIDS — most observers will assert that *someone* is morally required to provide the resources and to bring about changes in policies or social arrangements that will be necessary to eliminate or at least mitigate these problems. This is not to say that acute deprivation would be avoided completely even if all with responsibilities to address them did their share, but that the magnitude of acute deprivation in our world is due in part to the failure of some agents to meet their responsibilities. There are sharp disagreements, however, about which agents are responsible for addressing these deprivations, and which courses of conduct they must undertake.

Disagreements about these policies and practices are partly pragmatic — disagreements about the relative capabilities of different agents effectively to address the problems or about which institutional arrangements would suffice to alleviate them.[1] Yet they seem also to be rooted in deeper disagreements of value. Disagreements of value often relate to conflicting views concerning the appropriate principles for determining responsibilities to address acute deprivation.[2] These principles have two aspects: they function as *limiting principles,* which identify the agents that have responsibilities with respect to some particular deprivation; and as *allocative principles,* which determine the nature and extent of these agents' responsibilities to address this deprivation.[3]

Take the current debate about access to medicines, for example. It does not appear to be rooted in disagreements that have been the focus of much recent writing on "health equity" — disagreements about whether we should characterize health standards in terms of access to health-care resources, health outcomes, or opportunities for health, or about whether one ought to

---

[1]   In many cases, of course, these are not good-faith disagreements.

[2]   Principles are not the only area of value in which views may disagree. Disagreement may also concern the *subjects* — such as present and future individual persons, groups, communities, states or nations — who can be acutely deprived, and to whom one can bear responsibilities; the *aspects* of these subjects — such as their income, resource holdings, capabilities, functionings, levels of utility, or some weighted combination of the preceding — that are relevant for determining whether or not they suffer acute deprivations; the *threshold level* — the levels of income, resource holdings, capability, functioning, utility, or some combination of the preceding — under which these subjects will count as acutely deprived; the *aggregation function* — the weights attached to the *depth* and *incidence* of deprivation, and perhaps also to its distribution — for assessing the overall magnitude of acute deprivation, and for the purpose of setting priorities, the *agents* — individual persons or collective agents, such as nongovernmental organizations, corporations and states, or more dispersed and loosely affiliated groups and collectivities — who *can* bear responsibilities to address acute deprivation; and the *standards* for applying principles in real world contexts where there is often reasonable disagreement about whether, for example, specific agents are capable of alleviating or mitigating some deprivations, or about the extent to which they have contributed to them. The literature on all but the last two areas is enormous.

[3]   One might, for example, adopt the contribution principle as the sole limiting principle — holding that contribution is a necessary condition for having some agent's having a reason to address acute deprivation, but still hold that the strength of this agent's reason depends much more on other factors, such as her capability to do so at low cost, her associative connections to the sufferer, or her having benefited from the sufferer's misfortune, etc. In this case other principles would serve as the primary allocative principles.

use sum-ranking, maximin, or some indicator of inequality as an interpersonal aggregation function for assessing the fairness of the current situation. All participants in this debate seem to be committed to the idea that the suffering of all present and future human persons is, impersonally speaking, of equal concern, and that whether measured in terms of health outcomes, resources, or opportunities to achieve good health, the current situation is unacceptable. Moreover, all seem committed, verbally at least, to the idea that some universal minimum health standard should be secured for all. Their disagreements are rooted, rather, in divergent accounts of the appropriateness of different principles, and the appropriate *standards* for applying these principles in the real world.[4] With respect to debates concerning access to medicines, for example, three principles for allocating responsibilities have often been invoked. The first appeals to agents' *associative connections with those suffering*. The second claims that responsibilities ought to be allocated according to the *capacity* of different agents to discharge them. The third allocates responsibilities to agents based on whether and to what extent they have contributed, or are contributing, to bringing about the medical needs in question. We might refer to these as the *capacity*, *association*, and *contribution* principles respectively.[5]

2. Principles for determining responsibility: Some preliminary distinctions

Principles for determining responsibilities identify certain factors as providing moral reasons for agents to act in certain ways with respect to some other agent(s). Following Shelly Kagan (1992), I shall refer to those factors as *normative factors*. Principles for determining responsibilities to address some instance of actual or potential acute deprivation, therefore, identify certain normative factors as providing reasons for agents to undertake to remedy it or prevent it from occurring.[6] To claim that an

---

[4] I discuss the issue of standards for applying principles in section V below, and more exhaustively in Barry (2005).

[5] These principles are certainly not exhaustive of the principles that can be appealed to for determining responsibilities. One might adopt a 'beneficiary' principle, which holds that responsibilities should be allocated to those who have benefited from its occurrence, a 'risk' principle, which would allocate responsibilities according to the extent that they have contributed to the aggregate risk of their occurrence, or what Miller (2001) calls a 'moral responsibility' principle, which would allocate according to the culpability of different agents for its occurrence.

[6] The significance of different principles of responsibility will may vary depending on the context of their application. The principles deemed relevant for identifying those who

agent's contribution to (or capacities to alleviate) some acute deprivation provides her with a moral reason to address it does not entail that these reasons cannot be overridden. Nor does it entail that any contribution, no matter how minimal, triggers a responsibility to address it. To say that an agent has a responsibility to do X is to claim that she has moral reasons of significant weight to do X, and this may require that the normative factor be present to a high degree, e.g., that an agent have substantially contributed to or benefited from some deprivation.[7] In what follows, I will refer to reasons based on the factor of contribution as contribution-based reasons, and will sometimes contrast them with capacity-based reasons, association-based reasons, and reasons that are based on other possible normative factors.

3. Three claims about the contribution principle

Three claims might be made on behalf any principle for determining responsibilities. First, that it identifies the *sole* normative factor that is relevant. Second, that it identifies a normative factor that has a *special status*. Third, that the factor *is relevant*, though no more relevant (and perhaps less relevant) than other factors. In examining the plausibility of the contribution principle, therefore, we must assess three claims that might be made on its behalf.

(C1) An agents' contributing or having contributed to acute deprivation is the only normative factor that is relevant for determining whether and to what extent she is responsible for addressing it.

(C2) An agents' contributing or having contributed to acute deprivation is a normative factor of special significance for determining whether and to what extent she is responsible for addressing it.

(C3) An agents' contributing or having contributed to acute deprivation is a normative factor that is relevant for determining whether and to what extent she is responsible for addressing it, though nor more significant (and perhaps less significant) than other factors.[8]

---

should address situations in which reasonably well-off persons are deprived of some of their property will likely differ from those that identify those who should address acute deprivation.

[7] I realize this formulation is vague. I call a reason "significant" when it is often, though not necessarily always, decisive for determining what an agent ought to do. I draw here on distinctions in Raz 1975.

[8] Those rejecting (C1, C2, and C3) must claim that an agents' contributing or having contributed to acute deprivation is not a normative factor that is relevant for determining whether and to what extent she is responsible for addressing it.

Two versions of (C2) as an allocative principle can be distinguished.[9] The *strong* version of (C2) asserts that contribution-based reasons trump reasons provided by other principles. If A has contributed to B's deprivation but not to C's, then A must always prioritize addressing B's deprivation over C's deprivation, whether or not A has associational ties with C, can alleviate C's problems with greater ease, and so on. The *moderate* version of (C2) holds that contribution is a more significant normative factor than those identified by other principles. Minimally, this would require that, other things being equal, we give priority to addressing those deprivations to which we have contributed over those to which we have not contributed so long as the other normative factors are roughly equal.[10] This weight might be represented as a ratio, so that A's contribution-based reasons to prevent the 100 instances of infant mortality to which her past conduct will have contributed would be of equal weight as A's association-based reasons to prevent 200 instances of comparable deprivations to whose deprivations A has not contributed. There are thus also multiple variants of the moderate version of (C2), some giving greater weight to contribution-based reasons than others.

While (C1) seems unduly restrictive — few find it plausible, for example, that the fact that an acutely deprived person is one's close friend or relative could never provide a weighty moral reason to help — most of those who are engaged in debates on policy and institutional design seem drawn to a version of (C2).[11] All participants in the debate concerning access to medicines, for example, seem to agree that, were it to be shown that some actors have substantially contributed to these deprivations, it would be their responsibility (though perhaps not *solely* their responsibility) to try to address them, while there is little consensus regarding whether these actors ought to do so merely because they can do so at low cost. Indeed, the pains that various actors, such as pharmaceutical company executives, government

---

[9]   C1 could be rejected but it still maintained that the contribution principle was a limiting principle — that only agents that have contributed to deprivation have moral reasons to address them but that once they have contributed other normative factors may be relevant. Although I focus here on variants of (C2) but there are also different variants of (C3). A very weak version would hold that, while a basically insignificant factor, an agents' having contributed or contributing to some deprivation may give them ever so slightly more reason to address them than they otherwise would have. A stronger version would hold that contribution is an important normative factor, but no more so than others, such as having the capacity to alleviate at low cost, being strongly associated to the sufferer of, or having benefited from the deprivation.

[10] I leave aside here the obvious problems of measuring "degrees" of contribution, association, capacity, etc, and of making "interprinciple" comparisons between them.

[11] My sense is that most disputants are drawn to a variant of the moderate version of (C2) that gives very much greater weight to contribution-based reasons than other reasons.

ministers, and WTO officials and trade representatives, have taken to show that they have *not* contributed to these problems, or that more substantial contributions have been made by others, further illustrates how much importance is being attached to this principle (Barry and Raworth 2002).[12]

That the contribution principle should figure prominently in discussions of assigning responsibility for global problems should not be surprising. A commitment to something like (C2) appears to be an element of what Samuel Scheffler (2001) has referred to as the "common-sense" or "restrictive" view of responsibility, according to which "individuals are thought to be more responsible for what they do than for what they merely fail to prevent, and they are thought to have greater responsibilities toward some people than toward others."[13] More specifically, responsibilities with respect to acute deprivation to which one contributes are generally felt to have three features:

(1) They are especially *weighty*: we have strong moral reasons to refrain from contributing to others' acute deprivation regardless of any further connections that we may have to them, and we cannot so easily appeal to considerations of *cost* to ourselves to excuse our failure to act on these reasons[14];

(2) They bind a *broad range of agents*: these reasons are applicable not only to individual persons, but also to collective agents such as corporations and states which may otherwise not held responsible for preventing acute deprivation;

(3) They are *broad* in scope: they apply to these individual and collective agents with respect not only to what they *directly* do to others, but also to what they indirectly do to others through creating and maintaining shared social rules and practices that can themselves contribute to acute deprivation.

The contribution principle seems to make sense of various moral intuitions about hypothetical and concrete cases. Imagine, for example, that there are two poor countries A and B whose populations are of roughly equal size and whose populations suffer from comparable levels of acute

---

[12] Indeed, Pogge (2002a) has recently been suggesting that widespread commitment to the contribution principle is of great explanatory importance, in that it helps to account for why few well-off agents feel (unjustifiably, he argues) responsible for addressing acute deprivations.

[13] Scheffler 2001: 4. In a more recent article, Scheffler argues that something akin to the contribution principle is a condition of "our practice of treating one another as responsible agents." See Scheffler 2003.

[14] Compare with Kagan (1991: 897): "Although ordinary morality insists on the existence of options to allow harm, it rejects options to do harm. Only the minimalist believes in the existence of options to do harm for the sake of promoting one's own interests."

deprivation. Assume that the overall cost of eliminating these deprivations in A is substantially greater than in B. Suppose further that it is shown that some other country C has significantly contributed to the acute deprivation in A. Finally, assume also that C had significant associative ties to B but not to A. Most people would argue that C has weightier moral reasons to address the deprivations in A than in B, even though it has much greater capacity to address those in B and has much closer associative ties to B.[15] How much weight should be placed on such cases is, or course, open to dispute. The contribution principle can also be given a deeper rationale, however, since unlike many other principles it seems to take note of the importance of people's interests in security and autonomy. It recognizes people's interests in security — being free from serious harm and threats thereof — in three ways: (1) it demands that those who have brought about acute deprivations take action to remedy them or compensate for them; (2) it provides weighty moral reasons for agents to cease and desist from activities that are presently bringing about acute deprivation; and (3) it enjoins agents to take special precautions not to undertake courses of conduct that will bring about acute deprivation in the future and also to take action to ensure that their past behavior will not contribute to future acute deprivations.

It recognizes people's interests in autonomy — the freedom to define for oneself a conception of the good life and being left free to pursue it — because it does not demand that agents disrupt their plans whenever, for example, they are well placed to alleviate the acute deprivations of others.[16] It can thus be seen as linking two attractive normative ideals — that people should bear the costs of the burdens that they impose on others and that there should be, as Nozick (1974) has put it, a "presumption in favor of liberty."

Those who reject the idea that contributing to acute deprivations is of much greater moral significance than merely failing to prevent them must adopt one of three positions, each of which seems intuitively implausible.[17] The first is that contributing to acute deprivation is morally very bad and that failing to prevent comparable deprivation from taking place is equally bad. The second is that failing to prevent acute deprivation from taking place is not morally very bad, but neither is contributing to acute deprivation. The third is that the moral significance of an agent's contributing to or failing to prevent acute deprivation depends solely on other normative factors, such as the cost to the agent of conduct that would not lead to the deprivation or of

---

[15] Our intuitions may change depending on the extent to which these three factors (contribution, association, capacity) are in play, and it is not altogether clear that comparative assessments of the "degree" to which such factors are present can be made with much precision.

[16] See Brock 1991 and Thomson 1984 for further discussion of this value.

[17] The first two positions are discussed in Bennett 1995 and McMahan 1998.

acting in such a way that they were not causally relevant to it, or on their associative connections with actual or potential sufferers. The first position implies not only that morality is much more demanding than has generally been supposed, but that it may also permit acts that are widely held to be impermissible.[18] The second position entails that morality permits various acts that are widely held to be impermissible. The third position runs counter to a broad range of intuitions. It is generally thought, for example, that we may not legitimately ignore the plight of someone whose severe medical emergency we have contributed to in order to remedy a comparable emergency of a family member which we had no role in bringing about.[19] And while we do not typically think, for example, that agents are required to make great sacrifices (even of their limbs, perhaps) in order to prevent the acute deprivation of innocent strangers, we may require such sacrifices from agents whose previous conduct has substantially contributed to the stranger's risk of death.[20] This does not of course mean that none of these three positions can be sustained; only that a commitment to at least some version (C2) has strong initial plausibility.[21] In what follows, I will offer further support for the contribution principle by showing that two objections that might be advanced against it are implausible.

4. Is the contribution principle impractical?

This and the following section focus on objections that might be made to the contribution principle under *any* plausible interpretation of the meaning of "contribution." In order to help fix ideas, I will stipulate the following definition of what it means for an agent to have contributed to acute deprivation.[22]

Agent A contributes to Agent B's Deprivation if and only if:

   (a) A's conduct was *causally relevant to it* — it was a necessary element in a set of actual antecedent conditions that was sufficient for its occurrence;

---

[18] This is due to the fact that it may require that one contribute to acute deprivation when doing so enables the agent to prevent more severe or widespread deprivation. See the interesting discussion in Unger 1996, who refuses to grant weight to the contribution principle and accepts these consequences.

[19] See Pogge 2002d for an extended discussion of such cases.

[20] I owe this example to Thomas Pogge.

[21] The first position has been defended by Singer (1972) and Unger (1996), the second and third are supported by Bennett (1995).

[22] I will discuss different approaches to drawing this distinction in section VI below.

(b) A's conduct did not merely permit a causal sequence that had antecedently put B under threat of acute deprivation to play out, but rather *initiated, facilitated, or sustained* it.[23]

For the purposes of my discussion I will also assume that the target of the objections advanced in this and the following section is (C1), which I will hereafter simply refer to as the contribution principle.[24]

The first objection holds that the contribution principle is not a *practical* principle. There are two versions of this argument. The first version rejects the contribution principle on the ground that it is focused exclusively on (or at least overemphasizes) the past, making it of limited value for addressing the needs of agents who must decide how to act now and in the future. The contribution principle, this argument suggests, is primarily a principle of *corrective* morality or justice. What is needed, however, are plausible *forward-looking* principles that help agents understand whether and to what extent they have moral reasons to address acute deprivation. The second variant rejects the contribution principle not as impractic*al*, but as impractic*able* in complex social contexts because it supposedly places impossible or unreasonable informational demands upon agents.

4.1 The impracticality of the contribution principle

"Fruitful work in ethics or politics must be practical," Onora O'Neill (2000) has recently insisted. "It must address the needs of agents who have yet to act, who are working out what to do, not the needs of spectators who are looking for ways of assessing or appraising what has already been done" (O'Neill 2000: 7). Each of the arguments discussed in this subsection suggests that the contribution principle should be rejected because it fails fully to address the needs of agents who have yet to act.

The first argument claims that the contribution principle conceives of responsibilities in terms of what Iris Young (2003b: 39–44) has recently

---

[23] This type of interpretation is developed by Foot (1994) and Kamm (1983). Condition (B) clearly requires a great deal more analysis than I can provide here. The basic idea is that A's causally relevant conduct permits a sequence to continue rather than initiating, facilitating, or sustaining it if and only if (1) there is a high antecedent probability, independent of what A might do, that B will suffer acute deprivation, (2) B suffers acute deprivation, and (3) had B avoided suffering the acute deprivation, it would have been through A's assistance. This interpretation has a clear evaluative component, since assessments of whether the alternative to B's deprivation is that he would have avoided it through agent's aid will depend on prior moral judgment regarding A's and B's entitlements. See McMahan 1998 for discussion.

[24] As shall be clear, my defense of (C1) against these objections would also suffice to defend all variants of (C2).

called a "fault or liability model."[25] That is, it is primarily backward looking: "it reviews the history of events in order to assign responsibility, usually for the sake of exacting punishment or compensation" (ibid. 40). This model of responsibility can be contrasted, Young suggests, with another way of conceiving responsibilities, which she calls the "political responsibility" model. "Political responsibility," she explains, "doesn't reckon debts, but aims at results, and thus depends on the actions of everyone who is in a position to contribute to those results. Taking political responsibility in respect to social structures emphasizes the future more than the past" (ibid. 41).

While the contribution principle does maintain that an agents' past behavior can add substantial weight to their present moral reasons for action, this argument rests on a misunderstanding. Let us suppose that we have two agents, Owner, who owns a factory, and Worker, who is employed in Owner's factory, and who suffers from a debilitating handicap. According to the contribution principle, the strength of Owner's reason to address Worker's handicap depends on whether (and to what extent) Owner has contributed to Worker's condition. That is, according to the contribution principle, the only relevant facts for determining whether or not Owner has weighty moral reasons to compensate Worker or provide treatment to remedy his handicap concern whether her conduct satisfies conditions (a) and (b) above. If Worker's condition is due to a congenital handicap, for example, or even if Owner was causally relevant to his injury but did not initiate, facilitate, or sustain the causal sequence that led to its occurrence, then Owner lacks special moral reasons to address his handicap. If his conditions arose because Owner maintained extremely hazardous conditions in the factory, and these conditions were a necessary element in a set of sufficient antecedent conditions for Worker's injury, then Owner does have moral reasons to address it. In this sense, the contribution principle differs from principles that determine responsibilities in a way that is insensitive to facts about the past, such as the capacity principle, which holds that responsibilities for addressing acute deprivation should be allocated to whomever can do so most efficiently and effectively, irrespective of whether they have contributed to the problem.[26] According to this principle, Owner

---

[25] Of course, Young does not speak of the 'contribution principle' per se, but she singles out Thomas Pogge, whose account of responsibilities for addressing global poverty seems to stress it, as a philosopher who overemphasizes this model. Similarly, Miller (2001) criticizes principles that allocate responsibilities on the basis of causal connection on the grounds that they are "purely backward-looking."

[26] See Miller 2001 and Goodin 1985. As Miller points out, views of this kind may be sensitive both to the *efficiency* of different agents and institutions in bringing remedy, and the *cost* to these agents of doing so.

has less moral reason to address Workers' injury than the injuries of others whose needs she can address more easily or efficiently, no matter how much she contributed to Worker's, but not the others' injuries. And if other agents can more easily or efficiently address Worker's injury than Owner can, they have weightier reasons to take action than she does.

The mere fact that the contribution principle holds that information about the past can be relevant for identifying an agents' contribution-based reasons does not show, however, that it is *purely, mainly,* or even *overly* backward-looking. Let us imagine that Owner has recognized that she has contributed to Worker's injury, and that she can fully compensate him for it, but only by selling off what little safety equipment remains in her factory. Owner also knows that selling off this equipment will lead to the injuries of Worker 2 and Worker 3. If this argument were correct, then we might expect the contribution principle to demand that Owner sell the equipment to compensate Worker. But this is implausible. In assessing the weight of her moral reasons, Owner will assess not only the strength of her contribution-based reasons to address existing injuries to which she has contributed, but the contribution-based reasons that she *will have* with respect to Workers 2 and 3 should she sell her equipment. Let us refer to contribution-based reasons to address deprivation that has resulted from one's past behavior *historical contribution-based reasons,* and reasons to minimize the incidence of deprivations that present behavior is resulting in or may lead to as *prospective contribution-based reasons.* Both types of contribution-based reasons figure prominently in global policy debates. Joseph Stiglitz's arguments to the effect that the IMF and the US Treasury contributed to the East Asian financial crisis, for example, are intended not only to convey the responsibilities of these collective agents to mitigate the deprivations that the crisis has engendered, but also to present these agents with reasons to change their policies, since their present and future conduct will otherwise be likely to continue to contribute to comparable deprivations.

It could perhaps be replied that, although my example of Owner and Worker shows that the contribution principle does not always give *decisive* weight to historical contribution-based reasons, it will give them *extra* weight. But this too is false. Suppose that Owners' selling of the equipment to compensate Worker will lead to the injury only of Worker 2. If the argument regarding the relative weights of different types of contribution-based reasons were true, then we should expect the contribution principle to demand that Owner sell the equipment. But the contribution principle demands no such thing. It claims that contribution-based reasons are the sole normative factors for determining whether an agent is responsible for addressing acute deprivation, but it does not demand that agents privilege the remediation of deprivations to which their past conduct has contributed over the avoidance of deprivations that their present conduct is contributing to, or will contribute to should they fail to change it.[27] Nor, it must be noted, does it privilege prospective contribution-based reasons. It provides agents with reasons to minimize the overall incidence of acute deprivation to which they have contributed without compensation.[28]

It might still perhaps be argued that agents committed to the contribution principle will tend (in practice) to give more weight to past than to future contribution-based reasons. However imperfect our knowledge of the past, it might be claimed, it is more complete than our knowledge of the future. Since the contribution principle gives agents reasons to minimize the incidence of deprivation to which they have contributed, and because we have greater confidence in our ability to discern past contributions than to predict future contributions, adherents of the contribution principle will therefore tend to privilege past contribution-based reasons, since they can act on them with more confidence.

This claim about our epistemic relation to the past and future can of course be questioned. We are often much less confident in our beliefs regarding outcomes to which our conduct *has* led than in our beliefs regarding the actual or likely effects of our present and future conduct. Even if this claim is granted, however, the inference to the conclusion that adherents of the contribution principle would privilege historical contribution-based reasons is invalid. For even when we are more confident in our beliefs regarding the effects of our past behavior than in our beliefs regarding the outcomes that will result from our present behavior, we may still be less confident about what historical contribution-based reasons *require*. In order to act on a contribution-based responsibility, an agent must know more than that she has contributed to some deprivation. She must also possess the relevant information for determining what this responsibility demands. An agent may, for example, be very confident that she has contributed to B's deprivation through her past conduct and unsure whether her present conduct will, if unchanged, lead to C's future deprivation. But she may nonetheless be more confident with respect to what her possible

---

[27] This not to say that a version of the contribution principle could not be constructed of which it would be true. One could hold a principle that held that historical contribution-based reasons outweighed prospective contribution-based reasons, but nothing in the basic idea of the contribution principle demands it.

[28] This shows that, although it may be combined with deontological commitments, the contribution principle is not, as such, a deontological principle. If the contribution principle is not combined with a commitment to refrain from contributing to deprivations even when doing so will reduce the overall incidence of deprivation to which one has contributed, it may intuitively seem to permit too much. My helping break a person's leg to avoid an outcome whereby my past conduct would have helped to break the legs of two other persons is not generally held to be permissible.

prospective contribution-based reasons would require. She may know, for instance, that refraining from supporting a corrupt politician will all but eliminate the possibility of her contributing to C's deprivation, while remaining largely in the dark regarding the conduct options that will suffice to mitigate or alleviate an injury to which her past conduct has contributed.

To see why this can be so, consider what providing full compensation of past contribution will mean.

Nozick has characterized the idea of full compensation this way:

> Something fully compensates a person for a loss if and only if it makes him no worse off than he otherwise would have been; it compensates person x for person y's action A if x is no worse off receiving it (Nozick 1974: 57).

Whether or not one agrees with the details of Nozick's account, it is clear that any plausible characterization of full compensation must invoke a counterfactual for the purpose of determining the state of the acutely deprived subject had the contributing agent not intervened. In many cases, the contributing agent may have very little confidence in her beliefs regarding the truth of these counterfactuals. Indeed, determining the requirements of past contribution-based reasons becomes far more complicated when one departs from simple small-scale examples involving a few individual persons.[29] These considerations render implausible the claim that conscientious adherents of the contribution principle will systematically tend to privilege historical contribution-based reasons.

In conclusion, it is worth pointing out that there is a serious problem with the so-called political-responsibility model Young endorses (or, for that matter, with any model that de-emphasises the importance of past wrongdoing for determining present moral reasons). The problem is that the assessments of behavior that this model will yield do not appear to be intertemporally consistent.[30] This model simultaneously claims that those in a position to "achieve results" have weighty moral reasons to do so, while it is also committing to the view that, should these capable agents fail to take action, they should not be judged to have weightier reasons for addressing them *now* than they otherwise would have.

Young (2003b: 41) also criticizes the "liability" model on the grounds that thus assigning responsibility to some agents "has the function of absolving other agents." But this is also clearly false. It does not follow from

---

[29] For interesting discussions of the problem of determining the contribution-based responsibilities of collective agents and groups for the deprivations suffered by other individuals, groups, or collective agents, see Hill 2002 and Waldron 1992.

[30] This political-responsibility model may also provide rather dubious incentives to its adherents — a problem I will not explore here.

the fact that one agent has contributed to some deprivation that another agent has not also done so, or even that one agent's contribution-based reasons are lessened by the presence of other contributing agents.[31] That Owner contributes to Workers' handicap by maintaining hazardous working conditions in no way absolves the sourcing companies which, in the interest of maximizing their returns for shareholders, demand "flexible" production, "just-in-time" delivery, faster turnaround times, tighter specifications, and ever-lower costs from their suppliers. If the conduct of these agents forms a necessary element in a set of actual antecedent conditions that initiates, facilitates, or sustains Owner's resistance to upgrading the standards in her factory, they share responsibility for addressing any deprivations that result. As noted above, however, the political responsibility model that Young endorses does seem to absolve agents, since once they have failed to act when they can do so they need not fear that they will be assigned any special responsibility for making up for this failure.

Thus far, the discussion has shown that the contribution principle contrasts with other principles, such as the capacity principle, not by being backward-looking, but by being *forward looking in a different way*. When assessing different prospective courses of conduct, an agent who is committed to the contribution principle will take special care to ensure that she is not contributing to present deprivations, and that deprivations are not likely to arise from her past conduct or from her present (and anticipated) future conduct. The contribution principle provides agents with reasons to correct or compensate for deprivations to which they have contributed, to cease to contribute to deprivations if they are presently doing so, and to take precautions not to act in such a way that they will have brought them about in the future. If Owner's poor maintenance of her factory has contributed to severe health problems amongst her workers, the contribution principle will play a role in two *prospective* inquiries: (1) *Corrective/compensatory* — who should bear the costs/provide remedy to these problems? (2) *Forward-looking* — should Owner go on with the conduct or practice in question?

4.2 Impracticability

It was noted above that the contribution principle seems to figure in what Samuel Scheffler has recently referred to as the "common-sense" or

---

[31] Young draws parallels between singling out agents in the context of allocating responsibility for injustice in global labor practices with criminal law. This is misleading, however, since while determining that suspect A has murdered B will generally exculpate suspect C, this result cannot be generalized even to all aspects of criminal law, let alone torts. It seems less plausible still with respect to the determination of moral responsibilities.

"restrictive" view of responsibility. According to this view, "individuals are thought to be more responsible for what they do than for what they merely fail to prevent, and they are thought to have greater responsibilities toward some people than toward others" (Scheffler 2001: 4). This "restrictive view," Scheffler suggests, rests on an "implicit conception of human social relations as consisting primarily in small-scale interactions, with clearly demarcated lines of causation, among independent individual agents" (ibid. 38f). And this implicit conception, Scheffler argues, seems less than adequate in a world in which people's lives "are structured to an unprecedented degree by large, impersonal institutions and bureaucracies."[32] As we come to coexist under shared rules and social institutions (e.g., markets in capital and labor, systems of property rights, trading regimes, and constitutive features of the nation-state), we begin substantially to affect one another's livelihoods in ways that are difficult to predict or even to discern ex post. Almost all market participants, for example, will figure in the complete causal explanation of many acute deprivations. This is not only because their daily consumption and production activities affect people's lives *directly* — through their impacts on prices, the values of shares, and so on — but also *indirectly* — by shaping the production and investment decisions of entrepreneurs, and the decisions of policy makers regarding the allocation of government resources, tariff levels, and labor market restrictions. In such contexts, it becomes extremely difficult (if not impossible) not only to figure out what we are doing to others, but even to undertake the kinds of practical inquiries that could enable us to refrain from behavior that results in others' acute deprivations.

Because the contribution principle asserts that the strength of our moral reasons to address acute deprivations depends in part upon facts about what we have been causally relevant to, about what we are presently causally relevant to, and what we will have been causally relevant to in the future, the difficulty of predicting and discerning the causal impact of ones' behavior substantially limits its practical relevance.

In a complex and highly interdependent world, the impracticability objection claims, the contribution principle would either morally unburden agents from addressing deprivations which result from their conduct — since it is nearly impossible to discern the consequences of one's past conduct or to foresee the consequences of one's present conduct, and because one's behavior could not plausibly be seen to have run afoul of normative standards — or it would place "wildly excessive demands on the capacity of agents to amass information about the global impact of different courses of

---

[32] Ibid. 40. Despite his doubts about its adequacy, Scheffler himself does not reject the restrictive view, largely because he is skeptical about the existence of any real alternatives.

action available to them."[33] Since what is perhaps most needed are principles that can help guide agents who confront pressing practical dilemmas, the contribution principle's impracticability gives us reasons to reject it.

This objection raises several important issues but it does not provide sufficient grounds for rejecting the contribution principle. Two responses can be given to this objection.[34] A *deflationary* response would accept the premises of the impracticability objection, but deny that it should lead us to reject the contribution principle. The difficulties that attend the application of the contribution principle are not sufficient to reject it, it might be argued, because *any* plausible principle for allocating responsibilities will require information about complex facts concerning causally relevant factors. Principles asserting that agents' moral reasons to address an acute deprivation depend on their contribution to the aggregate risk of its occurrence, or on their capabilities to do so efficiently or at little cost, for example, would also require information about the actual and potential global impact of agents' behavior. Consequently, the impracticability objection shows not that the contribution principle is implausible, but that any norms governing the interactions of individual agents will be difficult to apply in a complex world.

The deflationary response has some merit, but it does not fully blunt the impracticability objection. While it is true that all principles require some knowledge of facts about causation, not all are as informationally demanding as the contribution principle. The association principle, for example, requires information only about the salient associational ties between sufferers of acute deprivations and those who could potentially assist them. And while the risk principle requires the assessment of the risks to which agents are exposing others, this task, while difficult, is often much easier than that of determining causation.[35] Indeed, one of the great challenges to the modern tort system is the difficulty of proving which of the agents who have negligently exposed plaintiffs to risks have actually caused them harm.

A more *robust* response to the impracticability argument challenges its premises. That is, it can be argued that the impracticability objection rests on

---

[33] Ibid. 43. The question of whether (C1) would morally unburden agents is discussed below.

[34] A further response to this objection, which I shall not discuss here, is that it merely shows the contribution principle to work poorly as a guide in everyday life, not that the principle is itself implausible. Many utilitarian thinkers have also stressed the need to separate ultimate from "use" or "public" criteria for moral assessment. On these distinctions see Hare 1981; Parfit 1984; and Pogge 1990.

[35] Though certainly not always: it is often much easier to know which agent has caused a deprivation than to know which have contributed (and to what extents they have contributed) to the aggregate risk of its occurrence. All of this also assumes, of course, that objective probabilities exist and can be known.

an unjustifiably limited view of the possible *types* of contribution-based reasons that agents can have, and an impoverished sense of the information that is available to individual agents who wish to act on these reasons. With respect to individual agents, for example, three types of contribution-based reasons must be distinguished — *interactional, organizational, and institutional.*[36] Individuals have *interactional* reasons not to contribute *directly* to others deprivations and to compensate those to whose deprivation they have contributed *directly*. It is with respect to these reasons that the impracticability charge is generally raised, since it is often difficult to identify the direct causal relevance of my conduct to various outcomes. It is important, however, not to overstate the difficulties involved in acquiring information that is relevant for determining the strength of interactional contribution-based reasons. For while it may indeed be difficult for agents to identify the remote effects of discrete *acts*, they can often discern or predict much more easily how their regular *patterns* of behavior are causally relevant to outcomes. The effects of my taking a speedboat onto a small lake on Tuesday May 15th 2004 may be difficult to determine. But information regarding the effects of my *practice* of regularly taking a speedboat out on the lake — including its effects on the quality of water in nearby streams that supply my neighbors with drinking water — may be much easier to obtain. And once we have acquired information about the likely effects of practices, our pleading ignorance regarding the causal relevance of particular acts loses its plausibility as a moral excuse. If I spill gasoline in the lake, for example, I cannot credibly excuse myself by claiming that I couldn't possibly know or predict that *this* trip would be causally relevant to some outcome, such as reducing the quality of my neighbor's water supply.

It must be acknowledged, however, that this does not suffice to answer the impracticability objection, since even the effects of ongoing patterns of behavior may be quite difficult to understand in sufficiently complex social contexts. Indeed, focusing exclusively on these interactional contribution-based reasons can lead to neglect of the important ways in which agents affect others through their membership in collective agents such as firms, churches, nongovernmental organizations, corporations and states. This neglect is particularly problematic because participation in organizations can erode the sense of connection that individuals feel with the effects of their actions, and because many of the most consequential ways in which we affect others is through our participation in such organizations.[37] Overlooking the contributions of organizations to acute deprivation can

---

[36] My discussion here draws on distinctions in Pogge 1992.
[37] This can engender, as Hardin (1996: 142) has recently put it "a semideliberate inattention" in place of "individualized attention."

easily lead to an understatement of individuals' capabilities to acquire information about the probable effects of their past and present conduct, since it is often much easier to trace the causal relevance of the conduct of organizations than of individuals. Once we understand the causal relevance of an organization to various outcomes, we can sometimes "trace back" to our own contribution by estimating our causal relevance to the conduct of this organization.

Nevertheless, directing agents to take account of both interactional contribution-based reasons and organizational contribution-based reasons, will still provide an incomplete picture of an agent's responsibilities, since they may thereby neglect the ways that these agents contribute to others' deprivations through their impact on shared rules. When a social order is characterized by weak or unfair social rules, then deprivations may persist that are not easily traceable to the actions of particular individual or corporate agents. And even where deprivations *can* be traced to the actions of individuals or groups, such as widespread corruption amongst political leaders, abusive police practices, and the organized violence of private associations, the prevalence of these practices may be strongly influenced by the prevailing background of social rules to which many other agents have contributed. Corruption and rent seeking among state officials are often the result of low salaries and much greater reward incentives offered to them by local elites or foreign entrepreneurs. Levels of private violence are often aggravated by lax domestic and international restrictions on the purchase of arms or by economic policies that lead to increasing inequality.[38]

Failure to attend to the effects of shared rules can seriously diminish agents' sense of their overall contribution-based reasons with respect to very serious deprivations. Indeed, as Rüdiger Bittner has recently pointed out, when situations are not clearly brought about by a *single* agent (whether individual or collective), or by a small number of *specific* agents, people tend not to assign little bits of responsibility to many persons but rather tend to stop ascribing responsibility to anyone at all (Bittner 2001). Indeed, one reason why some issues, such as lack of access to medicines, receive great attention while others (such as severe income poverty) do not is that some deprivations *seem* (at least) attributable to an easily identifiable class of agents (such as Western pharmaceutical companies) while others do not. Recognizing this *psychological* tendency, however, does not *justify* neglect of responsibilities in cases where a complex range of factors have contributed to bringing about acute deprivations. It is not implausible to assert that agents' extremely small contributions to institutional

---

[38] For discussion see the World Bank study prepared by Fajnzylber, Lederman and Loayza, (1998), and also Klare and Anderson 1996.

arrangements that engender widespread acute deprivation can entail weighty institutional contribution-based reasons for these agents to address them.[39]

Institutional contribution-based reasons include reasons to uphold and comply with just institutional arrangements when they are in place, to help reform unjust institutional arrangements to which one has contributed or is contributing, and to remedy the hardships brought about by such unjust existing arrangements.[40]

These reflections on the different types of contribution-based reasons that agents can possess seem to blunt significantly the impracticability charge. Investigations of institutional contribution-based reasons, for example, will involve assessments of the design and functioning of global institutional arrangements, the examination of the relevance of individuals' conduct with respect to these arrangements, and the exploration of practically feasible alternatives. This will involve complex empirical investigations, which are subject to uncertainty. But it need not place "wildly excessive informational demands" on anyone. Indeed, it is quite difficult to imagine a plausible account of normative responsibilities that would not demand that we engage in precisely this type of social assessment.

5. Does the contribution principle lead to counterintuitive results?

One reasonable method for assessing the contribution principle is to assume its truth, investigate the kinds of conduct and social arrangements that it would most likely require, and determine whether these offend or are supported by our considered moral judgments. This is not to say that our considered moral judgments are sacrosanct. Indeed, there are many instances in which clearly unacceptable moral claims and distinctions have had strong intuitive support, and we should certainly heed Goodin's warning not to reduce political philosophy to "the role of philosophical anthropology — mapping without comment the social practices we find around ourselves" (Goodin 1995: 40). Nevertheless, the idea that at least *some* of these

---

[39] For discussion, see Parfit 1984, chapter 3.

[40] Developing an account of institutional contribution-based reasons involves three elements. It requires a conception of the appropriate aims that a social order should be designed to realize, and it demands an understanding of the specific institutional arrangements that can realize these aims. It demands an account of individuals' actual contributions to existing arrangements. Rational argument about institutional contribution-based reasons, then, can be of three kinds. It can concern disagreement about aims — the goals, values, and ideals that a social order ought be designed to achieve, the particular *institutional arrangements* that can realize these aims, or the nature and extent of an agents' contribution to them.

intuitions about the acceptability of conduct and social arrangements provide (rebuttable, of course) evidence in support of or against candidate principles seems unobjectionable. It can be argued that the contribution principle must be rejected because it would entail wildly counterintuitive results. The first version of this argument holds that, were the contribution principle to be adopted, we would have to conclude that the vast majority well-off individual and collective agents lack moral reasons to address the majority of the world's acute deprivations. Given the magnitude of acute deprivation in our world, along with the evident capabilities of well-off agents to alleviate or at least mitigate it, this judgment conflicts with many people's considered moral judgments.[41] The second version of this argument holds that the contribution principle would require implausible institutional arrangements. More specifically, the principle's focus on ensuring that those agents who have contributed to acute deprivations should bear the cost of addressing them would demand legalistic institutions that would be overly intrusive and unmanageable. I address each argument in turn.

For the first counterintuitiveness objection to be convincing, the following conditional must be true: when there is no conclusive evidence that some well-off agents have contributed to specific acute deprivations, then the contribution principle entails that these well-off agents lack moral reasons to address these deprivations.

Many assume that both the conditional and its antecedent are true, and that this gives us sufficient reason to reject the contribution principle.[42] Others have argued vigorously that, whether or not the conditional is true, the antecedent is false since there *is* conclusive evidence that well-off agents have contributed to acute deprivation — whether through unfair trade practices, by shaping the policies of international financial institutions, due to their enthusiastic participation in the global arms trade, or through other means.[43] Since the antecedent is false, this type of argument might conclude, we have no reason based on counterintuitiveness to reject the contribution principle.[44]

---

[41] It may also be supported, of course, by the considered judgments of many others. Indeed, this may even be one of their reasons for taking this claim to be true. I examine this claim at length precisely because it is relevant to those who appear to accept (C1) for this reason.

[42] See, for example, Young 2003b; Green 2002.

[43] See, for example, Pogge 2002a; Sen 2002; and Stiglitz 2002.

[44] My focus here is on the counterintuitiveness of this principle in our world, not in all possible worlds. It is easy to show the counterintuitive results of this principle in fictional contexts involving, perhaps, well-off agents who discover a planet (with whose inhabitants they have had no sustained interaction) that is replete with widespread deprivation that these agents can remedy at little or no cost to themselves.

I am sympathetic with these critics, but in this section I shall offer a different response to the counterintuitiveness objection, by challenging the assumption that the contribution principle entails that agents bear little responsibility with respect to acute deprivations unless there is fairly conclusive evidence suggesting otherwise.[45]

When activists, policymakers, and scholars argue for increased allocation of aid, debt relief and new institutional arrangements for the resolution of sovereign debt, and other (often costly) measures that would help to address acute deprivation, they often support these proposals on the ground that developed countries have contributed to these problems and should therefore help bear the cost. Claims that the IMF in particular has contributed to acute deprivations through its activities (notably its structural adjustment programs) have featured prominently in such claims. There are several mechanisms through which such contributions have allegedly taken place, of which I will here note three. It is argued that countries undergoing structural adjustment (hereafter, adjusting countries) (1) have had to make cuts in programs that help the poor, (2) have undertaken too much devaluation (as a result of requirements that they focus on short term domestic and external macroeconomic imbalances), which has let to deep recessions and burdensome import competition rather than sustained growth, (3) have undermined the incentives for countries that have mismanaged their economies to undertake more fundamental reforms that would (in the long term at least) have benefited them.[46]

These empirical claims have been contested. Maasland and van der Gaag (1992), for example, contend that there is no evidence that indicators of acute deprivation such as infant mortality rates have increased in adjusting countries. Summers and Pritchett (1993), argue that the three elements of adjustment that affect the poor: changes in relative prices, overall reductions in absorption to achieve external balance, and the effect on government expenditures, often appear to be to the overall benefit of the poor.[47]

---

[45] My discussion in this section draws on Barry (2005).

[46] I draw here on Summers and Pritchett 1993. For a sustained presentation of the claim that structural adjustment substantially contributed to acute deprivation in many developing countries, see Cornia, Jolly, and Stewart 1987. I set aside here complexities related to the fact that the IMF is not a unitary actor, and that its policies and decisions result from a complex negotiating process involving various elements of the Fund's management and executive board (which in turn represent the political interests of different countries.) I also assume that developed countries generally exercise control over the Fund's policies and decisions and thus share responsibility for its activities.

[47] They claim that changes in relative princes generally favor the rural poor (in many countries the majority of the poor) though they may lower incomes of other poor persons. They cite a study by Schiff and Valdes (1992), which claims that eliminating the bias against tradables raises output prices and rural wages. Since complex policy interventions

Assessing whether the IMF's critics or defenders are correct in this dispute also involves very difficult methodological issues. Graham Bird notes that in assessing such programs:

> We must distinguish between changes that have resulted from a particular adjustment program and those that have occurred for other reasons: the problems of the counterfactual. In practice, there is no completely satisfactory means of making such a sharp distinction. Before-and-after tests implicitly assume that other things remain constant, which they do not. Target-actual tests rely on the appropriateness of the targets that are set. While with-without tests assume that it is possible to formulate an accurate view as to what would have happened in the absence of an IMF-backed program (Bird 1996: 496).

I raise these issues not to suggest that no conclusions can be drawn about such programs, but merely to indicate that the evidence of their contribution is likely to remain reasonably contestable.[48] If I am correct, then the main question regarding the application of the contribution principle is: how, in cases where it is unclear whether or to what extent some agent has contributed to the deprivation of another, should the former conceive of its responsibilities to the latter?

In responding to this question, we need to distinguish three different *standards of application* for the contribution principle:

(1) A *Burden of Proof*, which determines whether the IMF must prove that it has not contributed to the deprivations or its critics must prove that it has;

(2) A *Standard of Proof*, which sets the evidential threshold that must be reached for it to *count* as proven that the IMF has or has not contributed to these deprivations; and

(3) *Constraints on Admissible Evidence*, which specify what types of evidence can be invoked in assessing this claim.

---

such as structural adjustments affect different groups of relatively badly off individuals differently, the issues mentioned above in note 3 regarding the *threshold level* — the levels of income, resource holdings, capability, functioning, utility, or some combination of the preceding — under which these subjects will count as acutely deprived; the *aggregation function* — the weights attached to the *depth* and *incidence* of deprivation, and perhaps also to its distribution — for assessing the overall magnitude of acute deprivation, are of obvious importance here.

[48] For the most comprehensive review of structural adjustment programs (neither of which rely on any one of these comparisons but try to formulate an overall view by examine the evidence that is available with respect to each), see Killick 1995 and Bird 1995.

Standards of this kind are of obvious importance in institutional settings such as courtrooms and regulatory bodies, which must make determinations about the possible contribution of different types of conduct to social outcomes, but their importance is seldom recognized for the application of principles to determine ethical responsibilities. They are equally crucial in this domain, however, since the way these standards are understood will significantly affect the practical meaning of these principles. For example, if critics needed to prove beyond a reasonable doubt that the IMF contributed to acute deprivations in adjusting countries in order to show that the IMF (and the developed countries that exercise a great deal of control over it) have contribution-based responsibilities to address these deprivations, then it might well turn out (for reasons already discussed) that such responsibilities are quite limited. Indeed, if the burden of proof is placed on the critics of the IMF, and the standard of proof is as stringent as that adopted within US criminal law, then the counterintuitiveness objection to the contribution principle would have a lot of force.

As I have argued elsewhere, however, insisting that the contribution principle adopt such stringent standards is implausible. Whether or not a particular standard is reasonable depends on the morally relevant features of the context. One of these features is the possible cost to those falsely "accused" or "convicted" of contributing to harms. One justification for the stringency of the criminal law standards, for example, is that false convictions in this setting can impose can enormous costs on the falsely accused.[49] Such stringent standards are not adopted, however, in civil legal settings where the costs to the falsely accused are seldom so steep. Here, showing that a "preponderance of evidence" supports the view that an agent's tortuous act caused some deprivation is grounds for holding them responsible for compensating for it. Here too, however, the burden of proof is placed on the prosecution. This is partly due to the (potentially quite significant) monetary costs associated with civil liability. It also relates, however, to the non-monetary costs, namely, that one has been singled out as having caused significant harm through one's negligence.[50] With respect to decisions to regulate conduct, such as forbidding a manufacturer to sell a product consisting of chemicals whose effects on humans are not known, even a strong suspicion that they may be harmful to a significant number of persons is often deemed sufficient, even when forbidding the sale of the

---

[49] Aside from losing their rights, liberties, and perhaps even their lives, being identified as a criminal offender may seriously damage all of their personal and professional relationships and even erode (however irrationally) their sense of self worth.

[50] In cases where it is alleged that an intentional tort has taken place the social sanction is even worse.

product will be very costly to its producer.[51] Unlike criminal and civil proceedings, or even some kinds of regulatory action, assessments of contribution-based responsibilities do not single out agents for sanctions that are backed by the coercive force of the state or any other "official" agency. All that is at stake is a determination of what (if anything) they morally ought to do to address the deprivations in question. While (as discussed below) the contribution principle may involve an evaluative component, an agent can be held to have contributed to some deprivation without their either being particularly blameworthy or even having behaved negligently. It simply demands that because an agent has not only been causally relevant to some deprivations, but has initiated, facilitated, or sustained the causal sequence that has led to them, this agent is obliged to share the costs of addressing them, whether by directly compensating their victims or by undertaking changes in policy with respect to them. In the case of the IMF (and, by association, the developed countries) the cost of addressing deprivations to which they have allegedly contributed need not be great relative to their means. Considering only the cost to those falsely found to have contributed to acute deprivation, we have reason to conceive of the standards for applying the contribution principle as much less stringent than those relevant for criminal or civil legal contexts.

The costs to those falsely held to have contributed to some harmful outcome are not, however, the only costs to be considered in assessing the fairness of various standards. We must also consider the costs to those who go uncompensated when those who have contributed to their deprivations are falsely found not to have done so.[52] How great these costs are depends on several factors, including whether (and at what cost) the affected agents can through their own efforts recover from these deprivations and on whether there are other mechanisms in place, such as social insurance schemes, that address these deprivations and spread the costs of remedying them fairly. In our world, these costs would be rather significant. Many countries to whose hardships the IMF has allegedly contributed often lack resources fully to offset the acute deprivations of their citizens. Other's may have sufficient

---

[51] That we may be inclined to disallow comparable costs to be paid by a company for damage that has allegedly already been done by the chemical further highlights the relevance of non-pecuniary costs to the accused party in fixing standards in civil law. Whether or not suspicion of harmful effects is sufficient to forbid sale of the product will depend on other normative factors, including not only the general benefit of the product, but its benefit to those who are put at greatest risk by permitting its use. See Barry 2001 for discussion of these issues as they relate to the regulation of new technologies.

[52] Clearly, where the alleged harms are less serious — merely making relatively well off persons a bit worse off, for example — the costs would be less significant, and the case for lessening the stringency of standards for establishing contribution correspondingly weaker.

resources but fail to allocate them for this purpose because doing so would require them to sacrifice other desirable goals that they legitimately wish to pursue. Some countries may put such schemes in place, but it is not altogether clear that they have thereby substantially lessened the cost of the failure to allocate responsibility accurately. Rather, they may merely have passed it on to others. Imagine, for example, a relatively poor but extremely well governed and egalitarian developing country that puts in place a scheme of social insurance whereby those falling beneath (some reasonably specified) poverty line receive assistance from the state. This will certainly reduce the costs to the acutely deprived, but the raising of such revenues my place burdens on many other people who are not particularly well off. The costs to these persons — perhaps involving inferior educational, health, or economic opportunities — are real and must be considered. Indeed, why should these relatively badly off people have to bear the full burden of alleviating the deprivations of their compatriots when it is foreigners (with much greater resources at their disposal) who have substantially contributed to them? Were the developed countries exercising control over the IMF to contribute to a general burden-sharing fund that provided reliable and effective assistance to countries whose residents suffer acute deprivations, then the cost of failures to allocate responsibility accurately would be substantially lessened. At present, however, such a system is notably lacking.[53] Consideration of the costs to those who go uncompensated because of failures to allocate responsibility accurately suggest, then, that in our word, further relaxing the standards required to establish contribution with respect to acute deprivation would be justified.

The conclusions of my discussion in this section are limited but significant. I have not shown that, on the basis of available evidence, we should take the IMF to have contributed to acute deprivation in adjusting countries. Nor have I defended a detailed account of how standards for applying the contribution principle should be specified. I have however presented reasons for doubting that adopting plausible standards for applying the contribution principle would lead us to the conclusion that few well-off agents have responsibilities to address acute deprivation.

It may be objected that the contribution principle would require a legalistic system modeled on a court that would be charged with the task of assessing whether agents such as the IMF have contributed to acute deprivations through their activities. Such a system would, one might think, not only be unmanageable but would also lead to counterproductive finger

---

[53] All developed countries together spend only $4.31 billion (2002), one-sixtieth of 1 percent of their combined gross national incomes, on meeting basic needs in the developing world (http://millenniumindicators.un.org/unsd/mi/mi_series_results.asp?rowId=592).

pointing instead of concerted action to deal with the real problems of poor countries. There are two responses to this argument. The first is that it is far from obvious that it would be counterproductive to institute a complaint system in which countries could allege that they were harmed by the IMF or other collective agents. As Kunibert Raffer (2003, 2004) has recently pointed out, it is a notable feature of our international order that developing countries lack mechanisms by which they can formally complain and seek compensation form international financial institutions and donor countries, even where the harms they have suffered appear to have been caused by grave negligence. Raffer argues that the absence of such mechanisms for holding these agents financially accountable has not only failed to provide adequate disincentives to sloppy work, but has actually created strong incentives for lending institutions to make poorly conceived loans because "errors and negligently done damage tend to increase the importance of IFIs (international financial institutions), since damages caused by one project or adjustment program call for a new loan to repair them, thus increasing IFI income — IFI flops create IFI jobs" (Raffer 2004: 63). He proposes the establishment of (ideally) a permanent international court of arbitration or (more likely) ad hoc panels that would hear complaints about the effects of IFI conduct lodged by governments as well as by international and nongovernmental organizations.[54]

Second, it is far from clear that the contribution principle would demand such an institution were it to turn out to be an ineffective way of ensuring that those who contribute to acute deprivation shoulder the costs of alleviating or mitigating them. There is nothing in the contribution principle that demands an institution that decides responsibility for paying these costs on a case-by-case basis. Indeed, an adequately resourced system of international burden-sharing might actually work better, so long as its cost did not fall disproportionately on agents who have little contribution-based reason to address acute deprivation.[55] Instituting a better system of regulation of the IMF and other collective agents might also better realize the aims of the contribution principle than a court of arbitration. This section has shown that the assumption that agents bear little responsibility with respect to acute deprivations unless there is fairly conclusive evidence

---

[54] I am not here endorsing Raffer's proposal. Indeed, I think that his insistence on a negligence liability standard is too restrictive. If IFIs have taken due care but have still substantially contributed to acute deprivation, should they bear none of the cost of addressing them?

[55] Compare here the arguments with which Waldron (1995) and other legal philosophers have advocated replacing the tort system with generalized social insurance schemes in domains where a fault system with individualized case-by-case judgments is costly, often inaccurate, and intuitively unfair.

suggesting otherwise cannot be sustained. To think otherwise, I have argued, requires a commitment to a view of standards for applying the contribution principle that, while not implausible in some legal contexts, cannot be defended in the context of determining ethical responsibilities for addressing acute deprivations. To be sure, the contribution principle does entail that well-off agents lack moral reasons to address acute deprivations when there is conclusive evidence that they have not contributed to them. But, in the world as it is, such a conclusive case can rarely be made. And most well-off agents committed to the contribution principle therefore have reason significantly to revise their behavior. The claim that the contribution principle would call for problematic institutional arrangements has also been rejected.

6. What does it mean to contribute?

The contribution principle has strong intuitive appeal, can be given a rationale that seems to have some initial plausibility, withstands the objections examined in the previous section, factors prominently in most people's practical thinking, and seems to play a role in explaining the behavior of many agents. It is therefore an important question how one should mark the distinction between contributing to acute deprivations and merely failing to prevent them or being completely uninvolved in them is of. This question is also notoriously difficult to address, since there are many ways in which it may be answered, none of which seem fully convincing. This section does not attempt to provide an account of this distinction. Rather, it sets out the kinds of interpretive criteria that should be used to assess such attempts and then applies these criteria to two popular attempts at drawing the distinction.

Most importantly, an account of the distinction should capture most of our convergent intuitions regarding the appropriate classifications of agents' conduct. That is, it should explain why nearly all people will unhesitatingly offer coinciding judgments about whether agents in cases described to them have contributed to some deprivation or not. We might refer to this as the principle of *agreement*. This principle will only take us so far, however, since there may be many cases in which competent speaker of English will disagree, or be unsure how to classify conduct. While no account of the distinction may resolve all such conflicts, it should help explain why people's classifications of conduct diverge, and why they are unsure how to evaluate conduct in other cases. We might refer to this as the principle of *explanation*. Finally, given that contribution-based reasons are generally held to have significant and distinctive weight, an account of the distinction should either draw it (if possible) in a way that makes it seem at least initially plausible to grant it moral significance. We might refer to this as the principle of *charity*.

The most fundamental question regarding the distinction relates to its *status*. Is it purely empirical, so that we can classify conduct as having contributed to or having merely failed to prevent some acute deprivation without recourse to evaluative judgments? Or does the correct application of the concept, like democracy, liberty, and perhaps coercion, depend on evaluative judgments?[56] We can refer to approaches that provide different answers to the question of status as "pure empirical contrast" and "partly moralized contrast" approaches respectively. When philosophers have distinguished those acute deprivations to which an agent's conduct has contributed from those that she has merely "allowed," "let happen," or "failed to prevent," they have generally taken themselves to be basing these claims on non-moral facts about her behavior (see Bennett 1995: 136f).

This section will show, however, that existing attempts to interpret this distinction as pure empirical contrast fail in terms of the interpretive criteria identified above.

6.1 The pure empirical contrast approach

Two versions of the pure empirical contrast approach can be distinguished: *causal* and *non-causal counterfactual* accounts. Causal accounts draw the distinction in terms of the causal relevance of an agent's conduct to some acute deprivation. It holds that an agent's causal relevance to some deprivation is both a necessary and sufficient condition for their having contributed to it. While this idea may seem intuitively right, it cannot be defended.

To show this, it suffices to examine a slightly modified version of a set of cases first developed by Bennett:

Suit: A far away village is in need. I launch a lawsuit that deprives them of a thousand dollars.

Cancel: Same village, same everything, but this time I learn that my accountant thinks he is supposed to sign away a thousand of my dollars to the village, and I tell him not to.

---

[56] Even if a term is understood as purely descriptive, it may still be the case that it usually, or always, goes along with a positive or negative moral assessment. That a term is purely descriptive means only that one can decide whether or not it applies without recourse to evaluative judgments.

No-help: Same village, etc. This time I could but do not give the villagers a thousand dollars.[57]

In all of these scenarios, the villagers suffer acute deprivations. In which case(s) does Agent contribute to this outcome? Most people will judge that Agent is a contributor in Suit, and not a contributor in Cancel and No-Help. If contribution is held to be equivalent to causation, however, then Agent is a contributor in all three cases. This is so regardless of whether causation is interpreted as "strong necessity" or "weak necessity/strong sufficiency," the two leading philosophical theories of causation. In all three cases, Agent is strongly necessary for the outcome, since "but for" the fact that she launched the suit, cancelled the sending of the check, and neglected to send the money, the villagers would not have suffered acute deprivation.[58] And in all three cases Agent is weakly necessary and strongly sufficient for the outcome, since A's launching the suit, canceling the sending of the check, and neglecting to send the money were in each case necessary elements of a set of antecedent actual conditions that was sufficient for the occurrence of the consequence — a full causal explanation of why the villagers are acutely deprived must include mention of these facts about Agent's behavior.[59] These examples show that causation is both too broad a concept on which to base the distinction. It thus does poorly in terms of the principle of agreement. It also fares poorly in terms of the principle of charity, since it appears to be far too weak a basis for a plausible principle for allocating responsibilities. Almost all participants in markets, for example, will figure in the complete causal explanation of many acute deprivations. The causal interpretation of the contribution principle would hold all such agents responsible for addressing these deprivations. Put in legal language, they would be strapped with "absolute liability" based on mere causation.[60]

In light of the problems that were discovered for the first two causal accounts of the contribution principle (which are based on the two most widely accepted philosophical approaches to causation), it might be suggested that what is needed is a more "restrictive" causal account that captures our "common sense" or "paradigmatic" uses of causal concepts.

---

[57] The case is drawn from Bennett (1995: 103). He chooses to locate this village in Africa, presumably to suggest that it is far away and "other," but I have not followed him in this. I shall try to correct for the crudeness of the case by drawing parallels with (and showing its relevance to) comparable but much more complex real world situations involving different agents' relevance to shortfalls in health due to the inaccessibility of essential medicines.

[58] For a discussion of the strong necessity view, see Mackie 1974.

[59] For a discussion of the weak necessity/strong sufficiency view, see Mackie 1974 and Honoré 1999.

[60] For helpful discussions that demonstrate the implausibility of basing either ethical responsibility or legal responsibility in tort on *mere* causation, see Ripstein 1999, and also the classic treatment of this issue in Coase 1960.

Three attempts to characterize a "restrictive" causal account can be considered. The first account, which might be called the *single sufficiency* interpretation, holds that an agent has contributed to a deprivation if and only if she was singly sufficient for its occurrence.

The single sufficiency view is obviously inadequate as an analysis of the distinction. Acute deprivations typically result from many actors each of whose conduct contributes to them, yet none of whose conduct may have been singly sufficient for them. Shortfalls in health due to the HIV epidemic in South Africa, for example, result from poverty, poor health-care infrastructure, gender inequality, social mores against the use of prophylactics, the idiosyncratic causal beliefs of President Mbeki, declining targeted aid from developed countries, and restrictive patents on pharmaceuticals enforced under the WTO's Trade Related Aspects of Intellectual Property Rights (TRIPS) agreement. None of the agents whose conduct results in any of these conditions is singly sufficient for these shortfalls, yet is wildly implausible to claim that neither the Mbeki government, nor the agents supporting and enforcing WTO rules have contributed to them. This account thus does poorly in terms of the principle of agreement. Moreover, such a principle would also fare poorly in terms of the principle of charity, since it would implausibly absolve almost all agents of responsibility with respect to acute deprivation, since each of these agents could easily show both (1) that the set of actual antecedent conditions sufficient for its occurrence would have the conduct of these other agents amongst its elements, and (2) that "but for" the others' conduct, it would not have occurred. This point can also be simply illustrated by another imagined case — *Suit 2* — in which there are two agents A and B, each of whom launch a suit, both of whose suits depend for their success on the launching of the other (perhaps because each will introduce evidence that becomes relevant to the other which would not otherwise have been brought to the court's attention.)

A second view, building on the work of legal theorist Richard Epstein, might hold that an agent has contributed to a deprivation if and only if her conduct is a *paradigmatic cause* of it. For example, Agent A is a paradigmatic cause of B's deprivation if the deprivation results from A's exercising force on B, frightening B, compelling B, or setting conditions that are dangerous for B.[61]

---

[61] These paradigms are elaborated in Epstein 1980. It is not obvious why Epstein's paradigms are restricted to conduct that can be described by these particular active verbs. A's hurting B, for example, appears equally paradigmatic. See Coleman and Ripstein 1995 for discussion.

How then, would Epstein's paradigms classify Agents' conduct? For example, which (if any) of *Suit*, *Cancel*, or *No-Help* would count as "setting conditions that are dangerous" for the villagers? It is plainly impossible to tell. This is not only because his paradigms are vague, but also because classification of conduct into these categories would seem to require more information than is presented in the description of the case. In Suit, for example, Agent might be seen either as a contributor or a non-contributor to the villagers' suffering, depending on certain background conditions. If the villagers have stolen Agent's money, then he cannot plausibly be seen as "setting dangerous conditions" for them. If Agent is launching a suit that is spurious, but that he knows will succeed because his high-priced lawyers will overwhelm the poorly trained legal representatives of the village or because the court in which he tries his case is corrupt, then it would appear that he had set dangerous conditions for the villagers.[62] Our judgments in these cases, however, are clearly guided by normative considerations. This is not a problem as such. Indeed, the conclusion of this section is that any plausible account of the distinction will be partly evaluative. However, it does show that this conceiving the distinction in terms of 'paradigmatic' causation does not belong to the purely empirical contrast approach, even though it sounds purely empirical because it is dressed up in the language of causation. Epstein's "restricted" conception of causation is not really a conception of causation at all, but a combination of causation (which is never precisely defined) and non-causal normative criteria (which are also never precisely defined). Due to this lack of clarity, the concept of a causal paradigm doesn't help us to identify the distinctions between contributors and non-contributors at all.

A third "restrictive" account might build on H.L.A Hart and Tony Honoré classic discussion of the "common-sense" notion of causation in *Causation in the Law*.[63] According to this interpretation, Agent A causes B's deprivation if and only if A's conduct is the factor which "makes a difference" by interfering with, intervening in, or otherwise changing the "normal" or "reasonably expected" course of events to bring it about.[64] Causes are distinguished from "mere" conditions by their abnormality and by their being the result of voluntary human action.

Wright (1985) provides the following succinct characterization of their analysis:

---

[62] Compare here the case of US pharmaceuticals' suit against South Africa for infringement of the TRIPS agreement with respect to importation of generic anti-retroviral medicines.

[63] Hart and Honoré 1985, chapter 2.

[64] Ibid. 31–39.

A contributing factor is treated as the cause rather than as a mere condition if it was (1) a voluntary human intervention that was intended to produce the consequence (for example, deliberately breaking a vase) or (2) an abnormal action, event, or condition in the particular context (for example, a freak storm or driving at an excessive speed). If there are two or more contributing factors which satisfy one of these criteria, the last one to occur is treated as the cause. When searching for the cause of an injury, we do not trace back any further once we come across a deliberate intervention or an independent abnormal condition.[65]

Hart and Honoré's common sense causal view meshes with many of our convergent intuitive classifications of conduct. It diverges with many others, however, since many instances of conduct that we intuitively classify as failures to prevent may be abnormal or deliberate, and thus commonly considered their cause.[66] More important for the present discussion, however, is that the common sense causal view described by Hart and Honoré would not provide a purely empirical account of the distinction. At any particular time, the behavior of two agents may be empirically indistinguishable, yet the conduct of one of them may be noteworthy with respect to (and thus singled out as the cause of) some outcome because, for example, they have violated some normative standard. Agent may be the common-sense cause of the villagers' deprivation in either *Cancel* or *No-Help*, depending on background features such as whether she has led them to expect her funds, or dissuaded others from contributing their funds by providing assurances that she intends to do so. Indeed, Hart and Honoré's own discussion of the conditions under which behavior will count as voluntary (e.g., that the agent intended to so conduct themselves, and that their conduct did not result from cognitive failures, coercion, and was not undertaken to avoid even worse outcomes, etc.) makes it absolutely clear that attributions of common sense causation will partly depend on normative appraisal.[67] These are not grounds for rejecting common-sense causation as an element of the distinction between contributing and not-contributing to or failing to prevent some deprivation. Rather, they show that such a distinction would not be a pure empirical contrast.[68]

---

[65] Wright 1985: 1745f. The relevant passages in Hart and Honoré 1985 are at 38–39 and 129–31. For a clear and sympathetic discussion of their account see also Stapleton 1988.

[66] Should someone die in a car accident because their brakes fail, their mechanic's deliberate failure to check the breaks of a car during its last servicing will certainly be identified by most observers as a cause of her death.

[67] This aspect of their analysis is discussed in Miller 2001; Stapleton 1988; and Wright 2001.

[68] As natural as it may be to draw the distinction by identifying contribution with 'primary' causal responsibility (see, for example, McMahan 1993), analyzing it in this way will fail for similar reasons. There are simply no plausible purely empirical grounds on which such

6.2 Non-causal counterfactual accounts

The causal accounts of the distinction discussed above are either plainly implausible, or are partly moralized and require separate treatmentJonathan Bennett's analysis of the "making and allowing," and Alan Donagan's analysis of the difference between "intervening and not intervening" in the "course of nature," provide non-causal counterfactual accounts of the distinction.[69]

According to the Bennett view, Agent A's conduct contributes to Agent B's deprivation if and only if most of the ways A could have behaved at the time would not have led to B's Deprivation. According to Donagan's view, Agent A's conduct contributes to Agent B's deprivations if and only if B's deprivation would not have occurred had A "abstained from intervening in the course of nature." Neither of these variants agree with many of our convergent classifications of particular cases.

Each of these accounts would classify Agents' conduct in both *Suit* and *Cancel* as having contributed to the villagers' acute deprivations. This may seems a bit counterintuitive, but I do not think that it provides conclusive grounds for rejecting these accounts of the distinction, since peoples' linguistic intuitions may well diverge here. Examination of a further case (*Village 3*), however, demonstrates the implausibility of both of these analyses. *Village 3* differs only in that there is a second agent, Agent 2, who will see to it that the village does not receive the money, whether or not I bring the suit or cancel the sending of the money. In this case, both of these accounts entail that I have not contributed to the acute deprivations in *all three* scenarios. Surely, however, if anything should count as contributing to their acute deprivations, my launching a suit to deprive them of a thousand dollars should — at least in those cases where I am ignorant of Agent 2's intentions and capabilities. It is also clear that the contribution principle — so interpreted — would fail to allocate responsibilities in a way that has any plausibility, since it would follow that I would never have weighty moral reasons to address the acute deprivations that have resulted from conduct so long as those suffering them would have suffered at the hands of other agents had I not done so.

The problem with both the causal and counterfactual accounts of the contribution principle is that our judgments regarding whether or not agents have contributed to acute deprivations cannot be adequately captured in terms of the characterization of the behavior space or the causal relevance of

---

a distinction can be drawn. As Kutz (2000: 51) has put it, "Contributory, necessary causes are metaphysically equal and only normatively unequal."

[69] Bennett 1995, esp. 88–104, and Donagan 1977.

their conduct at a particular point in time. This is because they neglect background conditions, including the normative relations between agents, which seem to inform these judgments. Indeed, as McMahan (1993) has pointed out, the fact that many would classify Agent's conduct in *Cancel* as contributing to the villagers' plight seems crucially to depend on the fact that it is the transfer of Agent's own resources that is witheld. If someone else was providing the aid, they would most likely judge Agent's conduct to have contributed to the deprivation. These examples suggest that our intuitive classification of conduct as having contributed to deprivation depend significantly on factors that involve an evaluative component. Determining whether an agent is discontinuing assistance that they themselves were providing or interfering with the transmission of resources that rightly belong to the intended recipient simply cannot be determined through the use of metics such as Bennett's or through purely causal criteria. Yet it is precisely such derminations that appear to guide our use of the distinction.[70]

What follows from this conclusion? Does it show that the whole business of evaluating the contribution principle is a pointless exercise because identifying an agent's contribution partly depends on prior evaluation of their conduct? Bennett has claimed that it does, arguing that:

> Both sides in the debate about the moral significance of making/allowing have thought they were discussing the moral import of something that does not rest on any prior moral judgement; if they were wrong about that, the issue dies (Bennett 1995: 137).

This argument is valid, however, only if it interpreted quite narrowly. Even if a term does have an evaluative component, its correct application may not be decisive or even particularly significant for moral assessment. For example, that an act constitutes treachery, murder, or cruelty counts as a reason against it, but this reason may not always overide other reasons for it such as an agents' capacity to avert very bad outcomes. If identifying an agents conduct as having contributed to some deprivation depends partly on evaluation of its morally relevant features—such as whether it involves discontinuing assistance or infringing property rights—then at least some version of (C3) must be true. But even a moderate version of claim (C2) need not be true, let alone (C1) or strong versions of (C2). The mere fact that someone is deemed to have contributed to some deprivation because there were causally relevant to it and because their behaviour inolved the infringement of the deprived subjects property rights, does not show that their contribution-based reasons for addressing it are of substantially greater

---

[70] What, more precisely, the evaluative component involves has not been explored in this essay.

significance than association or capacity-based reasons. In short, the question of whether the distinction has any moral signifincance does indeed die, but the question of how much moral significance it has is not therefore preempted. It can only be settled through further substantive moral argumentation.

This essay has not settled the question of whether and which version of the contribution principle should be adopted. It is hoped, however, that is has successfully clarified the status of this principle, identified some of its attractive features, and shown that objections to which it is commonly subjected are unconvicing.

Chapter 8

World Poverty and Moral Responsibility[*]

Ser-Min Shei
Philosophy, National Chung Cheng University, Chia-Yi, Taiwan

I.

We all know that hundreds of millions of people worldwide are chronically malnourished and barely surviving. According to a recent estimate, the number of people who live below the World Bank's $2/day poverty line is about 2,800 million or 46 percent of humankind, and annually, 18 million people die prematurely from poverty-related causes (Pogge 2002a: 2). World poverty is not a situation intentionally brought about by any particular agent. It is caused not by one single factor, but by innumerably many factors, and no one knows, even if one cares to know, whether or not their everyday economic decisions have negative effects on world poverty, and if so, how and to what extent. But, despite its complex origin, it does not follow that the eradication of world poverty is beyond our reach no matter what we — humankind — collectively choose to do. On the contrary, whether we take ourselves to have compelling reason to eradicate world poverty will surely make a difference. If enough of us are convinced

---

[*] In addition to the Oslo Symposium on Global Justice, the previous versions of this paper were also presented at the Philosophy Seminar entitled "Poverty as a Violation of Human Rights," organized by UNESCO, 8–9 September, 2003, in Delhi, India, and at the Joint Tsinghua-CUHK International Conference on Political Philosophy, entitled "Justice, Community and Democracy," 14–16 October, 2003, in Beijing, China. For the critical and probing comments it received, I would like to thank David Archard, Richard Arneson, Christian Barry, Rüdiger Bittner, Bashshar Haydar, Martin Van Hees, Hon-Lam Li, Ernest Marie Mbonda, Gerhard Øverland, Thomas Pogge, Joseph Raz, Sanjay Reddy, Yuan-Kang Shih, John Skorupski, Terence Tai, Andrew Williams, and Ruey-Yuan Wu. Especially, I would like to express my gratitude to Thomas Pogge, without whose encouragement and helpful suggestions this paper would not exist.

A. Follesdal and T. Pogge, (eds.), Real World Justice, 139-155.
© 2005 *Springer. Printed in the Netherlands.*

that we have compelling reason to eradicate world poverty, it will be relatively easy to find an effective strategy or a scheme of coordination to achieve it.[1] But why aren't people, especially those who are, relatively speaking, affluent and able, mostly living in the developed states, convinced that they have compelling reason to help eradicate world poverty?

One simple explanation for the denial of compelling reason is that most people do not believe that they are *morally responsible* for the persistence of world poverty, or even *mistakenly* believe, in my view, that they are *not* morally responsible for the persistence of world poverty.[2] The explanation is suggested by the assumption that once people come to believe that they are morally responsible for a bad situation, say, someone's being harmed, normally they will also believe that they have a duty to respond to the situation appropriately, such as to take action to change the situation, reduce its badness, and/or to compensate the victims (if there are any) for their loss and suffering. And if the situation for which they think they are morally responsible is very bad, then they tend to think that this duty gives them compelling reason to take appropriate action.

Admittedly, the notion of moral responsibility in which this explanation is couched needs further clarification, if we also want to show convincingly that people are mistaken about the moral responsibility for the persistence of world poverty. At least, we have to specify the general criteria (or grounds) for determining

(1) who is (are) morally responsible with respect to a bad situation such as world poverty; and

(2) how the duty to take appropriate action is to be shared among those who are morally responsible for the bad situation.

Ability to change the current situation or to compensate the victims might be relevant to the second question, but not to the first; so is whether one has gained from the bad situation: those who gain nothing from a bad situation may be morally responsible for the bad situation as in cases in which one intentionally makes the situation worse for others, which in turn comes to

---

[1] Admittedly, even if a person takes himself or herself to have compelling reason to help eradicate world poverty, he or she might not take any action at all for the eradication of world poverty, because the person might believe that what he or she does will *not* make a difference for the eradication of world poverty, given what others choose to do. Hence it is extremely important to get people to do what they take themselves to have compelling reason to do against the thought that what they each do will make no difference to the situation.

[2] For alternative explanations, see Pogge 2002a: 3–11. He lists and discusses two causal explanations as to why most people in the affluent Western states do not find themselves have compelling reason to help eradicate world poverty. Pogge also considers and rejects four "reasons" as well as what he calls explanatory nationalism as defenses for acquiescence in world poverty.

hurt oneself. A simple example may help us understand this point. In a case in which someone is drowning (a bad situation), I am morally responsible for his drowning if I alone pushed him into the water intentionally, whether or not I benefit from his drowning. But I am not morally responsible for this person's drowning if someone else pushed him into the water (assuming I am not morally responsible for her doing so), even if I benefit from the victim's drowning. I take it to be obvious that I have weightier reason to respond to the first bad situation, by rescuing the victim, say, or by paying compensation, than to respond similarly to the second situation.

One advantage of separating the moral responsibility for a bad situation and the duty to respond to the bad situation appropriately is to make clear that those who are morally responsible for a bad situation have a *negative* duty to respond to the bad situation appropriately, while those who are not morally responsible for the bad situation have, if they do, only *positive* duties to respond to the same situation. A duty is negative not in the sense that one should never violate it, all things considered, but in the sense that it is *always morally wrong* not to take it to be a *sufficient* reason against our conduct that it will violate the duty. While we may sometimes have to violate a negative duty, all things considered (as when something important is at stake, for example, in the situation in which by not saving a person for whose drowning I would be morally responsible, I will be able to warn 1000 people who would otherwise die), it is also undeniably true that by violating this negative duty, we have harmed (wronged) the person.

Although I do not have a complete answer to the first question, I am convinced that most people are mistaken in thinking that they are not morally responsible for the persistence of world poverty. This paper is an attempt to show why we are all morally responsible for the persistence of world poverty, hence share a negative duty to help eradicate world poverty.[3] I shall argue that we are all morally responsible for the persistence of world poverty simply because each of us is a member of a collectivity, humankind, which can be viewed as having had full control over the ongoing global order, hence is morally responsible for the persistence of world poverty. That is, in my view, the persistence of world poverty is a failure for which humankind as a whole is morally responsible, and each of us, simply being a member of humankind, bears this responsibility and shares the duty to eradicate it. And this view entails that for the same reason those who are victims of the ongoing global order also bear the responsibility, but because

---

[3] It is reasonable to assume that those who have made substantial efforts to help the global poor may share less of the duty to eradicate world poverty than those who have done less. Perhaps we should add that those who have benefited more from the ongoing global order share more of the duty to help eradicate world poverty than those who have benefited less.

of their difficult situation, the current global poor might share much less of the duty than the rich and powerful to help eradicate world poverty (so as to protect people of future generations from severe poverty).

To be sure, from the fact that most people do not believe that they are morally responsible for the persistence of world poverty, it does not follow that they believe that they have no moral reasons for taking actions aimed at improving the situation of the global poor and reforming the ongoing global order. Many of them do. However, those who believe they have moral reasons to respond to world poverty tend to see these reasons as arising exclusively from *the duty of mutual aid*, which they believe applies to all, regardless of what people have chosen to do. The duty of mutual aid, according to common understanding, is the duty of helping others in need or jeopardy, provided that we can do so without great cost to ourselves, for instance, provided that helping them will not prevent us from having a meaningful life or from fulfilling other duties we have, such as the duty not to harm or injure another, the duty to enhance the interests of our family members and friends. And I take it that when only the duty of mutual aid applies, one is not *morally responsible* for the situation in which others are in need or jeopardy. The duty of mutual aid so understood, however, appears to be relatively weak. Very often when it is in conflict with other duties or with one's interests, one could legitimately ignore its normative force and take oneself to have weightier reason to act toward fulfilling these other duties and interests.

If the duty of mutual aid is the only moral duty that provides the relatively affluent individuals with reason for taking action to help eradicate world poverty, then there will be too many grounds each of them could invoke to justify not doing anything to improve the situation of the extremely poor, not only within one's own country, but throughout the world. To be sure, it is an open question whether the duty of mutual aid is indeed so weak. It may demand more than we think (Singer 1972). The relatively affluent individuals may have very strong reason based on the duty of mutual aid alone to eradicate world poverty. But in my view, whether the duty of mutual aid is weak or not, the relatively affluent individuals are morally responsible for the persistence of world poverty, and because of their favorable situation and the benefits they receive from the ongoing global order, they share more of the duty to help eradicate world poverty. That is, they have a more stringent duty than the duty of mutual aid for eradicating world poverty. Obviously, if this view is correct, then, with regard to the eradication of world poverty, relatively affluent individuals cannot just take themselves to be bound by the duty of mutual aid alone. The question that concerns this paper is to explain why the persistence of world poverty is something for which the relatively affluent individuals are morally responsible.

It might be said that the relatively affluent individuals failed in the past to discharge their duty of mutual aid toward the global poor, so they are morally responsible for the persistence of world poverty. This claim might be true. But the problem is that it does not seem to be true that every relatively affluent individual has failed to discharge his duty of mutual aid toward the global poor. In any case, my question in this paper is about whether we can show that each and every relatively affluent individual is morally responsible for the persistence of world poverty, even if some of them did not fail in the past to discharge their duty of mutual aid.[4] In what follows, I defend an affirmative answer to this question. I begin by clarifying how my view differs from the view, put forward by Thomas Pogge, which emphasizes that it is the duty not to harm others unduly though one's conducts that provides the relatively affluent with compelling reason to help eradicate world poverty.

II.

To start with, let us note that some philosophers are very skeptical about morality-based reasons for eradicating world poverty, even skeptical about reasons based on the duty of mutual aid. For example, Rüdiger Bittner contends that

> [world poverty] is an outcome of what a large number of people did, and in doing what they do these people may be pursuing the same or different, even opposite ends, or indeed ends unrelated to each other. Moreover, none of the actors involved overlooks their whole interplay. The outcome, therefore, is not clearly anybody's doing in particular. They did something together, that is true, but neither collectively nor individually were they master over what emerged (Bittner 2001: 29).

---

[4] It may seem exceedingly plausible to some that not every relatively affluent individual shares responsibility for global poverty. They may insist that those who have done a lot for the global poor do not share the moral responsibility for the persistence of world poverty. In reply, one might say that these people still share some moral responsibility, though less than that shared by those who have done little for the global poor. This paper is an attempt to make this reply sensible. My idea is that those who have made efforts for the global poor should not be blamed, but on the contrary, should be praised, yet it is a different matter whether they still share moral responsibility for the persistence of world poverty, and hence still have compelling reason to help eradicate world poverty now.

Consequently, he draws the conclusion that world poverty is a non-imputable situation, and that it goes beyond the scope of moral judgment. For Bittner, it makes no sense to say that relatively affluent individuals, or anyone else, are morally responsible for world poverty (Bittner 2001: 31). Less extreme but equally disturbing are the following remarks made by Samuel Scheffler:

> Much of the daily behaviour we take for granted is linked in complicated but often poorly appreciated ways to broader global dynamics of the greatest importance. ... What we appear to lack ... is a set of clear, action-guiding, and psychologically feasible principles which would enable individuals to orient themselves in relation to the larger processes and their effects in a morally satisfactory way. In view of the moral importance both of the processes and of their effects, the absence of such principles raises an obvious question about the adequacy of a system of normative responsibility that treats the individual agent as the primary bearer of such responsibility (Scheffler 2001: 44f).

Against this skeptical current, Pogge tries, in his recent important book, *World Poverty and Human Rights* (Pogge 2002a), to make a case for the following claim:

> In virtue of supporting or participating in the ongoing global economic order, which foreseeably engenders avoidable severe poverty worldwide, the relatively affluent individuals (primarily, but not exclusively, ordinary citizens in the developed states) have *harmed*, and are harming, the global poor *unduly*.[5]

According to Pogge, we have a *negative* general duty "to ensure that others are not unduly harmed through one's own conduct." (Pogge 2002a: 130) Hence, if by participating in the ongoing global order, the relatively affluent individuals have harmed the global poor unduly, then they have violated this negative duty. Accordingly, the relatively affluent individuals have a very strong reason to compensate the global poor for the undue harms the latter have suffered, and, equally important, a very strong reason to stop harming the global poor unduly by making efforts, with very high priority, toward institutional reforms that would eradicate world poverty. If Pogge's claim holds, then, clearly, we have a strong case for the view that the relatively affluent have other morality-based reasons to eradicate world poverty than those based on the duty of mutual aid.

---

[5]   This is not a direct quote from Pogge 2002a, but a reconstruction of what he says in chapter 5, especially, section 5.2.

However, for his claim to hold, Pogge has to defend a number of theses, which for some are controversial (LaFollette 2003: 908):

(1) that there is, in some significant sense, a global economic order;
(2) that this order foreseeably engenders avoidable severe poverty;
(3) that by supporting or participating in this order, the relatively affluent individuals not only have *harmed* the global poor, but also harmed them *unduly*.

In this paper I shall leave (1) and (2) aside, which I believe have been well defended by Pogge, and focus my discussion on (3). I want to examine whether (3) holds and assess the way Pogge argues for it. In my view, (3) does not hold. But this verdict, I have to emphasize, does not defeat the claim I want to defend, namely, that the relatively affluent individuals are *morally responsible* for the persistence of world poverty, for the global poor's being poor. As it stands, my view does not presuppose that the relatively affluent individuals are harming the global poor unduly. That is to say, one can *endorse* my view that the relatively affluent are morally responsible for the persistence of world poverty without having to endorse Pogge's view that they harm the global poor unduly by participating in the ongoing global order. The crucial question is whether one can *defend* my view without appealing to (3). This paper is an attempt to offer such a defense. Its main idea, as I have remarked at the outset, is that humankind *collectively* has had full control over the ongoing unjust global order, under which the global poor suffer, and accordingly is morally responsible for its injustice and their suffering, and that the relatively affluent individuals, simply by being members of humankind and also beneficiaries of the ongoing global order, share the moral responsibility and bear a large share of the duty to eradicate world poverty — even though they do not harm the global poor unduly. In my view, the relatively affluent have compelling reason to reform the global institutional order and to protect the global poor from its effects, because they are members of a collective entity which has had full control over the current global economic order and they *benefit* from this order, but not, as Pogge has it, from the fact that, by upholding this order, they are harming the global poor unduly.

III.

To raise doubts about Pogge's key claim, (3), let us now clarify what Pogge means by "harming others unduly through one's own conduct." According to Pogge, both "harm" and "unduly" are moralized notions (Pogge 2002a: 130). That is to say, the negative duty not to harm others unduly through one's own conduct cannot be properly understood without appealing to some moral concepts. We must take "harm" to involve "setback of one's *legitimate* interests," otherwise "harming others" will not be an issue worth paying attention to (cf. Feinberg 1984). Also we need to have a baseline for determining whether or not, and if so, *to what extent*, a person's legitimate interests are set back in the relevant context, so that we have some idea about whether a person is harmed to an excessive or unnecessary extent, namely, *unduly*, by someone else. Moreover, "harming a person" must mean something like "causing harms to the person in a way that is *morally problematic*." While what makes a certain way of causing harm to a person morally problematic may be context-dependent again, there is a general point about "morally problematic" that should be registered, though not emphasized by Pogge, namely, that to harm a person unduly through our conduct it is a necessary condition that we can be held responsible for his legitimate interests being set back by our conduct. It seems to me that if I am not responsible for someone's legitimate interests being set back by my conduct, as in a situation in which I am coerced with deadly threat to cause harm to another person, I cannot be said to have harmed the person. In any case, the negative duty Pogge insists must be understood not as forbidding us to harm others in any way in any circumstances, but as demanding that we may not set back others' legitimate interests in ways that are morally problematic. With such clarification of "harming someone unduly through one's conduct" in mind, let us turn to the way Pogge defends (3). Pogge tries to defend (3) by arguing that:

(4) The ongoing global economic order, which the relatively affluent support and participate in, is unfair or unjust to the global poor.

To strengthen his case for (4), Pogge often reminds us of the fact that the ongoing global economic order is something that the developed states coercively impose on the global poor. It is not something the global poor would consent to if they could choose otherwise. In addition, Pogge goes on to discredit the speculation that the global poor under the present economic order might be better off than they were in the state of nature, which some philosophers take to be the baseline for making morally relevant comparison and claim that their situation was not worsened by our imposition of the ongoing order. Some might still want to dispute with Pogge about (4). But I do not. I think he is right about the unfairness or injustice of the ongoing global economic order.[6]

But does (4) alone support (3)? I think not and let me explain why not.

Given our understanding of "harming others unduly," for (3) to hold, Pogge has to show, in addition to (4), that another condition holds, which is:

---

[6] It should be noted that for Pogge (2), i.e., the avoidability of severe poverty, plays a major role in supporting (4) — see Pogge 2002a, chapter 4 and sections 8.2.1 and 8.2.2.

(5) By supporting and participating in the ongoing global (or any serious unjust institutional) order, the relatively affluent *harm* the global poor.

This is for the obvious reason. Without harming someone, I cannot harm him in a way that is morally problematic. But does (5) hold? (5) allows at least two readings:

(6) By supporting and participating in the ongoing global order, the relatively affluent, *collectively*, harm the global poor.

(7) By supporting and participating in the ongoing global order, the relatively affluent, *individually*, harm the global poor.

In what follows, I shall show that (5), under either reading, together with (4), do not support (3).

Let us begin with (6). The morality of negative duty forbids us to harm others in ways that are morally problematic. But this prohibition, as a guide for action, makes sense only when it applies to entities with agency: entities that are capable of acting for reasons. They must be able to take it to be a decisive reason against their conduct (action or omission) that it will cause harm to others in ways that are morally problematic. At least, they must be able to take it to be a reason against their conduct that it will cause harms to others. Understood *collectively*, the relatively affluent, strictly speaking, do not constitute a community. They include those relatively affluent citizens in the developing states as well as most citizens in the developed states. They do not share aims, have no common projects, do not speak the same language, and much else. Accordingly, it seems to make no sense to view the relatively affluent as having agency. That is, since the relatively affluent do not constitute a collectivity with agency, it is not true that the relatively affluent harm the global poor unduly by supporting and participating in the ongoing global order.

Admittedly, whereas entities without agency cannot harm people unduly, they may still cause harms to people. The relatively affluent are a group, of which it is true that if all of its members had acted differently (had, say, withdrawn their support or refrained from participation), the global poor would not have been harmed by the global order. But even if it is true that the relatively affluent constitute such a group, it does not follow that everyone in the group harms the global poor. For the relatively affluent group might not be the smallest group, of which it is true that if they had all acted differently, the global poor would not have been harmed by the global order (Parfit 1984: 71). This means that even when some of the relatively affluent are not involved in the harming of the global, the counterfactual claim about the group of the relatively affluent as a whole might still be true. Thus, from the truth of the counterfactual claim about how the global poor would have fared, one cannot infer that the relatively affluent, as a group of individuals rather than as an agent, harm the global poor. To assess whether the relatively affluent, as a group of individuals rather than as an agent, harm the global poor, we have to turn to (7).

To assess whether (7) holds, it may help to clarify one more time what it is for someone to harm another. To harm someone, we have to be causally involved in some way. But it does not follow that we harm someone whenever we are causally involved in the event of his being harmed. What else is needed? Many conditions may be suggested, but I believe we could not avoid the following condition: that our conduct in fact *contributes to* the setback of the person's legitimate interests. Let us call it *the contribution condition*. To be sure, to clarify this condition, we need to give a plausible interpretation of "contribute to" which is not expected to be entirely morally neutral. As a first approximation, it might be suggested that my action does *not* contribute to the setback of a person's legitimate interests if, even without my action, the person's legitimate interests would have been set back to the same degree anyway and this not for the reason that someone else would take my position in the causal chain. This means that what I actually did, considered alone, has no marginal detrimental effect on his legitimate interests. The paradigmatic case in which one's conduct does not contribute to a certain outcome is that of a popular election with a large number of voters. In such a case, as is well understood, one's voting or not voting for a particular candidate makes no difference to whether she is elected or not. Similarly, whether or not one supports or participates in the ongoing global economic order makes no difference to whether it is unfair to the global poor: so long as enough other people support and participate in the global order and make it unfair to the global poor, your support and participation may make no difference to its unfairness. Similarly, one's support and participation may make no difference to the overall situation the global poor are facing. That is to say, what any of the relatively affluent individuals does in their everyday economic decisions and political decisions does not contribute to the setback of the global poor's legitimate interests — despite the fact that the global poor fare badly under the ongoing order supported and perpetuated by the relatively affluent individuals. That is to say, relatively affluent individuals, individually speaking, do not contribute to the setback of the global poor. Thus, none of the relatively affluent individuals harms the global poor simply by supporting and participating in the ongoing global economic order, even though this global order is unfair and the global poor fare badly in it.

It sounds paradoxical to many people that by supporting and participating in the present unjust global order, the relatively affluent individuals are causally involved in the setback of the global poor's legitimate interests, but (almost) none of them contributes to the setback of the global poor's legitimate interests. Some objections might be raised to this paradoxical claim.

A first objection attempts a counterexample. Suppose we get a few people to cause harm to someone through a set of buttons so wired that the victim will experience the same severe pain whenever one or more buttons are pushed. The contribution condition implies that, if several people are pushing their respective buttons, then none of them contributes to the victim's severe pain and none of them therefore harms the victim.

This objection is based on a misunderstanding of the contribution condition. Getting people together to do such a thing is itself an action, which, in this case, is obviously contributing to the severe pain experienced by the victim. If the collaboration is set up by a single person, then this person, at least, is harming the victim. Furthermore, those who participate in this scheme knowingly, if there are such people, should be viewed as a collective entity with agency: in this case they, collectively speaking, clearly do act for reasons. By contrast, it is unlikely that any particular affluent individual, or any group of such individuals, is deliberatively imposing the ongoing economic order to set back the legitimate interests of the global poor. Typically, each of them is pursuing his or her own projects without knowing how their own decisions and actions affect the well-being of particular individuals living far away.

A second objection maintains that, according to the contribution condition, one's burning a small piece of wood does not contribute to the pollution of the air because it makes no difference to the quality of the air. This seems implausible because, when millions of people burn wood at the same time, the air does get polluted, which shows that each person burning wood is contributing to the pollution.

In reply, we have to admit that the air is polluted, which is an empirical fact, hardly deniable. It must also be admitted that those who burn pieces of wood are causally involved. But we need not admit that an individual burning a small piece of wood does not contribute to the pollution of the air. Such an individual clearly contributions to polluting *some* air. Hence, it is not accurate to say that according to the contribution condition, none of these people pollute the air.

Now one might say that it is true of the relatively affluent, as well, that each of them contributes to the harm suffered by *some* global poor. But this claim is not as straightforward as the claim that every person who burns a piece of wood pollutes *some* air. It would be very controversial to say of a person's everyday decisions which harm no one close to him that they harm some particular persons far away. (Which particular person was I harming when I drank a cup of tea in my study room?) And if we have the global poor as a whole in mind, some might argue, it is not true that each relatively affluent individual contributes to the setback of their legitimate interests.

Against these defenses of the contribution condition, an opponent might correctly point out that for each relatively affluent individual there is some smallest group of which he is a member and of which it is true that, if all of its members had acted differently, the global poor would not have been harmed (or would have been harmed less). The opponent would then conclude that the relatively affluent, individually, harm the global poor, as (7) holds. This opponent deems it a mistake to take marginal contribution to harm as the only relevant factor for determining whether one is harming or not. According to her, one can be said to harm a person even if one's marginal contribution to the harm this persons suffers is zero.

This is a powerful objection to the contribution condition. In reply, a further distinction might be suggested between harming and acting wrongly. To determine whether one acts wrongly, one might argue, it would indeed be a mistake to take marginal contribution to the harming of others as the only relevant factor. But to determine whether one harms (or benefits) someone else, it is not a mistake to take marginal contribution to the harming of the person as the only relevant factor (Parfit 1984: 67–73). Thus, even though (7) is false, the relatively affluent nonetheless act wrongly by supporting and participating in the ongoing global order.

Whether or not this distinction between harming and acting wrongly is found acceptable, it is difficult for many people to accept the possibility that none of the relatively affluent individuals harms the global poor by supporting and participating in a global order that does harm the global poor. If this is counterintuitive, then it seems we should reject the contribution condition as well as, more broadly, any notion of harming that is based solely on an action's marginal contribution to the setback of someone's legitimate interests.

In my view, however, both the defenders of the contribution condition and their opponents are mistaken about "harming." To see this point, we need to replace the distinction between harming and acting wrongly with a more complex set of three cross-cutting distinctions. It will be easier to formulate these distinctions in terms of some *Agent* (any one relatively affluent person), his *Peers* (other affluent persons), and the *Victims* (the global poor to whom the agent and his peers are causing harm).

First, let me distinguish two senses of causing harm:

(a) Agent's action viewed in isolation has the effect of setting back a Victims' legitimate interests;

(b) Agent's action, but only when considered together with the actions of his Peers, sets back Victims' legitimate interests;

Next, we need to distinguish two senses of "causing harm to a person intentionally":

(c) Agent regards the fact that his action causes harm to Victims as a reason in favor of his action;

(d) Agent regards the fact that his action causes harm to Victims not as a reason in favor of his action, but he does regard this fact as not a decisive reason against his action.[7]

Given these two distinctions, we should agree that while it is not true that each of the relatively affluent individuals causes harms intentionally to the global poor in the senses of (bc), it is undeniably true that each of them causes harm to the global poor intentionally in the senses of (bd). In addition, we have to agree that *if* (b) should be counted as a species of harming, then (7) is vindicated. But this is a big *if* and, in my view, it is a mistake. I believe that, to judge whether one person harms another, we need yet a third distinction:

(e) Agent is morally responsible for the conduct of his Peers;

(f) Agent is not morally responsible for the conduct of his Peers.

I grant that each of the relatively affluent is intentionally causing harm to the global poor, in the sense of (bd), by participating in the ongoing global order. But it does not follow that each of them is therefore causing harm to the global poor in a morally problematic way. Although each relatively affluent person, by participating, causes harm in the sense of (b) and even *intentionally* causes them harm in the sense of (bd), he may nonetheless not be morally responsible for the global poor's legitimate interests being set back by the effects of his and other people's participation considered together. This is so because, with respect to a bad situation such as world poverty, a relatively affluent individual normally cannot be held responsible in the sense of (e) for what other relatively affluent individuals choose to do, because he could not, by persuasion or prevention, stop the others from participating. I am suggesting then that ordinary affluent people — because they intentionally cause harm to the global poor only in the sense of (bdf) and not in the sense of (bde) — should not be judged to be harming the global poor.

This suggestion does not defend all affluent people. It does not defend those who cause harm to the global poor in the senses of (ad). Clinton, for example, could single-handedly have shaped the emerging WTO treaties quite differently from how they were in fact shaped; and the same is true of Europe's top three politicians (the French President, the British Prime Minister, and the German Chancellor). Thus, it is reasonable to say of them that they are harming the global poor. But when we turn our attention to

---

[7] I borrow this distinction from Scanlon 2000.

ordinary citizens in the developed states, it is difficult to believe that they are causing harm to the global poor in the sense of (ad). Rather, as we have seen, each of them is intentionally causing harm to the global poor only in the sense of (bd). Even this suffices for a verdict of harming when persons are morally responsible for the participation of others (e). But most ordinary affluent people are not morally responsible for the participation of others. And, insofar as each of these ordinary affluent individuals, by participating in the ongoing global order, merely causes harms to the global poor intentionally without being morally responsible for the participation of others (bdf), it does not seem fair to judge him as harming the global poor in a way that is morally problematic.

In sum, my view is that when your action makes no marginal contribution to the setback of another's legitimate interests but does cause harm to that other when considered together with the actions of your peers, you should be judged to harm these victims only if you are also morally responsible for how your peers choose to act. You harm another if you either cause her harm single-handedly (a) *or* if your action, considered with those of others, causes her harm that you regard as a reason for your conduct (bc), *or* if your action, considered with others' actions that you are morally responsible for, causes her harm that you regard as not a decisive reason against your action (bde). If you are like most citizens of the affluent countries today, then none of these three disjuncts will be true of you. Rather, you are most likely causing harm to the global poor in the sense of (bdf): Your actions, together with your peers' actions for which you are not morally responsible, cause the global poor harm that you regard as not a decisive reason against your conduct but also not as a reason in its favor. Most affluent people do not, by participating in the ongoing unjust global order, harm the main victims of this order, the global poor. This is so because each of these ordinary affluent people does not have any detrimental impact on the global poor through his own conduct, does not regard the harm suffered by the global poor as a reason for acting as he does, and does not bear moral responsibility for the conduct of his peers.[8] This supports my rejection of (7).

---

[8] In contrast, it should be added that when the number of individuals gets smaller, it becomes more plausible to hold each individual morally responsible for what her peers choose to do if they know that what they do, considered together, will cause harm to an innocent person. That is to say, it becomes more plausible to say that each of them is harming the innocent person even when no individual's actions make a marginal contribution to the suffering of the innocent person.

IV.

Now, to defend Pogge's (3), some might grant that (7) does not help, but insist that (8) together with (4) are sufficient:

(8) By supporting and participating in the ongoing global order, *but without giving help to the global poor*, the relatively affluent individuals have harmed them.

Under certain circumstances, one may be able to help some particular poor person. If so, then, of course, whether or not one offers his help will make a difference to that poor person's legitimate interests. That is to say, if I do not offer my help, then my conduct (omission) may contribute to the setback of his legitimate interests. For example, when it was one of my alternatives to prevent the setback from happening to a particular person, but I did not prevent it, then my omission clearly contributed to the setback of that person's legitimate interests. Suppose my omission is harming him in that sense. The next question we should ask is: Do I harm the person in a way that is morally problematic? In this context, the relevant criterion is, in addition to the fairness or unfairness of the ongoing global order that is imposed on him, whether I have good grounds to justify my not taking it to be a decisive reason to offer my help that it will benefit that poor person. But then, we should notice, this is a question about whether *by not giving my help to that poor person*, I am harming him in a way that is morally problematic, which has to do with the duty of mutual aid, but not about whether *by supporting and participating in the ongoing global order* I am harming any of the global poor *unduly*, which means something more than failing to discharge my duty of mutual aid to the global poor. My concern in this paper is not about (8) but about (5), which is what I take Pogge's strategy for defending (3).

At this point, however, we should be informed that Pogge sometimes talks about (9) instead of (3):

(9) By supporting and participating in the ongoing global order, *but without compensating the global poor*, the relatively affluent individuals *harm* them *unduly* (Pogge 2002a: 135f).

But we may accept (9) without accepting (3), because even if (3) does not hold, we may still accept (9) as a consequence of accepting the claim that the relatively affluent individuals, by supporting and participating in an unjust global economic order, are morally responsible for the plight of the global poor, and thus owe them something based on the duty of compensation. The duty of compensation creates legitimate interests and, if it is not discharged, the global poor are harmed, and they are harmed unduly if without good grounds, the relatively affluent individuals do not take it to be a decisive reason for improving the situation of the global poor that this is what they owe them. To be sure, this justification for accepting (9) depends on the thesis I have not explicitly argued for, namely, that the relatively affluent individuals are responsible for the plight of the global poor. That task is what I must turn to now.

V.

The relatively affluent individuals, taken as a whole, do not have agency, but many would contend that their states can sensibly be viewed as having agency. If so, then we have to agree that the developed states harm the global poor unduly, because they are powerful and they do coercively impose the ongoing global order on the global poor, while foreseeing that this order is to the disadvantage of the global poor. But, again, for similar reasons, their citizens, individually, are not harming the global poor by supporting their states (though, I am sure, many citizens would deny that they support their states.) As I have emphasized repeatedly, this does not mean that such citizens bear no responsibility. Once the role of the states is recognized, some might argue that since the developed states are their states (with or without their support), the citizens are responsible for the harms they cause, simply by being citizens. This is one way of attributing responsibility to the relatively affluent individuals, but it can only explain why those relatively affluent individuals *living in the developed states* bear responsibility for the plight of the global poor. It may leave out those affluent individuals who are citizens of weak, developing states. To explain that they too share responsibility for the plight of the global poor, we have to appeal to the idea that in the end, humankind (humanity), personified, is responsible for the injustice of the global order, hence for the plight of the global poor. After all, the ongoing global order is what we bring to the world: it is our "product" and we are liable for the damage (the suffering of the global poor) it causes. If personifying humankind makes sense, then humanity as a whole is responsible for the plight of the global poor. The relatively affluent individuals who belong to developing states get their share of responsibility simply for being a member of humankind.

But does it make sense to personify humankind? Following Ronald Dworkin, I think personifying humankind makes sense and is the most general case of attributing group responsibility. Here is the example he gives for attributing group responsibility by means of personification:

> Suppose an automobile manufacturer produces defective cars that cause terrible accidents in which hundreds of people are killed. Set aside the question of law, whether the corporation is guilty of a crime or legally

responsible to compensate victims or their families. And the question of efficiency, whether imposing such liability would reduce accidents or contribute to a more efficient use of resources. We are interested now in the question of moral responsibility. [Suppose no one acted in a way we can judge wrong by personal standards of conduct.] What sense does it make to say that the corporation is morally responsible to compensate victims from the corporate treasury, with the consequence that its shareholders must bear the loss? (Dworkin 1986: 169)

Dworkin suggests that "the corporation must itself be treated as a moral agent," for "anyone who has had full control over the manufacturer of a defective product has a responsibility to compensate those injured by it," and in this case, "[n]o individual employee or shareholder has had that control, but the corporation has." (Dworkin 1986: 170) Similarly, we may say that no individual state, no individual state official has had control over the present global order. In short, we may claim that we, humankind as a whole, is responsible for world poverty. It is not simply because people could have done something in the past to prevent world poverty from happening and they did not do it. Indeed, even if it is true that if people in the past had all acted differently, world poverty would not have persisted, it does not follow that they knew what they each should have done in the past in order to prevent world poverty. But it cannot be denied that world poverty is an outcome that is engendered by the ongoing global order actually imposed and perpetuated by people, past and present, for which we, humankind as a whole, are responsible. So we may follow Dworkin's strategy by saying that humankind, personified as a moral agent, has had control over the present global order, hence bears responsibility for its injustice, and accordingly bears responsibility for the *disadvantages* the global poor have suffered under such an unjust order. Then the duty to reform the global order and to reduce world poverty ought to be distributed proportionally to every member of humankind, depending on how much he or she benefits from the ongoing global order and how much he or she has shaped this order. Some people share more of the duty to help reform the ongoing global order, to eradicate world poverty, simply because they have benefited more than others from the ongoing global order and/or because they have more influence on the shaping of the ongoing global order.

Chapter 9

The Principle of Subsidiarity

Stefan Gosepath
Philosophy, Freie Universität Berlin and Universität Potsdam

The question of subsidiarity

In social and political philosophy the principle of subsidiarity is a principle which states that in the relationship among communities, but also in the relation of the individual to any form of human community, the smaller social or political entity or institution ought to be given priority (e.g., the individual should come before the community, the community before the state, the state before the federation, and so on). In this context, it is an important, if not the most important, responsibility of the bigger institution to enable the smaller one to perform its tasks and to provide it with any necessary support (*subsidium*) (Herzog 1998).

After this fairly straightforward definition one may wonder why there would be any need for further philosophical clarification of the principle of subsidiarity. Let me start to answer the question of the principle of subsidiarity by giving a brief overview of the history of the term and the resulting unclear points.

Conceptually, there are numerous statements and insights dating back many centuries that are now considered to be expressions of the principle of subsidiarity although the technical term "subsidiarity" would not have been used in those days (Lecheler 1993: 29–43; Pieper 1994: 27–60; Herzog 1998). Etymologically speaking, the Latin term *subsidium* originated in the realm of the military and was used to refer to the third line of Roman soldiers, the Triarii, who would only join in a battle if the powers of the two front lines were insufficient. Once the military connotations had started to fade into the background, *subsidium* began to take on the more general meaning of "helpful support" or "used as an aid," i.e., it became a term

A. Follesdal and T. Pogge, (eds.), Real World Justice, 157-170.

describing the kind of support that, under ideal conditions, one would not need (Höffe 1997: 271ff).

Thus, even though the concept of subsidiarity goes back very far (Utz 1953; Blickle et al. 2002), the term and its current usage are quite recent. The term itself was only introduced in its classic form by Pope Pius XI in the encyclical *Quadragesimo Anno* in 1931, which was influenced significantly by the thinking of the Catholic social philosophers Gustav Gundlach and Oswald von Nell-Breuning (1962). In the encyclical, a danger of overburdening the state is diagnosed, and in the crucial paragraph 79, the principle of subsidiarity is offered as the solution to this problem. Going even further, the encyclical interprets the principle of subsidiarity as the single most important principle of social philosophy (*"in philosophia sociali gravissimum principium"*). To this day it is occasionally called on in social philosophy or social politics (mainly by Christian Conservative parties) as a "social principle," even though is has never been formally recognized as a universal principle of law. It is neither the constitutional basis of any country, nor can it sufficiently explain current social policies or the structure of social associations.

Beyond Catholic social teaching, the principle of subsidiarity is also recognized in other areas, although the object of the principle varies from context to context, which effectively blurs its meaning. Here are some examples.

In Roman law subsidiary laws are those universal norms that, although per se applicable, have to stand back in favor of other more specific legal norms. An example: the general freedom of action is subsidiary to the more specific freedoms, i.e., once a specific freedom (such as the freedom of opinion or the freedom to choose one's job) is concerned, the general freedom of action — although it is still applicable — does not enter into the equation any longer, despite the fact that both norms obviously have the same status (here: constitutional status). Similar relations of subsidiarity can be found at various levels of the law. This is based on a general principle of interpretation in Roman law, which states that the more specific norm should always take precedence.

Furthermore, there is another prominent legal concept of subsidiarity of a rather different kind, which is concerned with organizing responsibilities. In 1992, the idea of subsidiarity was adopted as an important structural principle for the construction of the European Political Union. It was introduced into a central passage in the Maastricht "Treaty on European

Union,"[1] which has even given it the status of public and constitutional law. The EU's responsibilities only comprise cases where member states cannot reasonably be expected to deal with an issue themselves in any meaningful way. Particularly this mention of the principle of subsidiarity in the Maastricht Treaty has subsequently caused a new and ongoing controversy about its interpretation, its boundaries and legal applications (e.g., Lecheler 1993, Pieper 1994). Since the principle has found its way into secular state and constitutional theory in accordance with its sociopolitical importance, it has also been recognized in modern theories of society such as systems theory (Glagow 1984) or communitarianism.

The principle of subsidiarity plays a rather new role in the debate about globalization. It is in the legal philosophical and state theoretical discussion of how globalization can be construed in a just way, internationally or transnationally, that the principle of subsidiarity is now being invoked fairly frequently (cf. Pogge 2002a). Subsidiarity is often thought to guarantee a plurality and hierarchy of state and sub-state institutions or entities against an overly powerful supra-national political union. This seems necessary for the following reason: according to a strictly normative, individualistic and universalistic concept of global justice, all individuals — in order to create justice, and out of a rational and moral interest — enter into a social order that is supposed to guarantee peace, freedom, security and justice for everyone by way of state sanctioned positive law. From such a concept of a social contract, which is built solely upon the universal and fundamental interests of all individuals, it is easy to move on to a position of moral cosmopolitanism that cannot recognize differences among different national or regional characteristics, between citizens and foreigners or among states, but which only knows persons. Once moral universalism is at last taken seriously in politics it will turn into cosmopolitanism. Since the fundamental interests of all people are identical everywhere, they are all equally in need of a rule of law. This establishes the consequent step towards a contract-theoretical foundation for the world state.

However, the idea of a single centralized world state is generally deemed problematic. Particularists, such as realists, communitarians, nationalists or patriots on the one hand, find this scenario unbearable. They consider such a theory as too far removed from reality and normatively inappropriate. Some universalists, on the other hand, have also voiced objections. For one thing, they fear, just like Kant did, the danger of a single global state becoming despotic due to the lack of constraint from other states that might offer

---

[1] The crucial reference here is the European Union Treaty, article 3b, newly introduced into the Maastricht Treaty. (Because of numbering changes resulting from the Amsterdam Treaty, this is now article 5 EUT.)

opportunities for emigration. Furthermore, even universalists and cosmopolitans seem to consider the concentration of sovereign power in just one world state not only dangerous but also beyond legitimacy with regards to the moral subjects of this global order, the citizens.

Proponents of the project "Global Justice," which has been moved forward especially by Thomas Pogge, have therefore emphasized the observation that moral cosmopolitanism does not necessarily have to imply institutional cosmopolitanism, i.e., a single global political authority. This is the case because there is a relevant distinction to be made (Pogge 2002a, 7.1.; Beitz 1999: 199) between a moral cosmopolitanism that defines principles of international justice, and an institutional cosmopolitanism which advocates the implementation of these principles through global political institutions. If one takes this distinction into consideration, moral cosmopolitanism is left with the problem of determining which could be, and ought to be, the most appropriate local through global institutions in a system of global justice. If it rejects the idea of a world state due to the danger of despotism, moral cosmopolitanism is left with two alternatives. Either global justice can be achieved through a just international order of the existing nation-states. Or, which seems to be the philosophically more promising approach in terms of achieving global justice, a set of moral principles could be included in the position of moral cosmopolitanism that can normatively, i.e., independently from any factual, existing state order, justify an institutional order. In this sense, institutional cosmopolitanism can essentially be restricted by the principles of subsidiarity and federalism, which are connected to other mechanisms of curtailing state power such as the separation of powers and democracy. For this reason, the principle of subsidiarity plays an important part in current discussions on global justice.

It would be interesting to investigate in more detail this peculiar and rather new evolution of the term and find out its underlying political reasons. My hypothesis is that the rise to the forefront of the principle of subsidiarity can be seen as a reaction to signs of a crisis. From a state theoretical point of view, the creative capacities of political institutions are reaching their limits, which has led to a "de-mystification of the state" (Wilke 1983). At the same time, the Western welfare state is in crisis. The "future of the welfare state" is now uncertain because of endogenous reasons, such as higher expectations and demands, increasing state responsibilities and counterproductive effects of state welfare, as well as because of mainly exogenous reasons like, amongst other things, the "crisis of the labor society," demographic and sociocultural changes, and scarcity of fiscal resources due to the globalized nature of markets for money, goods and services. Therefore, redesigning the welfare state is the dominant theme of social politics today (Heinze 1985). In government in general, and social politics in particular, agents other than state institutions increasingly ought to or have to — more or less voluntarily — fulfill functions that used to be government functions. Furthermore, the development of *global* systems of leadership creates a lot of anxieties around inappropriate concentrations of power. The principle of subsidiarity is thought of as a guarantee for a plurality and hierarchy of state and sub-state institutions or entities against an overly powerful supranational political union.

Subsidiarity (thus) generally has positive connotations and is supported widely. However, in the internationally well-known treatises on justice of our time, subsidiarity is hardly ever dealt with explicitly. It is also surprising to see, that this topic has found very little recognition in current philosophical discussions.[2] Since in social and political theory, as well as in current politics, the exact meaning and justification for this principle is controversial, its content, justification and status remain relatively unclear.

Therefore, there is a clear need for philosophical clarification. This requires us to answer the following questions, whose respective meanings will only fully unfold once the previous steps have been taken. 1. What exactly is it the principle of subsidiarity says? 2. What is the justification for this principle? 3. Does subsidiarity represent a priority rule? 4. Can the principle of subsidiarity solve questions of competency? 5. How does the principle of subsidiarity fit into the context of other principles of justice? By answering these questions, I would like to show first that subsidiarity is an essential and often neglected principle of justice that should be part of any theory of justice; and second that subsidiarity does not deserve as prominent a status as a central principle of the structural organization of states as Catholic social teaching and the Maastricht Treaty would have us believe. The principle of subsidiarity is actually subordinate to more general principles of justice.

1. Reconstructing the principle of subsidiarity

Subsidiarity is a *normative* principle of justice that refers to individuals as well as to institutions. It is because of these normative qualities that it is of interest to practical philosophy.

---

[2] An attempt at such a philosophical categorization and justification was undertaken particularly by Höffe (1996, chapter 10, 1997, and 1999, chapter 5.1–2). An historical overview of justifications for the principle of subsidiarity can be found in Millon-Delsol 1992 and Höffe 1997, a systematical overview in Follesdal 1998.

In its classic formulation, the principle of subsidiarity has a positive and a negative thrust, which correspond to three sub-principles that are interrelated.

SUB₁ The conceptually more fundamental positive version expresses a *Rule of Assistance*. The larger social entity or institution, ultimately the society or the state, ought to support the smaller one whenever the individual or the smaller institution cannot perform their tasks by themselves.

SUB₂ In its negative formulation the principle of subsidiarity prohibits the bigger social entity from interfering with the affairs of a smaller unit of affected individuals or of an individual. (*Ban on Interference*)

SUB₃ Thus, the kind and extent of support that are legitimate are restricted to "*helping others to help themselves.*"

This is the core of subsidiarity. All other aspects will have to follow from it or represent premises for its justification. Subsidiarity *seems* to constitute a priority rule for the political and moral distribution of responsibilities: smaller social institutions or entities take prima facie precedence over the larger ones. This brief definition and interpretation (as an answer to the first question) throws up four further questions concerning the principle of subsidiarity, which I will now discuss one by one.

2. Justifying the principle of subsidiarity for individuals

Any philosophical investigation of these issues has to be looking for a justification of subsidiarity. As a priority rule, subsidiarity gives smaller social entities formal argumentative precedence. It is a priority rule because it alleges that transferring responsibilities to higher level institutions needs to be justified, whereas the lower level institution performing the same tasks would require no such justification. The *onus probandi*, the burden of proof, clearly lies with the bigger institutions. In principle, this is consistent with any hierarchical structure for societies that are governed top-down, as long as reasons can be given for it. At the same time, however, formally awarding precedence to smaller social entities results in their prioritization because of a shift in the burden of proof, which makes it more difficult to justify the transfer of responsibilities to the higher level institution. What reasons can be given for construing the burden of proof this way? Priority rules are commonly justified by reference to their plausibility. In philosophical investigations, however, this is not sufficient. However in the relevant literature one can hardly find any reasons for taking this position. Therefore, I would like to propose my own attempt at giving reasons for the principle of subsidiarity: I believe it can be justified in the following six steps, provided that one presupposes a liberal democratic conception of justice (cf. Gosepath 2004).

(a) Any judgment about questions of justice should analytically be placed into a context of reasons. The individual (as the smallest unit) is the measure for any justification. The entire moral and political order ought to be justified in relation to all affected individuals. This is sometimes called the principle of normative individualism.

(b) The predicates "just" or "unjust" are only applicable when we are talking of voluntary actions, or failures to act, that agents can be held responsible for. The weather, natural disasters, natural untreatable diseases, etc. as such cannot be just or unjust. The appropriate use of the term justice is not based on the fundamental dichotomy of fate on the one hand, and man-made injustice on the other hand, for it is not crucial whether a human being is responsible for an event or not. Persons are responsible for circumstances where human corrections and interventions are possible; they cannot, however, be made responsible for misfortune or fate (Shklar 1990). One condition for the adequate application of the concept of justice is thus the presence of agents who are effectively in a position to alter institutional structures, practices, and actions corresponding to the principles of justice. Justice requires changeability and responsibility. Justice is primarily related to individual actions. Individual persons are the primary bearer of responsibilities (ethical individualism). The individual is responsible only for those things she can change. Because she would be overwhelmed by changing or improving all that is unjust in this world, and because she has to know that benefits and costs are distributed fairly, the individual gets together with others to create a just society, which they safeguard by means of positive law and state power. With the help of such institutions and structures, the individuals can collectively fulfill their responsibilities. Thus, the responsibility for justice lies secondarily with the collective.

(c) Within the frame-work of a "regime of justice" that guarantees universal, liberal and equal rights for all citizens, each individual has the right and the obligation to live his or her life in an autonomous and self-determined manner. Justice secures, amongst other things, the conditions for personal autonomy, political freedom and democratic self-determination.

From this one may conclude further:

(d) The individual has an obligation to help herself. There is no justification for a duty to help another person who could help herself without incurring any great loss. Such far-reaching claims would simply demand too much from others. Autonomy and freedom are both rights and duties at the same time. If the starting point is fair for everyone involved, each agent has to bear the consequences of their own autonomous actions (Rawls 1971, §12; Dworkin 1981). Primarily, it is the responsibility of the individual who has the power to change things to correct unjust arrangements, no matter what caused these circumstances. This is the reason for prohibiting the exploitation of others — albeit with a crucial qualification, which I will discuss further later on: the obligation to help oneself is only applicable within otherwise just arrangements.

(e) It is unjust if one person is worse off than another unless this is the result of his or her own free decision. Whoever is in need through no fault of their own is morally entitled to compensation or help, provided that the person in need cannot help herself. Otherwise, a person could suffer as the result of circumstances that, from a moral point of view, are coincidental, which would ultimately put them at an unjust disadvantage compared to others (Rawls 1971, §12; Dworkin 1981). Any causes that are morally arbitrary, and whose consequences can be influenced, ought to be compensated for by human beings. This is the justification for the rule of assistance.

(f) Since individuals have a fundamental right to freely live their lives with the same freedoms and universal civil rights and in an autonomous and self-determined way, other persons or social groups must not interfere in their affairs, not even with the best of intentions. This would constitute a bad case of paternalism. If an individual does not need any help, one must not "help" her. This justifies the negative version of the principle of subsidiarity, which defends the individual or smaller social units against interference from larger entities or institutions. Any justifiable intervention from external or higher level agents must aim at enabling the object of the intervention to live his or her life autonomously. Help must be defined as "helping others to help themselves."

This explicates the normative properties of the principle of subsidiarity, including its three sub-principles, in relation to individual persons. Helping those in need is a duty. Abusing the willingness of others to help is a breach of duty. Interfering in the affairs of others constitutes a violation of autonomy and freedom. The principle of subsidiarity for individuals follows the maxim: if in doubt, prioritize individual responsibility and freedom. In this context, freedom and responsibility are like two sides of the same coin. It should be clear, however, that all this is very much open to interpretation. Establishing the principle of subsidiarity is not the end point of this debate since what it means in detail (being in need, help, the affairs of others, etc.) is still an open question. Furthermore, what can be easily justified in relation to individuals can be problematic in relation to communities and political institutions or entities.

3. Justifying intermediary institutions

The principle of subsidiarity in its classic form explicates the conditions for its application very clearly: it is only applicable if smaller and larger social institutions and entities relate to each other like parts to a whole. Interpreted in this way, the principle of subsidiarity presupposes a hierarchical order and is concerned mainly with the internal arrangements of competencies in this order. Subsidiarity in its negative formulation as a ban on interference (sub_2) is a rule for distributing responsibilities within a given structure, and it is applicable wherever such a structure is organized in a part-whole relationship. The principle is applicable not only to individuals but also to social associations of various sizes (including states) and global political systems. This poses the question how, in the context of the principle of subsidiarity, one could possibly argue for intermediary institutions? Why should there be any such institutions at all? Two alternative strategies for their justification are feasible: either subsidiarity presupposes a hierarchically structured (political and social) order and regulates its internal distribution of competencies, or subsidiarity also establishes the hierarchical order of social associations, in the dual sense of creating the political order itself and clarifying the reasons for its justification.

(a) In its first, classic version, subsidiarity presupposes a hierarchy within a state or among states as historical fact. If this is the case, then subsidiarity cannot be a reference point for justification strategies, e.g., for rejecting centralized government. As long as we start with empirical facts and a certain "normativity of the factual," only the right to existence and self-preservation of any existing social and political institutions could be such a reference point. Is there any such existential right?

It seems advisable to remain skeptical about any existential right for collectives as they appear to be only of derived significance. Each social entity at state or sub-state level cannot be justified as an end in itself, but has to be able to justify its existence in reference to the welfare of the individual. Thus any such entity has to be grounded in the principle of subsidiarity. However, strict conditions for its justification are not required. We do not need to go back to the philosophical drawing board to reinvent the institutions of civil societies. As long as a community has been created voluntarily and in a just manner, the formation and organization of this union is entirely the business of its citizens.

From the point of view of justice, it is altogether more difficult to assess the merit of societies where one is not a member by choice. Rather than granting these societies an intrinsic value in a Communitarian fashion, one may recognize the justice of such *historically factual* and *particular* societies in a Hegelian manner in this way: any given society offers a pool of lifestyles (e.g., families, culture, etc. as social institutions) that could hardly be brought about *intentionally* by individuals or collectives and that are necessary for one's good life. To the extent to which social institutions are prerequisites to one's good life that one could not create oneself, there may be, on the one hand, obligations to contribute to defending or supporting and developing these institutions, while on the other hand, there may be obligations resulting from the existing institutions themselves. One may also accept these obligations as underlying conditions of one's good life even if one does not need or appreciate them.[3] Recognizing that social institutions are prerequisites of a good life that can hardly be created by individuals or collectives intentionally coerces everyone to also recognize the capabilities of factual, existing institutions. Of course, this does not mean that those institutions could not be changed and thereby improved.[4] Insofar as existing particular institutions are providing morally valuable services and do not violate universal principles of justice, they have a derived value. To that extent, one may as well trust them with subsidiary tasks and responsibilities.

(b) Those who are looking for normative reasons rather than empirical premises should agree more with the second alternative. According to this thinking, the principle of subsidiarity also represents a principle for establishing social associations. Its grounding in principle in the tradition of contract theories is as well known as it is correct. In this philosophical, abstract and rational reconstruction, communities are formed exactly because of the neediness of the individual. Thus, in order to establish the rule of law and justice, rational beings get together with others to create societies as artificial entities. These structures, however, comprise different layers, ranging from the community of families to private, civil unions and to public sub-state institutions and, finally, states. However, it is the requirement to have intermediary institutions that is relevant for the principle of subsidiarity and is in need of justification. Intermediary institutions, such as parishes, counties, individual states and federations, ought to be justified in reference to the autonomous individual in order to avoid the necessity of a single world state. I will present two arguments for this position.

---

[3] For example, I would be bound by convention to greet others even if I knew that it would be possible, or perhaps even better, if I did not greet them. Or I might be obliged to respect the products of one's culture even if I do not like them. Thus it may be morally and legally forbidden to destroy a painting by Rembrandt (or Roy Lichtenstein for that matter), even if I own it and come to believe that it would be better if it did not exist any longer.

[4] They can be changed, but this process cannot simply be initiated through better political and moral insight. Social and political processes are infinitely more complex. One may demand or even set off a revolution, for example, but one cannot make certain of its success.

The argument from the sovereignty of the people: the only morally legitimate rules and regulations are those that have been agreed on by all affected parties under conditions of autonomy, freedom and equality. These rules are justified because those affected by them have — nota bene in principle — decided so themselves. This procedural justification continues through in political reality, beyond any hypothesized consensus under ideal conditions, as the sovereignty of the people. This way, it legitimizes authority while at the same time securing the maximum possible amount of autonomy and equal political influence for all affected parties.[5] It is important to note that in the context of subsidiarity, the target group of a collective rule is identical with the authors of this rule: in both cases we are dealing with those (and only those) who will be affected by the matter that is being regulated. In effect, the argument from the sovereignty of the people fulfills the function of the second, negative formulation of the principle of subsidiarity (sub_2). Only affected members of a collective are allowed to make decisions regarding their own affairs. Others are not. This argument from the sovereignty of the people outlines who, according to which procedure and under which circumstances, may decide on the distribution of tasks. Thus, this argument bestows on the principle of subsidiarity the status of a procedural guarantee. However, this does not specify how an autonomous collective ought to be organized. Furthermore, the group of relevant people may vary depending on the subject matter to be regulated.

This argument is supplemented by a further *functional argument*: the generative principle of subsidiarity creates larger political entities in order to safeguard the smaller ones against overtaxing, and intermediary entities to safeguard the larger ones against excessive demands, a proliferation of red tape, losing touch with its citizens, as well as all kinds of ineffectiveness. This calls for the type of association that is best equipped to perform the tasks at hand in the most just, democratic and effective way. The respective objectives are set normatively by the interests of the affected individuals. This is echoed in social politics by the fact that modern societies only partly link the idea of subsidiarity to the solidarity of natural communities. The necessary and helpful types of association are justified rationally as means to an end and vary from task to task. The respective type of institution that is most appropriate to the task at hand is then, within a legal context, determined pragmatically or functionally.[6]

---

[5] In this context, the type of democracy that exercises this authority and its justification do not need to be specified.

[6] Possibly, this approach could also be used to justify social communities, such as families, as the most appropriate place, especially for children, for developing one's moral character (Aristotle 1996, I 2, 1252a2ff; Hegel 1821, part III).

Functional arguments on principle do not describe which of the smaller entities should be granted political authority. Thus, no decision will yet have been made on whether a political institution is well suited to taking on several responsibilities (as is commonly supposed to be the case with nation-states), nor is it clear whether the task-specific hierarchy of political institutions should follow territorial or purely functional boundaries. Which organizational models should be institutionalized is up to the members of society to decide in a free, democratic process, as long as the elected institutions fulfill their roles satisfactorily and justly. If the idea of subsidiarity is to become an effective principle for political and social order, it must be redeveloped in the context of a society organized according to functional criteria.

4. Prioritizing smaller institutions?

Both arguments, the functional one and the argument from the sovereignty of the people, if justified, threaten the status of subsidiarity as a priority rule. Whenever a hierarchical structure is presupposed, the criteria for assessing and distributing competencies and responsibilities are a matter of adequacy for effecting a stable, long-term, self-supporting, good and just fulfillment of given concrete tasks. Those criteria are *not* grounded in the idea of subsidiarity but they are, rather, functional criteria for measuring the need for and effectiveness of a given institution to perform its respective concrete task(s). In this context, subsidiarity is more of a heuristic method rather than a criterion (Homann and Kirchner 1995). After all, many bad experiences have been made with tendencies to centralize. At the same time, the size of any subsidiary institution is limited, not by the precedence given to intermediary units, but by the circle of affected individuals who are also simultaneously addressees and authors of the relevant positive law.

These insights have to correct our understanding of subsidiarity. It can no longer say "if in doubt prioritize the smaller institution or entity" but it has to give precedence "always to the institution that best serves the affected individuals" (cf. Pogge 2002a, chapter 7). I do not consider a general assumption that the smaller institution was always the more functional to be justifiable. Should we not interpret historical experiences as suggesting that larger entities are often *better* at securing the social conditions that can guarantee justice and prevent tyranny and the oppression of minorities? The basic rule to only create, support and functionally and democratically organize those political entities that best serve the affected individuals is a fundamental principle of the democratic self-organization of citizens. It is not a priority rule.

5. Attributing competencies

After making these necessary adjustments to the common understanding of subsidiarity, it should become very quickly clear that the principle of subsidiarity alone cannot solve all problems around the distribution of competencies, i.e., outlining clearly which distributions and applications of competencies are permitted within a certain political order (such as the European Union), which ones would be imperative, and which ones would be prohibited. The *right* to apply one's competencies in practice is assigned by the principle of the sovereignty of the people. The *distribution* of competencies must be done according to functional criteria. This insight is particularly relevant in the area of social justice to which I now briefly turn.

6. Subsidiarity and social justice

Following on from its origins in Catholic social teaching, the principle of subsidiarity has always been applied most frequently to issues of social justice. In this context, it does not regulate the distribution of competencies but the duty to support others financially, and thus it can refer to the positive formulation of the principle of subsidiarity (sub$_1$). In debates about social politics this principle is often used in a way that gives subsidiarity a conservative, market-liberal flavor since the burden of rectifying undeserved economic disadvantages is transferred onto smaller political institutions.[7]

If there are good reasons to stipulate a rule of assistance, the question that follows is which community of individuals is morally obliged to provide assistance and compensation. A priority rule that states that the smaller collective entity is the primary bearer of responsibilities for social and economic assistance seems particularly implausible. In this context, "natural" communities, such as immediate and extended families, and local political institutions, such as municipal authorities, are often called upon. But why should only the small institutions be in charge of looking after family members of members of the community who fell ill, became unemployed, or are generally in need of assistance? This seems implausible not only in cases where the members of those smaller political or social entities are not capable of providing such assistance, but also in cases where

---

[7] However, in the above justification for the principle of subsidiarity, provisions were only made so that individuals have to bear the consequences of their own decisions — provided that conditions and opportunities are otherwise fair for everyone. Undeserved disadvantages for individuals and their effects, on the other hand, have to be compensated for by the community. This is Rawls's (1971) famous argument of equal opportunities through compensating morally arbitrary disadvantages due to social and natural causes.

providing assistance would constitute excessive hardship for the entity in question. A middle-class family, for instance, might be able to provide care over twenty or more years to a close relative who was paralyzed by a stroke at a relatively young age, but in European welfare states, like Germany, for example, society has slowly come to realize that this kind of assistance and support — even if it could be undertaken by the family alone — should at least be supplemented, if not provided to a large extent, by the whole of a mutually supportive society. The underlying reason — this is my claim — is not just the possibility that the family might be overwhelmed by this task (in which case, according to the principle of subsidiarity, a bigger more able institution would have to take over) but also an aspect of distributive justice. Within a just society, we must not only distribute fairly any natural benefits (such as natural resources, land, etc.), but also at least certain natural disadvantages (such as the effects of illness and so on). The above intuitive example is supposed to show that, in the realm of social justice and politics, whenever principles of distributive justice apply, the prioritization of smaller institutions or of sub-state before state support cannot be justified. Since the principle of subsidiarity can only be justified in relation to individuals, and the size and hierarchical order of social institutions is justified according to democratic and functional reasons but not through a genuine priority of smaller institutions, the social idea of subsidiarity has to be seen as subordinate to general principles of distributive justice.

7. Conclusion

This investigation of the principle of subsidiarity has shown, first of all, that subsidiarity is an essential and often neglected principle of justice that ought to be part of any theory of justice. For subsidiarity, if we understand it as a principle for limiting the exercise of authority and power, can be justified by reasons that relate to theories about the justice of individual and collective autonomy, as well as on functionalist grounds. In my opinion, these capture the true essence of the three principles of subsidiarity. Secondly, however, it has become clear that subsidiarity does not deserve the high status as a central principle of the organization of states which it was given, for instance, in Catholic social teaching and the Maastricht Treaty, because we found no reasons in favor of arguing for a distribution of the burden of proof in relation to the principle of subsidiarity, only reasons against such arguments. The principle of subsidiarity is secondary to general principles of justice. This concludes my analysis of the principle of subsidiarity. More concrete interpretations and applications of the concept of subsidiarity cannot be found by theoretical, philosophical analysis alone.

Chapter 10

"It's the Power, Stupid!"
On the Unmentioned Precondition of Social Justice[*]

Alessandro Pinzani
Philosophy, Universidade Federal de Santa Catarina, Florianópolis, Brazil

A major criticism advanced by politicians, politically interested or engaged individuals and political theorists or philosophers is that the economic sphere tends to become more and more independent from the political and to escape every form of democratic control. I would like to question this criticism, not in order to show that politics still has control over the economy, but rather in order to show that this claim is based on a conceptual misunderstanding. My first thesis therefore is that the alleged loss of control of the political sphere over the economic is due precisely to the distinction between them — a distinction which is rooted in a wrong theoretical assumption (points 1 and 2). My second thesis is that we should consider every human interaction as an expression of power relationships (points 3, 4 and 5) and therefore (my third thesis) that the problem of world poverty presents a double issue: we should first eradicate the most immediate consequences of poverty, like poverty-related death and suffering, and we should secondly reduce the power gap between rich and poor, both on an international and on a domestic level (point 6). While many theories offer good moral arguments for the necessity of solving the first issue (which from a practical point of view obviously has priority, since it concerns immediate and present suffering), the latter issue goes far beyond the former, concerning the causes of poverty themselves, and the need for additional moral arguments. Therefore, while eradicating the immediate effects of severe poverty constitutes a priority both for theory (which has to offer arguments showing the moral necessity of corresponding actions) and

---

[*] I would like to thank Andreas Follesdal, Thomas Pogge and Thomas Mertens for their comments. Special thanks to Paul Harvey for his help in giving this paper an acceptable linguistic form.

A. Follesdal and T. Pogge, (eds.), Real World Justice, 171-197.
© 2005 *Springer. Printed in the Netherlands.*

praxis, eradicating the deeper causes of poverty may represent a further goal, whose practical realization may be postponed, but whose theoretical justification should already be an object for a theory of global social justice.[1] I shall not offer such a justification in this article, nor to lay the foundation of it, but only to offer some preliminary reflections on the role of power and on the space that power should receive in a theory of global social justice.

1. Globalization, power and traditional theories

If we consider the major political theories of the modern age, we can see that they offer a picture of society which does not correspond to the reality of present post-industrial society — particularly in times of sprawling economic globalization (Pinzani 2003a). This is not tantamount to criticizing thinkers of past times, since they could not possibly have imagined the growing complexity which characterizes our society. No all-encompassing vision or theory is now able to account fully for this complexity; and with globalization the centers of economic, and often also of political power have become even more opaque and inscrutable. This opacity has also limited citizens' democratic control on the shifts of economic, social and political power. Citizens have fewer opportunities to participate in decisions concerning the political and economic measures necessary to control the phenomena of globalization. Further, the complexity of the problems goes not only beyond the intellectual capabilities of the average citizen, but often seems to be too much for the decisional and organizational abilities of politicians. Moreover, we live in times in which economic, work, social and environmental politics are determined less by single national governments than by the so-called imperatives of the international economy.

Given these circumstances, it is no wonder that among the citizens of our democracies one can ascertain a growing resignation and electoral apathy which can be attributed much less to a missing civic spirit (as some theorists — particularly communitarians like Etzioni or Sandel, and New Republicans like Skinner, Pettit and Viroli — think) than to a consciousness of political impotence. It is not that people have lost interest in political affairs. The contrary is true: they still have a strong political interest and are still worried about the common good and their communities. This is shown by the fact

---

[1]   I share Rainer Forst's opinion that "a focus on only distributive justice may be insufficient and may even harbor the danger of leaving the unjust system basically intact by turning the hitherto dominated into mere claimants and recipients of goods" (Forst 2001: 176). In other words, they risk this danger when they only insist on the (re)distribution of goods without touching questions of (re)distribution of power. For the distinction between the two perspectives see below.

that more and more individuals get involved in political movements and groups which consider themselves to be alternative forms of political participation: NGOs, but also the so-called "movement of movements" which resulted from the protests in Seattle (November 1999) and elsewhere, and from the four editions of the World Social Forum in Porto Alegre (2001, 2002 and 2003) and in Mumbai (2004). These movements articulate a need for political participation, which cannot be satisfied through the traditional institutional instruments like, for instance, the election of representatives. Though the citizens involved in these initiatives are still a minority, they are testimony to the fact that there are many individuals whose answer to the growing impotence of traditional politics is to look to alternative options for political action. This involvement takes the shape of a peculiar international movement, of a constellation of locally active groups, which form a supranational, highly changeable network that cannot be controlled from a center (on this topic see Arrighi et al. 1989, Keck and Sikkink 1998b, O'Brian et al. 2000, and Follesdal et al. 2003). This is a plurality of movements which confront a common complex of problems but have different goals and use different strategies of action. They conceive of political participation as international involvement and they break with the traditional, "territorial" concept of democracy, according to which democracy is possible only in single, national states and can function only through certain institutional instruments (elections, parliament, separation of powers, etc.).

Many traditional theories about politics and the essence of political life are not able to understand these phenomena (globalization, new movements, new forms of political participation) for two reasons: a prima facie and a deeper one. The first reason is that they remain caught in the national dimension and therefore are not able to grasp the changed conditions under which economic, social and political power is distributed and exercised. They conceive democracy as something which is possible only at a national, domestic level and they suppose that a national government is able to establish and follow economic, social and environmental policies of its own, independent of external factors and actors. However, the second and real cause of this incapacity lies in the widespread claim that there are different fields or spheres of human action and that in each of them a different kind of power is exercised (religious power, economic power, political power, cognitive power, etc.).[2]

---

[2] Of course one thinks here of Michael Walzer (1983), but as a matter of fact this distinction is typical of most political thinkers since ancient times, even if they do not use this terminology.

In a sense, we can say that typologies of power are almost as old as philosophy (see Bobbio 1999: 102ff), starting from Aristotle's distinction among the power of the father over the son, the power of the master over the slave and the power of the ruler over the ruled, moving onto the typical modern distinction among paternal, despotic and political power (see for instance Locke, *Second Treatise on Government*, chapter XV), and arriving at contemporary typologies of power (like for instance that elaborated by Max Weber), which — according to Bobbio — are based instead on the different means through which the power-holder exerts power over the passive subject. One must distinguish therefore between economic, ideological, legal and political power. According to Bobbio, economic power concerns the possession of goods which are considered to be necessary in a situation in which these goods are scarce, so that those who do not own these goods are compelled to behave in a certain way such as selling their ability to work. Ideological power rests on the influence that ideas can have on people when they are formulated in a particular way, under particular circumstances, and by a particular person, and when they are disseminated through certain procedures. This is the case with religious ideas and the way priests control them, or with scientific knowledge and the way scientists and intellectuals manage it. Political power is founded upon the use of physical force (weapons, armies, police, etc.): it is a constraining power in the very physical sense. Bobbio assumes that political power is the supreme one, since it is the ultimate instrument to coerce and to force people to adopt certain behaviors. These forms of power establish and maintain a society in which inequality reigns, that is, a society divided "into rich and poor according to the first [type of power], intellectual and ignorant according to the second one, strong and weak according to the third one" (Bobbio 1999: 105). The social structure can therefore be seen as being formed by three sub-systems which are committed to organize productive forces, consent (as the result of the legitimation of society and its institutions offered by intellectuals) and constraint (as the instrument through which the strong exercise power over the weak) respectively.

The assumption of the existence of discrete fields or spheres of human action and of different kinds of power has a normative consequence — an implicit or explicit one, depending on the theory. The normative consequence is that there should be no trespass from one sphere into another. For instance, religious or economic power should not become political power and vice versa. Both the assumption and the consequence are the deeper, truer reason why most traditional theories cannot describe the reality of globalization. Since they conceive politics and the economy as two separate spheres, and since they give to this separation a normative character, they have difficulty in describing the de facto existing interaction of these spheres, or they just see this interaction as a proscribed interference (of politics in the economic world or vice versa) — an interference that they condemn on the basis of their ontological assumption, but one which they have difficulty describing in an appropriate way.

It is worth noticing in this context that while most political theories insist on the necessity of a justification or legitimation of political power in general (as legitimation of the existence of legal or state institutions at all) or in particular (as legitimation of single institutions or norms), almost no theory even takes into account the possibility of a legitimation of economic power. It is not clear at all why individuals, subject to legal and political power, should be entitled to demand a justification of such power, but not of economic power. In my opinion, this (mostly implicit) assumption is a completely unjustified consequence of the aforementioned separation of the economy and politics. One could reply that for most theories political associations are the result of a free union of individuals, of a contract whose result should be acceptable to everybody — an acceptance that can be reached only through the legitimation of legal and political power. But most contractualist theories (starting with Locke) also consider the market an arena which individuals join freely. The very idea of a political contract rests finally on the model of private contract which is the basis of economic relationships. If both the market and the *agora* result from the free union of individuals, why should they have different legitimation demands and standards?

A possible answer could be that political and legal power is connected to the exercise of force and needs therefore a greater legitimacy. While this is certainly a good reason for demanding the legitimation of such powers, it is not clear why this is not the case for economic power, since its consequences can be as devastating for the lives of individuals as the consequences of the use of force. Actually, notwithstanding the great number of wars afflicting the poorer regions of the world, most deaths there are poverty related, that is, they have an economic cause.

2. Money rules? Not quite …

One could object to the above-mentioned theories that religion, politics and economics are not discrete entities, and that they have never been such. Marx and theories which share his approach (but which are not necessarily Marxist theories) affirm for instance that the idea of State as a transcendent power (that is a power which takes a position high above the social level, that is above every other component of society) is just an *ideological* fiction used by modern political thinkers to conceal the fact that the real power lies somewhere else, that is, in the structures of production and trade.[3] This fiction was precisely a condition for the establishing and flourishing of the real power, the economic one. For such "ideological" theories[4] the modern State was from the very beginning just an instrument for the exercise of this power and political power is just a different face of economic power, since the law is the best instrument to protect the interests of the people who are economically better off.

These theories, while criticizing the ideological use of concepts like "State," "political sphere" and so on, use the same concepts and take over the distinction of the spheres of politics and economy in order to develop emancipating strategies that should create a different, more just society. They offer therefore an interesting vision of the history of legal and political institutions in Western societies in the last two centuries. According to this interpretation, it was only when the groups of people which were economically worse off (workers, women, etc.) began to use the law and therefore the State to improve their situation (for example, by imposing better standards in labor and social politics), that political power became at least in a minimal sense independent from economic power. Yet it could become independent only in a minimal sense, since it did not overthrow the economic system and therefore did not free itself completely from the interests of the economically stronger groups: even the most advanced welfare state recognizes and defends the private ownership of the means of production and considers capitalism (maybe in a more politically controlled form) as the only possible economic system.

In other words, disadvantaged people or classes have tried to improve their situation by using the very same instruments created by the dominating classes to defend their own interest (State, the law); they have fought for their rights and they have obtained important concessions both on the level of political participation (universal suffrage) and on the level of social legislation (the creation of a social security system, establishment of high health and safety standards for workers, right to unionize, the creation of State health care, of a State-funded educational system, etc.).[5] By doing this, it was the disadvantaged classes themselves who emancipated political power from the dominion of economic power: they *created* in a sense political power as an independent power that can be used against other forms

---

[3]   This is expressed in interpretations of the history of modern political thought like that
      offered by Macpherson (1962), introducing the concept of "possessive individualism."
[4]   I use the term "ideological" not in the sense that these theories have ideological character
      themselves but to mean that they conceive of State institutions as ideological instruments
      in the hand of economic powers.
[5]   This is typically the reconstruction of the changes in the social and legal status of citizens
      offered by Thomas Marshall (1950).

of power. This interpretation of social conflicts is the basis of theories like the ones elaborated by Habermas or Santos (Habermas 1984, 1987; Santos 2001). They take over the starting point of traditional liberal theories (the assumption that there are different kinds of power) in order to point to the emancipating potential which is hidden in the factual existence of State and law as instruments of domination by some individuals (the better-off) over other individuals (the worse-off). Thinkers like Santos and Habermas want to bring this potential to light in order to emancipate worse-off individuals from domination by those, who are better off. The establishment of an independent political sphere becomes therefore a precondition for human emancipation. The separation of the economic and political spheres could have in this sense a positive, emancipatory meaning, if it could be used to control the economy through political instruments (under the condition that the latter ones are used in a democratic way).

On the other side these theories are also aware of the difficulties connected to this emancipatory project. The main problem lies in the fact that for reasons which different theories identify differently (the fall of the Soviet bloc, the fact that the working classes were co-opted by the bourgeoisie through the enjoyment of welfare, the fact that citizens became clients of the State, and so on), the process of emancipation of an independent political sphere stopped and an opposite movement started: the economy took over and politics became again just an instrument of it. From this point of view, one can no longer speak of a separate political sphere since politicians, statesmen and officials are nothing but administrators following the commands of the economy. Furthermore States conceive their own task exclusively in doing everything to promote the economic growth of the country and to attract foreign investors — which is true not only for economically developing countries but also for industrialized ones. This change in both the nature and the goals of politics is particularly evident in the countries that had, in the last decades (or even in the last century), built some form of Welfare State. In almost all these countries economic politics seems at present to have only one goal: to help corporations and entrepreneurs by lowering labor costs, deregulating the labor market, privatizing public companies, multiplying tax exemptions for private companies, etc. This is not to say that the social State structures are being dismantled or that they are in jeopardy.[6] Nevertheless, reading the

---

[6] A similar position is shared by scholars like Paul Pierson. Basing his position on comparative research, he writes that while reform agendas vary, "all of them place a priority on cost containment. This shared emphasis reflects the onset of permanent austerity. Welfare states are not being dismantled. Efforts to achieve recalibration can generate interesting innovations and even extensions of social provision. Yet everywhere such adjustments occur in a context where the control of public expenditure is a central if

newspapers of most European countries one could have the impression that the main task of European governments is just to help the "national economy" — and by this expression they mostly mean the *private* economy. Here we are not simply facing a colonization of the political sphere by the economic one, rather we are witnessing a radical change in the nature of politics itself. Thus, according to these "ideological" theories, political power would become once again just another face of economic power.

This is not tantamount to saying that corporations, particularly transnational corporations (TNCs), are taking over and becoming the "new rulers of the world" (Pilger 2002); nor to claiming that managers or executives are no longer willing to try to convince politicians to do what they want, and prefer therefore to become politicians themselves (Derber 1998; Palast 2003).[7] Things cannot be that simple. There is no massive conspiracy of economic "powers" to seize political power as in a bad spy movie. According to a more sophisticated interpretation, reality is maybe even worse: executives do not need to become politicians themselves, since politicians (including so-called New Leftists like Bill Clinton, Gerhard Schröder and Tony Blair) are more than willing to decide exactly what executives would decide in their place. It is not that executives and corporations are taking over, but rather that the difference between the political and economic spheres is fading away, making therefore an emancipating use of politics impossible. This process cannot be reduced to the actions of single subjects (individuals or TNCs) but it seems to be inherent in the history of modern capitalism. As Santos and Habermas try to show, capitalism tends by its very nature to submit every other power (political power, communicative power, etc.) to economic power, not in the sense that politicians become controlled by executives (conspiracy theory), but in the sense that politicians start thinking like executives and not like politicians. It is not just economic interests that take over, rather it is an economic vision of things (of individual life, of Nature, of international relationships, etc.) that becomes predominant over other possible perspectives, therefore obstructing the path to emancipation.

---

not a dominant consideration. The core structure of most Welfare states are not in jeopardy, nonetheless the contemporary climate remains a harsh one for efforts to improve social provision for the vulnerable or to address newly recognized risks" (Pierson 2001: 456).

[7]   According to a quite simplistic diagnosis, it is not by chance that the current US president (politically the most powerful man in the world) is a businessman and that most members of his administration have worked for private corporations as executives, advisers, etc. (not to mention the case of Italy — one of the G8 countries — in which the country's richest man, involved in almost every economic field, simply became Prime Minister).

According to this interpretation, the predominance of the economy ought to be evident also in the sphere of international relations, since there economic power seems more relevant than military or political power (even if not in every circumstance). The preeminence of rich countries over the "poorer" is based on their economic power, not their military supremacy. If a poor country does not want to open its borders to the wares of a rich country, the latter will not threaten the former with war in a traditional sense — in the sense of a war that is prosecuted with weapons as in the past (here one thinks of commodore Perry and Japan or of the Opium War in China). The only war rich countries threaten to wage is the war on import duties or on loan conditions. They exercise therefore their power over poor countries through economic weapons (and sometime they wage such economic wars among themselves, particularly in the case of the USA and the EU). The exercise of political and military power, the waging of a war in its traditional sense, has very high costs and does not always achieve its goals (as the recent war in Iraq demonstrates), while the "conquest" of a country through "peaceful" means (such as big investments, acquisition of privatized former State companies, imposition of enterprise-friendly standards in the labor market and in its social politics) is more effective, cheaper and more likely to be accepted both by national and international public opinion (sometimes including vast sectors of the public opinion of the "conquered" country).

A similar approach is taken also by Hardt and Negri, whose book *Empire* (2000) found a wide echo because of its analysis of the transformations of power and of the exercise of power in the globalized world. Also Hardt and Negri move from the traditional point of view, according to which politics and the economy are two different spheres. In their view these two spheres are melting — a process which is caused by the global tendencies of the market and which provokes the crisis of the nation-state and of the idea of sovereignty. Capital, they say, "tends historically to destroy traditional social boundaries, expanding across territories and enveloping always-new populations within its processes. ... Capital sweeps clear the fixed barriers of precapitalist society — and even the boundaries of the nation-state tend to fade into the background as capital realizes itself in the world market" (Hardt and Negri 2000: 325ff). Hardt and Negri claim that capital is taking hold of the state and therefore is overtaking power. Power is therefore "made immanent," while "sovereignty transforms into governmentality" (ibid. 339), into simple administration. According to this position, capital would not only colonize the public sphere or the life-world (*Lebenswelt*), as Habermas theorizes: it would rather destroy the very essence of politics and of political life.

Nevertheless this is just part of the story. What I want to question is the idea that it is all about *economic* power. In other words: the idea that money rules or that it "makes the world go round," as a famous song says. Such an idea is just another formulation of the normative consequence driven by the theories of point 2, with the only difference being that this time the prohibition of interference is a one-way prohibition: economic power should not become political power but political power may (and according to some authors it should) exercise a certain control over economic power, and therefore should itself become — at least in part — economic power. This is of course an important difference for the political consequences of such a position compared to the one of the theories of point 2. While the position of these theories (where no interference at all is allowed) is typical for some forms of political or economic liberalism, the position of "ideological" theories (the only permissible interference is that of politics on economy) is more typical for "leftist" points of view, like, for example, social democracy, but also liberal positions which insist on questions of social justice (an example of the first kind of liberalism could be represented by Nozick, while social liberalism is at best identified with Rawlsian theories like the one developed by Thomas Pogge). Nevertheless both kinds of theories start from the basic idea of the existence of different spheres of human action and of different kinds of power.

3. A first attempt at defining power: its transcendental character

In order to question this idea, I shall refer to a less evident tradition of political thought — a tradition according to which human relationships are always power relationships. Based on this fundamental idea I shall attempt to lay the foundations for an identikit of the concept of power. As a first step I shall emphasize the transcendental character of power itself: power is the capacity to achieve goals, independently from how we define these goals. Furthermore I shall emphasize the relational nature of power: it implies the exclusion of other individuals from some goods, including the capacity to reach goals of their own. In this sense, power does not only affect people's actions; it also influences their *existential possibilities*. This becomes especially evident if we consider certain forms of power, for instance cognitive power — a power which is assuming a growing importance in our world at the cost of more traditional forms of dominance such as military power. A further consequence is that power needs not to be openly exercised — the mere possibility of its exercise can be enough to influence the life and actions of other people.

Some political theories do not recognize the existence of different spheres of human action, each one of which obeys different rules and principles, and which are organized on the basis of different forms of rationality or grounded on the distribution of different goods. These alternative theories are more holistic. They tend to reduce human action in all its variety of forms to a single element, to a common denominator: power in a very general, unqualified sense. They pass from the concept of power in the plural (political, economic, religious, social power, etc.) to an idea of power in the singular: power defined generically as the capacity of determining other people's actions and behavior. Sometimes we may consider such power relations as the expression of an unacceptable, illegitimate discrimination, and therefore as forms of power abuse. For example, this might be the case of an educational system hindering individuals belonging to certain groups (be they racial, national, social or gender groups) from enjoying its services; or of a political system excluding individuals from political rights because of their nationality, their religion, their social status, and so on; or of a world trade system which is disadvantageous for poor countries. However, we accept as legitimate the existence of other forms of power: the one that the loved one exercises over her lover; the one a religious chief has over his (very seldom of *her*) followers; the power of parents over small children; the power of a commission of scholars called upon to decide who among a certain number of candidates will get a fellowship, a prize or an academic position. We tend for some reason to believe that the latter ways of exercising power (in contrast with the former ways) do not need to be justified or legitimated — at least not in the same way. There may be some good reasons for this assumption. For instance, the fact that parental power is supposed to be exercised not for the power-holder's sake but for the subject's sake, or the fact that scholars are supposed to judge candidates on objective grounds and not on the basis of their race, gender, nationality or social status provide such reasons. However they cannot erase the fact that the power relationships we think of as perfectly legitimate and "natural" are nevertheless *power* relationships. This is the point that the above-mentioned theories insist upon. In my opinion, Machiavelli offers the best example of this position.[8]

Machiavelli's writings can be all considered parts of a quite (but not completely) unsystematic theory of power. All human relationships are reduced to power relationships — even the most intimate ones, even love, as shown in that great treatise on power and manipulation which is *La mandragola*, Machiavelli's most celebrated comedy (in Machiavelli 1961).

---

[8] I would like to mention another radical vision of power that of Elias Canetti, who, for instance, sees a power relationship even in the one between someone who is eating and her food: "Alles, was gegessen wird, ist Gegenstand der Macht" (Canetti 1980: 257).

In it, the young and rich Callimaco wants to win the love of old Nicia's beautiful (and young) wife Lucrezia. In order to realize his goal, he enlists the cunning Ligurio and the corrupt friar Fra' Timoteo. While the former uses a trick to persuade Nicia to let the young man sleep with his wife, the latter convinces Lucrezia that she will commit no sin by sleeping with a stranger. It is true that Callimaco's tricks reach their goal thanks to his economic power, which allows him to win for his cause (or better: to buy the services of) Ligurio and Fra' Timoteo, whose help is essential for the success of the whole enterprise. But Fra' Timoteo's success in convincing Lucrezia that she has to betray Nicia with Callimaco is based on his influence as a friar, that is on his religious power. And Ligurio is able to trap Nicia thanks to his rhetorical power and to his (supposedly) superior knowledge (in this case of the "miraculous" powers of the mandrake root). In Machiavelli's eyes everyone considers the others merely as instruments to reach her/his own goals; everyone tries therefore to control the others without falling himself/herself under their control.[9]

In *The Prince* Machiavelli points out an important aspect of power. The main instrument on which the Prince should rely to affirm his power is less physical force, rather the opinion his subjects have of him (Machiavelli 1940: 56ff). Whether it is best for this aim that they love or fear him cannot be judged a priori: different situations (and different people) call for different strategies of action (ibid. 66ff). Nonetheless it is decisive that power-holders are able to control the opinion of their subjects in order to control their behavior; and that they give the impression of force even when they do not have it at all. Machiavelli therefore separates power from force even if force may be essential to power.

More interestingly, while reducing every human relationship to a power relationship, Machiavelli points out that power is something qualitatively different from every other good that human beings can achieve. Power is the main instrument to reach every goal that one can decide to set oneself. Power therefore has a transcendental character since it is the faculty that makes it possible to achieve goals at all, independently of the definition of the particular goals themselves. Callimaco uses his power to obtain the favors of Lucrezia, the aspiring Prince uses his power to create a principality and establish his dominion. The latter example shows that power can be an instrument to achieve power. Contrary to other goods, the consumption of power can lead to an increase of power itself — and it does not matter

---

[9]   In Machiavelli this fight for power concerns not only relationships with the other human beings but also the soul and the mind of the individual himself who has to fight against the power of his passions. The fight thus becomes an internal one but it is still a fight for power and for control of human actions.

whether the Prince is transforming military or characterial power (his ability as a strategist, his charisma) into political or even economic power (creating a principality implies often accumulating wealth). Machiavelli would probably consider such a reading as an unnecessarily complicated description of the simple phenomenon of an individual using his power to gain more power, both defined in a generic way. From this perspective, political power is simply the possession of the means to control a territory and its population by the threat of the use of force, while economic power is the possession of wealth and of the means to control other people's wealth, cognitive power is the possession of knowledge that gives its holder an advantage over other individuals, and so on.

This intuition on the particular character of power will be developed by the other "bad guy" of modern political philosophy: in chapter X of *Leviathan*, Hobbes defines "the power of a man" as "his present *means*, to obtain some future apparent Good" (Hobbes 1996: 62, emphasis added). However, this is an incomplete definition, even from Hobbes's perspective. In a world without others, one would not have *power*: one would only have (or not) the physical possibility to get goods (food, shelter, etc.). Only if one had to compete with other animals to obtain these goods, we could say that he has power (if he succeeds in the competition). *Power implies exclusion.* Hobbes himself considers goods to be scarce, or at least available only in limited amounts and for a limited time, and this opinion is shared by most political thinkers.[10] From this point of view, power consists in the possession of those means which enable us to obtain some goods *while preventing other people from obtaining the same goods themselves*. By excluding other individuals from obtaining certain goods I demonstrate my superior power over them, at least with regard to those goods. The concept of power is in other words a *relational* concept: one has power *with regard to other individuals, not to things*. One further consequence is that power shows itself not only in the capacity to achieve one's own goals, but also in the capacity to prevent other individuals from achieving their own goals.

Therefore, if — as some political scientists claim (Stoppino 1990: 838) — we define power as the capability to determine other people's behavior (by command, persuasion, manipulation, etc.), we should consider this capability in a very wide sense. We may also determine other people's actions by not allowing them access to certain goods and therefore reducing their opportunities and possible action strategies. For instance, by not letting the poor countries participate on fair terms in the world economy (e.g., by

---

[10] Without considering, as many thinkers (including Hobbes) do, that men suffer under *pleonexie*, a boundless desire for new goods, no matter how many of them one may already possess.

imposing on them the very unfair conditions of the WTO agreements, or by imposing on them the not only unfair, but sometimes inhumane conditions necessary to get loans from the IMF and the World Bank), the rich countries are exercising their power over them and imposing on them certain strategies of action (like adopting certain labor and social policies).

In the present world, there are many examples of this way of exercising power as influencing the existential possibilities of actors rather than influencing only their actions. If we want to use a traditional vocabulary, assigning predicates to the term "power," we could say that, for instance, while traditional military power has lost its preeminence (remaining nevertheless very important), cognitive power has become central. In this way, we may not hold a meaningful debate on social justice in general and on global social justice in particular without taking into account the questions of intellectual property, of the availability of information, of the concentration of the media, of the independence of academic research, of the knowledge gap between industrialized and non-industrialized countries, of the brain drain from the latter countries, and so on. While everyone speaks of visible wars, very few theorists seem to notice that there is a more hidden war going on; the one on patents, which is assuming worrying dimensions, particularly since it has reached the biological field (as the race to decipher the human genome shows). The same can be said of religious power, as shown by the problems occurring because of different religious fundamentalisms, or of the ideological power of concepts like race and nation, as shown by recent events like the Yugoslavian wars, the Rwanda massacre, the many simmering or open ethnic conflicts in several regions of Asia (India, Indonesia, Sri Lanka) and Africa (Nigeria). We can define all these kinds of power by applying to the term a different predicate: cognitive, religious, ideological, economic, etc. Yet in its essence it remains power; it follows the same scheme, it obeys the same logic. It is a relationship among actors in which some of them may determine the behavior and/or the existential possibilities of the others. In this sense, a simple shift of goods from the richer to the poorer, while it may be of vital importance (literally saving lives) could not represent a real change if it would not cause a shift in the power relations, for instance, giving to the poor access to more knowledge or information (on this see point 6).

A further important distinction in this context is that between actual and potential power. A general ordering his men to attack is exercising actual power over them but he also possesses a potential power. Even if he does not command an attack, the soldiers would attack if he were to do so (Stoppino 1990: 841). In order to say that an actor A has power over another actor B, it does not need to be the case that A is actually exercising this power. For example, the State has a coercive power over its citizens even when it is not concretely arresting or punishing them for having broken a rule. When I sit down at my desk and fill in the forms to pay my taxes, I know that the State has the power to compel me to do this even if there is no state official sitting there with me and admonishing me. When a country B wants to do something which will not please a more powerful country A, B knows that A will react in a way which could be unpleasant for it; therefore B will probably modify its strategy of action. In this case A will have benefited from its power over B even without actually exercising it — maybe even without knowing it. The consequence is that B will try to act in a way which will please A even when A is not asking B to do this. The existence of a power relationship creates a constellation in which individuals conform automatically to the expectations of the power-holder. The creation of such expectations and the automatic adaptation to them of those who are subject to the power are essential elements of power itself. It is to this question that we now turn.

4. A second attempt at a definition: the dilemmas of power

Having defined power in its more general form, we ought now to take into account those aspects of it which have direct importance for questions of social justice. By doing so, we see that power tends to create and maintain expectations about people's behavior and therefore constitutes a central element of every form of social life from love relationships to the State. When considered as political or legal power it seems to lead inexorably to dilemmas that exclude the possibility of a democratic control of the economy or the solution of problems like environmental damages and world poverty. This will lead us, in the next section, to develop an alternative concept of power.

I shall start from Niklas Luhmann's reflections on this topic (Luhmann, 2000: 18ff, 2003: 60ff). According to Luhmann, power is a communicative medium (Luhmann 2003: 4ff) through which A determines B's choices among different action strategies according to A's own views. In this sense a power relation has the same structure as a love relationship, as Luhmann notes following Machiavelli (but without quoting him). Power implies uncertainty: A disposes of more than one alternative and for this reason she can provoke uncertainty in B, since B does not know which decision A will take (ibid. 8) — and in this sense there is an analogy between power and love (Machiavelli would have said that the power of the loved one has the same nature as that of a prince). On the other hand, while B has to choose from only a restricted number of options, A has no such restrictions. In this sense also A suffers uncertainty, while B knows with greater security that if he chooses a certain way of acting the reaction of A will be a rewarding or a punishing one. Therefore, when A reaches her goal of reducing complexity and establishing patterns of behavior for B, she loses at the same time her grip on B, since she reduces B's uncertainty about A's reaction. But if A would not do this, if she would exercise an arbitrary power over B, she would fail to meet an essential condition of power — the establishing of expectations about the behavior of B *and* of herself. By doing so, the power of A would lose legitimacy (intended by Luhmann in an empirical, not normative sense as the generic willingness to accept decisions taken by the power-holder). This is a crucial dilemma which power unavoidably incurs. For this reason if power wants to maintain itself, it has to renounce either legitimacy (and this could cause the revolt of the subjects) or its opaque and unpredictable character. Power must therefore unavoidably be institutionalized. Its arbitrariness must be reduced, and this happens through institutionalization. The acts of B are then to be judged not according the arbitrary will of A, but according to laws, rules, norms that are fixed once for all or that can be modified only according to certain procedures.

Luhmann obviously thinks of political power and of its partial transformation into legal or institutional power, but I wonder whether this reasoning applies to other cases and therefore whether he is not just describing a particular kind of power. It does not seem that economic power, cognitive power or the power of the loved one over the lover lead necessarily to the same consequence. Let us suppose that B is madly in love with A, and that A reacts highly arbitrarily to the acts of B. Due to that, A may either tighten her grip on B or "kill" B's love. However, there is no way to find an arrangement like institutionalization.

Moreover, the dilemma arises only in the case in which the power-holder A reacts to B's behavior. Yet this is just one possible way of exercising power and is typical of political power both before and after its partial transformation into legal power. But power may also consist in the capacity to exclude B from the achievement of certain goods like instruction, economic autonomy, and so on. Reducing B's range of choices does not mean compelling B to act or behave in a certain way, since it may also result in controlling the existential potentialities of B. Power is not only about what B may or may not *do* but it is also about what B may or may not *be*, that is, what kind of person she can be, what kind of life she can lead, what kind of social environment she may interact with (see above point 3 and see below point 5).

According to Luhmann's analysis, power increases with the increase of the nominal freedom of B: the more possible action strategies there are for B, the greater is the power of A (ibid. 9f). The power of a master over his slaves, for instance, is much smaller than the power of the chief of a national bank on the managers of the banks of that country — and this not just because of the number of people involved but because of the fact that even if the individuals subject to the power have a broad range of possibilities and may act in different ways, all of them can nevertheless be controlled by the single one who has power over them. In this sense, the real essence of power lies in the shaping of the will of the individuals who are subject to it. Power does not need to break the will of its subjects: instead it has to neutralize it. When the subjects themselves recognize the power and freely submit their actions to its control, when they stop deciding for themselves and just act as is expected from them — then power shows itself most. Power is a mechanism to reduce complexity, to generate expectations concerning behavior, and to provoke precisely the kind of behavior expected of its subjects. Luhmann goes so far as to claim that power does not influence the will of a subject; it rather *creates* that will first (ibid. 11, 21).

This is not equivalent to depriving B of every possibility to revolt or to exercise on his part some kind of power over A. According to Luhmann, power is based on the existence of alternatives which the power-holder would like to avoid. Once these alternatives are realized, power collapses. The power-holder must therefore threaten the individuals subject to his power with sanctions in case they choose a strategy which he would like them to avoid. The sanctions do not necessarily have to be positive acts of punishment (like, for instance, inflicting physical pain or depriving someone of her liberty), but can consist also in the deprivation of some positive performance (like, for example, stopping state subsidies[11]). In any case, when the individuals who are subject to power are able to provoke the reaction of the power-holder, they create a sort of counter-power. In a sense they control the behavior of the power-holder and reduce the uncertainty about it. They know that the power-holder will react with sanctions or with force. By provoking the power-holder's violent reaction, those who are subjected to his power exercise therefore a form of power over him and create a counter-power. For this reason both Arendt and Luhmann differentiate power from force or violence (Arendt 1970; Luhmann 2003). Moreover, violence (when it comes from the power-holder) implies renouncing control over the possible action strategies of the one who is submitted to the power. The latter has no more alternatives, since she is forced to act in a certain way (Luhmann 2003: 9).

---

[11] In a recent case, some US universities were threatened with the withdrawal of federal funds since they do not allow the US army to hold recruiting desks on campus because of the discriminatory policy of the US army against homosexuals — a policy that goes against the anti-discrimination rules of those universities (see on this question: www.law.harvard.edu/news/2004/01/13_solomon.php).

As I have already pointed out, Luhmann concentrates (in a quite orthodox way) on political power. He can therefore claim that in a highly complex society (like ours) political power is not able to fulfill its functions since there is an unavoidable gap between the growing need for quick decisions and the fact that in such a society power is always exercised through a long chain of decisional centers that unavoidably slow down the process of decision-making (ibid. 84ff). Political power cannot catch up with its "environment" — with the highly specialized problems it has to face. These problems are in part created by power itself, since every decision for a certain strategy can provoke, by excluding other possibilities, unexpected difficulties. However, the main reason why political power is not able to fulfill its function is the existence of *other* social powers which are not so pervasive and total since they concern only specific ambits, but which are nevertheless much more effective. Luhmann thinks primarily of bureaucratic power which can obstruct political power through a strategy of slowing down or even blocking the concrete realization of politically taken decisions (ibid. 84). Nonetheless, this is evidently also the case for family, economic, educational or religious power (one just needs to think of the supremacy of family ties over political duties which is typical of many cultures; or of the power of economic lobbies; or of the fact that only educated people have a real access to key social positions; or of religiously motivated conscientious objectors) (ibid. 92).

For Luhmann there are no ultimate solutions to these problems. A way of dealing with them is political planning. This consists in the control of the political agenda: what politicians should decide on is which questions need to be the object of political decisions. The process of decision-making itself, on the other hand, should follow established procedures and results finally in an act of administrative power. What Luhmann rejects because of their ineffectiveness are precisely two options that seem to be typical of the present situation: the extension of the legal sphere, that is, the inclusion in the legal system of more and more fields which are to be controlled through laws and juridical norms; and the extension of democratic participation both in a quantitative sense (concerning a greater number of decision-making processes) and in a qualitative sense (concerning a deeper participation in processes which are already democratic, like, for instance, through the creation of new participation forms beyond traditional ones such as elections, referenda, and so on) (ibid. 94ff). These two solutions are precisely those advocated by many thinkers who think that the problems of globalization can be solved only either through the creation of a global legal system (even in the form of a world state), or through the democratization of crucial decisions on matters concerning economy, environment, and so on. I shall come back to this aspect under point 6.

A final comment on Luhmann's concept of power would be that, even if it claims to be simply descriptive, Luhmann's theory presents a strong similarity to the theories of point 2 in at least one respect. Like those theories, Luhmann's position seems to have a normative consequence, namely that legal power and political power in its democratic form should not extend to other spheres of human interaction even if — as Luhmann concedes — it is precisely in these spheres that the major problems of a complex society arise.

5. A third attempt at a definition: an alternative concept of power

After having presented positions that consider power as an entity, as *something*, which one has (or does not), or as a mechanism, through which an actor A influences the behavior of another actor B, I would like to refer to an alternative concept of power, namely, that elaborated by Michel Foucault (1990: 85ff; 2003: 126ff, 202ff, 229ff, 300ff). According to Foucault, power is a relationship, not something that individuals *have*. There is therefore no power-holder. Instead power shapes individuals, it gives them a certain role, a position with regard to other individuals. For instance, power makes of an individual the loved one who can influence the behavior and feelings of the lover; it makes a certain individual the ruler over other individuals who become then subjects to his authority. Power has therefore a constitutive nature, creating as it does social roles, causing institutional arrangements, giving birth to knowledge by defining what is true and false, what is correct and incorrect.

Foucault speaks of the omnipresence of power: "Power is everywhere; not because it embraces everything, but because it comes from everywhere" (Foucault 1990: 93). "Power is exercised from innumerable points," it is immanent in every human relationship, from sexual relations to economic processes, and therefore it "comes from below; that is, there is no binary and all-encompassing opposition between rulers and ruled at the root of power relations" (ibid. 94). A consequence of this is the existence of asymmetries of power, of fields in which there are differences in its density. Contrary to most theories, power is not centrally controlled, starting from the authority of a greater power-holder like, say, Hobbes's Leviathan.[12] Central power

---

[12] "Neither the caste which governs, nor the groups which control the state apparatus, nor those who make the most important economic decisions direct the entire network of power that functions in a society (and makes *it* function)" (Foucault 1990: 95; italics in the original).

results rather from the intersection of many power relationships. Power manifests itself in a plurality of situations and places: in schools, prisons, hospitals, universities, churches, families, and of course also in parliaments, stock exchanges, battlefields. There may be a thickening of such power relations in the so-called centers of power (understood as cores of economic, political, educational, cognitive power embodied in the "dominating" elites) but they do not form a unitary entity. There is no unique will, no unitary strategy, no all-encompassing controlling agency (ibid. 94f).

Society is based on the existence of power relations ("A society without power relations can only be an abstraction"), that is, on the existence of differences: "Every relationship of power puts into operation differences that are, at the same time, its conditions and its results." Such differences are of many kinds: "juridical and traditional differences of status or privilege; economic differences in the appropriation of wealth and goods, differing positions within the process of production, linguistic or cultural differences, differences in know-how and competence, and so forth." Correspondingly, power can be exercised in the pursuit of different objectives ("maintenance of privileges, accumulation of profits, the exercise of authority, the exercise of a function or a trade"). Further, it can be exercised in different modes ("by the threat of arms, by the effect of speech, through economic disparities, by more or less complex means of control, by systems of surveillance, with or without archives, by rules, explicit or not, fixed or modifiable, with or without the material means of enforcement"). It can be institutionalized in different forms ("traditional conditions, legal structures, matters of habit or fashion") and at different degrees of rationalization (with regard to the "greater or lesser technological refinements employed in the exercise of power" or to "the possible cost") (Foucault 2003: 140f).

Instead of identifying different spheres of power or different functions of power, one could therefore speak of different ways in which power expresses itself by establishing certain differences among actors. This is, I believe, a decisive difference: there are not many forms of power, only many forms in which power can be exercised. When a corporation influences government policy, we should not speak of an unwarranted interference of economic power in the political sphere or of a transformation of economic into political power. Rather we should speak of the establishing of a power relation between an actor (the corporation) and another actor (the government) with further consequences for a third actor (the citizens of the country as far as they are affected by the politics of their government). This different perspective allows us not only to describe this kind of phenomena in a different way (that would be quite irrelevant) but also to conceive of the relationship among the actors in a different way. If a corporation exercises power over the citizens of a country (through the power it exercises over their government), the citizens may exercise a counter-power *and this will be fully legitimate.* Actually, it does not even need to be deemed legitimate, it is just a matter of fact whether they react or not. Again, it is Foucault who points out the necessary connection between power and counter-power or resistance to power: "Where there is power, there is resistance, and yet, or rather consequently, this resistance is never in a position of exteriority in relation to power" (Foucault 1990: 95) and "in order to understand what power relations are about, perhaps we should investigate the forms of resistance and attempts made to dissociate these relations" (Foucault 2003: 129). The reaction to power may be of course very weak or even so feeble that it practically does not exist. Nevertheless at least the possibility of a resistance, even if hopeless, is always there. A small child can resist the power exercised by her parents by going off in a huff, a student can oppose the decisions of an examining board by protesting or by appealing to a court, a lover can break up with her partner, a consumer can boycott the products of a certain company, a government can resist the pressures of foreign corporations, of international investors, of the IMF, etc.

Counter-power may articulate itself in many ways — exactly as power does. At present this is happening, for instance, in the movements I mentioned above (see point 1). When a political movement, say a party or an NGO, calls for a boycott of a company because the latter supports a dictatorship, or because it is exploiting child labor, or because it is destroying the environment, resistance is taking place. That resistance is resistance against the power exercised by that company over the subjects of that tyrannical government, over those children (and indirectly even over workers in other countries and over governments that ban child labor), over the people living in that environment. It does not matter whether the company is exercising its power legally (e.g., in countries with low standards for environment preservation or for child-care): it is exercising power over people, and people react with a counter-power, whether this resistance be legal or not. Legal power is just a way of exercising power. Moreover it is not always a legitimate one, since the judgment of the legitimacy of the legal exercise of power should be given by the people subject to that power and this is something that happens very rarely in cases like the ones mentioned above. The resistance that is articulating itself in new social movements, in the political activity of NGOs, in initiatives like the World Social Forum, is the expression of interests which are often very different from the interests of TNCs, of shareholders, of financial markets, of financial speculators, and even of governments. Legal systems tend to express more the latter interests, showing that they are nothing but ways of exercising power. Yet no power is eternal and specific interests can be supplanted by different interests, namely, when counter-power becomes the dominant power. In this sense the emancipative ideal of the theories above which I referred to as "ideological" can be maintained and reformulated in terms of a global attempt to give voice to alternative interests and to establish alternative power relations, in the sense not of eliminating power in itself (that would be impossible), but of creating new relations of power among the actors — and therefore of creating new actors beyond the usual ones (States, companies, unions).[13]

Concerning this latter point, Foucault's idea of power can also be useful in another way. As a commentator says, "Foucault's re-elaboration of a theory of power subverts power in the formal juridical sense of negative constraints located in laws and legal institutions, insisting instead that power is an all-pervasive, normative positive presence … . We are what we learn, internalize and reproduce as knowledge and the language through which it is understood" (Evans 1995: 114). Foucault claims that power is not something exercised by a subject A over the subject B, but a relationship which shapes the subjects themselves and gives them their peculiar nature. An individual is the person she is because of certain power relations which made her that kind of person. This is true both in an immediate and in a more indirect sense. Foucault points out the first aspect and emphasizes the role of power relations which take place in the family, education, the socialization process, State, religious and social institutions like barracks, hospitals, schools and universities, prisons. I think we should also consider the second aspect: we are what we are also because we are born in a certain country in a certain time. Our existential chances are determined by such facts even more than by, say, education. An illiterate poor person in Germany has at present a completely different set of existential choices than an illiterate poor person in Ethiopia. The chances that the former will starve to death are nil and he can count on services (offered both by the State and by private actors) which will ease his suffering, help him to improve his economic situation, maybe even to find a job — his life is completely different and therefore he is a different person, just because he was born in an affluent country with a strong social system. So-called external factors of someone's life, like time and place, are not neutral with regard to the identity and the existential possibilities of an individual. They are expression of those power relations that created precisely that situation for that place in that time. If at the beginning of the 21st century Germany is more affluent than Ethiopia, and therefore poor people living in Stuttgart are better off than poor people living in Addis Ababa, then this is not simply by chance but a consequence of certain historical events which made Germany an economic world power

---

[13] This is not tantamount to claiming that counter-power is always used for what is normative good. Actually history gives us examples of morally questionable, or even morally wrong uses of it.

and Ethiopia one of the poorest countries in the world — events which were determined, beyond geographical aspects, by the different power of the two countries.[14] History is not a succession of natural events or happenstance, but in the first place the history of power relations among groups (and therefore also among countries). If I have a high education and become a philosopher, I owe this not only to my personal capabilities and to the sacrifices my parents have made to allow me to study, but also to the fact that I was born in a rich country in which higher education is available. However, this country did not become rich by chance but through its history which was, among other things, also a history of colonization, wars, exploitation.

This is not the same as saying that rich countries do not deserve their richness or that their economic preeminence is unjust or is the fruit of injustice. I merely make the observation that the so-called external situations of one individual's life (country, historical moment, etc.) are an expression of more general power relationships involving the country that individual is born in or is living in or the social group she belongs to. This quite trivial but often forgotten fact leads us to further considerations concerning the question of international social justice. I would like therefore to conclude this paper by presenting some reflections both on power in the globalized world and on the role of contemporary political theories of justice.

6. Power and global social justice

International relationships form a complex network of power relationships that often are not easy to read. Very few IR-theories (including the ones on international justice) really takes this fact into account: Rawls's *The Law of Peoples*, for example, certainly does not do it (power in general is scarcely mentioned in this book and only as a synonym for "internal political power"). A reason for this could be the conceptual vagueness of power and the difficulty of clearly attributing power to the different actors on the world stage. Paradoxically, this is particularly true of states: oil-producing countries, for instance, have power in a sense, but they are weak in another, since their power depends finally on the oil demand and on the "benevolence" of industrialized countries, since their governments know that they would be toppled quickly if they would not deliver their oil at a "reasonable" price.[15] Another example: the US has a huge military power to

---

[14] Geographical factors are important but not decisive. Otherwise one could not explain how, for instance, Denmark is a richer country than Brazil even if it does not have all the natural resources (mineral resources, biodiversity, etc.) of the latter.

[15] I thank Thomas Pogge for calling my attention to this point.

defend itself, but can nevertheless be very vulnerable, as shown on 9/11. Among the few theorists who try to discuss the question of power in the globalized world there are, again, Hardt and Negri. They define power as a deterritorialized entity, since the world no long forms an arena in which discrete entities (the States) establish power relationships among themselves (Hardt and Negri 2000: 186ff). According to them, what has changed is that power-holders are no longer States but either impersonal entities like markets, or other institutions like corporations. Hardt and Negri move closer to Foucault's position that power is no longer an individual quality, something you can predicate of a subject in the traditional way (X has power). This is particularly evident in the case of entities like the market which does not have power in the way States have (or are said to have) power. In this sense, such entities do not have power at all, it is rather power that defines them. The market is a network of power relations among certain subjects, whose role is defined precisely by their relationships to one another (like, for example, the seller and the buyer).

One could object that the same was true of States, that as power-holders they were nothing but a fiction or a theoretical construct, that power has always been running through channels other than political and legal institutions and that States were always acting on the international level just as agents of economic interests (as Marxist theories claim) or simply as actors among others (companies, churches, markets, educated elites).

One could also claim that it would be more appropriate to distinguish between governments, States and peoples: a distinction one can miss very often in the literature on international relations, from the first documents on the law of peoples to Rawls's book (Rawls 1999). While governments and peoples can be considered actors in a traditional sense, since they really *act* (they stipulate contracts, they either take decisions or revolt against them, and so on), States do not. States are (as the word suggests) static entities, states of things. A State is an ensemble of institutions which form a frame in which individuals act either according to expectations, or violate them, or act in a way that is indifferent to them. These expectations often take the shape of laws, of legal norms, but they may be also social rules, social expectations.[16] States are mechanisms to perpetuate (but also to create and to change) these expectations, mostly through the creation of legal norms, but

---

[16] As an Italian citizen, for instance, I am supposed not only to respect Italian law, but also to act in a certain way, for example, to be patriotic, to love the Azzurri (the national soccer team), to follow a certain mentality, to show certain traits of character which are considered to be peculiarly Italian. This is not the same as suggesting that the State and national culture necessarily coincide. One can also have social expectations of citizens of multinational, multicultural States. A Swiss is supposed, for instance, to be a Swiss patriot independently of her status as Swiss-German, Swiss-French, and so on.

also connecting generic social expectations (like loyalty towards the group) to the institutionalization of collective identity.[17]

States and their institutions are therefore instruments to perpetuate power, since one of power's main attributes is the creation of expectations (I have already referred to the potential character of such a power, introducing the example of the conscientious taxpayer). State institutions do not really *act*, rather they *react* to actions which could represent a threat to the status quo. They tend to "freeze" a certain situation, inserting the current power relations into a legal frame. For instance, private property finds its way into the civil code (and its defense finds its way into the penal code). This is not to say that they tend to freeze the flux of power; rather they try to channel it, to let it flow between dams (the law) in order both to keep it at least under the nominal control of political and legal authority and, above all, to avoid big shifts of power. Law is inherently conservative with a small "c". Interestingly, we may now see that law has become for many leftist thinkers a barrier against wild predatory capitalism. Such authors stress the democratic character of law and see in it the only instrument to carry forward an emancipatory project (see particularly Habermas 1996a). They are conservative insofar as they are fighting to maintain a certain political control over economic forces, assuming that the Welfare State (where legal norms pose stronger limits to capitalism) is more respectful of individual autonomy than the Minimal or Nightwatchman State, which is the ideal of the dominant ideology at present: economic liberalism. Being conservative in this sense means nowadays rebelling against the supremacy of predatory capitalism and fighting for the rights of individuals against an impersonal, often inhumane economic power. It is not by chance that theories of social justice normally advocate the maintaining or the creation of a *legal* frame that should guarantee a fairer distribution of goods (either only on the domestic level, or both on the domestic and on the international level). In other words, these theories start from the assumption that the economic and financial world may be controlled politically so that the latter may force the former to share the costs of the morally necessary indemnification. Most of these theories try, therefore, to offer the moral basis for the claim that the political sphere should control the economic through certain institutions.

A very good example is offered by Thomas Pogge's theory of social justice (2001a and 2002a). Pogge's approach is more an ethical than a political one, since he tries to demonstrate that the actual state of things in

---

[17] Through Italian citizenship one becomes Italian in a much stronger sense — stronger than when there was no Italian state and Italians were just Neapolitans, Lombards, Tuscans, etc. and were legally subject to Spanish or Austrian rulers, but also stronger than in the case of foreigners living in Italy or of descendants of Italian emigrants living abroad.

the world — with few rich countries on the one side and a majority of people suffering for the behavior of the affluent inhabitants of the privileged countries on the other side — is contrary to our moral belief. Pogge tries to show that poverty is produced by the attitude and behavior of the rich countries (for instance, by the fact that they impose — through the WTO — certain rules of international trade or — through the World Bank and the IMF — certain conditions for international money loans over poor countries) and that therefore the rich countries should repair the poverty caused by their politics, according to a principle deeply rooted in their own moral ideas (that who bears responsibility for an injustice should make up for it).[18] To reach this goal one should create new (or modify existing) international rules and institutions.

Pogge and theorists sharing his approach, from Rawls to Habermas and Santos, tend to consider legal or political power as *the real* power, the power able to control all other forms of power if correctly used, where they mostly take in consideration only State or State-like institutions (e.g., the UN). Alternative theories — like for instance the theories of global governance[19] — do not share this positive vision of State and of political power. They think, on the contrary, that precisely the traditional centers of power like private companies, churches and religious groups, educational institutions or even families and clans (Rosenau 1998) should assume the role of emancipating individuals. In other words, this task would be fulfilled more effectively by institutions independent from the State like churches and markets, or by State-controlled but quasi-autonomous institutions like universities.

---

[18] This approach, while doubtless convincing on the whole once one accepts the moral point of view of the dominant rich countries, may incur some difficulty when it comes to specifying the identity of those who actually bear responsibility for the present state of things. This is a decisive step if we want to turn to the practical application. If it is "we, the affluent," who are responsible for the poverty of millions of individuals, we should bear the costs which are necessary to correct the situation and eradicate poverty. But who are the "we" exactly? Who should concretely bear the costs? National governments? And why not the private enterprises which seem to profit most from the present situation in poorer countries? It is mostly companies and corporations that look for cheap raw materials or cheap productive forces and that therefore take advantage of (or even create) phenomena like corrupt authorities, low working standards, low wages, scarcely organized trade unions (when they are allowed by the government), tax exemptions for foreign investors and practically non-existent social policies. Once we have established that "we, the affluent" should correct the injustice and the harms that we produce, we should also decide how to do this, who is supposed to bear the costs of it, and in which proportion. These are no longer ethical, but political questions, as Pogge points out.

[19] On governance and its dangers, see Pinzani 2003b.

These theories consider therefore social actors (States, churches, TNCs, NGOs, unions, etc.) as subjects that are defined once and for all, and that have power (theories of points 2 and 3) or hold power relationships among themselves (Luhmann, but finally also Negri and Hardt). According to Foucault, on the other hand, power is something liquid, a fluid penetrating into the social body that isolates and connects at the same time the single elements of that body, while at the same time regulating their relationships to one another. From this point of view, power in the globalized world identifies, connects and correlates those elements in a different way. While States (both as institutions, as governments, and as people or citizens) have "lost" power (as long as one can use this verb in relation to this noun), other actors emerged on the global scene, gaining a role they previously did not have — at least not so openly. Put another way: power took different shapes from the traditional ones, as shown by the examples I mentioned above (see point 3), concerning so-called cognitive, ideological or religious power. There I claimed too that a simple shift of goods from the richer to the poorer would not represent a real change, since it would not represent a shift in the power relations. By saying this, I do not want to minimize the importance of a partial redistribution of wealth as demanded by many contemporary theories of justice. I am just pointing out a deficiency they may present. As theories of political justice (e.g., Held 1995, Held et al. 1999, Höffe 1999, Rawls 1971 and 1999), they insist on the necessity of legitimating political power but do not consider at all the legitimacy deficit in economic power. As theories of social justice (e.g., Pogge 2002a) they discuss questions of distributive justice and focus on the (re) distribution of goods, but by doing so they only bring into question (a) some form of power like military or economic power, (b) some instruments through which power is exercised like the free market or the so-called Westphalian model of international relationships, and (c) certain outcomes of the power relations which are objects of their analysis. In doing so, they do not question the legitimacy of our economic system, rather of certain negative aspects of it; and they do not discuss the question of the real nature of the power relations which cause the social problems they would like to solve. Above all, they do not discuss the nature of *power itself.*

As I stated at the beginning of this paper, it was not my aim to offer an exhaustive definition of power but rather to advance some general considerations on the nature of this phenomenon. In this sense, I hope that this work will be seen as a contribution to such a debate.

Chapter 11

Egalitarian Global Distributive Justice or Minimal Standard? Pogge's Position[*]

Véronique Zanetti
Philosophy, Universität Bielefeld, Germany

On what principle do we want to base the theory of global justice? On a principle of equality (of chances, opportunities, resources, etc.) or on a minimal standard, to which every individual has a justified claim? I shall address two positions, both of which endorse the opinion that affluent and powerful groups of people have a special moral responsibility with respect to poorer groups and that they are bound to strive for a more balanced distribution of the advantages and burdens that stem from international cooperation and environmental resources. Whereas the two positions are in agreement about this moral requirement, they differ in their characterization of injustice. According to the one position, injustice lies in "the violation of elementary, absolute standards of justice," which makes it impossible to live a life worthy of a human being (Krebs 2000: 21). For the other position, injustice lies in the violation of a substantive requirement of equality. In other words, the first position takes a "need-based approach" (Sen 1984: 301), the other an "equality-based approach." In the following, I distinguish these two basic principles and attempt to demonstrate their concrete implications for global justice (1). In the second part I examine the arguments that led Rawls — in the context of the theory of international relations — to reject the egalitarian premises of a theory of distributive justice within individual societies (2). In the third part I review arguments in favor of a principle of assistance, which defines a minimal standard of elementary needs (3). In the final section (4) I show, on the basis of Pogge's theory, that the non-egalitarian critique is mistaken in treating the principle of equality as a derived principle. My argument can be summarized as

---

[*] I would like to thank John Michael and Donna Orange for their precious help in translating this essay.

A. Follesdal and T. Pogge, (eds.), Real World Justice, 199-213.

follows: if the idea of a minimal standard is necessary for the realization of basic rights on a global scale, it is nevertheless not a sufficient condition for the realization of justice. The concept of justice is closely bound to that of equality (cf. Gosepath 2001: 406). I will also show, however, that as Thomas Pogge advocates this position, his global egalitarianism shifts slightly in the course of his publications. In making certain concessions to pragmatism along the way, he even comes close to positions encountered in anti-egalitarian theories of justice.

1. Egalitarianism within individual states and non-egalitarianism on a global scale?

It is debatable what role the basic principle of equality should play in the distribution of goods and burdens. In the wake of Rawls's *A Theory of Justice* (1971), many theorists have invested the principle of equality with a moral value, which they consider decisive in assessing the legitimacy of the distribution of basic social goods and burdens.[1] Others — especially in recent years — have called this very principle into question, and thereby also its appropriateness as a basic value to be acknowledged.[2] True, as George Orwell wrote: "a fat man eating quails while children are begging for bread is a disgusting sight" (George Orwell 1938: 115). Nevertheless — argue the advocates of non-egalitarian justice theories — if this example is shocking, it is not because of the unequal distribution of goods, but because of the destitution of the hungry. The inequality between two people — so they continue — is not shocking or outrageous when both people have sufficient means to lead a life worthy of a human being. What is shocking is not that some have more than others, but that some do not have enough at all.

According to advocates of a non-egalitarian conception, a theory of justice should not insist on regarding equality as an end in itself. On the contrary, it should strive to secure the conditions of a worthy life. Whereas the egalitarians[3] employ the principle of equality in a relational (namely, a comparative) sense, the non-egalitarians support the principle of justice by

---

[1] Some of the best-known among the authors writing in English are Dworkin (2000), Sen (1980, 1992) and Nagel (1979). As for the literature in German, see Tugendhat 1997 and Gosepath 1998, 2001.

[2] See Raz 1986, chapter 9; Frankfurt 1987; Anderson 1999. These texts are collected in Krebs 2000.

[3] I am taking into account only the moderate version of Egalitarianism mentioned by Parfit 1995. The radical version — according to which any inequality is an evil in itself, even when it would improve everyone's overall condition — does not merit serious consideration.

appealing to the ideas of "sufficiency," "standards" (Frankfurt 1987: 37) and "priority" (Parfit 1995), which establish a threshold of needs necessary to be met. In other words: what counts from the perspective of non-egalitarian criticism is that everyone has access to the goods necessary to lead a decent life, i.e., that they have enough to eat, a roof over their heads, clothes on their backs, an elementary education, access to medical treatment, and that they live in a natural environment that will not cause them to become ill (Krebs 2000: 31). The list of such goods can become considerably long.

Granted, Rawls's thoughts about "primary goods" contain something like the notion of a "set" of basic goods, which the fundamental institutions of society are to guarantee in order to assure stability ("for the good reasons"). But, although these goods are in fact defined (the list includes rights, freedoms, opportunities, salary and wealth, along with the social foundations of self-respect), the lowest level of satisfaction of needs is oriented towards the most disadvantaged members of a society. Hence the right of the underprivileged to a greater share of basic goods is not absolute, but relative to their position in the social scale. The concept of a minimal standard, on the other hand, implies no such comparison. The standards determine the order in which people are to be helped.

Thus it is clear that the principle adopted to support a theory of justice has concrete consequences for the realization of the theory. Harry Frankfurt writes that "situations involving inequality [are] morally problematic only to the extent that they violate the ideal of sufficiency" (Frankfurt 1987: 37). So consideration for justice would demand that everyone be guaranteed a minimal standard. On this view, the poorest people would not have a unique claim to assistance because they have less than others but, rather, because they do not have enough to live lives worthy of human beings. Involuntary destitution is an evil in itself. At the international level this viewpoint calls for an effective assistance pact, the goal of which would be to eliminate squalor in the world.

But, on the other hand, if the principle of justice is developed on the basis of the principle of equality, then it implies the task of organizing the structure of social institutions in such a way that everyone has equal access to those goods that are necessary for a decent life. The goal of such an exercise of law — as well as the means it would call for — differs from that of an effective assistance pact. A just political and social system would aim to create a general state of social cooperation "for the right reasons." This means that the justified claims of participants in social cooperation would be fulfilled when the fundamental principles that govern the distribution of goods are such as they would have chosen in a "fair" selection process. "Fairness" means that the interests and freedoms of all participants are taken into consideration in agreeing on the rules governing social organization.

The corresponding means differ as well: participants do not content themselves with a guarantee of a minimal standard of subsistence but, rather, evaluate political and social institutions according to whether they offer everyone equal access to basic goods. On a global scale, this means that the practice of global justice could not settle for the exercise of a duty of assistance. Fundamental egalitarian international structures would have to be created as an extension of those structures that exist within individual just states.

2. Rawls: Non-egalitarianism on a global scale

Rawls's theory of justice reflects precisely the aforementioned tension between the two fundamental principles of distribution — the egalitarian and the non-egalitarian. It is well known that Rawls refuses to apply the egalitarian premises of a theory of distributive justice to international relations. International institutions are not designed to create distributive justice among peoples. It is not among the goals of the normative principles of international law that the enormous differences between the gross domestic products of rich and poor countries be leveled. Nor do these principles seek to correct the natural inequalities that endow some states with immense resources and deprive others of any. Moreover, they do not even envision any regulation of the distribution of wealth, such as would guarantee the poor an acceptable life. What drives Rawls to such diffidence?

To put it briefly, the upshot is that Rawls constructed his theory of international relations upon two premises: the first is to be found in the notion of the self-sufficiency of societies, the second in the idea that the principle of economic equality among societies is less cogent than the principle of equality among individuals. Individuals left to themselves are in a situation of defenselessness that simply does not apply to peoples or states. Individuals must cooperate with others in order to survive, whereas states are already organized such that they enjoy a certain minimal autonomy — that is their *raison d'être*. Hence the imperatives of justice which provide the basis of a just society cannot be applied in working out a comprehensive body of legislation to govern cooperation among and coexistence of societies. In the context of international relations, there can be application of the difference principle according to which any inequality in the distribution of cooperative goods must benefit everyone, especially the disadvantaged.

To summarize: according to Rawls, there are several reasons why it would not be sensible to assume the principle of just global distribution:

1) It would contradict the basic liberal principle of tolerance by assuming that "all persons must have the same civil rights in a constitutional democracy" (LP 82).
2) It would place an unnecessarily strong burden upon the preservation of relations among states: wealth is not indispensable for the creation of respectable political institutions.
3) In the long run, it would lead to relations of dependency. One of the primary tasks of justice is to help political communities to achieve autonomy at the international level.
4) It could produce unjust consequences by penalizing certain economic decisions. Countries that increase their wealth by industrialization or by significantly decreasing their expenditures would be punished by the re-distribution of wealth, whereas countries that undertake no financial exertions would benefit.
5) Finally — an objection that is not normative but empirical — the demands of justice are bound up with the reciprocity of the benefits individuals derive from mutual cooperation. Hence the obligation to justice ends where this cooperation is interrupted. Yet the world, according to Rawls, does not consist in a cooperative partnership akin to that characterizing the relations within states.

And so we see that John Rawls espouses in his theory of international relations a position that is not far removed from the notion of a minimal standard as envisioned by the non-egalitarian conception of justice. While just global distribution would remain persistently dependent upon the institutions responsible for distributing basic goods, the duty of assistance would be limited by a "cutoff point."[4]

Such a duty of assistance would however depart from the ideal of satisfying basic needs, since it establishes not a subsistence threshold but a political one. What disadvantaged societies need, in Rawls's view, is to be assisted at certain points in creating suitable political institutions and thereby joining the international community. Thus the principle of assistance is not intended to decrease the differences in gross domestic product between rich and poor countries by adjusting the level of affluence in disadvantaged societies. Paradoxically — and contrary to appearances — it would also stop short of assuring the citizens of the neediest societies the minimal income requisite to a life worthy of human beings. In fact, not all — but only well-ordered or "respectable" — societies would be suitable benefactors of

---

[4] Rawls 1999: 119. "The question to ask about it is whether the principle has a target and a cutoff point. The duty of assistance has both: it seeks to raise the world's poor until they are either free and equal citizens of a reasonably liberal society or members of a decent hierarchical society. That is its target. It also has by design a cutoff point, since for each burdened society the principle ceases to apply once the target is reached" (ibid.).

subsidies from the international community. To offer humanitarian
assistance to a society with a corrupt or despotic political regime would
amount to tacit support of injustice. Clearly, Rawls's position lags well
behind egalitarian as well as non-egalitarian ambitions. Satisfying
everyone's minimal basic needs simply has no place on the agenda of his
duty of assistance. This is regrettable, because his theory *thereby* abandons a
large number of needy individuals to their fates, and collectively punishes all
those who are undeservedly subjected to authoritarian regimes. Indeed, those
who also happen to live below the poverty line are doubly punished.

So it is not surprising that one encounters arguments at the level of
international relations that were originally applied within non-egalitarian
criticism to interpersonal relations "within individual states." They can be
summarized as follows:

- Equality has no intrinsically moral, but only derived value.
- Affluence is not a necessary condition for the realization of a just society.
  Inequality in the distribution of natural resources does not demand
  compensation.
- The egalitarian principle of redistribution is not applicable worldwide;
  such a broad application would not reflect the complexity of the content
  and extension of the concept "justice."
- The egalitarian principle of redistribution penalizes those (individuals or
  societies) whose wealth is the product of productivity and economic
  efficiency. Egalitarian principles frequently lead to wastefulness.

3. A minimal standard

For non-egalitarians, the satisfaction of a minimal standard does not
presuppose participation in any particular forms of cooperation. The demand
it imposes is universal in nature: it seeks to enable *everyone* to live under
conditions worthy of human beings.[5] Hence the basic principle of a
sufficient minimal standard could in fact lead to a global reallocation of
resources in the interests of the needy, as long as the reallocation increased
the total number of people attaining the minimal standard. But non-
egalitarians reject the notion of such a reallocation proceeding from the
intention to achieve an equal distribution of goods.

---

[5]   "When it is more important to help one person than another because the former is more in
need, then it is irrelevant whether they belong to the same society or are even aware of
each other. The greater urgency to support the one person is not dependent upon her
relationship to other people, but upon her absolutely worse standing" (Parfit, in: Krebs
2000: 97).

As non-egalitarians see it, the distribution of goods is unjust if not all people are in possession of sufficient goods. Inequality is for them not morally significant if it does not endanger anyone's supply of basic goods. It becomes relevant only when it manifests itself in the inadequacy of some people's provisions.

How ought we to delineate the level of subsistence? There are various contextual restrictions that need to be taken into consideration (cf. Nussbaum and Sen 1993). I cannot go into great detail here, but shall content myself with the following remarks:

- The idea of a minimal standard rests upon a substantialist and universalist conception of the necessary goods that make up what one calls quality of life. Despite the variety of social and cultural needs, this conception assumes a core of material and immaterial goods — the scope of which depends upon the specific conception — that are necessary for anyone to unfold her personality. This core may contain quite a long list of goods, as for example in the case of Martha Nussbaum, who espouses a "thick conception" of the good life as a basis for an intercultural ethical-political conception (Nussbaum 1990).
- The domain of the exercise of justice includes everyone, irrespective of nationality. With respect to the definition and preservation of standards, the citizens of every country are *normatively* considered equal. This absolute access is, however, de facto compatible with a certain relativism of empirical variables, which reflect the standard of living in a particular country.[6]
- The subsistence-oriented conception of just distribution is subsidiary: first and foremost, the individual states are obliged to guarantee their citizens minimal conditions of subsistence. Only when political and economic conditions do not enable every citizen to provide sufficiently for herself must external distributive agencies offer their help (Kersting 2002: 98).

One may raise the following critical objections:

- It may be objected that a weak conception of the good, which is limited to the necessary conditions for subsistence, is insufficient. What use is it to the poor to be supplied long-term with food from rich countries, if world markets are persistently closed to them and international regulations give priority to the rich?
- A second possible objection: a strong conception of the good may make far greater demands of political and social institutions than a liberal

---

[6] "Even under an absolutist approach, the poverty line will be a function of some variable, and there is no a priori reason why these variables might not change over time" (Sen 1984: 328-9). Cf. Nussbaum's (1990) distinction between plural and local specification.

egalitarian conception would (cf. Nussbaum 1990). Hence the question arises as to whether these demands can be met at the global level. What global agencies would be commissioned to fulfill these demands? To what extent could — or should — they intervene in the case of inadequate social and political institutions in individual countries? It may be that the Aristotelian approach — involving a strong theory of the good — can be defended against the objection of paternalism (Nussbaum 1990); but it will not be able to ignore the far-reaching consequences that strongly interventionist global politics have within the domestic sphere, should the chosen criteria be guaranteed.[7]

4. A principle of equality for global justice

Egalitarian theories are in agreement with the advocates of a substantialist theory of the good insofar as they regard the right to subsistence as more fundamental than civil and political rights, since it is often a basic precondition for the realization of these other rights (Shue 1996). Rawls, they argue, is wrong to think that corrupt or tyrannical political structures are the primary cause of the conflicts in the world and of the enormous inequality among countries (Rawls, LP 108). Corruption, repressive regimes, and bloody internal conflicts cannot be explained merely by referring to failed political structures. To claim that would be to ignore the significance of the mutual dependency of countries. Certain corrupt administrations are only able to remain in power because they are supported by other governments. Indeed, the poorer a country is, the more completely is it exposed to pressure from multinational corporations and other governments — and all the more susceptible to giving in (Pogge 1989, 2001b, 2002a). Guaranteeing every individual a minimal living standard is simply not enough if the goal is to secure an increase of global justice, even if such a guarantee would undoubtedly constitute an advance beyond the current situation. Rather, the basic structure of societies and communities of states must be reformed. Presently, global economic structures are shaped by agreements and contracts concerning trade, investments, environmental protection, the use of natural resources, etc. These agreements and contracts are negotiated for the most part by wealthy countries and serve their

---

[7]   Nussbaum admits this and observes that the Aristotelian approach cannot work "without a strong intervention from the political side" (Nussbaum 1990 German trans. 1999: 78). "Freedom of choice is thoroughly compatible with the kind of political reflection about the good and the kind of intrusion into laissez-faire politics that the Aristotelian approach involves — indeed, it requires both" (ibid.).

interests. Unequal distribution of wealth among countries leads to unequal distribution of power. The injustice is that the unequal distribution of natural resources among countries puts some countries in control of the manner in which the distributive regulations for goods and services at the level of international trade are administered. A principle of assistance is a necessary, but not a sufficient condition for the realization of global justice. As long as the procedural rules for global institutions — along with the significant consequences they have for the independence of the countries subject to them — do not *equally* reflect the interests of all countries affected by them, there can hardly be any chance for an improvement in the condition of poor countries.[8]

It must be emphasized that it is less a *result* than a *rule* of distribution that stands at the center of a theory of distributive justice. What counts is the effect of regulation upon the production and distribution of the goods that are to be distributed. In other words, the system of rules must itself be evaluated according to the opportunities it offers those who are subject to it — especially those who are the most disadvantaged.

Those who are familiar with the reception of the theory of global distributive justice in Germany will know that some authors have very harsh words to say against it and against Pogge's theory in particular. Even when the critique does not come from right-wing economic liberalism, it accuses the theory of being unrealistic and dangerous, and of leading to a totalitarian socialism. For Wolfgang Kersting, the main representative of this critique, global distributive justice is like a huge central bureaucracy that inevitably leads to the creation of a despotic world-state.

Kersting becomes so overwrought against the theory of global justice because he continues to interpret it as a redistribution of the "social pie" in equal parts, a distribution therefore that would cut off what the rich have in excess and give it to the poor (he speaks of the "administrative dispossession of the citizens" (2002: 62)), for the sake of an ideal of egalitarian material provision (Kersting 2002: 99f).

Kersting's caricature of the global theory of distributive justice — as a gigantic distributive apparatus, beholden to a cosmopolitan despotism which degrades the members of privileged economies to "productive slaves in a globally impersonal distributive arrangement" — is false (Kersting 1997b: 342). It assumes that the goal of a theory of global justice must be materialist

---

[8] "We must stop thinking about world poverty in terms of helping the poor. The poor do need help, of course. But they need help only because of the terrible injustices they are being subjected to. We should not, then, think of our individual donations and of possible institutionalized poverty eradication initiatives ... as helping the poor, but as protecting them from the effects of global rules whose injustice benefits us and is our responsibility" (Pogge 2002a: 23).

egalitarianism, whether in terms of the possession of goods or of well-being "in the sense of an egalitarian ideal of material endowment" (Kersting 2002: 99f). An equal distribution of goods need not be an end in itself. According to a different conception of distributive justice — like Thomas Pogge's — what "is to be evaluated [is] not a distribution, but a system of rules and institutions, i.e., an economic order" (Pogge 2002c: 221). The system of rules must be evaluated not only on the basis of data concerning the distribution it tends to bring forth, but also in view of the kind of causality "through which this system produces particular goods and burdens for its participants" (ibid.). This point of view deflects the evaluation from the product of distribution to the responsibility of agents for the *rules* of distribution. At this level, the principle of equality takes on an essential and indispensable function. The appropriate notion of equality in this context simply does not refer so much to the effects of distribution as to the establishment of institutional procedural principles. The conception of justice at issue here is essentially procedural.

Pogge unmistakably advocates this position. By putting the emphasis on institutional and individual responsibility for social injustices, however, he abandons the position of global egalitarianism which his earlier writings suggest as an alternative to the Rawlsian model of international relations. Hence Pogge's position winds up being less radical than the reexamined version of Rawlsian egalitarianism would be if applied consistently on a global scale. In his most recent articles, he even approaches certain anti-egalitarian theories of justice (e.g., that of Martha Nussbaum) when he makes the pragmatic choice in favor of a "thin conception of human flourishing," which presents the attainment of a "standard of living" as a criterion of justice ("Human Flourishing" in: 2002a: 36, 39, 48). In this last part, I will show that Pogge's position, though pragmatically strong, is not entirely compatible with the original theory that motivated his criticism of Rawls.[9]

Pogge shares with Rawls the conviction that the social position of the least advantaged should be the touchstone for assessing our basic institutions. He differs from Rawls, however, in that he argues in favor of a starting point that immediately addresses the world at large. In "An egalitarian law of peoples," he states the three egalitarian components of Rawls's conception of domestic justice and underlines his commitment to all three at the global level: "My own view still is that all three of the analogous egalitarian concerns are valid in a world characterized by the significant political and economic interdependencies that exist today and will in all

---

[9]   For a more thorough presentation of this line of criticism, see Merle's text in this volume.

likelihood persist into the indefinite future" (1994: 196). Thus the difference principle is one of the egalitarian principles that should be applied globally.

In his criticism of Rawls's conception of international justice, Pogge says: "the ground on which Rawls holds that fair equality of opportunity and the difference principle constitute requirements of background justice militate against confining these requirements within national borders." Indeed, "if excessive social and economic inequalities are unjust domestically, how can like inequalities arising internationally be a matter of moral indifference?" (1989: 250). The incoherence he denounces is an incoherence at the level of the moral imperative; to admit two diverging moral principles at the national and international levels means adopting a double morality. This double morality might not deserve condemnation if it could be shown that the unequal division of wealth had no impact on justice within societies. Yet this is not the case. In Pogge's words, "In a world with large international inequalities, the domestic institutions of the poorer societies are vulnerable to being corrupted by powerful political and economic interests abroad" (1994: 213).

Pogge must therefore maintain the validity of the difference principle as a demand of global justice. Theoretically, the difference principle holds insofar as there is an unequal distribution of wealth, even when the beneficiaries have attained a suitable level of development. This principle does not allow a "cutoff point." Granted, its application demands a great deal from richer countries. But, as Pogge retorts to a potential interlocutor, its absence would require much more from the most disadvantaged (1994: 213).

In his later writings, however, Pogge nuances his position. "Modesty is important if the proposed institutional alternative is to gain the support necessary to implement it and is to be able to sustain itself in the world as we know it" (2002a: 205). "When social institutions work so that each person affected by them has secure access ... to minimally adequate shares of all basic goods then they are, according to my proposed core criterion of basic justice, fully just." This minimal adequate share of all basic goods is to be understood as a "standard of living" (2002a: 38, 39). Although this standard is thinner than Martha Nussbaum's list of basic goods, it is close in the essentials: "Though disagreements about what human flourishing consists in may prove intractable, it may well be possible to bypass them by agreeing that nutrition, clothing, shelter, certain basic freedoms, as well as social interaction, education, and participation are important means to it, which just social institutions must secure for all" (2002a: 36, 51). In this version, global distributive justice seems to admit a target and a cutoff point that the first version rejected.

Therefore, an important question arises here: why must we be content, at the international level, with achieving a minimum standard? By subjecting the global economic order to weaker demands than any national economic order, does not Pogge apply the same double standard of moral assessment he accuses Rawls of applying? As he says critically of Rawls: "we owe the global poor an account of why we take ourselves to be entitled to impose on them a global economic order in violation of the minimal moral constraints we ourselves place on the imposition of any national economical order" (2002a: 109). What reason can we give to the least advantaged for choosing, on the domestic level, a principle of justice oriented to the poorest, even if the poorest people in our own country have a standard of living far higher than the minimum standard with which we expect the poorest of other countries to be content?

The question can be formulated in another way: does the requirement of a minimum standard at the international level suggest that we abandon the ideal theory and content ourselves with a non-ideal theory? Or does it indicate a change within the theory of global justice? In other words, does it mean that Pogge's "pragmaticism" renounces the *egalitarian* requirements of justice? In "An egalitarian law of peoples" Pogge denies this: choosing a minimal standard would signal a conviction that it is the most just solution among the feasible and morally accessible avenues of institutional change as we now can make it. But this pragmatic choice would not imply a denial that it would be morally preferable to apply the difference principle on the global plane or to adopt the global perspective right from the start (cf. Pogge 1989: 260). Even if, for practical reasons, Pogge contents himself with a minimal standard, he is not doing this because he rejects the principle of equality as a basic principle. Our current global institutional scheme is unjust and its injustice does not just mean that many persons today are very badly off, but also that they are disadvantaged by existing institutions.

If this is so, then by aiming to achieve a minimum standard at the international level and by admitting it as a cutoff point, we seem to have entered the domain of the non-ideal theory rather than to have modified the theoretical premises of the conception of global justice. Hence Pogge's strategy might be characterized in the following way: after having denounced Rawls's ungrounded double standard of morality and shown through his criticism how a global theory of justice should look, he takes a step backward and turns to those who are not even ready to admit Rawls's premises. Even then — it could be argued — we are compelled to admit the existence of global obligations of justice by: a) the universality of a minimal standard of fundamental rights; b) the historical responsibility of prosperous countries; and c) the economical interdependency among nations. In other words, Pogge's minimalism is a pragmatic concession meant to accommodate all those who are not ready to endorse the ideal of global liberalism. But if this is what Pogge has in mind, we would expect him to say so clearly — and this he does not do.

In the following, I will show that this pragmatic concession is in reality not compatible with Pogge's individual egalitarianism. Even as a provisional measure, it would come at the price of abandoning the moral premises at the foundation of the theory of justice.

Pogge defends an individualistic theory of global justice, which supports equality of opportunity worldwide. Yet he differs from the egalitarian position and from its consequences in that he does not derive the principle of redistribution from the egalitarian requirement but, rather, from the responsibility borne for unjust institutions. Radical inequality represents neither a sufficient nor a necessary condition for the derivation of a negative responsibility on the part of the more advantaged. For that, a causal responsibility between the poorest and the richest must be established, or it must be established that there exists a relation of structural dependence in which the richest profit at the expense of the poorest (cf. Pogge 2002a: 198ff).

Pogge's work surely goes beyond Rawls's theory of international relations, but it does not on this account adopt a global egalitarianism. Pogge emphasizes economic interdependence among nations and its importance for those nations placed outside the processes of elaborating international regulations. He denounces the vulnerability of the governments of poor countries within the power relations that falsify economic and political negotiations. On the other hand, he does not think that rich countries or materially advantaged people are by the mere fact of their advantages obligated to the poorest. The redistribution imperative, in other words, is not driven by the egalitarian demand but rather by an imperative of corrective justice: it is not because certain countries are miserable that rich countries have a moral obligation to help them. If they have an obligation, it is because they bear a responsibility for this misery, whether for its appearance or for its maintenance. "We are asked to be concerned about human-rights violations not simply insofar as they exist at all, but only insofar as they are produced by social institutions in which we are significant participants" (1992: 93). This responsibility may be linked to violations created in the past; it may also be tied to the establishment and maintenance of a world economic order that privileges developed countries.

In this, Pogge's position might ground the duty of justice more convincingly than does either moral utilitarianism or global egalitarianism. Indeed, why should it be the duty of those who find themselves in materially privileged circumstances to lessen the suffering of others, even of those with whom they have no particular tie? By showing that we profit from a historically unjust situation and that we contribute to perpetuating an unjustifiable inequality in the way people are treated, one points exactly to the reasons that give birth to a moral duty of justice. This position, however, unquestionably retreats from the three egalitarian principles which Pogge still considers valid at the global level. The question we should raise at this point is whether this position is compatible with Pogge's global moral individualism. Indeed, in view of the requirements of global justice, we not only need an account of when agreements are free (which is the requirement of procedural justice) but also of when the social circumstances under which they are reached are fair. Now, these circumstances can only be fair if the rich are unable to use their greater bargaining power to capture a greater share of the social product than they would if the egalitarian requirement were applied right from the beginning. By interpreting the injustice of the social system as being a result of prior wrongdoing and not of an unequal distribution, the possibility is left open that inequality resulting from wrong choices made by individuals or institutions — in the absence of any wrongdoing — might remain uncompensated. And yet Pogge criticizes Rawls precisely for introducing a morally unjustified structural disanalogy between the domestic and the international level. Indeed, only at the domestic level does Rawls accept the difference principle, which would allow persons to be penalized for their parents' wrong economic decisions solely if their social position would still be better than under all economic alternatives. In the case of societies, however, Rawls expects their members to bear the entire responsibility for the economic and social decisions made by former members of the government. This discrepancy contradicts Rawls's individualistic convictions in matters of social justice, all the more that the contingency of nationality makes it problematic to hold individuals responsible for decisions made by their government, all the more so for those made by a previous one.

The principle of assistance should assure that a society not fall *below the level of a minimal standard* through punishment for previous bad economic choices or because of unfavorable natural circumstances. As we have already mentioned, however, the principle of assistance is not intended to decrease the differences in gross domestic product among states. Moreover, it is limited by a cutoff point, which may be reached when the minimal standard is fulfilled. The principle of assistance, in other words, is a principle of corrective justice, which applies until a fixed limit is reached and as a result of particular causal circumstances. The principle of distributive justice, on the other hand, should apply constantly and independently of the cause of inequality. The structural disanalogy, therefore, not only implies different requirements in the exercise of justice, but in fact reflects double standards of morality.

In conclusion, it is clear that Pogge's cosmopolitanism is no "expansive statism of a leviathan-like dimension" (Kersting 2002: 62); it does not lead to an "administrative dispossession of the citizens" (ibid.) for the sake of "an ideal of egalitarian material provision." Indeed, according to Pogge's causal theory of justice, what is unjust is not so much the unequal distribution of natural resources as the fact that this inequality actually results from acts of violence which the international institutions endorse by giving themselves an institutional legitimization that allows them to resist reforms. A more fair distribution of natural resources is not an aim in itself derived from an egalitarian premise, but a possible means of compensating for injustice and of partially repairing its damages (cf. Pogge 1992). On the other hand, the equality toward which the theory of justice should strive is not related to redistributive effects, but to the elaboration of institutional rules. We are essentially concerned with a procedural conception of justice. In this sense, the principle of equality requires not only more than the achievement of minimal standards, but above all, it demands the realization of justice for other reasons. If global institutions are unjust, this is not only because a significant number of people live below the poverty line and have no real hope of ever living in better conditions. If these institutions are unjust, it is because the norms with which they operate (laws and the powers they grant as well as the burdens they give) impose globally an order that perpetuates poverty in a great part of the world population that is subjected to this order without any means of resisting it.

I agree with Pogge's diagnosis of the injustice prevalent at the international level, and am convinced the duty of realizing justice lies primarily with those who are responsible for the injustice from which they profit. Pogge's position is a strong and convincing one because it puts its finger precisely on the source of the immense inequality at the global level and on the structural reasons for the growth of this inequality. My doubts concern the compatibility of this position with the content of his critique of Rawls. The question Pogge addresses to Rawls remains: how can we justify to the global poor our holding the difference principle as just on the national level, while abandoning it for pragmatic reasons on the global level?

Chapter 12

Responsibility and International Distributive Justice[*]

Alexander Cappelen
Economics, University of Oslo

1. Introduction

A natural focus of the debate on international justice has been the inequalities between the rich and the very poor, and often totalitarian, countries. However, important questions of distributive justice also arise among relatively affluent countries with well functioning democracies. This is typically the case within unions or associations of countries such as the EU and NAFTA. Considerations of distributive justice are also important in the design of bilateral or multilateral agreements with distributional consequences, such as tax treaties, trade rules and environmental regulations. In this paper I shall explore the implications of a liberal egalitarian, or luck egalitarian, approach to the distribution of resources in such situations. I will focus on the question of when it can be justified, not only for incentive reasons, to deviate from a strict egalitarian distribution in an international context. In particular, I shall discuss how a liberal egalitarian theory of international justice can take account of national autonomy and the extent to which national autonomy might justify some international inequalities. The fundamental question addressed is, in other words, to what extent, and under what conditions, we should hold nations responsible for the inequalities that result from factors under their control?

The distinction between inequalities that are a result of factors under the control of an agent and inequalities that are outside her control is pivotal in

[*] I would like to thank Cornelius Cappelen, Andreas Follesdal, Thomas Pogge and Bertil Tungodden for valuable comments on the paper. The usual disclaimer applies.

A. Follesdal and T. Pogge, (eds.), Real World Justice, 215-228.
© 2005 Springer. Printed in the Netherlands.

liberal egalitarian theories of distributive justice. Such theories seek to combine the values of equality, personal freedom and personal responsibility. The contemporary focus on this relationship can be traced back to the seminal work of Rawls (1971). The ideas of Rawls have been developed further, notably by Dworkin (1981), Arneson (1989), Cohen (1989), Le Grand (1991), Roemer (1993, 1996, 1998), and Fleurbaey (1995 a,b), where the main achievement has been to include considerations of personal responsibility in egalitarian reasoning. Liberal egalitarian ethics can be seen as consisting of two parts. The first part is the egalitarian principle that the effect of differences in factors outside the agents' control should be eliminated. We can name this the *principle of equalization*. In the context of income distribution this principle implies that all individuals making the same choices, or exercising the same effort, should have the same income independent of their circumstances (see Bossert (1995) and Bossert and Fleurbaey (1996)). The second part is the liberal principle that agents should be held responsible for factors under their control. We can name this the *principle of responsibility* and it tells us that there might be justifiable inequalities if these inequalities reflect differences in choice or effort. It is important at the outset to point out that the principle of responsibility does *not* imply that individuals should be held responsible for the actual consequences of their choice. The actual consequences of choice will typically depend on a person's circumstances. To hold a person responsible for the actual consequences of choice would therefore violate the principle of equalization. I shall return later to the question of what it means to hold agents responsible for their choices if it does not mean that they should face the actual consequences of their choices.

An appealing feature of the liberal egalitarian view, compared with the standard strict (or outcome) egalitarianism, is that it is able to take account of strong intuitions about individual responsibility. Strict egalitarianism does not allow any inequality among agents, and hence is not at all sensitive to differences in choices. It can be criticized on two accounts. First, it is inefficient; second, it is unfair. The former criticism is well known and has been a major concern in the design of redistribution mechanism such as progressive tax systems. But incentive considerations are not the only reason why liberal egalitarians object to strict egalitarianism. Liberal egalitarians also find it fair that agents are held responsible for their choices even if doing so does not have any effect on individual behavior. It would, for example, be fair to reward a person who works long hours with a higher income even if the labor supply was inelastic.

This paper analyzes what implications the liberal egalitarian view has for international distributive justice and asks how the principle of responsibility and the principle of equalization should be applied when the agents are nations rather than individuals. I shall argue that this approach allows us to combine the ideal of national autonomy with an ideal of international equalization. I shall furthermore argue that the liberal egalitarian approach to international distributive justice provides a way to justify an asymmetry between domestic and international justice without arguing that we have different and more extensive obligations towards compatriots.

In the context of income distribution, liberal egalitarianism raises two fundamental questions. First, where do we draw the "cut" between those factors that are under the agents' control and those factors that are outside the agents' control? The second questions concern how it is possible to reward choice or effort without simultaneously rewarding factors outside the control of individuals. These two questions also arise in the context of international distribution. First, we need to ask what factors should be considered to be under the control of each nation. Secondly, we must address the question of how differences in factors considered to be under the nation's control should affect the international resource distribution. An additional question arises when liberal egalitarianism is applied to the issue of international distributive justice: what are the conditions under which it is acceptable to hold individuals accountable for the decisions made by their governments? I shall discuss these three questions in the following, but I start out by presenting a first approximation to a liberal egalitarian theory of international distributive justice.

2. A liberal egalitarian approach to international distribution

Let us start by assuming that we can hold all individuals in a democratic country responsible for decisions made by national institutions. What do the principles of equalization and responsibility then imply for international distribution? To answer this question, let us start by noting that factors that are beyond the control of each individual in a group often are within the control of the group as a whole through collective decision-making. All individuals are members of many groups, but nation-states stand in a special position because they are the locus of collective decisions that have all-encompassing effects on the opportunities of their members. The opportunities an individual has to pursue his idea of the good life will, to a large extent, be determined by decisions made by institutions under democratic control at the national level. Even individual preferences and social norms will typically be affected by collective actions in the long run. To illustrate this point, consider a person who wants to improve her economic situation. Individually she can do this in several different ways: she can work longer hours, she can try to develop new skills and find a new job, or she can save her earnings. In making the decision about what to do, she would take important parameters, such as her hourly wage, the education system, available job opportunities and the return to capital as given because these factors are outside her control as an individual. However, she could also pursue her goal through the political system. She could participate in the political system so as to influence public policies, such as the tax system, the education system, trade policy, etc., that would promote her goal. By participating in democratic processes she is able to affect, at least in principle, factors that were outside her control when she acted on her own. I shall refer to these factors simply as national choices. However, there are also factors that are outside the control of the country. A country can, for example, do nothing about the international distribution of natural resources or its location relative to important markets. Most countries also have little influence over the basic structure of international cooperation and economic interaction. I shall name these factors that are outside the control of each country as national circumstances.

Different countries often face different national circumstances and thus have different opportunities to pursue their goals. Due to such differences, countries that pursue the same policies and make the same collective effort, e.g., in terms of forgone consumption or leisure, will not necessarily get the same outcome in terms of GDP per capita, economic growth or supply of public services. Applied to an international context, the principle of equalization then implies that international differences stemming from national circumstances should be eliminated. International justice requires, in other words, that the opportunities different countries have to pursue their goals are equalized. Two countries that make equal effort in the pursuit of the same national goals should achieve the same national outcomes. It is, for example, obviously unjust that resource-rich countries, such as Norway and Saudi Arabia, are allowed to keep all the revenues from the resources extracted within their territory. These countries can achieve their goals, for example, a certain quality of public education or a low tax level, without the same sacrifices as less resource-rich countries. This inequality therefore calls for international transfers between those countries that have favorable national circumstances and those countries that have less favorable circumstances.

However, liberal egalitarian reasoning can also justify international inequalities if they appropriately reflect differences in national policies and decisions. According to the principle of responsibility, we should hold agents responsible for those factors that are under their control. If we assume that we can hold individuals within a country responsible for democratic decisions, this implies that these individuals also should be held responsible for factors under national control. International inequalities in GDP per capita or in the public services level can thus be justifiable if these inequalities reflect differences in national priorities rather than national circumstances. To illustrate, consider two affluent democracies that initially face the same national circumstances. One of the countries decides to forgo consumption in order to invest a considerable part of its total production in research and development and human resources. As a result, the GDP in this country will over time be higher than in the other country. However, this inequality does not call for international redistribution. If countries are to be held responsible for their choices, there should be no redistribution among countries that are identical with respect to their national circumstances, even if these countries are unequal with respect to per capita production.

The aggregate effect of individual preferences, to the extent that they are outside the control of the nation, can constitute an important part of national circumstances. Systematic differences in preferences and the aggregate effects of individual behavior play an important role in determining the income opportunities in a country. We know, for example, that there are systematic differences in savings behavior in different countries and that these differences cannot be reduced to differences in national policy. Assume that the international differences in savings behavior are caused by systematic international differences in individual time preferences. Individuals in some countries have on average a lower discount rate than individuals in other states. Assume further that a high level of saving has positive external effects on the income opportunities of people living in the same country. Systematic differences in preferences can, in other words, create differences in individual opportunities across countries even if both national policies and national circumstances are identical. If our ultimate goal is to equalize individual opportunities, this inequality calls for international redistribution so as to equalize the income opportunities.

It is, however, important to note that the goal of such redistribution should only be to eliminate the effect of differences in income opportunities, not to eliminate any income inequality among the countries. Even if individuals in both countries face the same opportunities, they might choose to use these opportunities differently if there are systematic differences in individual preferences in the two populations. Consider a situation in which the population in one country places more weight on family life and leisure than the population in another country. As a result of these preferences, the average working time and the labor market participation rate is lower in the first country, but this has no external effect on the income opportunities in the economy. This will, in turn, result in differences in per capita income in the two countries. However, these inequalities simply reflect differences in individual preferences. If we accept that people should be rewarded for their effort in a national context, there should be no reason to eliminate differences in aggregate effects of such inequalities at the international level.

Applied to international distribution, liberal egalitarianism thus implies that international inequalities that are a result only of national policies should be accepted while inequalities that are a result only of national circumstances should be eliminated. However, this simplified presentation makes three important assumptions, each calling for further elaboration. First, we have assumed that national policies appropriately reflect individual preferences and that citizens legitimately can be held responsible for national policies. Second, we have assumed that it is possible to identify those factors that are under a country's control and those that are outside a country's control. Finally, we have assumed that inequalities either can be traced back to differences in national circumstances or to differences in national choices. All three assumptions are problematic and will be discussed below.

3. Should individuals be held responsible for national policies?

It is not possible to hold a country responsible for its decision without holding the individuals living in that country responsible at the same time. The net transfers a country receives will affect all individuals in the country, either through higher tax payments or a lower public service level. It is therefore necessary to address the question of whether or not it can be justified to hold individuals in a country responsible for the policies made by their government. Clearly, there are situations where it would be unreasonable to do so. An illiterate farmer in a totalitarian regime can hardly be said to be responsible for national policy in his or her country. Incentive considerations might demand that even transfers to such regimes should be made conditional on its policies. In particular, it might be necessary to design international transfers so as to promote certain institutional or policy changes. However, the justification for this type of conditionality cannot be to hold individuals in the country responsible for the decisions made by their government.

In order to hold individuals in a country responsible for national policy decisions, they should be able to influence these decisions through democratic procedures and should have the education necessary to make use of their democratic rights and to know the likely outcome of different policy alternatives. The existence of a well-functioning democracy and a minimum level of education are therefore conditions that have to be satisfied if we are to hold individuals responsible for national policies. However, it could be argued that it is problematic to hold individuals responsible even in situations where these conditions are satisfied. One objection is what we could name the *humanitarian objection*. According to this objection, we cannot allow people in a country to starve even if their poverty is a result of democratic decisions, e.g., the result of some failed economic experiment. In order to answer this objection it is useful to observe that extreme poverty typically is the result of bad decisions made under bad circumstances. It is almost inconceivable that extreme poverty should result from well-informed democratic decisions in a situation where national opportunities were equalized internationally. If poverty in a country partly is a result of unfavorable circumstances, it does not necessarily follow from the liberal egalitarian perspective that we have no duty to help. In section 5 I return to the question of what it means to hold agents responsible for their decisions in such situations.

Another objection is what we could call the *minority objection*. Well-functioning democracies with informed voters are typically characterized by pluralism. There will always be a minority that disagrees with — or dissents from — the national policy. Holding a country responsible for its policies will therefore necessarily involve holding individuals who disagree with these policies responsible as well. If people were perfectly mobile across countries, one could still argue that all citizens tacitly accept the national policies by remaining in the country. However, it is as a rule not possible for individuals to move freely across international borders. This is, in particular, true for the least advantaged citizens of poor countries who also lack the financial resources to establish themselves in a foreign country. We can therefore not view citizenship as a voluntary commitment.

An important instance of the minority problem concerns the extent to which international transfer systems should try to eliminate the effect of past decisions. The most important determinant of a country's GDP per capita is not the policy decision made this year, or even the last few years. It is a result of national decisions made in the past, partly by individuals who no longer live in the country. It is therefore important to determine to what extent a country should be held responsible for decisions made in the past. To illustrate this problem, consider the role of expenditures on R&D and human resources. The aggregate level of such expenditures will depend on both public policy and on individual preferences. It will depend on investment opportunities, demography, the saving culture, etc. It also depends on factors such as political stability, tax incentives, and so on. Clearly, historical differences in expenditures on R&D and human resources among countries will generate differences in wealth and national income. Should this type of inequality be accepted or should an international transfer system aim to eliminate inequalities that arise from past decisions of this kind? The argument for eliminating such inequalities is that a great number of people living in the country today have had no influence over these decisions. To hold young people in states that historically have had a low level of expenditures on R&D and human resources accountable for the decisions made by their ancestors seems to violate the principle that we should eliminate inequalities that arise from factors that are outside their control. However, if this argument is drawn to its extreme, we cannot hold countries accountable at all because new citizens are born every day.

If we are to hold a pluralistic democracy responsible for its decisions, we have to accept that some individuals are held responsible for decisions they did not take part in. It is important to point out that the problem of dissenting minorities is an inherent problem of any democratic procedure in the absence of unanimity. To the extent that nations are given some autonomy, we cannot avoid such decisions having an effect on national minorities. Furthermore, if we use the transfer system to insulate the present generation from the effects of decisions made by their predecessors, we effectively eliminate the opportunity people have to better the economic condition of their descendants through the use of national institutions. There is no easy solution to this dilemma. Given the second-best nature of international redistributive policies, we will either have to transfer too much to certain groups in the country or too little to another group. Decisions about how far back in history we can hold a country responsible will have to be a trade-off between these two considerations.

4. Drawing the cut between circumstances and choices

An inherent difficulty faced by liberal egalitarian theories of distributive justice is to determine what factors are under the agents' control and what factors are outside their control. The answer to this question determines to a large extent what implications the liberal egalitarian theory has for income distribution. If we believe that those factors that determine an agent's income mostly are outside the control of the agent, then liberal egalitarianism implies that income should be equalized to a large extent in the absence of incentive considerations. If, however, we believe that inequalities to a large extent can be explained by differences in factors under the agent's control, then a liberal egalitarian theory could justify large inequalities in income. It is, therefore, not surprising that the political parties on the right traditionally focus on the importance of individual effort when they explain economic inequalities, while parties on the political left typically explain such inequalities in terms of social and economic circumstances outside the individual's control. The question of where we should draw the cut between factors outside the agent's control and those under the agent's control is therefore important for any interesting specification of the liberal egalitarian approach.

Above I argued that the "cut" between circumstances and choice should be drawn differently in the context of domestic justice than in the context of international justice. In the context of international justice, drawing the cut amounts to clarifying to what extent the factors that affect a country's economic growth and affluence are under the control of national institutions. Different liberal egalitarian theories of distributive justice can be interpreted as giving different answers to this question. One way to illustrate the importance of this question is to consider the different liberal egalitarian theories of international justice presented by John Rawls and Thomas Pogge. One important difference between these authors is that they draw the cut between factors outside and factors under national control differently.

John Rawls's liberal egalitarian theory of distributive justice, as it was presented in *A Theory of Justice* (1971), was explicitly developed to address questions of national redistribution. It was first in his essay "The law of peoples" (1993b), and later in the book of the same name (*The Law of Peoples* (1999)) that Rawls applied his framework to the question of international justice. There is an interesting asymmetry between Rawls's theory of domestic distributive justice and his theory of international justice. Rawls argues that an individual's pre-tax income is morally arbitrary insofar as it is determined by factors outside individual control. He therefore concludes that domestic inequalities in lifetime income and wealth among social groups suitably defined should be eliminated. Deviations from strict equality can only be justified by appeal to incentive considerations (the difference principle). According to Rawls, rich Western societies have a duty to assist so-called "burdened societies" in their development to be just and well organized. There is, however, no international equivalent to the difference principle and a broader range of international inequalities in income is seen as morally acceptable.

This feature of Rawls's theory of justice can be seen as a result of where he draws the line between national circumstance and national choice, and the extent to which he believes international inequalities are a result of factors within national control. Rawls suggests that international inequalities primarily are a result of differences in national policies and political culture, as well as the preferences or character of the individuals in each country. To eliminate international inequalities due to such factors would not be justifiable, according to Rawls, since it would unfairly burden societies that have been responsible in their economic affairs and benefit those that have not. Rawls's argument for this position mainly consists of stylized examples, designed to show us why international redistribution is unfair. The first example is a good illustration of how Rawls reasons. He introduces two well-ordered societies, liberal or decent, initially endowed with the same amount of capital and of similar size. However, different collective decisions make for unequal distribution of wealth between the two countries in a second period. The first society decides to industrialize and to increase the rate of savings; the other society does neither, valuing perhaps consumption today higher than consumption tomorrow. Some decades later, the first society is twice as wealthy as the second. Given that both societies in this stylized example are liberal or decent, and thus capable of making their own decisions, it is unfair to burden the first society with a redistributive and global tax.

Like Rawls, Thomas Pogge (1989, 1994, 2002a) can be interpreted as having a liberal egalitarian approach to international distributive justice. However, he draws quite different conclusions with respect to the legitimacy of international inequality. One important source of this difference between Rawls and Pogge is to be found in a disagreement about where to draw the line between national circumstances and national choice. Pogge argues that domestic societies are only partly responsible for their affluence. While Rawls seems to believe domestic institutions are the only determinant, Pogge has emphasized the importance of external factors beyond national control, such as natural resource endowments and position in the international economy.

Pogge does not reject the importance of culture or other national factors in explaining international differences. He argues, however, that the distinction between factors that are outside and factors that are under national control is difficult to draw in an integrated world economy. The global economic order plays a substantial causal role in shaping how the culture of each poor country evolves and by "influencing how a poor country's history, culture and natural environment affect the development of its domestic institutional order, ruling elite, economic growth, and income distribution" (Pogge, 2002a: 46). Global institutional factors therefore contribute substantially to the persistence of severe poverty.

In the following I shall assume that national policies and democratic decisions have a substantial impact on economic growth and national productivity, but also that Pogge is correct in his assertion that the effect of national factors partly depends on factors outside the control of each nation. Given this assumption, the fundamental question for a liberal egalitarian theory becomes what it means to hold countries responsible for their democratic decisions when the consequences of these decisions partly is a result of factors outside their control.

5. What does it mean to hold nations responsible?

The fundamental challenge for any system of international transfers is to give all countries equal opportunities and at the same time hold them responsible for their decisions. How can we design an international transfer scheme that satisfies the principle of equalization and the principle of responsibility at the same time? Even if we agree on how to make a distinction between circumstances and choice, there is no straightforward answer to this question (see Bossert (1995), Fleurbaey (1994, 1995b, 1995c), Bossert and Fleurbaey (1996), Cappelen and Tungodden (2002b, 2003)). The reason is that it is not always possible to separate the consequences of choice and the consequences of circumstances.

If we had full separability between the consequences of choice and the consequences of circumstances, i.e., if the consequences of the one factor did not depend on the other, then the natural solution in the liberal egalitarian approach would be to reward choice with its actual consequences. If, for example, individuals freely could choose their work effort and if an increase in work effort gave the same marginal increase in pre-tax income for all individuals independent of factors they could not control, such as social background or IQ, then the principle of responsibility would tell us that work effort should be rewarded with its marginal return. However, full separability is the exception. Typically, the marginal return on a person's effort depends on a wide range of circumstances outside her control. This is certainly also the case when the agent is a nation and not an individual. The consequences of changes in national policy, such as a tax increase, investments in research and development, or a reform of the education system, depend on a wide range of factors that are outside the control of each nation and that differ among them. It is therefore not possible to separate the effect of national choice and national circumstances.

When full separability does not hold, the two liberal egalitarian principles do not imply that effort should be rewarded with its marginal return. It would, for example, be unjust to reward effort in the labor market with marginal productivity, because a person's productivity for a given effort to a large extent is outside that person's control. According to the ethics of responsibility, an agent should be held responsible for his or her effort, but not for being a person under specific circumstances making a particular effort. It is not obvious what it means to hold a country responsible for its national choices if it does not mean to hold it responsible for the actual consequences of their choice.

The principle of equalization implies that people should be treated as if they were identical with respect to factors outside their control (Cappelen and Tungodden 2002b and 2003). In the context of international distributive justice, this implies that all countries should be treated as if they were identical with respect to their national circumstances. We need, in other words, to establish a "reference circumstance" and treat all countries *as if* they had these circumstances. To illustrate, consider a situation in which the size of the tax base and the price level in each country are outside national control, while the tax rate can be set at the discretion of each country. The principle of equalization then implies that two countries that make the same tax effort, i.e., set the same tax rates, should be able to provide the same level of public goods. The international transfer scheme should, in other words, aim to equalize the fiscal capacity of each country. In order to do so, one would need to decide on a reference or standard fiscal capacity and then transfer resources among countries so as to ensure that all countries are able to provide the public goods they would have been able to provide if they had this reference fiscal capacity. The choice of reference fiscal capacity obviously affects the distribution of revenues among jurisdictions with different tax levels. The difference in public goods supply in two countries with different tax rates will be equal to the difference in public goods supply these countries would have had in the absence of international transfers if both countries had the reference fiscal capacity. An important question for any international transfer scheme is, therefore, how to determine the reference fiscal capacity.

More generally, the choice of reference circumstances will determine how distribution of resources will be related to national effort. It is possible to defend specific choices of reference circumstances (Bossert and Fleurbaey 1996 and Cappelen and Tungodden 2002b and 2003). One way to approach this question is to place restrictions on the type of effects that we allow changes in policies in one country to have on other countries (Cappelen and Tungodden 2002b and 2003). However, I shall not defend any specific reference circumstances in this paper.

Several implications for a system of international transfers are important to note. First, a liberal egalitarian transfer scheme would have to be conditional in the sense that the net transfers a country receives would depend on the democratic decisions made and the policies the country implemented. A liberal egalitarian transfer system would therefore not be similar to a so-called foundation grant system, well known from the literature on fiscal equalization at the local and municipal level. Under a foundation grant system, the transfers given to each jurisdiction are determined by certain features of their circumstance (e.g., each jurisdiction receives transfers so as to be able to finance a standard level of public services with a standard tax rate), and their choice of policy does not affect the transfer level. A foundation grant system can only ensure equal opportunity at one effort level (Cappelen and Tungodden 2002a) and will thus violate the requirement that national opportunities should be equalized. Equal opportunities can only be achieved with a system of transfers that are conditional on the policies chosen by each government.

A second, related feature is that the transfer system must be open-ended and that the total level of transfers will depend on the decisions made by different countries. This might seem like an undesirable feature of international distribution because it implies that other countries might be adversely affected when one country changes its policies. However, it is easy to show that this is a necessary feature of any transfer system if it is to satisfy the principle of equalization in a situation without additive separability (see Bossert and Fleurbaey (1996) for a proof). If we accept that equalization implies that some agents sometimes are rewarded with more or less than the actual consequences of their decisions, we must accept that other countries are affected when they change their policies.

Finally, there is an important link between the degree of national autonomy and the level of redistribution. A world order in which countries have a large degree of autonomy would also be a world in which more factors were under national control. Since the aim of the redistributive system is to compensate for differences in factors outside the control of nations, this would obviously affect the degree of redistribution. Furthermore, we would expect that more autonomy would be accompanied by less redistribution. Such considerations would clearly be important in a discussion about the appropriate degree of national autonomy (for a discussion of this issue, see Follesdal 2001).

To the extent that this is correct it could also justify an asymmetry in redistribution at the international and the local level. Other things equal, we should redistribute more among lower level jurisdictions within a country than among countries. The reason for this is that countries generally have more autonomy than lower level jurisdictions. Important features affecting individual opportunities are outside the control of a local jurisdiction, but under the control of a country. Important examples are monetary policy, national infrastructure and trade policy. A country thus has more control over its own destiny than a local jurisdiction within a country would have. This could justify some asymmetry between intranational and international redistributive policy.

6. Conclusion

The main aim of this paper has been to argue that it might be justifiable to hold individuals responsible for national policy and that this might create an asymmetry between domestic and international distributive justice.

However, as emphasized above, a claim that certain types of international inequalities might be justifiable does not amount to a claim that *any* inequality can be justifiable. The most important inequalities in the world today can only to a very limited extent be attributed to differences in national preferences. Furthermore, the poorest countries in the world typically do not satisfy the minimal conditions required to hold individuals in a country responsible for national polices.

An important conclusion in this paper is that the correct way to hold a country responsible for its policies is not to hold it responsible for the actual consequences of its policies. The focus on national responsibility does therefore not imply that we should hold these countries responsible for their own poverty, even if it could have been avoided by different national polices. The appropriate transfer level will depend both on a country's policies and on its circumstances.

The aim of the analysis has been to discuss the possibility of establishing an independent fairness argument for holding countries responsible for their policy choices. For this purpose, it has been useful to ignore incentive considerations. Clearly, incentive considerations can provide powerful arguments for making transfers conditional on behavior. It will sometimes be necessary to deviate from an egalitarian distribution in order to promote certain policies or induce certain types of behavior. However, the argument presented in this paper has not relied on such forward-looking consequentialist reasoning.

Chapter 13

From Natural Law to Human Rights — Some Reflections on Thomas Pogge and Global Justice

Henrik Syse
Ethics Programme at the University of Oslo, and International Peace Research Institute, Oslo

My purpose in this article may seem overly theoretical, bearing in mind the practical purposes and concrete subject matter of the current book. Yet, in helping to clarify the conceptual basis of what I dare to call our common endeavor — to address global injustices and to increase the motivation to find meaningful measures to correct those injustices — I also hope to make us better equipped to pursue that endeavor. I take this also to be a central part of Thomas Pogge's work on human rights and world poverty, which I take as my point of departure.

The main forerunner of modern theories of global ethics and international justice in the Western philosophical tradition is undoubtedly the natural-law tradition. The idea itself, that there exists a morality higher than that of positive law or custom, is probably more ancient than the oldest written records we have of humankind. But as an organized and identifiable teaching within our culture it was developed by early Latin thinkers in the period from the Middle Stoa and Cicero to the early Christian philosophers Ambrose and Augustine (admittedly inspired by the earlier Greek philosophies of the pre-Socratics, Sophists, and not least Plato and Aristotle). This early natural-law theorizing teaching centered around the idea of a *ius naturale*, i.e., a system of right which is natural and as such common to all people, available to humankind as a measuring stick of right and wrong.

While this teaching's original intention was surely not egalitarian — it had little to do with social justice at all, but was rather conceived of in anti-relativistic terms — it has always carried a critical potential against unjust aspects of existing social orders. One of the first to explore this explicitly was the Sophist Antiphon in the 5th century BC, who reflected on the distinction between human conventions, such as slavery and discrimination

A. Follesdal and T. Pogge, (eds.), Real World Justice, 229-237.

of foreigners, on the one hand and the order of nature on the other.[1] While most Sophists — including Antiphon — used this distinction between *physis* and *nomos* to defend more or less relativistic or egoistic teachings, it was among the Sophists that such ideas were (even if only on occasion) used to promote what we would call social justice, such as criticism of slavery. We also know the idea of natural law from a source that predates Plato's teaching on the forms or ideas, namely, Sophocles's *Antigone*, where certain laws of this world are denounced as wrong because they conflict with what is right according to a higher, divine law.

The Stoics and the early Christians developed the concept of natural law[2] and made it more *universal* than it had been among the Greeks, encompassing not just one gender within one social sphere within one linguistic community, but ideally including the whole of humankind in a transcendent community. This was a natural result of the widening of the world which occurred in the shift from the Greek city-state to what became the Roman Empire, and it was certainly also inspired by the radical emphasis on the equality of all in the face of God formulated by Christianity. The contrast between Plato and Aristotle on the one hand and the Stoics, Cicero, and the early Christians on the other must not be exaggerated on the political plane, however, since they all thought in terms of a "higher law" and a pre-conceived social order that humans can do relatively little to change in this world. According to this line of thought, socially embedded inequalities are part of the social order which humans should naturally accept, without thereby losing their dignity or worth.

I will not go into further details on these origins and developments of natural law, as I have tried to do so elsewhere (Syse 2002; 2005). It is rather to Thomas Pogge's elaboration of the idea of natural law that I will now turn.

---

[1] See Striker 1996: 211f, who stresses that Antiphon's teaching was not primarily meant to instigate progressive social change. Rather, he most probably meant to stress the relative character of law, and the freedom of each individual to discard its letter for the sake of self-interest. Nonetheless, the teaching that nature can overrule law is obviously conducive to being used for radical social causes. See also Waterfield 2000 for a number of fragments from Antiphon and other Sophists.

[2] We could here just as well say "natural right" as "natural law," since many writers (such as St. Augustine) employed the term *ius naturale* to cover what we mean by natural law — indeed, the two concepts can be used more or less interchangeably in the pre-modern context. However, we must make sure that we do not confuse this sense of "natural right" (which is normally expressed in the singular) with "natural rights" (in the plural).

1. Natural law and natural rights in Thomas Pogge

In his article "How Should Human Rights Be Conceived?,"[3] Thomas Pogge sketches a development from natural law, via natural rights, to human rights, claiming that this is the route along which the moral (as distinguished from the strictly legal) notion of human rights has evolved. This is certainly a plausible claim, since several important thinkers and schools in Western political philosophy indeed formulated the concept of rights — and later of natural rights and human rights — within the framework of natural-law theory.[4]

Pogge describes the plan for his discussion of these concepts as follows:

> The moral notion of human rights has evolved from earlier notions of natural law and natural rights. We can begin to understand and analyze it by examining the continuities and discontinuities of this evolution. I do this by focusing on the shifting constraints imposed, ideas suggested, and possibilities opened and closed by the three concepts rather than on the particular conceptions of them that have actually been worked out (Pogge 2002a: 54).

The following comments aim to explicate and complement Pogge's portrayal of the relationship between these concepts.

Pogge holds that all three concepts — natural law, natural rights, and human rights — express "a special class of *moral concerns*, namely ones that are among the most *weighty* of all as well as *unrestricted* and *broadly sharable*" (ibid., emphasis in original). He adds that the characteristic of being broadly sharable also implies that these moral concerns "are capable of being understood and appreciated by persons from different epochs and cultures as well as by adherents of a variety of different religions, moral traditions, and philosophies" (ibid. 54f). This is, in many ways, a secularized version of the idea that there exists a higher law that is somehow recognizable by all human beings, having been "written in the hearts of men," to use St. Paul's often-quoted expression from *Romans*, 2, 15.

While the above characterization represents a plausible and unified definition of natural law — that we are speaking of something moral, weighty, unrestricted, and sharable — there are also nuances and discrepancies within the tradition that should be noted. Indeed, throughout its many-faceted history, the concept of natural law has been subject to

---

[3] From *Jahrbuch für Recht und Ethik*, vol. 3 (1995), reprinted in Pogge 2002a, 52-70; my page references are to the latter.

[4] It should be added that Pogge's reason for sketching out this historical road map is his wish to single out what are the basic features of human rights — which is, incidentally, not the same as delineating what rights there actually are.

heated discussions and subsequent often dramatic theoretical developments. There are several such developments that we will not touch on here, but only mention in passing, such as the questions of (a) the relationship between God and natural law, (b) the relationship between will — divine and human — and natural law, (c) the bearing natural law has and should have on politics, and (d) the scope for human freedom and conscience within natural law.

The most significant and far-reaching debate (and subsequent dramatic change) within the tradition happened, however, when the meaning of the term *ius* was enlarged not only to encompass the idea of "rightful order" but also to mean "claimable right." This happened in a decisive manner only with the development of liberal political theories in the 17th century, but it had its roots in medieval developments in philosophy and law, especially in the canon-law movement of the 12th and 13th centuries and the voluntaristic ethics of the 14th century.[5]

For Pogge, too, this is a crucial turn, pointing toward the development of later human-rights doctrines. This turn from law to rights contributes to a secularization of the natural-law idea, toning down individual commitment to the harmonious order of the cosmos as created by God — which had been so central to most earlier natural-law thinkers — and focusing instead on certain moral demands human beings have against one another, these demands being understood to be natural.

It is important to remember, however, that this doctrine of natural rights is still a *moral* teaching in the true sense of the word. While Thomas Hobbes's development of a natural-rights idiom, which was influential as well as controversial, may be said to have made the care for one's natural rights an egoistic concern rather than a moral one, the main trend in natural-rights theories was clearly to be other-regarding and not merely self-preserving or self-regarding. This comes out in such enlightenment protagonists of the natural-rights idea as Samuel Pufendorf, John Locke, and later Thomas Reid and Immanuel Kant. They all adapt the new natural-rights idiom to an emphasis on the duties of human beings to respect the rights of *other* human beings, and they all see this reciprocity as absolutely crucial to freedom, law, and order in political society.[6]

---

[5]   See several articles in Tierney 1997 and chapter 2 in Syse 2004.

[6]   Strauss 1953 famously holds that many of the seemingly "other-regarding" contract theorists after Hobbes, most especially John Locke, in essence shared with Hobbes a thoroughly egoistic outlook, but hid this under a veneer of pious respectability. I will not enter into that debate here, but merely point out that Locke, when read at face value, clearly regarded duties to others and duties to God as indispensable parts of the social fabric, without which stability, peace, and welfare would be impossible.

Pogge points out that three categories of moral duties that were central to the natural-law idea are left out by the natural-rights idiom: duties to God, duties to oneself, and moral demands towards animals or non-human nature (see Pogge 2002a: 56), the main reason being that neither God, oneself, nor animals can meaningfully make claims on me. This in itself is certainly a contested part of several modern rights theories: they seemingly remove human beings, morally speaking, from that larger reality within which human beings exist as natural entities. Now, this can be claimed to be both a strength and a weakness of natural-rights theory: it sets human beings free from obedience to more or less arbitrary conceptions of hierarchies and natural or divine lordship and clearly gives each human being access to equal, rightful claims that forcefully gainsay the reduction of individuals to defenseless beings whose low status is naturally or divinely instituted. The weakness of such a line of thought lies in its potential divorce of individuals from responsibilities toward the larger context and environment on which these individuals to a large extent depend, since all legal and moral responsibilities seem to be reduced to relationships among human beings.

This leads us naturally to the following observation: prior to the High Middle Ages the term *ius* (right) was rarely used about something one could have or own. A language of claims — for instance, in law courts — was admittedly present in both Greek and Latin (and surely in other social and linguistic communities). But the idea that it was possible to *have* a right, and especially to think of *natural* right (*ius naturale*) as something that could be had, owned, or claimed, seems to have been foreign, or at least very rare. It was primarily jurists in the 13th century who started using the term *ius* in a way that lends itself to genitive constructions, and most historians of law today agree that medieval jurists had a relatively developed notion of rights. Less frequently do we find *natural* rights (*ius naturale*) being used in this sense at that early stage, but the historian of ideas Brian Tierney has shown that it is not impossible to find even that.[7] Yet, it is only with Thomas Hobbes and the contractarians who followed his lead in the 17th and 18th centuries that we find the clearly expressed idea of innate rights of nature belonging to all human beings.

Now, if these innate rights — or natural rights — are something I *have*, they are possibly also something I can dispose of. This point was eagerly picked up by the contractarians, such as Hobbes and Locke, who imagined natural rights being traded in for security, with a stable political system as the result. However, others cannot dispose of them for me, at least not in theory — they are *my* property. Indeed, being natural, not merely conventional, they are mine to interpret and defend. This constitutes a

---

[7] See Reid 1991 and Tierney 1997 for several interesting observations.

crucial turn in the history of Western philosophy. It accompanies the broadly capitalist turn — if we follow the portrayal of C. B. Macpherson on the left and Leo Strauss on the right[8] — inaugurated by the early liberal political philosophers. I am thinking here of the increased emphasis on ownership and the right to dispose of one's own property freely. Applying this line of thinking to one's natural rights does not imply that there can be no extra-human limits at all to the exercise of those rights. After all, several of the contractarians, most notably Locke, portray the God-given law of nature as a general limiting condition on the exercise of individual rights, emphasizing in particular the duty this implies not to worsen the situation for others by one's own amassing of property. Nonetheless, it is true to say that the moral relationship among human beings is to a significant extent changed into a relationship among "owners" of rights.

This has several ramifications. Firstly, we have hereby gained an immensely powerful tool for expanding the number of people able to formulate moral claims against others — even against the most powerful — from very few to virtually *all*. No one is without chips to trade in, since everyone is the owner of natural rights. And secondly, the natural-rights idea constitutes a version of natural law compatible with deep disagreement about the good. It is not necessary to have a common view on the ultimate meaning of life or the highest moral good in order to recognize one another as holders of natural rights. The focus is on capabilities and interest, rather than moral aims or religious truth. The latter may still be just as important in each individual's and community's life as they were before, of course, but they are no longer in a position to dictate the political order.

Yet, the emphasis on human beings who *own* and *pursue* these claims could seem to favor the more active and willing over those with limited abilities to fight for their rights: children and the mentally retarded most particularly. This could be solved, as Pogge (2002a: 56) also indicates, by saying that children can be viewed as people who *in the future* will make such claims, and, for instance, the senile elderly or even the dead can be thought of as people who made such claims *in the past*. But the problem remains in the case of those who, for some reason, are not able to make such claims at all — they seem to become utterly dependent on others making the claims for them. Whether this emphasis on the (potential or actual) *ability* to make claims as autonomous, rights-holding human beings is a possible weakness of the natural-rights idea is a question I will not attempt to formulate a decisive answer to here. Yet it should be noted that the natural-rights language moves us away from the basic natural-law idea of human beings *belonging within a moral order* to a more radical and individualist

---

[8] See Macpherson 1962 and Strauss 1953.

idea of every human being *owning* the powers (i.e., natural rights) that make it possible to lead a decent human life within a just societal order.

2. The move to human rights

In the 20th century the natural-rights idea lives on, but the favored expression becomes that of *human* rights. As Pogge (2002a: 57) rightly points out, this takes us one step further along the process of secularization: the claim that there are certain basic rights that all human beings have comes across as "political" rather than "metaphysical," to use John Rawls's (1985; 1993a) formulation — no contested claims about human *nature* are made. It also makes it even more clear that human rights belong to humans only, and that they belong equally to *all* humans, in the sense that all human beings are — in spite of their differences — equally human. Hence, natural differences, which in theory could be taken to lead to differences in *natural* rights among individuals, become theoretically indifferent within the human-rights idiom.

Pogge also points out that the human-rights language has tended to limit itself to rights against governments and their officials, or against armies and large corporations and organizations. The natural-rights language had not as clearly done so, encompassing even rights claims among individuals.

Pogge sums up that "[a] commitment to human rights involves one in recognizing that human persons with a past or potential future ability to engage in moral conversation and practice have certain basic needs, and that these needs give rise to weighty moral demands" (Pogge 2002a: 58).

There is, however, one more crucial feature of human-rights as opposed to natural-rights language, which Pogge does not discuss explicitly[9]: the idea of natural rights clearly includes a conception of the *origin* of rights. They come from nature. Being natural, they cannot be taken away by or at will — except possibly by my own will, as was pointed out above, since they have been donated to *me*. They are *donated* not by any human act or agent, but by nature or God, and are as such an integral part of who I am as a natural being. The concept of human rights involves no such specification of origin or donor. While the idiom is meant to convey much the same idea as that of natural rights, namely, that these rights belong to humans *qua* humans, they also open up the possibility that the origin of these rights is human, and that they therefore have all the instability, uncertainty, and limitedness that characterize human affairs in general.

Is this a crucial argument against the concept of human rights? We can only hope not, since the impossibility of gaining universal acceptance for

---

[9] It is implicit, however, in his discussion of human rights as political, not metaphysical.

one, unified metaphysical theory or religious faith to underpin and explain the existence of human rights is manifest in our world — something the framers of the UN *Universal Declaration* of 1948 certainly came to see. Yet the argument is not insignificant. One of the key facets of human injustice throughout history has been the arbitrariness with which rulers — whether political, feudal, or clerical — have conferred and revoked rights. Rights to food, shelter, political participation, or fair legal treatment have been commodities over which the less powerful individuals in most societies have had no say. They have been, to put it somewhat paradoxically, *human* rights indeed, since they have been donated by human will and susceptible to no extra-human appeal or defense.

3. Conclusion

In sum, serious reflection on the development from natural law to human rights makes us aware of at least three crucial aspects of the tradition out of which the idea of human rights has grown, and which we ought to bear in mind as very real challenges.

First, in the turn from natural law to natural rights we see how the moral fabric of the world is made to evolve around the question of *having* or *holding* rights. Thus, the ability (potentially or actually) to "own" rights, and to pursue that ownership through the formulation of claims, becomes central to one's standing in the world.

Second, in the turn from natural rights to human rights, we see — even more explicitly than in the first turn from natural law to natural rights — the moral commitment to a larger reality, of which human beings are part, being lost.

And third, we see rights becoming a human rather than a metaphysical concept to such an extent that the sanctity and reverence of their origins — and thus of their permanence — can easily be called into question.

All these developments are historically quite natural, in the sense of having arisen within social contexts that encouraged them. And they are certainly, to a large extent, to be welcomed: they have made it easier to express, in a society where people hold different views about nature, God, and the good life, the basic idea that all human beings have a claim to be treated with respect and dignity. In fighting world poverty, such an idiom of human rights is indispensable. Yet the problems of a potential egoism, encouraged by the idea that each human being is the shepherd of her *own* rights first and foremost, are real. These problems are part and parcel of a world where the rights language has become all-pervasive and conceived of in highly individualistic terms. Human rights can thus become a shield behind which may hide comfortable living and a refusal to help the less fortunate, instead of acting as a real tool for change.

In replying to this claim, it is easy to point out that the older natural-law idioms were part and parcel of societies that accepted inequality and political oppression more readily than we do today. In such a light, the human-rights idiom must be termed a definite success. However, that should not stop us from reflecting on the moral ideas and perspectives which that older way of thinking had to offer. I am not advocating a full-fledged "return to the ancients" or a charter of "human duties" to accompany that of human rights,[10] nor am I claiming that the modern human-rights language has made it impossible to find meaningful ways of expressing philosophical or theological ideas about law and duty. All I am claiming is that there are resources in the natural-law tradition out of which the human-rights idea has grown, which the human-rights idea itself has changed significantly or left by the wayside. And much of what has been lost may not be so easily replaceable.

---

[10] It should be noted that the UN *Universal Declaration of Human Rights* actually does include a clear manifestation of duties, in article 29: "Everyone has duties to the community in which alone the free and full development of his personality is possible."

.

Chapter 14

Deliberation or Negotiation? Remarks on the Justice of Global and Regional Human Rights Agreements[*]

Regina Kreide
Philosophy, Johann Wolfgang Goethe Universität, Frankfurt

Human rights, the nucleus of a just global order, are commonly described as two-sided. From the perspective of moral philosophy, they appear as moral rights. As such they formulate moral claims on the institutional order, securing the satisfaction of basic human needs. Their normative substance does not depend on the outcomes of real political struggles concerning the status, content or reach of obligations linked to human rights. In this formulation, other conceptions of human rights do not make very much sense, as they require that one give up the idea of preserving the normative, prepolitical content of human rights that protect citizens from arbitrary state power. [1]

From a political point of view, another side of human rights comes to the fore. They can also be seen as legal rights that are part of either binding international law or of a constitution that is valid for a certain legal community. In this version, international human rights conventions are the object and result of a nation's power calculations, and constitutional law depends on the political and judicial interpretations of political representatives and executive organs.

Following this dualism, there can be either only one *correct* (moral) interpretation of human rights, or many incommensurable political

---

[*] For helpful critical remarks and constructive advice I thank the participants of the Philosophical Colloquia, Union College, Schenectady (New York, February 2003) and those of the "Global Justice" Symposium (Oslo, September 2003), especially Andreas Follesdal and Thomas Pogge. I am grateful for critical reading to Felmon Davis, Ana Garcia and Peter Niesen.

[1] For this "institutional" notion of human rights see Pogge 2002a: 64–7. For the difference between moral and legal human rights see Habermas 1996a, postscript, Wildt 1998: 124–46 and Michelman 2000.

A. Follesdal and T. Pogge, (eds.), Real World Justice, 239-264.
© 2005 *Springer. Printed in the Netherlands.*

interpretations, which may express various ideas about collective identity or political power. The dichotomous view attempts to leave one side of human rights in the dark. However, a cynical conclusion that follows from the idea of interpretive pluralism is that there are no standards for evaluating political practice and the legitimacy of law. Moral right claims are then only one argument among others within political debates. Marx's criticism that human rights are only an instrument to cement the unjust distribution of power and property in bourgeois society starts here (Marx 1988: 354, 362, 364–8).

But even if one admits that political theory should be vigilant concerning the misuse of human rights as an instrument of power, the cynical conclusion is not convincing in its claim that morality and politics are necessarily identical and that moral utterances always serve to mask political intentions. Even though this is a widespread assumption in Marxism, systems theory, and also in the political theory of realism, these theories needlessly surrender the critical, normative point of view required to render judgment against humiliating and abusive practices.

Another, "moralistic" version attempts to resolve the tension between moral and legal human rights on the side of morality. As law is under suspicion of being corrupted through power, a switch to prepolitical rights is held out as an option for preserving the critical, normative content of human rights. This approach becomes "moralistic" only if it entails a direct deduction of moral rights from legal ones. But one need not agree to Jeremy Bentham's criticism of moral (natural) rights to see what is problematic with this approach. Bentham, a skeptical critic of natural law, doubted that one could deduce real rights from abstract, imaginary rights at all. The basic metaphysical and ontological presumptions of natural law are already much too pejorative, and are therefore a serious threat to public order.[2] Another problem, however, remains even if one does not defend a natural law approach to moral rights: how can the enforcement of rights be legitimized without prescribing the motive for following a legal norm and compelling its addressees? In spite of its coercive character, law must offer an opportunity to follow it out of utility calculations ("There is too much of a burden if I do not submit") and not just on the basis of a certain conviction. Otherwise there is the danger of enforcing conscience.

In this article I will rebut the "realist" assumptions of international human rights negotiation as well as the "moralistic" short circuit between morality and law-making, and will proceed to the question of under what circumstances an agreement on internationally binding law can be called just.

---

[2] Bentham 1987: 72f. It was in this context that Bentham penned his famous sentence that natural rights are "nonsense upon stilts."

To answer this question, the relationship between moral and legal human rights has to be clarified in some detail. To this end I will discuss two strategies for human rights legitimation that, at first glance, show some family likeness, but which upon closer examination have distinctive methodological and normative differences. I am interested in how far both positions, which lie between the cynical and the moralistic versions, acknowledge the fact of plural human rights interpretations, without sacrificing a normative point of view. Then I address the question of which approach most convincingly explores the relationship between morality and politics for the legitimation of international lawmaking processes. Against the first one, the Deliberative Model, which possesses a tight interlocking between moral and political discourse with view to law-making procedures, I will posit the Model of Fair Bargaining. In this model the moral justification of human rights is largely decoupled from the political discourse, but it is held that minimal normative procedural conditions can yield a just agreement at the international level. This procedural approach guarantees that the "ideal theory" accommodates the empirical, "non-ideal" societal conditions — in our case, for the pluralism of human rights interpretations. Moreover, law can remain the object of permanent normative criticism, which is not under the suspicion of serving as a mere instrument of power.

I proceed in three steps. First, I will briefly characterize the current, predominant notion of human rights and sketch out three main objections as well as counterobjections (1). On the basis of this reconstruction, I will discuss the already mentioned two models of law justification, mainly with the intention of determining which of the two recognizes different convictions most appropriately and, at the same time, identifies those arguments that support human rights — violating practices (2). As we will see, law that is the result of a fair procedure can, but *need not* be legitimized through generalizable, moral arguments. A just agreement can be reached despite a pluralism of reasons only if fair procedural conditions are given. Human rights, however, do not necessarily lose contact with morality completely. I will lay out in the third part that moral arguments play an often underestimated role in political negotiations. I will illustrate this by examining the process that led to the *Universal Declaration of Human Rights*. However, there is still the danger that human rights discourse can degenerate into mere "human rights rhetoric" in the service of states and also transnational corporations (3).

1. Criticism of the "Western" interpretation of human rights

The question of the just conditions for agreement on human rights may seem surprising at first glance. One can point to the *Universal Declaration of Human Rights*, the *Convention on Civil and Political Rights* and other examples that obviously express a shared idea of global justice. Furthermore, the permanent International Criminal Court, which came into existence in 2002, offers a legal means for prosecuting the gravest international crimes — a radical innovation in the history of international law that expresses more than anything else the reality that there already is a consensus on human rights.

Human rights activists, and some theorists of international law as well as philosophers, are convinced that nowadays there exists one correct human rights interpretation that rightly claims to be universal. For others, there is no doubt that this interpretation represents the typical "Western" idea of human rights, which is based on culturally biased notions of reason and the individual, which, moreover, are misused to pursue national interests. As a reaction to the dominant human rights interpretation, regional human rights declarations, such as the *Bangkok Declaration* of the Association of South East Asian Nations (ASEAN), the *Banjul Charter* of some African countries, and the two Islamic *Declarations* were developed. These declarations highlight the incompatibilities with the central concept of human rights, especially their universality, the protection of the individual, and equal treatment of individuals.

The *Bangkok Declaration*, together with the other two, share the fact that they emphasize obligations instead of rights, group rights and the protection of the family instead of claims of the individual, and, moreover, they underscore the importance of social rights by neglecting civil and political rights. Furthermore, they stress the "Right to Development," which demands fair international trade relations among states — a right that addresses collectives and not individuals. So we in fact are confronted with a variety of interpretations that claim legal or at least normative validity.

1.1 The predominant human rights interpretation

Now we can turn to the question of what characterizes the predominant human rights interpretation. The best way to approach this question seems to be through a historical-systematic reconstruction of how the human rights idea has developed — a task that I can only carry out here very roughly. The concept of "human rights" is relatively new (Burns Weston 1992: 656). It found its way into everyday speech only after the United Nations was founded in 1945. Before that, the phrases "natural rights" and later "the rights of man" — concepts that can be seen as predecessors of modern human rights — were more common (Thomas Pogge 2002a: 54–9).

In its very early period, natural rights were seen as given by God. Thomas Aquinas described natural law as the eternal law of God-given reason. And it was only after the Treaty of Westphalia (signed in 1648) that a qualitative change took place in how natural law was perceived. Subjects were allowed to make claims against the state and other subjects for the first time. In the theological reading of natural law, an individual subject of rights was unknown, and the violation of God-given natural law was a contravention against God's world order but not against a single subject. That freedoms of religion and conscience were guaranteed after the *Augsburg Religion Peace* in the different principalities, and the fact that religion — at least the faith of the heretic minority — became a private matter, and that the protection of dissenters became a task of the state, was a milestone in the development of human rights: for the first time, the individual was both the addressee and the source of rights.[3]

One problem with the natural law approach, however, was and still is the fact that the notion of human nature is highly contested. Despite this theoretical shortcoming there is some continuity between the natural law approach and today's predominant idea of human rights. Human rights are still described as being characterized by three elements: they are universally valid (or at least that is what they claim to be); they address the individual and not a specific group; and their content is very general. It is because of these elements that human rights claim to be valid independent of future historical developments and cultural diversity (Pogge 2002a: 52–71). There are at least three further characteristics that cannot be traced back to the natural law tradition and which are not much contested in the international human rights debate. I mention them here for reasons of completeness.[4]

---

[3] The idea that individuals have rights just because they are born human spread quickly. The English parliament passed the Habeas Corpus Act in 1679, establishing the right to be protected against arbitrary detention or imprisonment. England's revolution in 1688, which led to the Bill of Rights a year later, provided juridical security and security of property but also free elections and freedom of speech. It was John Locke, inspired by the Glorious Revolution, who argued that individuals as human beings possess rights of life, liberty and property, and who — together with Montesquieu — became the important theoretician for some of the main actors in the American and French revolutions. See Locke 1960, and also König 1990. When Thomas Jefferson, one of the founding fathers of the American *Declaration of Independence*, stressed that "all men are created equal, that they are endowed by their Creator with certain inalienable Rights, that among these are Life; Liberty and the Pursuit of Happiness," John Locke's ideas were very present.

[4] Nowadays, moral human rights are rarely legitimized with reference to natural law but rather "in relation to" another conception. Human rights therefore claim to be universally valid but they are legitimized "in relation to" a conception of morality or of discursive

The first aspect refers to the addressees of human rights, i.e., those who are responsible for the protection and realization of human rights. The natural law approach, as well as the utilitarian positions (to mention just one example), are based on an interactional understanding of human rights: every right corresponds to direct obligations that have to be fulfilled by all individuals and governments. For the institutional approach, this reading of human rights is not sufficient. Human rights are not only claims on different goods or measures we "owe to each other" (Scanlon 1998), but are also claims on the international and domestic institutional order that allows secure access to the goods and services postulated by human rights (Pogge 2002a: 64–7). This means citizens and representatives are not just asked to work on a domestic realization of human rights. The change of perspective also affects the evaluation of global interconnections: the results of international trade negotiations and financial transactions should meet human rights standards.

In mentioning this, I have already touched on another characteristic: human rights are not only a matter of national concern but are of international interest. This becomes clear if one realizes what a *violation* of human rights means. One says a human right is violated only if people are hindered from accessing vital resources or are murdered, humiliated, or harassed in a way that attracts transnational attention and raises the question of who (aside from the state that is obviously neglecting its obligations to protect its citizens) is obliged to change the unbearable situation (Follesdal in this volume).

The issue of human rights violations brings another aspect to the fore. We only speak of human rights violations if they have been carried out or at least tolerated by government officials. We do not say, for example, that the human right to possession has been violated when thieves break in, steal valuables, and destroy a home. If a state does not take action to catch and punish the perpetrators, and does nothing to prevent future encroachments, and, moreover, initiates the break-in with the intention of forcing people out of their homes, then one indeed would talk about a human rights violation (Pogge 2002a: 59–63).

---

rationality. A human rights conception in relation to morality is offered by Tugendhat 1993 and Gewirth 1996; for one that refers to discursive rationality see Habermas 1996a, 1996b and Rainer Forst 1999a, 1999b.

1.2 Objections and counterobjections

This interpretation of human rights has been criticized from different angles. I will concentrate on three important objections, acknowledging that there are many other voices.[5] With the selection offered here, I try to discuss certain aspects: the notion of "the person" that is at the foundation of the conception of human rights, the reasonableness of religious assumptions regarding rights, and the persuasive power of reason.

— Community vs. individual

One often raised objection to human rights is that the concept of the individual that is embedded in human rights discourse is not compatible with the "Asian" ideal of acting responsibly towards the community, nor is it compatible with community-focused practices in some African cultures.[6] Moreover, the legal form itself prescribes an individualistic perspective that is incompatible with these traditions. In a "Confucian" society, it is argued, close personal relationships are emphasized and the virtues of selflessness, *dana* (generosity), and non-violence are stressed (Pannikar 1982). Self-determination cannot be understood in terms of individual self-realization, but must be seen as cooperation within a community of relatives, ancestors, and descendants. Individual human rights might be a reasonable answer to the individualized "megamachine" in a world of "techniculture" (Pannikar 1982) but they are useless in a world with close ties to mythical traditions. "Western" individualism, according to this position, undermines political trust because of a widespread culture of "fighting for elbow room" and leads to unwanted social losses.[7]

---

[5] For more detailed analyses of objections against the "Western" interpretation of human rights see the contribution of Follesdal in this volume. He identifies nine objections, which he extracts from the *Bangkok Declaration* and which he rebuts respectively. The three objections in this article have more illustrative meaning. It shall be demonstrated how the two different models of justifying human rights deal with objections, and on what grounds they respectively reject them.

[6] See, for example, Howard 1990: 159–84. At this point it is worthwhile noting that a similar argument has been given by the so-called "communitarians." They criticize — from within "Western" discourse — the dominant liberal Western idea of a person, which expresses the possessive, individualistic striving for freedom of the individual. The "unencumbered self" (Sandel 1982) carries out actions according to rational calculation and neglects social ties and solidarity with others.

[7] This is also the interpretation of Charles Taylor who refers to a reformistic articulation of Theravada Buddhism. Taylor discusses the movement of the late Phutthathat (Buddhadasa) who tried to purify Buddhism by turning it away from rituals around heaven, hell, gods and demons, and focusing it on Enlightenment. Enlightenment here not

— Theocracy vs. secular state

Some theoreticians argue that human rights have their roots in the 1400-year-old teachings of Islamic scholars.[8] They claim that the right to life, security, individual freedom, and equality of all human beings can be found in the Quran, either explicitly or by interpretation of its texts. This notion became known to the general public through the 1981 *Universal Islamic Declaration of Human Rights* of the Islamic Council for Europe, a nongovernmental organization. It was also echoed in a later document — the *Declaration of Human Rights in Islam* — drafted by the representatives to the 1990 "Organization of the Islamic Conference," in Cairo. The belief that there are human rights of Islamic origin facilitates identifying points of intersection between Islam and the UN *Universal Declaration*. But on the other hand, claims regarding the historical and theological roots of the Islamic *Declarations* tend to leave room for only one *correct* interpretation of those rights, which is incompatible with the dominant "Western" interpretation.

A main incompatibility between the two Islamic *Declarations* and the UN *Universal Declaration* is that in some parts of the Islamic world Shari'a is not just a system of rules for personal religious practice; it is also the foundation for civil and criminal law. Shari'a law has direct juridical influence in at least two controversial areas of human rights, especially freedom of religion and gender equality.[9] Converting to another faith is regarded as heresy in some Islamic countries and can be punished by juridical sanctions such as compulsory divorce and/or loss of parental custody of children.[10] Religious faith also still influences personal status in Islamic countries: marriage between Muslims and atheists or polytheists is

---

only means to be concerned with one's own liberation, but also with that of others (Taylor 1999: 124–44). See also Sivaraksa 1992.

[8] See Mawdudi 1976. For a comprehensive overview and critical evaluation see Bielefeld 1998: 131ff.

[9] Cruel physical punishment is a third contested aspect but it persists in just a few countries, such as Mauritius, Sudan and, as of recently, in some parts of Nigeria. Nevertheless, from a Christian-Catholic perspective it is sometimes argued that the publicly inflicted and suffered pain of someone who violated the religious order can serve as atonement, which undoes the committed crime. This admittedly uncommon view is not widely held in the secular world. See Taylor 1999: 142.

[10] This violates Article 18 of the *Universal Declaration*, where religious conversion is explicitly protected as a component of freedom of religion. Nasr Abu Zaid, a well-known Egyptian literary scholar, was accused of being a "heretic" and, as a consequence, excluded from *umma*, the community of the believers, and forced to divorce his wife.

not permitted for men or women.[11] Secondly, family law is not based on the idea of gender equality: it is much easier for men to obtain a divorce, and polygyny is believed to be permitted by the Quran, but not polyandry.[12] And furthermore, women are entitled to inherit only half of what their male relatives may inherit.[13] Any decoupling of religious and political affairs means — and this is seen as the main problem — a dilution of religious beliefs and practices. What is praised as the neutrality of the state in the West is inextricably linked to the demise of religion.

— Universal use of reason

Human rights, say some critics, are a "Western" achievement that has come to the fore through the "Occidental" idea of reason, but which can bring about its own contradictions and trigger unwanted effects. Whereas on the one side reason stands for the inclusion of all those endowed with reason, it has always disguised the exclusion of parts of the population, and worse, it has at times facilitated colonization and oppression in the name of alleged civilization.[14]

Another aspect, namely, the critique of reason through reason, has a long tradition even within Western philosophy. Martin Heidegger and later Richard Rorty defined what one can call an "abstractive fallacy."[15] Reason, originally based on Platonic thinking, "forgets" its own local context of emergence by claiming universal validity, thereby ignoring that every historical or cultural context has its own ideas of what makes an action right or wrong.

Of course, in international human rights discourse, all these objections are confronted with counterarguments that claim to weaken the above-

---

[11] A Muslim man is allowed to marry a member of one of the other monotheistic religions, but this is not an option for a Muslim woman, see Mayer 1991.

[12] See, for example, Othman (1999: 169–92), a leading member of the "Sisters in Islam," an autonomous, non-governmental organization of Muslim women. Through the second half of the 1980s and throughout the 1990s, there have been many attempts by Malaysian authorities in several of the thirteen states (under control of the Islamic Affairs Departments) to allow polygamy as a matter of principle (ibid. 179).

[13] See the comprehensive study on the realization of women's rights in Pakistan by Weiss (2003). And for this aspect also Taylor 1999: 142.

[14] Poor workers, women, blacks, gypsies, and children have long been excluded from the community of right bearers. The rights of asylum seekers, homosexuals, and animals are still highly contested in Western countries. And the concepts of "civilizing missions" and — already — "humanitarian interventions" were used to legitimize the imperialistic politics of powerful Western states from the late nineteenth to the early twentieth century (Yasuaki 1999: 105). See also Fisch 1984; Paech and Stuby 2001: 102ff.

[15] For this expression, see Habermas 2002: 204 and Rorty 1993.

mentioned readings of human rights and to offer another, more convincing interpretation. For example, some refute the claim that human rights contravene the idea of community and presuppose a self-interested self. Defenders of liberal theory, however, argue that it is mistaken to say that liberal theory finds people to be "atomistic" and not interested in community matters. Rather, liberal theory describes people as having a sense of justice, which includes the ability to see other people's points of view and to interact on a reciprocal basis (Forst 2002: 8–16)[16] — a necessary precondition for social interaction.

With respect to the second point, regarding the role of religion, one may claim that in fact the neutral, secular state is a successful answer to the religious wars in Europe, pacifying antagonistic ideas about "true believers." Liberalism demands from its citizens that they reconcile religious convictions with the basic principles of the constitutional state, including respecting religious freedom. Given the existing plurality of convictions, it becomes necessary to relativize one's own "comprehensive doctrines" and accept that, even though different ideas on religion and "the good life" are incompatible, they can exist together in society. The fact that religion loses public relevance thereby becomes a small price to pay for peaceful coexistence.

And finally we come to the idea that universal reason may have first appeared in the comments of "Western" philosophers. The practice of reason-giving, defenders say, is an integral part of communicative action, which itself rests on the idea of reciprocal communicative relations (Habermas 2002: 212). In international human rights discourse, participants who aim at a common understanding of interpretations have to orient their actions according to certain presuppositions. Among them is the idea of symmetrical relations among participants, which is expressed through reciprocal respect and taking over the perspective of others as well as the willingness to see one's own tradition from the perspective of the other (Habermas 2002: 213). Taking these normative assumptions into consideration, it is possible to track down injustice in every cultural context; they undermine the normative preconditions that have to be fulfilled to come to a consensus.

---

[16] For Michael Walzer, often misleadingly named a "communitarian," the liberal self is not a pre-social self but a post-social one (Walzer 1990: 21).

2. Deliberation versus fair bargaining

At this point, the question arises of how, in view of these conflicting interpretations, one can reach a just agreement. Which arguments are "permitted," and which are not? And what are the criteria by which to judge the appropriateness of the arguments offered? Asking these questions has a long tradition in philosophy after Peirce's linguistic turn, and the assumption is quite common that what is characterized as a "good" argument depends on the conditions under which it was raised. In the following section I will discuss two models of human rights justification, the "Deliberative Model" and the "Model of Fair Bargaining," which both offer different suggestions about fair conditions for the legitimation of law.[17] Both have in common that they propose ideal legitimation procedures. Furthermore, by definition, they maintain contact with different historical and cultural contexts because, as procedures, they are open to all arguments that might arise in a debate. And finally, these models do not rest on metaphysical premises, nor on a "comprehensive doctrine" (John Rawls), but on an impartial procedural basis by which to judge arguments and come to a fair agreement. The procedural conditions must themselves be "acceptable" for the participants.

However, the models differ in some respects. First, they rely on different normative procedures. Second, they vary in the ultimate content and character of the agreements they produce. Third, the kinds of reasons employed in the procedures have different status, and, finally, the operational concept of the person varies.

---

[17] The distinction between the two models is based on an ideal-typical reconstruction of different but similar approaches. For the Deliberative Model see Habermas 1996a, 1996b; Michelman 2000; Forst 1999a, 1999b. For the Model of Fair Bargaining see Hampshire 1999; Maus 1992, 1995; Rawls 1993a and, although different in many respects, Elster 1989, 1998. Similarities and differences with respect to the legitimation of rights in the theories of Maus and Habermas have been very clearly presented in Niesen 2002.

2.1 The Deliberative Model

The Deliberative Model (DelM)[18] proposes a "constructivist" procedure where the results of the procedure as well as the procedure itself rest on the hypothetical presupposition of reasonable justification. The participants come to a fair agreement through an organized exchange of arguments based on normative preconditions that include some procedural arrangements and a certain notion of personhood.[19] The human rights conception that is accepted by all participants can be understood as the result of a "discursive constructivism" (Forst 1999a: 45, 1999b: 152): The way to the aim, the aim itself, and also the different phases passed through on the way to reaching the aim are created " hands free" by the people, i.e., without further given rules or content that may restrict a free exchange of arguments. We will only see later that there are in fact built-in restrictions in this model. The participants, however, stand with both legs on the ground of cognitive competences: it is assumed that they are all willing to get involved in the argumentative practice and that they also possess the competences necessary to argue with one another and to convince other parties of their own convictions. This presumes — and this is also true for the Model of Fair Bargaining — that the "habit of playing the game of argument" (Hampshire 1999: 37) has become widespread internationally.[20]

Rainer Forst, a proponent of "discursive constructivism," has described the procedure of legitimation as a two-level procedure, where a first step of moral justification logically precedes a second step of political justification (Forst 1999a: 43, 1999b: 151).[21] In the first phase, the procedure is located in a moral context. The members of the hypothetical community of all human beings agree on those moral principles to which they in the end must submit. This includes that principles formulate conditions of norm-setting as well as

---

[18] I refer mainly to Habermas' theory of law. Habermas has coined the expression "deliberative politics" to a great extent. He has worked out his ideas on the legitimacy of law in *Between Facts and Norms* (1996a) for the democratic constitutional state. Later works, in which he also addresses the legitimacy of international law, are, with view to the normative presumptions, much more modest. In "Die postnationale Konstellation" (Habermas 1998: 164–7) he proposes two criteria, which at least should be fulfilled: rationality of the communicative and decision processes and transparency of decision-making processes. Nevertheless, one can assume that the idea that legally binding human rights conventions should not contradict moral human rights remains an important idea. Rainer Forst has worked on this topic in 1999.

[19] Cf. Forst 1999a, 1999b whose approach differs from Habermas's in some respects, which I will point out in the following. See especially Forst 1999a, 43ff and 1999b, 151ff.

[20] Hampshire notes, however, that the rules of the game may vary from context to context.

[21] Michelman (2000) distinguishes also between moral and political justification of human rights.

norms (and moral rights), which also are the result of the discursive practice. Within the argumentative practice, all reasons if they fulfill the following two criteria are acceptable (Forst 1999a: 44): they first must be "reciprocally non-rejectable" (Thomas Scanlon), which means they must be agreeable on the basis of insight. This would prevent an author of a rule from demanding anything he or she never would submit to because he or she in fact finds the rule to be useless or inadequate. Therefore, part of the conception of a person within this model is that — along with being capable of adopting the perspective of the other — people must have a sense of justice that makes it clear that oppressing or dominating others is socially unacceptable.

Secondly, reasons must be general, which means that they must be addressed to all those who may be affected by the norms or by the actions that follow from those norms (Forst 1999a: 44). Only those who have been the author of a rule are required to submit to it. The two criteria together make for a fair procedure of justification. Forst entitles this as a "basic right to justification" (Forst 1999a: 44). This very basic moral principle allows every individual a "veto-right" (Forst 1999a: 44) towards all reasons one finds unacceptable according to the two criteria, and it obliges all participants to publicly explain proposals and actions. The right to justification is itself a normative presupposition that one cannot forgo.[22] That means that agreements on the rules of procedure must also meet the normative assumptions of reciprocal justification.[23]

The second phase of legitimation requires a change of perspective: through the morally justified principles, the constructivist procedure is placed within the context of a political community of law. As a result, it is no longer the aim to come to an agreement on moral principles, but instead to arrive at consensus on the political "basic structure" (John Rawls), i.e., on the rights and other political rules that enable people to live together. The procedure is identical with the one for moral principles, but in addition to moral reasons, other reasons that reflect the social and political conditions are allowed (Forst 1999a: 48).

As we turn to the micro-level of argumentation of the DelM, an important aspect comes to the fore: there are different categories of reasons and the category employed in the justification has enormous influence on the results. The arguments can be distinguished from one another by their

---

[22] Whereas in Forst's theory the principle of justification is of a moral nature, the very similar discourse principle in the theory of Habermas is based on a notion of reason.

[23] The principle of justification is a (transcendental) principle of reason, which cannot be justified without committing a "performative self-contradiction" (Karl-Otto Apel). The question "Why be reasonable in this practical way?" asks after the reason for giving reasons and presupposes what it asks for. The recourse to other authorities does not help either as the same question of legitimation again occurs (Forst 1999c: 192).

content, but also by their degree of abstraction. In the course of the discursive practice, the participants proceed from the most concrete to the most abstract level. Jürgen Habermas calls this the "logic of questioning" (Habermas 1996b: 1534) within a discourse that results from the structure and aim of the different discourses.[24]

From the perspective of discourse theory one can analytically distinguish three different ideal types of discourses in which respectively different subjects with different kinds of arguments appear. Within the *pragmatic discourse*, preferences and interests are clarified and political or social programs are evaluated.[25] This discourse deals with questions such as whether certain social programs fulfill their purposes as they relate to determined targets. For example, are affirmative action programs effective in integrating women into the workforce? The *ethical discourse* focuses on the authenticity of a community and its self-understanding. It refers to the question of what our collective, political self-description looks like. How do we want to understand ourselves as a community? And as it relates to the topic here: is gender equality a formative element of our political community?

The *moral discourse*, however, is detached from contingent historical and cultural conditions, from heteronomous decisions that are fed by value preferences and personal interest. From the perspective of a reason-driven morality, only those reasons that meet the general interest of all are acceptable. To stick to our example, the question becomes whether gender equality is a value that everybody in society can and should support? This perspective entails that those affected have to be convinced in *the same way* so that it becomes possible to agree with the *same reasons*.[26] This is the unique condition required for saying that an agreement is in fact a

---

[24] The code of law, according to Habermas, is insensitive to the material "sorted" through the questioning but this at the same time is very useful as it allows juridical argumentation without restricting it: it sets off external discourses (Habermas 1996b: 1535).

[25] For the different discourses see Habermas 1996a, 157–68, and 1996b.

[26] Why, however, are shared, "correct" reasons necessary for cooperation? With view to the assumptions of the DelM this is because correct reasons become part of a person's convictions and these are not easily changed. Also, what strikes one as compelling becomes something that deserves to be seriously evaluated by others as well. Coming to terms with what we think is true — even if it is just for the time being — can only be reached intersubjectively. However, a rational consensus can only occur if all participants feel compelled by an argument in the same way (Wellmer 2000: 265). In non-moral discourses, by definition, an agreement cannot emerge from shared reasons. From a pragmatic point of view, the rational interests of the parties may overlap, but even then they still remain the interest of somebody in particular. And in ethical discourse, reasons need to express the insight that one is identical to what one wants to be, and not what everybody else thinks it would be good to be.

consensus. As it is an agreement based on shared reasons, I call it a *monolithic consensus*.

While practicality is the criterion for a good argument within pragmatic discourse, the criterion for a good argument in ethical discourse is authenticity, and in moral discourses it is whether it meets a "generalizable interest." The procedure of the DelM works according to a certain logic and classifies the arguments according to the different kinds of discourses so that it results in a "hierarchy of reasons" (Niesen 2002: 44f). If an unresolvable dispute arises within a discourse due to preferences, then the participants must, according to the "logic of discourse" (Habermas 1996b: 1534), change to the next, more abstract level of argument. From this more distant perspective on the dissent, they can try to solve the disagreement with more abstract arguments.

The hierarchy of reasons begins at the level of pragmatic questions, is then followed by ethical ones, and is finally "trumped" on the moral level. This is the bargaining-arguing-route. More specifically, one can answer contested pragmatic questions if one focuses on these problems from a more distant point of view and clarifies the more general questions of identity and authenticity of the whole community. Agreement on this more abstract level facilitates a decision back at the level of interest. If we cannot decide about the efficacy of women's rights, we should clarify whether we want to be a society where women and other social minorities are represented equally. If values conflict on this level, then the disputing parties will again have to "change discourse" and shift to the moral level. And if the parties disagree as to whether society regards itself as one in which women should play an equally important role in public as men, then one has to switch to the moral question of what is in the interests of all.

What does all this mean for the arguments for and against the predominant human rights interpretation? This question gets at the heart of our earlier question on the relationship between moral and political constructivism. In the DelM there exists, as we have seen, a tight interconnection between both perspectives. Examination of the micro-level of argumentation showed that moral arguments "trump," as they are very general and stand at the end of the road to universalization. The priority of moral arguments is inherent in the practice of reasonable argumentation.

The "basic right to justification" is simultaneously of a moral nature and the undeniable basis for moral and political justification procedures. As the shape of the procedure is more or less given through the moral principle, there is a priority of the moral principle of justification in contrast to all other principles, which possibly may be the result of the procedure. That is why the moral claims — and moral human rights — that moral persons grant reciprocally build the core of each basic political structure (Forst 1999a: 50).

The important assumption is that all other rules should neither contradict this principle nor undermine the principle of justification. The rights that citizens agree on are either moral human rights or come in their concretized variations after having been discussed politically. This is a first problem of the DelM. The concretization of moral human rights is problematic, as becomes clear if one considers what this means on a practical level. One can ask, does the right to property also entail the right to inheritance, or should free availability of wealth and possession be linked to a principle of efforts, where one has property only if one "deserves" it? This type of question foreshadows the fact that "concretizing" of moral principles always hides a potential, other interpretation that one should also deliberate. Merely spelling out an already determined meaning would only infer positive rights from moral principles, which would be presented to the citizens as "moral facts."[27]

Another problem with the DelM is that the consensus even among moral theorists will be quite narrow. This relates to the highly demanding criteria that must be fulfilled in order to come to an agreement. As mentioned above, all the reasons have to express universal interests and, more demandingly, an agreement can only be reached by shared reasons. A consensus based on these assumptions will not have the support of (human rights-friendly) philosophical traditions, which are skeptical of deontological justification, such as rule-utilitarianism. And it also excludes those approaches that support human rights but criticize reason-based approaches and instead, for example, refer to human needs, compassion, or sensitivity. Those theories might present good reasons in support of the well-known list of human rights fixed in the *Declaration*, but their reasons vary, such as maximizing happiness for the greatest number, or derivation from shared human needs, or the universal idea of sensitivity; and so they will not pass the "moral filter." It can now easily be said that in the DelM, the above-mentioned predominant human rights interpretation gets acceptance on the basis of good reasons, whereas the objections do not pass the "moral filter." They do not express a generalizable interest. Regional human rights declarations, such as the *Bangkok Declaration* or the *Banjul Charter* are, we can conclude, not legitimized according to this standard. The agreement of the proposed list of human rights is only supported by a few moral theories.

The tight interconnection between morality of reason and law also presumes that the motivation to consent to a right is not at the free disposal of the individual, but is directly linked to moral conviction and, through this,

---

[27] A consequence that Forst (1999a: 50) refutes. But it remains unclear how the demand for independent political justification can be redeemed as long as moral and political constructivism are so closely connected.

to the individual's insight into the correct way of acting: a human rights regime that is based on legally binding international law is valid only if one can prove that all those affected respect the codified human rights and submit to it out of inner conviction. But exactly what the moral-based justification presumes is problematic and contradicts its very own preconditions: human rights guarantee subjective freedoms, including freedom of conscience; so the protection of plural, reasonable interpretations through human rights cancels out the idea that there is only one correct (moral) interpretation for the debate on the political level.[28] The enforcement of codified human rights infringes directly upon the level of conscience: because citizens can only agree with moral reasons and submit as moral persons out of inner conviction and respect towards a human rights regime, a political minority that favors another interpretation has no other option than to bow to the "correct" insight.

Furthermore, the idea of a moral-based international law underestimates that law has a tendency to uncouple from political influence; rather it is inclined to become insulated against non-juridical influences and is hardly open to new interpretations and every kind of changes. Meanwhile, some comprehensive sociological studies have shown that in the course of increasing juridification, global and regional legal sub-systems have developed and there is a tight net of regulations ("constitutions") to address such different spheres as politics, economics, the Internet, science, and sports.[29] That is the reason why, at the international level, one finds considerably fewer negotiations embedded within communicative contexts that can serve as a source for political human rights interpretations. In the DelM, citizens have to come to a common insight about their local interpretations of human rights, which at the same time must have an acceptable, universalizing reading that permits codification of moral human rights. De facto, however, the development of "poly-contextual" law (Brunkhorst 1999b: 382) is far from any law-setting procedures that come close to the addressed standards of justice (cf. Habermas 2002).

Because of its *"morality-ladenness,"* the deliberative model of law-making fails to get a hold on another phenomenon: with the unregulated spontaneous evolution of international law, we see the emergence of a growing number of spaces not covered by any law — the most prominent example is Guantánamo. The reason is that codified law always possesses

---

[28] Cf. Maus 1992: 180f. The danger of restricting freedom through trumping moral arguments has been presented also by Niesen, who especially stresses that the freedom to break off communication in moral contexts no longer exists (Niesen 2002: 51f).

[29] Cf. Teubner 1996; Fischer-Lescano 2002; as well as Brunkhorst (1999a), who approves the sociological description of how law develops, but criticizes the lack of democratic legitimation of international law.

inherently the power to exclude (Agamben 1998). The unleashed power of international law is expressed in the potential to arbitrarily determine who is protected by law and who is not. If morality is an inherent part of law then its critical normative content is already exhausted with the codification of law: human rights can easily become corrupted and perverted by political power into their opposite, a force for exclusion instead of inclusion. The danger of moralizing politics becomes obvious in the growing competencies of the UN Security Council which now is authorized to conduct humanitarian intervention with "best moral intentions" or to do nothing as it sees fit without having to contact the UN plenary assembly and respond to any other authority.

This development does not do the idea of human rights a good service. "Morally loaded" human rights implemented by an executive use of force are hardly an appropriate means to peaceful communication about divergent interpretations of moral, cultural and religious human rights. An alternative to the DelM would require making a clear distinction among moral human rights, which offer a normative critical point of view, and positive human rights, whose legitimation is procedural and morally neutral (Kreide 2003).

2.2 The Model of Fair Bargaining

To avoid the problems of the DelM, the Model of Fair Bargaining (FaiB) starts off from other theoretical and empirical presuppositions.[30] Even under ideal conditions, free from the influence of domination, complex societies are confronted with the impossibility of extracting a generalizable interest from the variety of diverging interests, whether in the domestic or the international context. This holds even under the assumptions that discussion proceeds under fair conditions with all available information and that deliberators can claim their interests meet the criteria of generalizability. John Rawls has coined the term, "burden of reasons" (Rawls 1993a: 54–8) for this kind of argumentative deadlock brought on by the fact that conflicting religious, pragmatic and also moral arguments can make equal claims to being reasonable and unobjectionable.

The FaiB assumes (reasonable) incommensurable readings of conflicting interests. Law-making processes aim at coming to an agreement but the way to agreement is highly contested. The fact of plural notions of justice implies that the assumptions that go into the basis of procedure can only be normatively modest, especially since procedure itself needs to be acceptable to all participants. If we want to get the most comprehensive agreement, it is

---

[30] For the Model of Fair Bargaining see Elster 1989, 1998; Hampshire 1999; Maus 1992, 1995; Rawls 1993a.

helpful to create procedures that do not presuppose too strong normative assumptions. In the FaiB, all those affected by the principles or rights in question should have an equal chance to participate in deliberation and to be heard. To listen to the view of others — *audi alteram partem* — is a basic, minimal principle of every kind of procedural justice.[31] Internationally, this practice has become so common that one can speak here of a universal normative principle (Hampshire 1999: 27, 77) — just think about the political practice of NGOs demanding rights of participation at WTO negotiations.

But whereas the DelM makes an implicit assumption of reciprocity of reason-giving and the generalization of these reasons, this does not hold for the FaiB. What can be reasonably expected from others is also object of dispute. Whereas the DelM assumes a symmetrical representation with no bargaining advantages on any side, the second model makes do with less. The FaiB also proposes a deliberative setting, we have seen, but threats or coercion are not completely excluded, nor are all power constellations leveled out. Material resources — for example, the speaker's prestige and slanted argumentation disguised as in the public interest — may influence the outcome. And whereas the first model relies on the idea of undistorted impartiality, the second is satisfied with at least the pretence of impartiality.

Jon Elster has shown that these assumptions come close to political reality but not too close to be completely absorbed by power struggles. One can see in political debates that both norm-orientated action and strategic action are interconnected (Elster 1998). Politics, to Elster, is too complex to be reduced to a matter of efficient regulations and economic agreements. The main purpose of many political processes is to create living conditions that are appropriate for all the members of society. Getting to this point is only possible for an adept perspective that is in the equal interest of everybody. Elster (1998) illustrates this pattern of deliberative process, in which different types of negotiation are combined, with reference to the historical constitution-making processes of Philadelphia 1776 and Paris 1789–1791.

Social action is not based solely on strategic utility calculation — that is the fact Elster wants to show in his historical analyses and which he thinks represents a universal phenomenon. To portray society as the coordination of action on the basis of opportunistic utility calculation betrays complete ignorance of the real world. Rather, social action is determined through social norms whose appropriateness is not accepted because of their effects

---

[31] This "principle of affectness," as I called it in Gabriëls and Kreide 2002, is a minimal normative principle, that forms the basis of every democratic order.

but because they are justified.[32] Social norms that appear in political practice cannot be reduced to action oriented towards strategic rationality. A proof of this is that whether political deliberation is convincing as acceptable depends very much on the degree to which the speaker can show it satisfies the public interest and not merely his own interest. As long as the public is inclined to endorse ideas that aim at the general interest and to reject blatant self-interest, strategic action is possible only if it is subtle: "The civilizing force of hypocrisy," according to Elster, "is a desirable effect of publicity" (Elster 1998: 111).

Also, because of these "empirical facts," FaiB can do without giving special priority to moral arguments. The different types of argumentation (pragmatic, ethical and moral) stand on the same level. A just agreement is the one that prevails at the end of a dispute under fair procedural conditions. What the negotiating parties reach at the end is not a *monolithic consensus* based on shared reasons as we have in the DelM, but a fair *polygenic consensus*. This is a consensus where the participants agree on the basis of *different* reasons but ones which they find illuminating. These are the best reasons they have, they fit in with their overall convictions and are their "first choice." Moreover, the result of the agreement is the best they would like to get, representing the best solution for all. This is different from a *compromise*: a compromise is their second-best solution, often reached on the basis of reasons they actually do not find convincing; but as they know that this agreement is better than none, they accept.[33]

However, the "pluralism of reasons" (Niesen 2002: 44) of the FaiB explains why it can result in a regional human right convention — and in one that is just. To illustrate how under "non-ideal" procedural conditions ethical, religious and moral arguments are engaged in the process of coming to an agreement, I will look at the debate about women's rights in Pakistan. After Pakistan had ratified the CEDAW (*Convention on the Elimination of all Forms of Discrimination against Women*) in 1996, a lively public debate

---

[32] An example of a social norm that is shared among all members of a society is "respect of human dignity" and the "prohibition of cannibalism."

[33] A further type of agreement could be called the "polygenic compromise": even though people can stick by their overall convictions and thus maintain their reasons of "first choice," the result does not express their first priority. Think of someone who defends a theory of needs and someone who is in favor of a neo-liberal theory, and both want to come to an agreement on social security measures. Both may agree that some basic subsistence is necessary for the poor. From a need-perspective this satisfies the idea that people who have needs and cannot satisfy them should get subsistence, whereas from point of view of a neo-liberalist, supporting the poor helps to stabilize social peace. For the first party (need-theory), however, the measure does not go far enough; for the second it already demands too much. So the result is a compromise (second-best option for both) but they agree on the basis of their very own first-order convictions.

emerged about what is discrimination against women, what are women's rights, and how can they be implemented in an Islamic state.

The American sociologist Anita Weiss describes how women's groups tried to win over the public by offering a not too radical interpretation of the Quran. The director of the New Islamic Institute for Women in Islamabad, Farhat Hashmi, offers an interpretation of women's rights derived from Islam which seems strange to most of us. She points out that women and men both have basic responsibilities: men work outside the house and women in the home. It is not forbidden for one to do the work of the other. But Hashmi proposes that they are permitted to carry out the tasks of the other once they have fulfilled their own responsibilities.[34] She considers this is a progressive interpretation which does not violate traditional sentiments too much. Other women's groups have criticized Hashmi's opinion for not going far enough.[35]

If you want to win the fight, you have to learn about your opponents' strategies and to think about which arguments usually win, regardless of

---

[34] Weiss 2003: 589. Also much effort has already been undertaken to derive context-specific notions of freedom, autonomy and individual choice out of the diversity of "Asian value systems." In the complex ideas of Confucius, for example, nobility of conduct has to be achieved in freedom, and in the Indian tradition one can find a variety of views on freedom, tolerance and equality (referring to the writings of Emperor Ashoka). The hope of some human rights theorists and activists is that a comprehensive political consensus can be reached by a local reconstruction of values which might pass the intercultural test of political agreement (Tatsuo 1999: 52).

[35] Through the second half of the 1980s and throughout the 1990s, there have been many attempts by Malaysian authorities in several of the thirteen states (under control of the Islamic Affairs Departments) to allow polygamy as a matter of principle (Othman 1999: 179). Women's groups argued that acknowledging polygamy as a man's right violates the Islamic notion of a woman's right in marriage, also referring to the Quran. Muslim feminists have pointed to the sociocultural bias built into the interpretative process because of the fact that exclusively male experts were doing interpretative legal reasoning. For example, the *Islam Sisters*, a NGO in Malaysia, argued that since in Islam a woman cannot be forced into marriage without her consent, it is not possible that the husband has a right to unilaterally change the circumstances of the marriage contract (Othman 1999: 180.) Moreover, they and other scholars suggest laying out sources in the Quran and *sunna* which are controversial according to international human rights standards and explaining them in historical context. What is needed is a contextualized reexamination of exegetical and jurisprudential texts. The inequality of men and women stems from the traditionalists' decontextualized exegesis of the Quran, where inappropriately meaning is transferred into universal principles. The obligation of family economic responsibility applied to men does not mean that men generally have authority over women, so some feminist argue. But the required obligations, especially for widows and divorced women, have to be explained in the context of a clan-based society of Prophet Muhammad's time (Othman 1999: 182); for this approach see also An-Na'im 1990c. The Quran also provides arguments that Islam in principle promotes gender equality. See, for example, Mernissi and Lakeland 1993.

whether they will be the ones which pass the test of generalization. Sometimes in real political debates it is not helpful to argue that women should be treated as equal because they are born equal or possess the same cognitive competencies. In their abstraction, these claims are not very telling as they are not responsive to social and political context. What the face of discrimination looks like, what opponents might say, what a change in law will mean for cultural identity, are important questions which cannot be easily sorted out, even by the local participants. The struggle to gain rights arises at the local level, set off by the experience of injustice and struggles against oppression, and by the pursuit of a more adequate interpretation of human rights. On the other hand, already existing legally binding international agreements, their interpretation and implementation, can influence the understanding of human rights elsewhere, as in the case of Pakistan. The interpretation of human rights sometimes begins locally, triggered off by newly experienced violations and later appeals to international agreements. The debate on human rights is characterized by an interplay between universal and local interpretations, as well as between international and local political requirements.

The *Bangkok Declaration*, for example, can be interpreted as a document which expresses the political will to come closer to the *Universal Declaration* by reconstructing local knowledge on human dignity in the form of law (Rechtsform). To this extent this regional convention refers to a not yet existing but coming universalization. But it can also be read as a statement separating parts of the Asian world from "Western" traditions and political practices. Then it becomes a symbol of incommensurable but well-founded interpretations of law.

We could describe the difference of the FaiB from the DelM by referring to John Rawls's notion of "pure procedural justice": regardless of what principles the parties agree on under fair conditions, they are just (Rawls 1993a: 72). In contrast, the DelM is based on "perfect procedural justice" which assumes independent criteria beyond the conditions of fair procedure: whether an outcome is just or not is determined by these criteria as the procedure is constructed from the start as a kind of "moral filter" that guarantees the result will fulfill the criteria. In the DelM, we have seen, legal human rights collapse into moral human rights. This has the negative effect of blurring the borders between legislative procedures that are disinterested in the motives of the participants and procedures that require from them correct insight into the principles. In the FaiB, motives in the process of reason-giving are not restricted. Rather agreement can be based on arguments people are convinced of even if they are not shared by everybody. "Morality-laden" human rights conventions neither take account of the pluralism of existing (and sometimes universalizing) interpretations, nor do they help to prevent a "moralization" of executive enforcement practices in the hands of the United Nations or some hegemonic authority. The FaiB distinguishes between legal and moral human rights and their legitimation, and frees the legislative procedure from linkage to a specific (Kantian) idea of morality.

Model of international procedural justice	Deliberative Model (DelM)	Model of Fair Bargaining (FaiB)
Concept of procedural justice	Procedural justice: reciprocity and generality	Procedural justice: equal chances to be heard
Order of reasons	Hierarchy of reasons — "Moral filter"	Pluralism of reasons
Concept of person	Sense of justice	Rational interest
Result	Monolithic consensus	Polygenic consensus

3. The performativity of normative arguments

So far, the FaiB seems to be on the winning side of the discussion. But one can now ask whether we are approaching a slippery slope by giving up too quickly on a normative point of view which would permit criticism of procedural outcomes. Does the FaiB allow too much to be given up of the human rights vision under unfavorable power constellations, especially of its universal claim? It would be a misunderstanding, though, to conclude that with the FaiB there is no normative evaluation left. First, there is the fair procedure of law-setting which guarantees that all those affected by the norm are heard. And secondly, one can rely on moral *norms* (not legal rights) which one can say are already built into the core of international politics, so, for example, the norm that human beings should not be murdered, hurt, humiliated, or have to live in poverty through official misdeed or negligence. Some of these uncontested core principles are most of all moral human rights. Moral human rights — and this is an important point here — do not directly legitimize political actions; rather one can understand them[36] as normative claims on a just institutional order that guarantees that all those affected have secure access to vital goods and services (Pogge 2002a: 64). The implementation of moral claims should proceed by creating international procedures for law-making. But this, nevertheless, does not mean that one can work towards some single comprehensive moral ideal for the international level which is supposed to

---

[36] Cf. Pogge 2002a: 168–95, 1988b, with special focus on the role of moral values in international relations.

be non-negotiable. Still, the more widespread these normative ideas, the more they are reflected in codified human rights conventions.

The prospects for a "moral cosmopolitanism" (Pogge 2002a: 169) are not that bad. Contrary to the opinion of the "realist," not only economic-pragmatic but also moral arguments have "performativity." Performativity here does not assume a causal relation between normative practice and action but norms do, it is claimed, have efficacy, e.g., they can, though they need not, have effects in the world and can influence how people live. For instance, they may trigger processes of self-reflection with the result that people perceive their situation differently — maybe see it as unjust and act accordingly and, as a result, fight for their rights.[37]

This aspect of efficacy can be illustrated by looking at the process by which the *Universal Declaration of Human Rights* was set up. Just after a draft version of the *Universal Declaration* had become public in 1947, the character of this political agreement began to change. It was no longer a mere preliminary political act in good faith. The agreement became a powerful instrument for the oppressed.[38] Petitions inundated the Commission of Human Rights. People wrote about suffering from racial discrimination, religious prejudice, the sexual abuse of women, hunger, and lack of medical treatment. The most prominent petition came from W. E. B. Du Bois who,

---

[37] Austin (1962) introduced the idea that when one utters a sentence like "You're fired" or "This meeting is adjourned" one performs an act. He calls this "explicit performative utterances." The theory of speech acts, which he developed, claims that one does more things by help of words than just convey information. For the idea that normative institutions affect people's actions see Peters 1993: 325. The notion of performativity used here refers to Peters' notion: arguments may have an effect on others, but the effect depends on the context in which they were uttered.

[38] The French *Declaration*, for example, once institutionalized, triggered debates regarding what is meant by the "Rights of Man and of the Citizen." Yet in 1791, new articles were added specifying that freedom of thought and worship also apply to Protestants and Jews — two groups who had been persecuted under the Ancien Regime. Economic and social rights were added to the canon of constitutional rights after a bloody revolt by the poor. Olympe de Gouges proclaimed the *Declaration of the Rights of Woman and the Female Citizen*, saying that the "woman is born free and remains equal to man in her rights" (Gouges 1995). And the slaves of Saint Dominique, today's Haiti, demanded equal rights, relying on the newly established rights in France when they launched their massive revolt (Lauren 1998: 18). Other struggles for the recognition of rights followed. It took some decades before the obvious truth that all men are equal by nature also included non-whites. In 1857, Abraham Lincoln ran against Justice St. A. Douglas to represent Illinois in the US Senate. He lost, but his campaign for the abolition of slavery triggered a lively debate. His opponent objected that it had not been the intention of the founding fathers that the *Declaration of Independence* should include blacks — otherwise they would have specified it, as slavery had been common then. Lincoln replied that the founder's aim was not to preserve a certain state of society, but to come closer to the meaning of rights all the time. Abraham Lincoln's Springfield Address, June 26, 1857, cited from Eide 1995: 36.

on behalf of the National Association for the Advancement of Colored People, submitted a detailed complaint about the denial of rights to blacks. He argued that this was not only a national but an international question, comparing the position of blacks to the situation of people in the colonial states.[39] This was exactly what governments began to fear during the process of composing the *Universal Declaration*: that an internationally established ideal of individual and collective self-determination might lead to unrest in their own populations, and that other states would be allowed to interfere with what occurs within national borders. However, the process of becoming aware of one's rights and going public was inevitable. The reactions from all over the world reveal the performativity of symbolic and normative political practices and of arguments arising from the experience of injustice.

Normative utterances however do not only trigger the development of a sense for injustice but they can create a certain "pressure to perform" on the producer of negative effects. Transnational corporations, for example, which voluntarily submit to "codes of conduct" and announce their respect for human rights standards in job security, minimal wage, the prohibition of child labor, etc., are measured by their announcements. They cannot fall behind what they have promised without losing credibility. One could say they have "talked themselves into moral discourse," entangled in their own moral standards which raise expectations.[40]

But people learn to play the normative scale. Even if work conditions have improved in some places of the world, one cannot overlook the fact that propagated self-obligations very often have the character of mere "human rights rhetoric." Nike, for example, is a prominent member of the "Global Compact,"[41] a pact among private actors (TNCs, representatives of economic

---

[39] For lengthy discussion see Lauren 1998: 226ff.

[40] See the anthology on the already achieved successes of the voluntary codes by Hartman, Laura P., Arnold, Denis G. and Wokutch, Richard E. 2003. Thomas Risse 2000 shows that argumentation, deliberation and convincing play an important role in international negotiations. He speaks of "moral entrapment": even those participants who enter the negotiations with a strategic intention at one point have to switch to discursive rules and an attitude orientated towards a common understanding ("verständigungsorientiertes Handeln").

[41] Besides the UN High Commission for Human Rights, the International Labor Organization (ILO), representatives of the UN Environmental Program and about 50 corporations take part, among them Nike, Shell, BP Amoco and Rio Tinto. The deal is that the corporations have to go public on the Global Compact Internet site by describing their progress in implementing human rights standards. In turn they are allowed to use a logo of the UN for their advertising. NGOs fear that the prestige of the UN will be damaged if its name is closely linked to corporations that have not respected human rights in the past. Besides this, corporations also agreed to voluntary *codes of conduct,* some even with external control. See also Kuper's evaluation of the "Global Compact" in this volume.

associations), the ILO and the United Nations, brought into life through Kofi Annan in January 1999 with the aim of moving more transnational corporations to adopt codes of conduct. The company has been sued by an American labor law activist, Mark Kasky, for false or misleading statements in advertising. Nike had assumed that work conditions in their subcontracting firms had improved — an assumption Kasky said was not true. A month later, in September 2003, Nike, which claimed it was engaged in fully protected free political speech, agreed to a settlement out of court and paid 1.5 million dollars to a fair trade organization.[42] Without persistent and thorough-going empirical and theoretical investigation into people's living conditions, human rights codes of conduct can just become another racket.

---

[42] Greenhouse 2003. A comprehensive study on corporation strategies and the legitimation through "moral fictions" is offered in Mark-Ungericht 2002.

Chapter 15

Human Rights and Relativism[*]

Andreas Follesdal
The Norwegian Centre for Human Rights at the Faculty of Law and ARENA Centre for European Studies, University of Oslo

Few governments today admit that they violate central human rights such as freedom of speech, or prohibitions against slavery and torture. Violations of human rights are denied or excused, but seldom defended (Schachter 1982: 336). The *Bangkok Declaration* of 1993 changed this. In this declaration, representatives of Asian states dismissed civil and political rights as contrary to "Asian values." Their statement has received much attention, particularly since it appeared immediately prior to the 1993 Vienna World Conference on Human Rights.[1]

Human rights are universal and critical norms constraining the allocation and exercise of state power, so it should come as no surprise that some governments object to human rights. The *Bangkok Declaration* insists that states have the primary responsibility for the promotion and protection of human rights, and the primary responsibility to remedy human rights violations. It falls to the government to determine trade-offs where appropriate, and to secure rights through such institutions as each government decides. Human rights

---

[*] The article was originally prepared for the International Human Rights Network of Academies and Scholarly Societies, under the auspices of the National Academy of Sciences, Washington D.C. Samuel Scheffler generously provided perceptive comments and constructive advice, and Tore Lindholm kindly suggested pertinent literature. The project was partially funded by the Norwegian Non-fiction Literature Fund, and pursued at the Minda de Gunzburg Center for European Studies at Harvard University. The author is grateful for the hospitality and support received from the Center, and from Barbara and William Graham and Patricia Pepper of Currier House, Harvard University, as well as for comments at the Oslo conference and from Thomas Pogge.
[1] Cf. Kreide's contribution to this volume for more discussion of the *Bangkok Declaration*.

A. Follesdal and T. Pogge, (eds.), Real World Justice, 265-283.
© 2005 Springer. Printed in the Netherlands.

must be considered in the context of a dynamic and evolving process of international norm-setting, bearing in mind the significance of national and regional particularities and various historical, cultural and religious backgrounds.

The *Declaration* insisted, in short, that national sovereignty entails non-interference in the internal affairs of the State, including the "non-use of human rights as an instrument of political pressure."

1. Nine challenges to human rights

From the *Bangkok Declaration* one may extract at least nine objections to human rights, which will be presented and discussed in the following. I will conclude that all of these objections are unconvincing.

1) *Human rights are based on atomistic egoism*
Human rights are unduly based on a Western conception of the individual as self-interested and atomized. For societies not sharing this conception, human rights talk amounts to objectionable Western cultural or ideological imperialism.

2) *Human rights ignore human duties*
A focus on human rights ignores or detracts from the duties of citizens to abide by the commands of their heads of family and government.

3) *Human rights ignore communal ties*
The concern for human rights ignores, or is incompatible with, individuals' local duties, to members of their own community and to the interests of their own society.

4) *Human rights ignore social and economic needs*
The focus of international or Western attention on civil and political rights is skewed. Non-Western conceptions of human rights include concern also for individuals' social, economic and cultural needs. Such rights require hard choices and trade-offs with civil and political rights.

5) *Human rights violate respect for individuals' tacit consent*
Respect for individuals does not require respect for their "human rights," but instead, requires that foreigners do not interfere with the society which individuals accept. The tacit consent of individuals should be respected, even when their government fails to respect human rights.

6) *Human rights violate respect for other cultures*
Human rights violate respect for other cultures by imposing a blueprint which conflicts with many non-Western societies. Respect for other cultures requires that societies should be left to flourish as they see fit.

7) *Human rights ignore non-governmental threats*

The human rights focus ignores the very real threats to human well-being wrought by non-governmental agents and other states. Under non-ideal situations, such as civil war or noncompliance by other states, any human rights obligations of states are canceled.

8) *Human rights violate state sovereignty*
Foreign protests and intervention of any kind violate the long-standing and generally accepted principle of national self determination.

9) *Human rights threaten world stability*
Human rights protests ignore the risk of global instability created by foreign intervention in the domestic affairs of other states.

These objections suggest that human rights should be dismissed as an objectionable exercise in Western ideological imperialism.

2. Premises: States, individuals, and human rights

Before addressing these objections, the underlying assumption about an East-West divide regarding human rights should be questioned. Some deplorable Western traditions have dismissed human rights well into this century, and there are strands and components of theories of human rights in many non-Western normative traditions. A rejection of "Western" human rights on the basis of "Asian" values is therefore unfortunate, for several reasons. When a government insists on distinct and unified Western, Asian, or African traditions, it ignores the diversity of cultures within and across geographical boundaries (Sen 1997). Moreover, such labels serve to hide discrepancies between the views of the government and the citizens. There are shared values across "civilizations," and disagreements within them, sufficient to question whether conflicts about human rights are due to a "Clash of Civilizations" (*pace* Huntington 1996).

The response to the nine objections will show that very many theories of human rights and moral traditions condemn the behavior which human rights serve to protect against. Indeed, most of the nine objections to human rights fail to hold against a wide range of human rights theories spelling out their basis and content. The remaining objections do not repudiate human rights, rather, at most they support some accounts and specifications of rights over others.

This section presents an overview of theories which regard human rights as safeguards for individuals within states. To develop this account, we start with some comments about sovereign states and the role of the state in promoting the "common good," then include some observations about the role of human rights regulations before discussing how human rights regulations secure significant interests.

2.1 The system of sovereign states

Our world order is a system of sovereign states. Conceptions of "sovereign" political powers can be found from the 9th century onwards in the writings of the Islamic scholars Ibn Abi-al-Rabi and Al-Farabi (Ahmad 1965: 54f). An important step in the development of the system of sovereign states is the principle of exclusive territorial control associated with the peace settlement at Westphalia in Germany, which ended the Thirty Years' War in 1648.

Each independent state enjoys legal sovereignty which may be regarded as two complex bundles of legal authority: internal and external (Weber 1972; Bull 1977). A government enjoys *internal* sovereignty over the population within a territory insofar as it claims a monopoly on the legitimate use of force, and is supreme over all other actors within that territory. And the government enjoys *external* sovereignty in the form of legal immunity against any agent beyond state borders: states are regarded as equals, not subject to any other government. This model allowed governments to provide domestic order and some security from outside domination, even under conditions of international anarchy.

State sovereignty has never been unrestricted within this world order of states. Some standards of legitimate governance which we now recognize as human rights were included in this arrangement from the start (Krasner 1993). The Peace of Westphalia required that the prince of the land must respect his citizens' freedom to exercise their religion (*Treaty of Osnabrück* article 5, section 28, 49). International agreements in the 18th and 19th centuries further regulated the treatment of religious minorities. For instance, in 1830, Greek independence was ensured in a protocol signed by Britain, France and Russia, on the condition that religious groups were to receive equal treatment. Treaties after World War I secured minority protections. Since the Second World War, several international conventions have recognized a wide range of human rights as binding on governments as a matter of international law. Historically, these recent efforts continue a long-standing tradition of regulating existing institutions and government practices according to normative theories of human rights.

2.2 The role of states: to secure the common good

Humans are social beings: we are dependent on an orderly society to develop fully as human beings and to live full lives. Even though all interests are interests *of* individuals, this does not entail that individuals are atomistic or egoistic, nor that associations and other individuals are simply of instrumental value for us in the pursuit of our own individual interests. We also value the well-being and flourishing of others. Moreover, many of our interests and projects consist in relationships and joint activity with others, or require coordination. Consider, for instance, participating in organized worship, the role of labor unions in wage negotiations, or voluntary interest associations. Indeed, many of our projects can only be expressed as cooperative ventures and achieved in cooperation with others. Many aspects of the good life for the individual can thus be considered the "common good" both in the sense that the good life for each has similar components, and in the sense that the good life can only be achieved in common with others.

Such accounts of the "common good" are shared by a wide range of philosophical traditions, including the Western natural law tradition (Finnis 1980: 168), and the Islamic philosophers Ibn Abi-al-Rabi (9th century), Al-Farabi and Ibn Khaldun (1332–1406) (cf. Ahmad 1965; An-Na'im 1990a).

In a sovereign state, it is ultimately the state which grants individuals all legal rights, powers and immunities. So the state is the source of benefits and legal rights enjoyed by the individual. Modern states make it possible for individuals to secure their basic needs and other conditions for a good life. It is therefore misleading to suggest that the relationship between individual and state is fundamentally conflictual. Similarly, conflicts between "community interests" and "individuals' interests" are not best regarded as conflicts between the interests of individuals and the interests of some other entity, but rather as conflicts among the interests of individuals, where some of these interests are in the shared activities of members of the community. But these interests are still interests of individuals, present and future, living in the community.

A long-standing and broadly shared view on the responsible use of state power is that it must be used for the common good, understood as the good of present and future individual members of society. This view is found in several Western traditions, and in the Confucian and Islamic traditions referred to above. Human rights provide a specification of the common good and how it should be pursued by governments, by regulating how benefits and powers should be allocated among individuals.

This concern for human rights does not assume that humans can exist independently of society. Nor does it deny that individuals have a duty to obey the commands of government, as long as those commands are within certain limits. Rather, a concern for human rights is compatible with accepting that individuals are social beings, with binding obligations towards their community. The focus of human rights is to identify the bounds of these requirements, by exploring their grounds. For even though the state is the source of legal rights and other benefits, a legitimate state may not allocate benefits and burdens any way the government desires.

2.3 Characteristics of human rights

Internationally recognized human rights are constitutional or other institutionally embedded legal protections and directives that regulate legislative and executive authority and discretion. The internationally recognized human rights thus affect both internal and external sovereignty: the authority governments enjoy over individuals, and the authority international bodies enjoy vis-à-vis domestic governments.

Internationally recognized human rights can be taken to have several characteristics (cf. Pogge 2002a for another, broadly similar account).

a) They are requirements that should often be embedded, constitutionally or otherwise, so as to regulate the laws and policies of the land;
b) They are universal, that is, rights of individuals living in any state;
c) They are directed towards governments, regarding their laws and policies;
d) They serve a critical and constraining role vis-à-vis actions by governments against their citizens and among one another (Schachter 1981, 1982; van Boven 1982);
e) Their violation is considered a matter of international concern, and some violations might warrant international assistance, protest or intervention.

It is by no means clear that the current set of such internationally recognized human rights is justifiable as it stands. Indeed, many critics of current human rights law do not deny that this set of human rights is part of international law. Instead, the challenge concerns whether these internationally recognized human rights can be justified on grounds which do not presuppose objectionable "Western" values. Other critics of current human rights law argue for other modifications, by appeal to what are claimed to be plausible theories of human rights.

2.4 The roles of human rights

Human rights can be seen as serving two important roles in shaping and maintaining a just system of states, corresponding to internal and external sovereignty.

Internally, human rights spell out some of the minimal conditions of domestic legitimacy. That is, human rights are necessary though not sufficient conditions for granting a government a valid moral claim that citizens should respect its decisions. A government must secure human rights for a population to be morally bound to obey (Schachter 1982: 351; Alston 1989; An-Na'im 1990b: 49; Donnelly 1989). Thus the *Universal Declaration of Human Rights* states

[I]t is essential, if man is not to be compelled to have recourse, as a last resort, to rebellion against tyranny and oppression, that human rights should be protected by the rule of law (Preamble to *Universal Declaration of Human Rights*).

The recognition that constraints on government are needed is not uniquely Western. Other civilizations have also claimed that government must be legitimate to command obedience, and that in this context all individuals have equal worth — though the conditions have not always been expressed in terms of human rights.

Confucius held that for a governor to be fit to govern, he must avoid several evils. Two of these are "Terror, which rests on ignorance and murder. Tyranny, which demands results without proper warning" (*Analects* 20.3). However, the great Confucian thinker Mencius (372–289 BC) went further and permitted the assassination of tyrants (cf. Gangjian and Gang 1995; Wood 1995: 170; Chan 1999).

Kautilya (c. 360–280 BC), an Indian Brahmin and minister to Emperor Chandragupta Maurya, is known as the author of *Arthashastra*, a treatise on government. He there lays out conditions of good governance expressed as duties of the king. "The king shall provide the orphans, the aged, the infirm, the afflicted, and the helpless with maintenance. He shall also provide subsistence to helpless women when they are pregnant and to the children they give birth to." In the happiness of the subjects lies the happiness of the king; in their welfare, his own welfare. The welfare of the king does not lie in the fulfillment of what is dear to him; whatever is dear to the subjects constitutes his welfare" (cf. Hay 1988).

Many Hindu traditions are in clear conflict with human rights — particularly the caste system, since it denies the equal worth of all human beings. Hinduism also stresses submission, hierarchy and loyalty toward the existing social order. However, we also find Hindu traditions which present standards of legitimate governance and the right to protest unjust rule, for instance, in the tradition of Mohandas Gandhi, and discussions of the duties (*dharma*) of the state found in *RigVeda* and *Mahabharata*. There, the duty of the state is said to ensure the well-being of the people, punish criminals, and protect its citizens, acting in the interest of all the people. Dharma of the state is for the general well-being of humankind. And loyalty to government has been limited according to long-standing Hindu traditions. For instance, Rammohun Roy (1772?–1833), a representative of Hindu enlightenment, was deeply critical of the government policy of permitting widow burning (*suttee*) (van Bulert 1995).

Some Islamic scholars state standards for assessing governments. 'Ali Shari'ati (1933–1977), one of the ideologues of the Iranian Islamic revolution, interpreted the Qur'an so as to criticize even Islamic religious states if they led to exploitation and alienation (Wessels 1995). There are Islamic scholars who argue for egalitarian readings of the Qur'an and the ethical and legal norms expressed in Shari'a more than thousand years ago (e.g., Taha 1987, An-Na'im 1990a). These scholars challenge the distinctions in Shari'a between the rights of Muslims and non-Muslims, and between Islamic men and women.

The second important role of human rights concerns external sovereignty. Compliance with human rights is regarded as sufficient for a state to have good standing in the international community. This is not to say that any human rights violation by a government justifies military intervention (Buergenthal 1979; Hoffmann 1981). A government's misuse of its powers does not logically or legally entail the right or obligation of any other party to intervene militarily (Kratochwil 1995: 35). Two important reasons for caution are the likelihood of failure even when military intervention is well intended, and the risks that authority to intervene may be abused (Schachter 1984; Donnelly 1989: 264). Nevertheless, in principle there may be circumstances and procedures which make such international practices acceptable.

External sovereignty may also be restricted through non-forceful means of protest and intervention, without such risks of setting off international wars. Such action may be international, i.e., involving other governments or intergovernmental bodies, or transnational, undertaken by non-governmental entities. Action may include humanitarian intervention, diplomatic protests or economic pressure to alleviate massive human rights violations. Actions may also seek to inform the domestic population of the violations perpetrated by their government. A "consistent pattern of gross violations of human rights" may warrant international response (ECOSOC 1970). If efficacious, such modes of protest may indeed be required of the international community.

Given these two roles of human rights in restricting and assessing legitimate sovereignty, it should come as no surprise that human rights are scorned by some governments. The critical role of human rights fosters such responses, so these reactions do not demonstrate that human rights are too restrictive. To assess such criticisms we must ask two questions. First, we must determine whether some human rights constraints on government can be justified. Secondly, we must consider whether the current international legally binding human rights are consonant with such justifications, or whether these existing components of international law should be modified. The first of these two questions is addressed by normative political theory concerning how state power may be justified. Responses to this question draw on the assumption that the legitimate role of government is to secure the common good, understood as the good of present and future individual members of society. Human rights standards seek to hold governments to this task.

2.5 Human rights as institutionalized safeguards for significant interests

The various justifications of human rights ground them in a conception of human interests or related notions such as needs, well-being, flourishing or dignity. Human rights require that social institutions and practices protect these interests against a variety of standard threats in a system of sovereign states.

On virtually all such accounts, a broad range of mistreatment is ruled out, such as torture, and violation of civil rights. Some differences among human rights theories stem from different views about which interests are significant. For the purposes of responding to the criticism of "Asian values," the most important difference among these theories is between those accounts that support "negative" rights of noninterference, and those that also support "positive" rights to opportunities.

Some theories of human rights concentrate on the interest in being free from coercion by others, particularly from the government, to exploit one's resources according to one's own ability and interests (Hart 1955; Berlin 1969). Such considerations support human rights that grant individuals immunity from government interference in the form of "negative" rights.

Many theories of human rights also recognize further interests of individuals. One important interest of individuals may be the ability to actually select certain options that they have reason to value (Gewirth 1978; O'Neill 1986; Sen 1985b). These accounts may therefore require intervention by the state to provide the individual with the appropriate opportunities. "Positive" government intervention may therefore be required to secure the satisfaction of basic human needs, some means for pursuing projects and relationships, or to prevent suffering, a central concern in all world religions.

Theories which only acknowledge individuals' interest in freedom from coercion may conclude that only "negative" liberties are human rights. Such views might be criticized for drawing on "Western" conceptions of the individual. But note that many "Western" scholars acknowledge a broader range of significant interests, including material needs, which justify "positive" rights. The following observations draw on the latter of these two positions, while acknowledging that there are disagreements about which interests are significant, about whether "interests" is the best term, and which modes of government action best secure these interests.

Legal or constitutional safeguards are of two kinds. Certain institutions may be required — "obligation of means" — or certain conditions may be placed on the outcome of institutions — "obligation of result" (Schachter 1982: 349f).

Thus human rights considerations require that some quite specific mechanisms be in place. Examples are legal immunities in the form of civil rights, freedom of speech, association and religion. Governments are also required to ensure that there are judicial remedies available to those whose legal rights are violated. Other specific requirements concern freedom of the press and freedom of speech, coupled with democratic political rights. Note that the reason for these political rights need not be the importance of negative liberty or the intrinsic value of autonomous living. Many of these liberties serve to secure individuals' ability to make well-informed decisions among political candidates. Democratic rule, as compared to non-accountable political power, is important not only if one values self-determination, but also to prevent risks to individuals' vital needs. Thus Amartya Sen has argued that freedom of the press and democratic competition among political parties protect against famines (Sen 1988).

Such arguments for political rights and freedom of speech are not based on a contested "Western" assumption of the intrinsic value of individual autonomy, or on an assumption that government power will always be abused. Rather, the argument is comparative, that other allocations of political power pose greater threats to the satisfaction of important interests.

Human rights considerations also support some legal obligations of result. Individuals' significant interests do not always require that governments pursue a particular policy, or that they establish specific institutions. Rather, the significant interests may be ensured in a variety of ways, allowing governments to take account of local circumstances, culture, and resources (Sohn 1982: 21). Many of the significant interests surveyed above require legal regulations under the social conditions typical of modern sovereign states — but any one of a variety of institutional arrangements may do.

Consider a society where all foodstuffs are bought and sold in markets. Then money is necessary to satisfy basic nutritional needs. Thus government policies must facilitate opportunities for paid labor and for income substitutes, leaving the institutional specifics to be determined by culture, history and majority rule. Governments may, for instance, be required to pursue a plausible strategy for agricultural or industry development, with the ultimate goal of securing the survival of the population. Such requirements are found in the Constitution of India, which includes a directive that the government pursue an agricultural policy securing food for all. Similarly, the

Spanish and Norwegian Constitutions require the government to have policies aimed at full employment.

Thus several arguments for economic and social human rights support legal obligations of result against the domestic government, while many civil and political rights are obligations of institutional means. Both kinds of arguments rely on empirical assumptions about the system of states and the risks to significant interests that arise within sovereign states. Still, these arguments support universal human rights, for all human beings live within states which claim internal and external sovereignty. Governments with centralized power pose similar threats to individuals everywhere, threats which human rights seek to protect against. Thus no government claiming to secure the common good can reasonably claim that human rights need not constrain them (Tomuschat 1985).

On these accounts, it might appear that only governments can violate human rights. To be sure, individuals' significant interests may also be systematically violated or threatened by individuals or organizations, by exploitation, violence or terrorism. Many such threats also constitute human rights violations, in one of two ways. The perpetrators violate legislation which is required by human rights theories, and the government fails to use its sovereign powers to prevent such systematic illegalities. Important questions of responsibility for violations of significant interests arise when state sovereignty is reduced or absent, vis-à-vis such diverse agents as multinational enterprises, paramilitary death squads, and international financial markets. The urgency of these issues notwithstanding, they fall beyond the challenges raised by the *Bangkok Declaration*.

3. The nine objections reconsidered

Defenses of human rights as sketched above offer grounds for alleviating or rebutting the nine objections to human rights.

1)   Human Rights are based on atomistic egoism

Human rights are inappropriately based on a Western conception of the individual as self-interested and atomized. Insisting on human rights is an exercise in objectionable Western cultural or ideological imperialism.

Historically, some arguments for individual rights have indeed appealed to an ideal of human flourishing which prized individual autonomy, or which focused on the individual as agent. For instance, Immanuel Kant and John Stuart Mill argued along such lines, and Alan Gewirth and Onora O'Neill have presented such arguments more recently (Gewirth 1978, 1982; O'Neill 1986, 1996). However, they do not assume that individuals are fundamentally self-interested, nor do they dismiss the importance of social institutions for ensuring the human good.

The arguments for human rights sketched above hold that human rights are important to protect individuals against standard threats by governments to their significant interests. But few of these arguments rest on controversial assumptions that only individual autonomy matters. For instance, one important reason for individual political rights and civil liberties is their instrumental role in preventing misery and starvation.

2) Human Rights ignore human duties

The focus on human rights ignores or detracts from the "human duties" of citizens, to abide by the commands of their government and their heads of family.

It is a mistake to hold that human rights are in fundamental conflict with a duty of obedience towards legitimate government. To the contrary, Thomas Aquinas, John Locke, and other central contributors to Western political thought all assumed that there is a duty to obey legitimate authority. Theories of human rights seek instead to lay down some limits on such obedience. In particular, human rights identify some conditions beyond which a government can no longer expect obedience on the part of its subjects.

There is no assumption that a society is better insofar as its members conduct their interaction on the basis of individual rights and legal considerations, rather than on the basis of friendship and mutual respect. The point is rather that some protections in the form of human rights are valuable final checks on government power, where friendship and respect are insufficient. Thus, this view is compatible with a broad range of world views, including the Confucian view that rights and laws are fall-back options, when virtue fails (Chan 1999).

3) Human Rights ignore communal ties

Human rights ignore, overrule, or are incompatible with normatively significant local ties and duties to the citizens' own community.

Human rights place some substantive constraints on domestic and international political orders. Therefore, in one sense this criticism is correct: there are existing laws, policies and cultural practices which are incompatible with human rights. But this is not to say that human rights prevent personal ties, common projects and shared commitments. Indeed, insistence on human rights does not prevent the acknowledgment of human duties and patriotism in general. Rather, the concern is to make clear when governments' claims to such duties and ties are morally binding on citizens, and when they are not. Duties towards compatriots and local communities are compatible with human rights as long as these duties and ties do not violate the constraints laid down by human rights. Indeed, in article 29, the United Nations *Universal Declaration of Human Rights* states that

> Everyone has duties to the community in which alone the free and full development of his personality is possible.

We can insist on human rights, and still acknowledge a broad range of "community interests," namely, those that are best seen as interests of individuals, in undertaking practices jointly with others. Any conflicts that arise, then, between the interests "of society" and those of the individual are fundamentally regarded as conflicts among the interests of different individuals — none of whom need be "atomistic." For instance, the human rights to religious freedom, rights of the family, and rights of association are centrally regarded as rights of individuals to engage in practices jointly with others. This is not to deny that some normative theories may hold that some of "the interests of society" may be irreducible to the various interests of individuals. However, this account of human rights shows that it is possible to adjudicate conflicts between community interests and other interests of individuals without holding that community ties are of no moral significance.

4) *Human Rights ignore social and economic needs.*

The focus of international or Western attention on civil and political rights is skewed in ignoring individuals' social, economic and cultural needs.

This objection is correct as leveled against some theories of human rights — in particular, those which regard negative liberty as the sole significant interest of individuals. However, justifications of human rights based on individuals' interest in *positive freedom*, i.e., in a realm of options open to actual choice, or interest in *well-being* more broadly conceived, recognize the social, economic, and cultural preconditions of a decent life. A broad range of theories of human rights provided by Western theorists support both sets of internationally recognized rights, as does the UN's *International Covenant on Economic, Social and Cultural Rights.*

The apparent focus of Westerners on violations of civil and political rights, rather than on the whole panoply of rights may be due to several factors.

Firstly, violations of social and economic rights are difficult to ascertain. States are typically required to take appropriate steps to ensure the realization of rights such as the right to be free from hunger. This right is not a legal right to food enjoyed by each individual, but an obligation by states to undertake political measures designed to improve production and distribution of food. Likewise, states must take steps to prevent, treat and control "epidemic, endemic, occupational and other diseases." Such obligations may be fulfilled even where people are starving or dying of epidemic diseases, since the government may be willing, but simply unable to prevent these disasters. It is thus difficult to ascertain whether economic rights are violated by a government.

Secondly, it is not clear that media attention in the West about violations of economic and social rights is an effective way to improve the situation. Lack of criticism is therefore no indication that Western states or Western ideologies regard social, economic and cultural rights as less important. For instance, one important mechanism for fostering compliance is through the reporting obligations of states signatory to the *Covenant on Economic, Social and Cultural Rights* (Alston 1989 and 1992; Gomez 1995). This arrangement holds states accountable to international bodies for their policies. Such international reporting seeks to improve compliance with the economic and social human rights, without international sanctions or pressure from media. Moreover, Western signatories to the *Covenant on Economic, Social and Cultural Rights* must also contribute reports, and citizens of Western states are members of the boards receiving and assessing such reports. Thus it is misleading to claim that Western states and citizens are not concerned with these rights.

One objection against the focus on violations of civil and political rights is that these rights must sometimes be traded off against social and economic rights. For instance, some governments of developing countries argue that the right to development can only be pursued by curtailing the right to political participation. Political rights must be sacrificed for economic development.

However, there is little economic evidence to support this claim, that a trade-off is required in practice, either in the short or in the long run (Beitz 1981a, 1981b; Alston 1989; Donnelly 1989; Olson 1993; Sen 1993; Goodin 1979).

One example of the alleged trade-off is presented by the Chinese government in its *White Paper on Human Rights* (1991):

> The problem of food and clothing having been basically solved, the people have been guaranteed with the basic right to subsistence. This is a historical achievement made by the Chinese people and government in seeking and protecting human rights. ... The people's right to subsistence will still be threatened in the event of a social turmoil or other disasters.

China has indeed had an impressive record of reducing and eliminating endemic starvation (Sen 1981: 7). The view presented in the White Paper holds that democratic rights and other threats to political stability are incompatible with securing subsistence. However, this claim must be challenged, on two grounds.

Firstly, even though China has had impressively well-functioning systems of food distribution, the White Paper seems to ignore the Chinese famine of 1958–61, during which 16.5–29.5 million people died. Thus, a stable government does not ensure that the vital need for subsistence will be met. Secondly, one important justification for political rights is precisely that acute famines do not occur in democracies — though political rights are not sufficient to prevent endemic hunger (Sen and Dreze 1990). Therefore, the alleged trade-off between economic rights and political and civil rights is not substantiated by the Chinese example. Indeed, people's interest in subsistence supports political and civil rights.

5) *Human Rights violate respect for individuals' tacit consent*
Respect for individuals entails that their actual compliance with the laws of the land should be regarded and respected as an expression of tacit consent, even when human rights are violated.

But actual compliance with the laws of the land is not the final word regarding the legitimacy of social institutions. More would need to be said about the reasons for actual acquiescence before accepting that this constitutes tacit consent in a significant sense. Where basic liberties, freedoms and basic needs are not protected, silence can easily be due to fear. We should not agree with a totalitarian government's interpretation of silence and acquiescence as tacit consent, if those who criticize the government risk immediate death or imprisonment.

6) *Human Rights violate respect for other cultures*
Human rights violate respect for other cultures by imposing an institutional blueprint which conflicts with many non-Western societies. Respect for other cultures requires that societies should be left to flourish as they see fit.

An important challenge to a theory of human rights is to lay down both the grounds and the limits of cross-cultural toleration. The defense of human rights outlined above seeks to respect cultural pluralism in several ways. Firstly, the theories of human rights are based on a limited set of significant interests, common to all individuals in states as we know them, and compatible with a broad range of moral traditions. Secondly, they offer minimum standards of legitimacy for governments, and do not seek to provide institutional blueprints. For instance, internationally recognized human rights which specify obligations of result leave the choice of policies to the domestic government. Finally, the theories of human rights respect existing cultures by offering conditions of legitimate government to be used principally by the domestic population in their efforts at change. Interventions, militarily or otherwise, are only considered as means of last resort.

When human rights are violated, the government pursues policies which are not in the interest of the population. Objecting to domestic and international protests by appealing to the importance of respecting culture begs several important questions. It must be made clear whose culture is to be respected: that of the government, or that of the citizens. And reasons should be presented for why culture should be respected when significant interests of individuals are at stake.

7) Human Rights ignore non-governmental threats

Human rights ignore the very real threats to human well-being wrought by non-governmental agents and other states.

It is correct that the accounts of human rights sketched above do not take up the question of how other agents than states can threaten the well-being and indeed the survival of individuals. However, two comments are appropriate.

Firstly, insofar as a government claims internal sovereignty over a territory and a population, it takes on responsibility as the first protector of the population against threats from third parties. Thus the government has an obligation to ensure just domestic order, including police protection to ensure security of persons (*Universal Declaration of Human Rights*, article 3.) One of the major threats to individuals' significant interests is indeed a government which provides no such protection.

Secondly, international law, as well as normative political theory, acknowledges that governments' responsibilities may be different in times of crises and non-ideal situations, such as civil war. The exercise of some civil rights, including freedom of expression, may be restricted by law in order to protect national security or public order (*ordre public*), public health and "morals." Thus the *International Covenant on Civil and Political Rights* holds that some rights are derogable in "time of public emergency which threatens the life of the nation and the existence of which is officially proclaimed" (article 4). But such derogations are carefully circumscribed, permitted "to the extent strictly required by the exigencies of the situation, provided that such measures are not inconsistent with their other obligations under international law and do not involve discrimination solely on the ground of race, color, sex, language, religion or social origin." The declaration also insists that some human rights are not derogable. These include procedures for death penalty, the prohibition against torture, slavery, forced labor, retroactive laws, and the freedom of thought, religion and conscience.

Thus a defense of human rights is compatible with the recognition that non-state actors can threaten individuals' significant interests, and may require exceptional state action — though within limits.

8) Human Rights violate state sovereignty

Foreign protests and intervention of any kind violate the long-standing and generally accepted principle of national self-determination.

However, recall that unrestricted external sovereignty has never been a principle. Even the Treaties of the Peace of Westphalia required princes to respect religious freedom. Furthermore, as a matter of international law, human rights violations are not properly regarded as "internal" affairs of those states that are signatories to the *International Conventions on Human Rights*. These treaties have clearly moved human rights violations into the sphere of international concern. Thirdly, some legal scholars hold that some human rights have a strong claim to the status of customary law, binding regardless of government ratification. Examples include slavery, genocide, torture, mass murders, prolonged arbitrary imprisonment, and systematic racial discrimination. "In declaring that such basic rights are part of customary law, we are asserting that all States are internationally responsible for violations attributable to them" (Schachter 1982: 336f).

Finally, it is appropriate to ask proponents of this view of unrestricted sovereignty to present convincing reasons for this position. Such a claim to state sovereignty can of course not merely appeal to international law, since international treaties are dismissed as a Western construct, and do not support unrestricted sovereignty anyway. The proponents of unrestricted sovereignty have to present arguments for at least the following three claims.

1) Sovereignty should be respected, even when a government violates its mandate as laid out by the various normative traditions adhered to by its citizens. Reasons must be offered why their citizens should accept a government which, for instance, violates the limits of sovereignty offered by Ibn Khaldun in the Islamic tradition, or by Confucius, or by a wide range of other religious and philosophical traditions.

2) Other governments are sometimes required to participate in international cooperation aimed at satisfying economic, social and cultural rights (*Universal Declaration of Human Rights*, article 22). The account of unrestricted sovereignty must explain why these other governments — typically Western — have such obligations.

3) Some exercises of internal sovereignty are nevertheless to be internationally condemned and regarded as issues of international concern. China and other Asian states have rightly condemned the practices of colonialism (1961 *Declaration on the Granting of Independence to Colonial Countries*) and apartheid (e.g., 1968 *Proclamation of Teheran* and 1973 *International Convention on the Suppression and Punishment of the Crime of Apartheid*). Arguments must be offered for this right to condemn human rights violations elsewhere.

9) Human Rights threaten world stability

International protests against human rights ignore the very real risk of instability created by allowing governments and foreigners to intervene in the domestic affairs of other states.

Liu Huaqiu, head of the Chinese Delegation to UN World Conference on Human Rights, put this objection starkly:

> To wantonly accuse another country of abuse of human rights and impose the human rights criteria of one's own country or region on other countries or regions are tantamount to an infringement upon the sovereignty of other countries and interference in the latter's internal affairs, which could result in political instability and social unrest in other countries (Quoted in Davis 1995b: 17).

Against this objection, we should first agree that human rights violations sometimes give rise to instability in the country where violations occur. However, this social unrest is not removed by preventing foreign protests. The best way to remove such unrest is to comply with human rights.

Secondly, observe that the human rights policy pursued is not one of military intervention at any breach of human rights, but of less forceful forms of protest and public pressure. The aim of these interventions is not to topple a regime, but to affect particular policy changes. The role of the international community in promoting human rights abroad is primarily one of nonviolent, civil protest, with no threat of military intervention.

Also note that the criteria for international military intervention are more stringent, partly due to the risks. The theories of human rights sketched above regard human rights as conditions of legitimacy, that is, as necessary for a government to have a valid moral claim that citizens should obey its commands. Rules for when military intervention is justifiable are a different matter. Even though violations of human rights would seem a necessary condition for intervention, such violations are not sufficient to justify military intervention on humanitarian grounds. The main roles of international protests against domestic human rights violations are instead twofold: a reminder to governments that they violate the common good entrusted to them and an important aid for the domestic population trying to determine whether their government and politicians are worthy of support (Schachter 1982: 351; Alston 1989; An-Na'im 1990b: 49).

4. Conclusion

Human rights are not Western in an objectionable sense. For instance, there are many grounds for human rights beside the allegedly "Western" conception of the individual whose only significant interest is one of non-interference and legal immunity against the government. Human rights may be defended, and violations protested by the international community, on many other grounds.

Human rights can be regarded as attempts to regulate the use of state power within a system of sovereign states, to prevent abuse of governments' drastic power over the lives of their citizens. Many theories and traditions join in condemning human rights violations such as torture, genocide, slavery-like practices, arbitrary detention, abuse of psychiatry for political aims, and the imprisonment of individuals for their religious beliefs, or for their non-violent protests against illegal government action. Respect for the internal affairs of other states should not prevent such protests, which are not unjustifiable foreign interference in their domestic affairs, nor illegitimate exercises in ideological imperialism against non-Western societies.

The objections raised by the *Bangkok Declaration* against "Western" human rights protests are found wanting. Most objections fail to hold against a broad range of defenses of human rights theories. The remaining objections do not repudiate human rights, since they can be met by several theories which regard rights as safeguards for individuals' significant interests against governments.

Chapter 16

The Nature of Human Rights

Leif Wenar
Philosophy, University of Sheffield, United Kingdom

Contrast two conceptions of human rights which, following Beitz, we can call the orthodox and the practical conceptions (Beitz 2004). The orthodox conception defines human rights as those rights that each human has against every other, at all times, in all places, under all conditions, and simply in virtue of her humanity. This orthodox conception is familiar from the philosophical literature on human rights, and any philosopher will know how to construct an orthodox theory of human rights using the standard tools of a consequentialist or deontological moral theory.

The practical conception of human rights is quite different, and is more familiar from international politics than from the philosophical literature. On the practical conception, human rights define a boundary of legitimate political action. Human rights specify the ways in which state officials must and must not act toward their own citizens, where it is understood that violations of these human rights can morally permit and in some cases morally require interference by the international community. This practical conception of human rights is what one finds in the various proclamations and treaties on human rights, such as the *Universal Declaration* and the *Convention against Torture*. Here I will explore why it is worthwhile for philosophers to theorize more about human rights understood in this second, practical way, and also say a few words about how such theorizing might be done. Thomas Pogge's account of human rights (2002a: 27–70) will provide the mileposts for the exploration of this topic.

To an orthodox theorist, the practical question about human rights will appear misguided. The practical question turns on legitimate action by the officials of modern states, and is especially concerned to find rights whose violation will permit or require outside intervention. Yet why this emphasis on legitimacy, modernity, and intervention? And why, in particular, this

A. Follesdal and T. Pogge, (eds.), Real World Justice, 285-293.

obsession with the state? After all states are not the only sort of agency that endangers individuals through violence, coercion, and neglect. Strangers, family members, and multinational corporations also endanger individuals — in fact quite often these other agencies will threaten individuals more than does their state. Why then should we take the actions of state officials as a special topic for normative theory?

The answer is that, until recently, the state was to outsiders a moral black box. Until World War II state officials violated, coerced, and neglected those within their territories with almost total impunity, appealing to the Westphalian ideal of state sovereignty to immunize themselves from external criticism and intervention. Before the Second World War there were virtually no commonly accepted standards for justifiable interference into what was called the internal affairs of a state. State officials were almost incorrigible with respect to their treatment of humans within their borders, and this is what distinguished state officials from other actors like family members and corporations.

The Second World War showed that the state could not remain a moral black box to outsiders. After the Holocaust it became clear that standards were required for official conduct toward citizens, such that violation of these standards could license or even necessitate an international response. The language that postwar political leaders used to describe these standards was the language of human rights. Human rights were meant to fill the void in the space of moral evaluation and action that was created by the concept of state sovereignty, given that this void had become morally intolerable. The human rights documents that were endorsed after the war were attempts to spell out what officials should never again do to those within their territories (cf. Donnelly 1998: 3–17).

Human rights so conceived are obviously immensely important for our politics, and so understanding which rights are such human rights should be a proportionately important topic for philosophical theory. Indeed a parallel from history may help to show how significant this kind of practical theorizing is. Before the seventeenth and eighteenth centuries, the official treatment of citizens was a moral black box not only to outsiders, but to those within the state's borders as well. State officials in this era claimed incorrigibility regarding the treatment of those within their territory — not under the Westphalian idea of state sovereignty, but under the older theory of the divine right of kings. The divine right of kings allegedly gave officials unlimited discretion over the treatment of subjects, such that no internal resistance to the crown was legitimate. The classic social contract theorists illuminated the justificatory darkness defined by the divine right of kings. Practical rights theorists such as Locke set out accounts of natural rights that marked out the boundaries of legitimate state action, where it was understood that violation of these rights could justify citizens' resistance and rebellion. The classical social contract theorists laid out standards of legitimacy that officials must meet on pain of suffering justified internal revolt, just as practical human rights theory lays out standards of legitimacy that officials must meet on pain of suffering justified external intervention. This parallel highlights the significance of practical theorizing about rights. It also incidentally shows that the natural rights theorizing familiar from classical social contract theory is actually more closely related to the practical approach to rights than it is to the orthodox theorizing with which we might ordinarily associate it.

1. Human rights and the question of legitimacy

The practical conception of human rights is an appropriate object for philosophical investigation. Any complete account of the rights of individuals will have a place for human rights so conceived, at least as long as the actions of state officials continue to have significant effects on the fates of those who reside in their territories. Yet of course once we understand human rights in this way, we want to know what human rights there are. Since asking the right question is often halfway to getting the right answer, I will first try to frame our question about practical human rights more precisely, before going on toward the end to suggest different ways that theorists might go about answering it.

Here is a more precise version of what I believe is the guiding question about human rights, practically conceived. The question is this: what are the considerations that state officials must and must not take into account when acting in ways that will affect the possibility of those in their territory leading dignified lives, such that failures to take these considerations into account will constitute a failure of legitimate state action, which will permit or require outside intervention when such is both feasible and appropriate?

This question has several parts; we can address its components singly. First, the question asks us to search for human rights conceived as moral claims which are in the first instance claims that individuals have against the officials who govern their territory. Individuals have human rights against the officials that have power over them, and if these officials fail to respect their rights then individuals may have secondary claims on outsiders to intervene. The rights claim is primarily against officials in the domestic government, and secondarily on outsiders who can act in the case of official failure.

Second, the question characterizes human rights as a criterion of legitimacy, which is the most primitive concept of normativity for political action. Officials who fail to fulfill the human rights of the citizens of their state forfeit the mantle of legitimacy for their actions. Such officials fail to attend sufficiently to the dignity of the individuals whose good they have been entrusted with, and insofar as they fail can be seen only as agencies of might, not of right. Human rights thus set the most basic standards of normative recognition for state action, drawing a line that separates the legitimate exercise of power from official crimes of violence, coercion, and neglect.

Third, the question specifies that the violation of these basic standards of legitimacy can permit or require intervention by outside agencies. Such intervention can in extreme cases involve military force, but as Beitz has noted (2001a: 269–81), it can take other forms as well. Intervention in response to non-fulfillment of human rights can also include economic sanctions, refusing entry to trade organizations such as the WTO, denial of development aid, or the provision of emergency assistance. What individuals in a country have a right to when their government fails to secure their human rights is that, under certain circumstances, outside agents act in some way that will remedy the breach and prevent further infractions. To do this, outside agencies may sometimes provide the object of the human right itself, as when foreign governments ship in food supplies. Or the outside agencies may take more indirect paths, for example, by putting pressure on a national government to improve economic equity so that an adequate standard of living becomes possible for all its citizens. As Pogge says (2002a: 69f), what is important is that individuals have secure access to the object of their human right, by whatever means will be effective in creating this access.

Fourth, outside intervention is only morally permissible when this would be both feasible and appropriate. Outsiders are only permitted to intervene when their intervention could be expected to be effective, and when it is not excessively costly for them. Moreover, since intervention is itself a potentially illegitimate political action, outsiders are only permitted to intervene when any coercive or violent means of their intervention can be justified by the evils they are attempting to prevent (Beitz 2004: 14).

Finally, the question about human rights is framed in terms of the considerations that state officials must and must not take into account. For example, we will explain the human right against torture by saying that officials must not take into account the fact that they could further their personal or political goals through torturing those who are subject to their power. And we will explain the human right to an adequate standard of living by saying that officials must work to create conditions in which all citizens can obtain decent food, clothing, and shelter. Human rights are here cast as direct constraints on official action and official inaction, and this is one place where we must diverge from Pogge's account.

On Pogge's understanding (2002a: 38–48, 64f), human rights are primarily moral claims on social institutions, and secondarily moral claims on those who shape and support these institutions. What individuals have a right to is that institutions secure for them access to certain goods. "Secure" here is defined probabilistically: what is important to Pogge is whether individuals are above or below some threshold of risk of lacking access to some good. Pogge asserts, for example, that whether an individual enjoys the human right against torture turns not on whether the individual is actually tortured, but turns rather on the *probability* that that individual will be tortured under the prevailing social conditions. This focus on probabilistic thresholds explains why Pogge prefers to speak of human rights as being fulfilled or unfulfilled, instead of their being respected or violated. Probabilities fulfill rights, while actions violate them.

Probabilistic considerations do have a place within human rights doctrine. Yet the unnatural ring of Pogge's language should make us suspect that probabilities cannot plausibly be built into the very definition of human rights as Pogge recommends.

Here is an example that shows why. On Pogge's understanding, there could be no human rights non-fulfillment even if officials of the Indian government ordered the kidnapping and torture of ten randomly selected Indian citizens — either for the officials' own entertainment or to complete some secret medical experiment. This could not count as a human rights non-fulfillment on Pogge's definition because there is no way that these tortures would push the average Indian citizen below any worrisome risk-threshold of insecurity regarding torture.[1] Yet this result is implausible. Torture occurs, but allegedly no one's right against being tortured has been left unfulfilled. We must find a characterization of human rights that captures the fact that the Indian government's torture of ten citizens would indeed violate human rights, and the characterization of human rights that I am recommending does capture this fact. On my characterization we can say that officials must never under any circumstances take into account that they could further their personal or political goals through torture, and if they act on such a consideration they will in each instance violate a human right.

On the characterization of human rights recommended in this article, we can take probabilities into account where they are relevant and leave them aside when they are not. For example, we can say that officials must never

---

[1] "A person may fully enjoy X [a basic good] even while her access to X is insecure (as when persons relevantly like her, say blacks or vocal government opponents, are beaten or threatened). Conversely, a person may be temporarily deprived of X, through a crime by a rogue government official perhaps, in a society that is very effective in preventing crimes of the relevant type … . My institutional [understanding of human rights] regards only the first case as a human-rights problem" (Pogge 2002a: 65).

under any circumstances take into account that they could further their goals through torture; while also saying that officials must act so as to keep all citizens above some probabilistic threshold of being safe from violent assault in the streets. We can say that some human rights are violated by discrete official actions, and that others are violated if officials fail to create the social conditions where access to some good is reasonably secure. This characterization allows for the important probabilistic feature in Pogge's account, while not permitting it to consume the whole definition.

2. The role of international political documents in human rights theory

I have suggested that the right question to ask about human rights practically conceived is this. What are the considerations that state officials must and must not take into account when acting in ways that will affect the possibility of those in their territory leading dignified lives, such that failure to take these considerations into account will constitute a failure of legitimate state action, which will permit or require outside intervention when such is both feasible and appropriate. How, then, to proceed when answering such a question? There are of course many different ways of setting out a theory. Here I will suggest a basic norm and a starting point, and then four possible paths for developing the theory of human rights practically understood.

In developing a theory of human rights we are searching for standards of legitimacy. We are searching for standards of legitimate state action, which when violated will legitimate outside intervention. Because our target is legitimacy, we should use, I believe, a basic norm of reasonable acceptance. This norm requires us to find standards for the exercise of political power that all individuals who are subject to this power would have reason to accept, whatever their cultural background or conception of value in life. This norm of reasonable acceptance is a variation on the Kantian imperative to respect the humanity of each individual, and it has been developed in different directions by theorists in the Kantian tradition like Rawls and Scanlon.[2] The norm is particularly appropriate when developing a theory of political legitimacy, since it mandates that those with political power be able to justify their exercise of authority to those whose freedom and well-being may be diminished by their actions.

---

[2]   For the importance of the idea of legitimacy in Rawls's work see Wenar 2002 and 2004. For the relation between Scanlon's norm of reasonable agreement and international duties of assistance, see Wenar 2003a.

Now in adopting a norm of reasonable acceptance we will be making things harder for ourselves, because we have so little to work with. I mentioned before that any philosopher will know how to construct an orthodox theory of human rights, using the standard tools of a consequentialist or deontological moral theory. Yet using a norm of reasonable acceptance makes it particularly hard to know how to proceed in theorizing about practical human rights. How to begin the search for standards of legitimacy, when our only theoretical constraint has such minimal internal structure?

We could start back in the philosopher's study, trying to arrive a priori at universally acceptable standards for state action and outside intervention. Yet I believe we should, rather, begin with the political documents about human rights such as the *Universal Declaration* and the various conventions that have been widely ratified. When looking for what could reasonably be accepted, that is, we should start with what has actually been accepted. The theorist's task, then, will be to develop theory that rationalizes, that corrects, and that extends the accounts of human rights in the various declarations and conventions — to extrapolate from what political leaders have actually accepted to what all individuals could reasonably accept. There are two reasons to begin here in what could be called the global public political culture. The first is simply that starting with content "out there" instead of "in here" will tend to reduce the personal and cultural biases to which we all are subject. Second, and more importantly, there is a second-order norm of reasonableness that says that under good conditions the most reasonable starting point for determining what people could reasonably accept will be the focal point of that which has already been agreed.

3. Strategies for theorizing human rights

The political documents on human rights have only received the actual agreement of politicians, which is not the same as the reasonable agreement of all individuals. We can see this as an opportunity for theory, instead of as an impediment. One way to go about theorizing human rights is simply to check the documents already agreed to for biases that are predictable artifacts of the process of their endorsement. For instance, since it was political leaders instead of citizens who have directly endorsed and ratified the documents, we should expect the documents to be biased toward those interests that all political leaders have in common. For example, all political leaders share an interest in being free from scrutiny over corruption. Moreover, we should also expect the political documents to be slanted toward Western or perhaps better enlightenment values, since the nations professing these values have been politically much stronger in the times the political documents have been affirmed. Putting these two sources of bias together, a theorist might reflect on the fact that a human right against political corruption has not been declared in any of the various political documents that political leaders have agreed to, even though such a right may in many circumstances be just as important as the human right to democratic participation which has often been proclaimed.

I will close by mentioning three other paths of theorizing about human rights, beyond this path of correcting the biases we could expect from the political process of their endorsement. The most obvious path is to work on the internal coherence of the list of rights that have been declared in the international human rights documents. The goal here is to find theory that lies beneath the lists of rights, to give these rights congruity, and to explain why some rights should be on the list while others should not be. One example of this kind of theorizing is Henry Shue's (1996) work on basic rights, which emphasizes the incoherence of acknowledging civil and political rights while denying subsistence rights, as the United States continues to do.

Another example at a deeper level is Pogge's development (2002a: 27–51) of a thin conception of human flourishing. Pogge's thin conception is a piece of theory intended to give a unifying account of the diverse sets of goods that are alleged in the political documents to be the objects of human rights, and to be used as a tool for evaluating which of the human rights that have been declared are genuine. Pogge's explanation is that these diverse goods are those that all could agree are necessary for developing or realizing a worthwhile life. Pogge emphasizes that the demand for reasonable agreement explains why human rights are and should be framed in terms of less controversial means to flourishing like nutrition and education, rather than in terms of more controversial components of flourishing like spirituality. The elaboration of such a thin conception of human flourishing is an excellent example of how theory can increase the internal coherence of the human rights documents that have achieved political assent.

Another path for theorizing is to extend human rights theory so that it coheres with related areas of rights. For example, a theorist might attempt to link the rights that define legitimate governance to the rights that define legitimate military action. Just as the conventions of human rights profess to set standards that officials must follow concerning the citizens whose good is in their care, so the *Geneva Conventions* profess to set standards that officials must follow concerning citizens of states against whom they are waging hostilities. One could use this conceptual isomorphism to inform the theories on both sides. For example, we should presume that whatever standards bind officials in their treatment of "enemy" civilians should also bind officials in the treatment of their own civilians. So the Geneva norms against collective punishments and forcible transfers should be translatable into norms of human rights, giving us a new language for condemning, for example, what Saddam did to the southern Shi'ites after the first Gulf War. We might also be able to work in the other direction, for example, using human rights norms of the presumption of innocence and the requirement of fair trial to develop the theory of enemy combatants. If that kind of theorizing were successful, it could shed light into the dusky area of international law in which the prisoners in Guantánamo Bay currently exist.

The final and most ambitious strategy for theorizing human rights is what might be called vertical integration. We might here attempt to extend human rights theory to apply to moral relationships that are as yet unstructured in the global political culture. As we have seen, rights set standards for agents who are entrusted with the good of their own citizens. The laws of war set standards for agents whose actions will affect the welfare of citizens of hostile nations. Yet we can also go beyond these relations, to explore the moral standards for agents whose actions can affect the well-being of foreigners, but who are neither officially entrusted with these foreigners' well-being, nor at war with their countries.

This is what Pogge has done in some of his most challenging writings.[3] Pogge's work on the limits of sovereignty argues for the necessity of extending human rights standards to apply directly to the conduct of international leaders and even to the actions of privileged individuals — that is, you and me. Pogge's main moves are to expand our awareness of the coercive nature of the global institutions such as the World Trade Organization, to highlight the pervasive effects of these institutions on individual well-being, and then to extend the definition of human rights to comprehend entitlements against all those who support coercive institutions, whether these institutions are domestic or international.

All of these moves are bold and deserve further scrutiny. We might, for example, wish to discuss at greater length this final step of stretching the very definition of human rights so that these rights apply in the first instance to both national and international institutions. Yet Pogge's work in amplifying the central idea of human rights so that it reaches to global threats to human dignity should serve as one model for theorists who are looking to deepen and to extend our understanding of human rights, practically conceived.

---

[3] Pogge 2002a, especially chapters 4–8.

Chapter 17

Severe Poverty as a Human Rights Violation — Weak and Strong[*]

Wilfried Hinsch and Markus Stepanians
Philosophy, Universität des Saarlandes, Saarbrücken, Germany

1. Introduction

From a philosophical point of view, the UNESCO project "Poverty and Human Rights" may be seen as an attempt to explain the idea of morally unacceptable poverty in a way that makes acquiescence to dire poverty a violation of human rights. Though many agree that severe poverty is a serious moral evil, it is as yet unclear whether severe global poverty can be generally perceived as constituting a human rights violation. Witness the ambiguous language used by the United Nations and their representatives when addressing the issue of poverty and human rights.[1] In 1992, the UN General Assembly recognized in Resolution 134 that "extreme poverty" is a "violation of human dignity" which, depending on circumstances, may "constitute a threat to the right to life" (General Assembly Resolution 134, December 18, 1992). However, a possible threat to a human right does not yet amount to a violation of it, and it is worth noting that the term "violation of human *dignity*" has been chosen instead of the rhetorically stronger phrase "violation of human *rights*." That "extreme poverty" violates human dignity is reaffirmed in numerous statements of the UN Commission on Human Rights (see, for instance, the resolutions 1993/13 and 2001/31). In the 1993 resolution, the Commission also maintained that the elimination of

---

[*] We thank Armineh Stepanians and Dickran Manoogian for many extremely helpful grammatical and stylistic improvements of our English.
[1] Thanks to Annali Kristiansen and Alex Folscheid for providing us with material for this paragraph.

A. Follesdal and T. Pogge, (eds.), *Real World Justice*, 295-315.

poverty and the full enjoyment of all human rights are "interrelated goals" and that there is "a contradiction" between the existence of extreme poverty and the duty to guarantee full "enjoyment of human rights" (Commission of Human Rights Resolution 1993/13). This statement may be understood to imply that severe poverty violates human rights, but it is does not say so explicitly and it remains ambiguous.[2] The 2001 resolution of the Commission on Human Rights reaffirms that "extreme poverty violates human dignity" and recalls that the elimination of poverty and the full enjoyment of human rights are "interrelated." It adds, however, that the right to life includes an "existence in human dignity with the minimum necessities of life." Although this may be seen as another step forward, it still falls short of an explicit official recognition (Commission on Human Rights resolution 2001/31). Finally, on October 17, 2002, the International Day for the Eradication of Poverty, UN Secretary General Kofi Annan "recalled" in a message "that poverty is a denial of human rights." To our knowledge, this is as close as the organs and representatives of the UN get to unambiguous statement that severe poverty constitutes a human rights violation (UN Press Release SG/SM/8431 OBV/297).

2. Some remarks on motivation

Before we make explicit the conception of rights we favor for an analysis of the idea of severe poverty as a human rights violation, we should perhaps pause for a moment and ask after the motivation for doing so. Why should we care whether severe poverty counts as a human rights violation? Why is its recognition as serious moral evil not enough? One reason may be the desire to shape up our political rhetoric in order to make it a more effective tool to persuade people that dire poverty is not only a serious evil but that there is an urgent moral duty to eradicate it here and now. The classical human rights (e.g., the right to life, liberty, and security of person or the right not to be subjected to torture or cruel and unusual punishment) are by now widely accepted as universal standards of individual conduct and political action. Most people nowadays think that the violation of these rights is a serious moral wrongdoing, and this belief enhances their willingness to change things for the better. If the emotionally loaded notion of a human rights violation could be shown to apply to the non-fulfillment of

---

[2] In the same year, the World Conference on Human Rights (June 14–25, 1993) declared in Vienna that the "existence of widespread extreme poverty inhibits the full and effective enjoyment of human rights" and that "extreme poverty ... constitute[s] a violation of human dignity." *Vienna Declaration and Program of Action.*

claims arising from morally unacceptable want, this would certainly bolster the willingness of people who care about human rights to fight poverty. Another reason to think about poverty and human rights along the lines of the UNESCO project would be to find out more about our duties towards those in dire need and about the specific kind of moral wrongdoing that is involved in tolerating the existence of poverty.

Both motivations are perfectly reasonable. Yet, there is reason to be skeptical about the idea of shaping up our political rhetoric. Even if successful, this may prove to be a mixed blessing. Any attempt to broaden the sphere of possible human rights violations so as to cover not only the so-called first generation rights but also valid social and economic claims has to rely on a broader understanding of the concept of a human right. However, as we shall see, the requisite widening of the concept of a human right has a price tag. It introduces considerable vagueness and uncertainty concerning the identity of the corresponding duty-holders and the precise content of their obligations. This indeterminacy is likely to weaken the concept's motivational impact considerably — my belief that someone should do something to help seems perfectly compatible with my not doing anything. On the other hand, removing this indeterminacy requires such serious and far-reaching cooperative efforts on a global scale (see section 6) that it may appear somewhat utopian at the present time. Still, in view of the urgency of the problem, reaching a lasting consensus concerning the theoretical and practical consequences of recognizing severe poverty as a human rights violation is certainly worth the effort. The lessons to be learned will, in any case, be instructive and useful for a more thorough understanding of the mechanisms and institutions required if human rights are put to concrete work for the benefit of their holders.

3. Regulative force and the relationship between rights and duties

What is presupposed by the idea that severe poverty constitutes a violation of human rights? First and obviously, it must be the case that persons living under conditions of severe poverty have a human right *not* to suffer severe poverty. We may understand article 3 of the *Universal Declaration of Human Rights* of 1948 to grant such a right if we take the right to life, as seems natural, to include a right to the means of subsistence.[3]

---

[3]   This is assumed by Rawls (1999: 65n) who mentions Shue (1996) and Vincent (1986) in support. It finds institutional backing in Resolution 2001/31 of the UN Commission on Human Rights from which we have quoted above. Article 25 of the *Universal Declaration*

Secondly, since there can be no violations without a violator, there must be somebody directly or indirectly responsible for the destitute condition of the right-holders. This, third and finally, requires the existence of sufficiently specific duties or obligations (we will use these terms interchangeably) associated with the right in question, such that not to act upon them is to violate it. Consider again the family of rights guaranteed by article 3 of the *Universal Declaration*: "Everyone has the right to life, liberty and security of person." Here we have three fundamental values life, liberty, and security of person, and we have the idea of protecting them by requiring that others perform, or abstain from, certain actions. To say that someone has such a right is thus to imply that at least one other agent has certain obligations corresponding to that right. Violating it consists precisely of a failure to act upon at least one of the associated duties.[4]

That violating someone's right presupposes both, the existence of a right as well as the existence of a duty that has not been discharged, is hardly more than a conceptual truism. Moreover, it seems highly plausible to assume that it must be possible (at least in principle) to violate a right. If so, however, all rights have to be closely associated with duties whose breach constitutes their violation. An argument to the same conclusion focuses on the protective function of rights. The very point of having a right lies in the protection it affords for the well-being of its holder. It does so by imposing duties on others. What makes rights such valuable commodities for their holders in the first place is the immediate consequences they have for the behavior of others towards the right-holder — what they may and may not do to her. This is the feature H. L. A. Hart calls their "peremptory force." A right possesses peremptory regulative force since having it cuts off further deliberation by its addressees about how to treat the right-holder with respect to the content of that right.

---

also seems to imply a right not to suffer severe poverty: "Everyone has the right to a standard of living adequate for the health and well-being of himself and of his family, including food, clothing, housing, and medical care and necessary social services."

[4]   Hence, proceeding from the human right stated in article 3 of the *Universal Declaration*, we may promptly arrive at the prohibition of article 4, "No one shall be held in slavery or servitude," which imposes on everyone negative duties of not holding other human beings in slavery or servitude. Or, take the human right of equal recognition as a person before the law (article 6) and of equal protection of the law (article 7), and you readily derive not only the prohibitions of article 9, "No one shall be subjected to arbitrary arrest, detention or exile," imposing certain negative duties on courts and state agencies, but also positive duties of public recognition and protection. Violating a human right, in this context, means the non-fulfillment of rather clear-cut negative or positive duties that go along with this right and account for its respective regulative force.

The "classical" theory of rights we favor takes the aforementioned points very much for granted, at least for the paradigmatic cases of rights.[5] The tight relationship it assumes between rights and duties is an attempt to vest rights with a maximum of regulative force. The demand that rights *must* have direct consequences for the behavior of others is given a *logical* interpretation: "must" is interpreted as logical necessity and "consequences for the behavior of others" as referring to duties towards the right-holder. Thus, the peremptory regulative force that allows rights to fulfill their protective function is taken to have *logically conclusive* force. Someone's having a right does not give its addressee just another, perhaps negotiable, reason to be considered while deliberating about how to treat the right-holder. Everything else being equal, if A has a right against B, then B has no choice but to perform the duty associated with A's right. Having such a right-based duty is more than merely "having a good reason" to do something. It is more since not acting on the implied duty is to violate the corresponding right, whereas good, but inconclusive reasons can be overridden by better reasons without necessarily wronging anyone.[6] It is because of their protective function that classical rights theorists insist that rights are essentially interpersonal in the sense of being directed *towards* or *against* some (at least one) other person, namely, a duty-bearer. The classical general form of a simple right is "A has a right to X against B," and it is taken to imply, as matter of logical necessity, the existence of a corresponding duty: "Necessarily, if A has a right to X against B, then B has a duty to X towards A."[7]

---

[5]   In the literature, the names "rights to a service" or "rights of recipience" can be found for this central type of right, but today it has become standard to use Wesley N. Hohfeld's term "claim-right." Since the right not to suffer severe poverty seems to be a clear case of a claim-right, there is no need to take other types of rights (Hohfeldian liberties, powers or immunities) into consideration. Thus, we follow Hohfeld in using "right" throughout this paper to refer exclusively to rights-in-the-strict-sense, i.e., claim-rights.

[6]   This does not prejudge the question whether, and under what circumstances, the addressee may be justified in disregarding the duty and violating the right. In situations of irresolvable conflicts between rights, if they are possible, we may have no choice but to wrong right-holders for the sake of other, more important rights or values.

[7]   Note, first, that it is not part of the classical view, as we understand it, that the implied duties must be enforceable. The insistence on enforceability seems to us to have its source in questionable sanction theories of duty that seem to be at odds with the existence of moral (and possibly even some legal) duties that cannot be properly enforced. It is in any case not the existence of institutionalized enforcement mechanisms that gives practical importance to rights in the first place, but the individual and social recognition of the implied duties. There is no denying that established institutions and recognized practices typically enhance the regulative force of (moral) rights. Indeed, they are, practically speaking, prerequisites of any form of social order that effectively protects the moral rights of individuals. Nevertheless they are, according to our view, not constitutive

It is important to keep in mind the motivation behind the strictures built into the classical concept of a right for the proper assessment of a recent challenge posed to it by Neil MacCormick, Joseph Raz and Jeremy Waldron, among others. Their main contention is that it is wrong to assume a *necessary* connection between rights and duties. Instead, they argue, it should be replaced by a considerably weaker and merely contingent link according to which rights are reasons that "justify holding some other person or persons to be under a duty" (Raz 1986: 166). This attitude of "holding others to be under a duty" is disjunctive: it is either to believe that others already have that duty or that they do not have it yet, but that it should be imposed on them (ibid. 179). According to Raz, the classical view has been decisively refuted by Neil MacCormick who has "convincingly argued ... that rights can exist independently of duties" (Raz 1970, Postscript, 225). Waldron agrees that the view to be found in the works of Hohfeld, Feinberg and Hart "is no longer reputable. Neil MacCormick has shown that even in technical legal relations, the determination of who has a right often precedes the determination of who has the corresponding duty and in some cases may even form part of the reason for assigning duties" (Waldron 1993: 16). Since this is not the place to enter this intricate controversy,[8] two brief remarks must suffice to indicate why we nonetheless remain faithful to the classical view. First, to hold with MacCormick "that rights can exist independently of duties" is to believe in the possible existence of rights which by themselves offer at best a very diluted form of protection for their holders. These rights without implied duties seem to be no more than interests to be taken into

---

elements of the concept of a right. Second, this conceptual implication from claim-rights to duties should not be confused with a considerably stronger and highly controversial thesis that generalizes from claim-rights to rights tout court and asserts also the opposite implication, from duties to rights in general. In the literature, this more ambitious thesis is often discussed under the title "the correlativity of rights and duties," and can be stated as follows: "Necessarily, A has a right to X against B *if and only if* B has a duty to X against A." According to Paul Sieghart, the correlativity thesis not only underlies international human rights law: "In all legal theory and practice, rights and duties are symmetrical ... if I have a right, *someone else* must have a correlative duty; if I have a duty, *someone else* must have a corresponding right" (Sieghart 1985: 43). But despite Sieghart's assurance to the contrary, the "right to left" implication from legal duties to legal rights is, at least in this unqualified form, doubtful and highly controversial. Many lawyers hold that having a legal duty towards someone is a necessary, but by no means a sufficient condition for someone's possessing a corresponding legal right. Moreover, *moral* theory and practice seems to allow for "imperfect" moral duties towards others without those others having corresponding rights. Candidates for such imperfect duties are duties of charity and benevolence toward everyone. However, for our purposes in this paper we do not have to answer the question whether there are duties without corresponding rights.

[8] For some good responses to Raz and MacCormick from a classical point of view, cf. the contributions by Matthew Kramer and Nigel Simmonds in Kramer et al. 1998.

consideration but not necessarily acted upon. In view of their almost complete lack of regulative force, it is hardly a consolation for these right-holders that their rights "form part of the reason for assigning duties" by some authority (who?) at some point in the future. As John Maynard Keynes pointed out, at some point in the future, we are all dead. Second, Waldron is wrong to suggest that the classical view is somehow committed to denying that "the determination of who has a right often precedes the determination of who has the corresponding duty." To ignore this obvious fact would indeed be odd. We certainly often do know that someone has a right without knowing who has the corresponding duty — and we may perhaps never find out. But there is nothing in the classical view that suggests otherwise. Those who defend that view are only committed to holding that *there is someone* with a corresponding duty, not that they actually know her by name and address. In any case, if severe poverty is a human rights violation, there must already be duties associated with the relevant right. And if this is so, it must be permissible to inquire after the bearers of those duties. As we shall see in more detail later, this question gives rise, in particular with respect to human rights to positive services, to what we call the "allocation problem": the problem of identifying the relevant duty-bearers and of specifying their concrete duties (see section 6 below).

Thus, our preference for the classical view of rights is not an attempt to legislate first how the term "right" has to be used and then to ask where this leaves us with severe poverty. We agree with Waldron that "we must take care not to put the analytical cart before the substantive horse. Our concept of a right is loose enough to be defined in a way that accommodates what we want to use it to say" (ibid. 16). The question, however, is not only what we want it to say but also what we want it to do for us. That is, we want rights to function as protectors of the well-being of persons. We take this to be an essential ingredient of the substantive issues involved and find it hard to see how rights can play this role unless they have some intimate and, indeed, necessary connection with duties.

4. The right not to suffer severe poverty as a universal, but special moral right

Besides its well-motivated insistence on strong regulative force, the classical theory has further advantages for an analysis of the idea of severe poverty as a human rights violation. Understood broadly enough, it allows for a unified general account of rights that covers legal rights well as moral rights, complex rights as well as simple rights. Perhaps like most philosophers, we think of human rights primarily as moral rights that may at the same time be legal rights in so far as they are part of international and domestic law. We take the difference between legal and moral rights to lie solely in their respective justifications. Legal rights are justified with reference to legal principles; moral rights by appeal to moral principles (cf. Feinberg 1970). In particular, what makes a right a *moral* right is the fact that ascribing it can be justified with exclusive reference to the value basis at its core. That is, people have moral rights because of the importance of the core value for their well-being as human persons. The claim that human rights are *universal* moral rights may then be explained as follows: they are (a) universal in the sense of having a value basis whose values (e.g., life, liberty, security) are of such significance for a worthwhile human life that their protection normally[9] cannot be reasonably denied to any human being. In virtue of their universal value basis, human rights are (b) universally valid claims, i.e., valid claims all individuals have to certain goods. They are universal in the sense that every person has these rights. We shall discuss the question whether the claims of need arising from severe poverty should be acknowledged as universal moral rights in the next section. In this section, however, we would like to point out some general formal features of this type of right that we believe to have significant consequences for their recognition and analysis.

Perhaps most important, a right not to suffer severe poverty would be a "positive" claim-right. That is, the obligations associated with it are not only negative and passive duties of non-interference but will often require positive and active assistance from their addressees. As is well known, however, these demands pose special problems. One of them arises from the fact that typical formulations of human rights, as they can be found in the *Universal Declaration* and elsewhere, do not expressly mention the bearers of the corresponding duties. We shall later (in section 6) discuss and reject the view, popular among international lawyers, that they are exclusively directed against "the state." As *moral* rights, however, it appears more plausible to regard some universal rights as holding against *everybody*, whereas others seem to be directed only against *some* natural and non-natural agents. Independent of the problem that concerns us in this paper, there is an important general distinction to be drawn between rights *had by everybody or somebody* and rights *held against everybody or somebody*,

---

[9]   "Normally" because there are situations in which the protection and realization of human rights values cannot be secured for all individuals. Sometimes there are trade-offs to be made between protecting and realizing these values for different individuals. In this context the term "normally" refers to a paradigmatic situation that meets certain feasibility conditions in order to explain the meaning of universal validity regarding human rights; it must not be taken as implying any empirical claims about how often such situations actually occur.

where "somebody" has its usual logical sense "at least one, perhaps all." We mark this distinction by calling a right "universal" if and only if everybody possesses it; but it is a "general" right if and only if it is held against everybody.[10] This allows for the possibility of non-universal, but general rights as well as universal, though non-general, i.e., special rights. However, since it is normally taken to be characteristic of human rights that every human being has them, non-universal rights do not qualify as human rights. Moreover, propositions of the form "A has a right against everybody (or somebody)" are complex in a way simple propositions of the form "A has a right against B," where "B" is a singular term, are not. The classical theory offers a unified reductionist account of the dichotomy between complex and simple rights by reducing complex rights to simple rights. According to the classical theory, rights held by or against more than one individual turn out to be disjunctive or conjunctive multiplicities — logical sums and products — of simple rights relations between exactly two individuals.[11]

The significance of these distinctions between general and special universal rights on the one hand and complex and simple rights on the other for our problem is as follows. A human right not to suffer severe poverty seems to be a special right. In this type of right, all of us are *candidates* for the corresponding duties, but only some of us are actually bound. Because of the referential opaqueness of the term "some," however, human rights of this kind give rise to what we call "the allocation problem," i.e., the task of identifying the relevant duty-bearers and of specifying their concrete obligations. Solving it requires that we provide for the complex right not to suffer severe poverty a reductionist analysis in terms of a logical sum of simple rights between exactly two individuals. We shall say more about this process in section 6. At this point, we merely wish to stress its significance for the recognition of positive human rights like the right not to suffer severe poverty. It lies in the fact that universal complex rights to abstract values against anonymous "somebodies" have at best weak regulative force unless they are supplemented by a determination of their concrete addressees with their specific active duties. In the course of this process, A's abstract and weak right against somebody is dissolved, as it were, into a multitude of concrete and strong rights between the right-holder and (ideally) one other agent with specific active duties towards her. Thus, the necessity to solve the allocation problem is the necessity to bestow strong regulative force on a weak and abstract right.

---

[10] For a clear view of this distinction and its importance, cf. Koller 1998; for neglecting it and the resulting confusion of doing so, cf. O'Neill 1996: 129ff.

[11] An example of the kind of analysis we have in mind is Hohfeld's proposal to analyze (complex) rights *in rem* in terms of (simple) rights *in personam* (cf. Hohfeld 1923: 72). However, Hohfeld's account may need some refinement.

The abstract characterization of a right not to suffer severe poverty and the consequences of its recognition will become more concrete in the rest of this paper. Moreover, we have accumulated some intellectual debts that we shall begin to discharge in the next section with a discussion of the question whether, and in what sense, there is a universal moral right not to suffer severe poverty in the first place.

5. Claims of need

It is controversial whether severe poverty can be seen as constituting a human rights violation *in sensu strictu*. There is widespread agreement, however, that it is a serious evil that cannot be tolerated, and that people suffering from severe poverty have valid claims to the assistance of others who are better off, assuming that it can be provided at moderate cost. The existing disagreements about claims of need and their moral basis, however, seem not to be about the question whether there are any valid claims of need and corresponding positive duties of assistance at all. Most reasonable people grant this. Rather, the disagreement seems to concern the allocation problem, namely, the problem of identifying the relevant duty-bearers and the assignment of their specific obligations.

But what are valid claims of need and what is their connection with rights? Perhaps we should begin by making explicit the main elements of our understanding of human rights as moral rights: there is, first, a fundamental human value the right is meant to protect for the right-holder. It is at the core of every human right, and it forms what we call its *value basis*. Often this value basis is merely alluded to in a very abstract way, as in loose talk about rights to "life, liberty and security of the person." Second, the value basis is the source of *claims* that arise from that value. And finally, there are the *duties* implied by the right, which are a necessary condition for its existence. The claim arising from a value remains weak as long as it fails to imply concrete duties against identifiable duty-bearers. Therefore, for such abstract claims to qualify as strong rights against agents with clear-cut duties, we have to solve the allocation problem and determine who they are. In this process, the abstract hints at values are replaced by descriptions of valuable actions. The abstract claim to "life," for example, thus becomes a moral claim that others perform certain actions that protect the claim-holder's life.

For the purpose of moral argument, we can define severe poverty as a condition of *morally unacceptable want* that gives rise to specific *claims of need* whose fulfillment is a matter of high moral urgency. Article 25 of the *Universal Declaration* gives us a rough idea of the content of these claims: "Everyone has the right to a standard of living adequate for the health and well-being of himself and of his family, including food, clothing, housing and medical care and necessary social services." Indeed, we may explain "morally unacceptable want" or "severe poverty" in terms of the claims of need it gives rise to. People living in severe poverty are lacking adequate food, clean water, clothing and shelter, basic medical care, and elementary security. The reason severe poverty is morally unacceptable is precisely that human beings have a claim to at least a minimal provision of these goods. However, severe poverty is a threshold notion. It is a necessary (though perhaps not sufficient) condition for valid claims of need that an individual's provision with these goods falls below a critical threshold with the threshold's being fixed by the requirements of a minimally decent life. In this regard, claims of need are close relatives of Henry Shue's "basic rights." They express "everyone's minimum reasonable demands on others" (Shue 1996: 19).

Grammatically speaking, "to need something" is transitive. We need things *to* do or *to* achieve other things. Hence, claims of need have a teleological structure, their *telos* or aim being the realization of certain values. Valid claims of need are value-based in the following sense: the goods or services they are claims to are necessary for a minimum realization of values deemed essential for a minimally decent life for the claimants. Typical values of this kind are the values of personal agency (i.e., the capacities necessary for rational action and social cooperation), sufficiently good health and physical condition, self-respect, and social recognition. For the purpose of our main argument in this paper, it does not matter much how we specify these values and which values we put on the list. It suffices to think of a minimally decent life as a life in which certain familiar values are realized to an extent that meets a (admittedly indeterminate) critical threshold. Moreover, in order to justify poverty-related claims of need, we do not have to assume that the values defining a minimally decent life are the same all over the world. Nor is it necessary to assume that people everywhere need the same kind of goods to realize these values in a minimally adequate fashion. We do not have to rely on the Rawlsian premise that there is a fixed number of *basic goods* which all individuals need in order to develop and exercise the basic capacities constitutive of their moral personality and elementary well-being. Nor do we have to presuppose a list of *basic capabilities* (as Amartya Sen, 1985a and Martha Nussbaum, 1992 and 1993, conceive of them, including personal capacities and social opportunities) which universally define the conditions of individual well-being. Indeed, the very assumption that there are universally desirable goods or capabilities that all human beings need for a good life is questionable. It seems possible to describe for any candidate for such a list a rational (but perhaps highly idiosyncratic) individual life plan that — in a given nondegrading cultural and social setting — can be carried out without the good in question, and which perhaps even requires its absence. However, to deny that there is something that every person needs as a matter of elementary well-being does not imply the denial that everybody needs *something* in order to have a minimally decent life. All we have to presuppose for valid individual claims of need is that it is possible to identify for every person some goods that, *given her particular cultural, social, and individual circumstances*, are necessary for a minimally decent life as she conceives of it. It is these goods, then, that are the objects of a person's valid claims of need. Depending on the (cultural, social, and individual) circumstances of a person's life, different things may be practically necessary.

More specifically, what is practically necessary depends on whether the need for those goods is merely instrumental and contingent for the realization of the values of a minimally decent life or whether it is constitutive and conceptually necessary. In the first case, we have a means-end relation between the goods needed and the values to be realized, as between adequate food and good health. The values at stake can be described independently from the means of their realization. Specifying the relevant claims of need, in this case, is a matter of choosing causally adequate means for realizing an independently specifiable end under given factual circumstances, and different circumstances may require different means. In the second case of a conceptual or constitutive relationship between the values of a decent life and the goods necessary for their realization, however, the values at stake cannot be described independently from the goods or services needed to realize them. To have such goods *means* (at least partially) to realize the values and vice versa. Take, for instance, the value of social recognition that we mentioned above as one of the values of a decent life, or the good of being recognized as "a person before the law" claimed as a human right in article 6 of the *Universal Declaration*. Recognition as a person before the law is instrumentally valuable in many ways because it provides individuals with social protection against others and against arbitrary treatment by courts and other agencies of law enforcement. As far as the value of social recognition is concerned, however, recognition as a person before the law is not a merely instrumentally valuable good. It is part of what it *means* to be socially recognized in minimally adequate ways. Depending on the cultural and social context, different legal specifications of what it means to be recognized as a person before the law may seem "practically necessary" for a minimal social recognition. In a liberal democracy nothing short of full equality before the law can be minimally adequate, whereas in other societies something less then full equality may meet the standard of minimal decency (cf. Rawls 1999, part II, on the criteria of a decent society as opposed to the criteria of full liberal justice).

How, then, can we decide for a given person in a given cultural and social setting which goods or services are practically necessary for a minimally decent life in a particular setting? How do we find out which claims of need are justified or valid? A general account of how to answer these questions with regard to claims of need is given in Hinsch 2002, chapter 6. For the purpose of this paper, however, it is enough to point out that the most elementary claims of need deriving from severe poverty — claims to subsistence and basic security — must certainly be valid claims, if human beings have any valid claims at all. Even if a minimally decent assignment of food, water, clothes, shelter, medical care, security, and social recognition may not be something everybody needs regardless of the chosen life plan, it is obvious that for those of us who do not pursue potentially suicidal life plans, a minimal provision of these goods is an indispensable prerequisite. Being in need of these most basic goods and not being able to provide them for oneself qualifies as a situation of morally unacceptable want that demands public recognition and gives rise to claims of need the fulfillment of which is a demand of basic justice.

One last remark before we turn to the allocation problem in the next section. It is sometimes suggested that at least some of the people living in severe poverty are themselves responsible for their plight. If that were so, it would seem as if their situation could not lead to valid claims against others. Self-reliance, it may be pointed out, is an important value and it is hard to deny that much of the globally existing poverty (though not, of course, all) is primarily due to factors within the poverty-stricken countries of the so-called Third World themselves. Why, then, should citizens living in better-off countries recognize any obligation to respond to claims of need beyond their own political communities? Responsibility has a retrospective, backward-looking and a prospective, forward-looking dimension. Retrospectively it is concerned with how a situation came about as the causal result of a series of individual and collective actions in the past. Prospectively the question is who can do something to change it for the better irrespective of who brought it about. Thus, a person may be (prospectively) responsible for the continuation of a situation because she is in a position to provide relief even though (retrospectively) she did nothing to cause it in the first place. We shall confine ourselves to two brief remarks on retrospective responsibility. Firstly, the severe poverty existing in the Third World today has a complex causal history that includes a period of violent colonial exploitation of Third World countries by the colonial powers from the fifteenth century until the middle of the last century. In view of this historical background and the predominant responsibility of the Western industrialized countries for the post-World War II international economic system, the claim that those living today in the Third World have actually forfeited their claims to assistance lacks credibility. It is certainly impossible to forfeit *all* your claims of need against others just because you are *partially* responsible for your own mischief. Secondly, even to the extent that some of the (retrospective) responsibility lies within the poverty-stricken countries themselves, it is primarily corrupt and kleptocratic elites that must be blamed and not their victims. Moreover, we must take into consideration that many of those who suffer the worst had yet no chance at all to forfeit any claims on others for the simple reason that they are innocent children.

In determining the scope of valid claims of need deriving from the globally existing severe poverty, responsibility matters mainly because of its prospective dimension. One of the fixed points of our considered judgments on need-based claims and duties of assistance is that, to the extent a person in need is capable of helping herself, she does not have valid claims on others. However, we agree with Henry Shue that the discussion about the validity of the claims of those who are healthy and can work to get themselves out of misery is largely academic and without much practical relevance. As Shue rightly points out, most "of the malnourished ... are probably also diseased, since malnutrition lowers resistance to disease, and hunger and infestation normally form a tight vicious circle. Hundreds of millions of the malnourished are very young children. A large percentage of the adults, besides being ill and hungry, are also chronically unemployed, so the issue of policy toward healthy adults who refuse to work is largely irrelevant" (Shue 1996: 23). It is a truism that external help cannot be a substitute for the self-governed productive activity of those who live in poverty. All it can do is provide a basis and support for self-help. Nonetheless, there is a morally significant difference between those who need help to help themselves and those who do not.

By way of concluding this section it can be said that there are valid moral claims of need deriving from severe poverty that have to be met by those in more fortunate circumstances. Indeed, all those capable of helping are candidates for a natural duty of assistance. We owe the fulfillment of this duty to others simply because they are human beings in a situation of unacceptable want. As natural duties, they are binding on us irrespective of existing personal or institutional relationships. This implies, among other things, that these duties go beyond borders (to use a phrase by Stanley Hoffman) and address claims of individuals we may not even know about and may never meet in person. It can be said, then, that severe poverty is a violation of basic human rights in the sense of being a condition in which morally valid claims of need remain unfulfilled, e.g., those claims expressed in article 25 of the *Universal Declaration*. However, as we have seen in section 4, abstract claims, however urgent, have only weak regulative force unless they are supplemented by a determination of their addresses and their specific duties. Normally, situations of morally unacceptable want can be dealt with in various ways involving different agents. As a consequence, a mere description of an existing situation of want and of the abstract claims of need arising from it remain much too vague to give us any specific idea of what has to be done by whom in order to meet the valid claims of need deriving from global poverty.

6. The allocation problem

Given their usual formulations, many human rights neither lend themselves easily to a determination of the duty-bearers involved nor of their duties. This is a point Onora O'Neill and others have often made (cf. O'Neill 1996, chapter 5.2 and 2001; Feinberg 1970; see also Stepanians 2005).[12] Take again the rights guaranteed by article 3 of the *Universal Declaration*: "Everyone has the right to life, liberty, and security of person." This formulation leaves little doubt as to who the holders of the right to life, liberty, and security are. In our terminology, all three are universal rights held by every human being. But who are their addressees, the bearers of the corresponding duties? And what is the exact content of the duties that counts as fulfilling them? For classical rights-theorists, who regard rights essentially as relations between at least two persons, such formulations are in a serious way incomplete.

The obvious way out is to supplement these formulations with a term for the missing addressee. According to many legal theorists, nothing is easier. At least for the human rights acknowledged in international law, they say, the addressee is a legal person by the name of "the state" (cf. Sieghart 1985: 43). If this is correct, the supplemented version of article 3 of the *Universal Declaration* reads: "Everyone has the right to life, liberty, and security of

---

[12] The point has to be stated with care, however. Contrary to O'Neill's suggestion (1996: 129ff), it has nothing to do with the rivalry among classical rights theorists between champions of the "choice" or "will" theory on the one hand and the "interest" or "benefit" theory on the other. O'Neill adopts, without argument, a choice theory of rights and does not address the well-known difficulty, explicitly acknowledged by its most prominent modern defender H. L. A. Hart, that the choice theory is incompatible in principle with the existence of inalienable rights (cf. MacCormick 1977: 195ff). Since at least the fundamental human rights are generally regarded as inalienable, it is misleading to object to positive human rights on the ground that it is in their case unclear against whom one has the power to waive these rights. A short answer to *this* problem is simply that such fundamental rights involve no powers of waiver.

person *against the state*." There is much to be said in favor of this view. First, there are important human rights that only states or state agencies can honor or violate in the full sense. This is true for all rights whose content cannot be explained without reference to state agencies or state-like institutional arrangements like due process and habeas corpus rights, or rights to political participation. Secondly, if we line up behind Henry Shue (1996: 193n) and John Stuart Mill and hold that a right is something "which society ought to defend me in the possession of" (1861, chapter 5), it becomes obvious that human rights imply claims against the state, given the factual need of enforcement and of coordinated social action aimed at upholding human rights. Finally, even with regard to those rights that imply primarily negative duties of non-interference (not to kill, not to rape, not to torture, not to starve, etc.), there arise what Shue calls "default duties" of protection and aid that must be discharged if the corresponding rights to life, security and subsistence are to be sustained (Shue 1996: 170–8, passim). Again, given the need for coordinated social action to support these rights, states and state-like institutional arrangements are natural addressees of human right claims.[13]

However, from an analytical point of view the exclusive focus on states, social systems, and peoples rather than on individuals in constructing a normative theory of human rights is unfortunate. There is no denying that states are important, perhaps even primary addressees of human rights, but it is highly implausible to regard them as the only ones. Indeed, the very notion of the state as having duties to uphold the rights of its citizens suggests that also non-state agents have duties derived from these rights. Moreover, in our world there is no such thing as "the state," but a plurality of states. Which is the one against whom everyone has the right to life, liberty, and security? Is it the state in which the right-holder is a citizen? Or perhaps the state on whose territory the right-holder happens to be? Or do *all* states that have signed the *Universal Declaration* have the corresponding duties towards every right-holder? Even if international lawyers have clear answers to these questions, as they certainly do, it is obvious that not only states are capable of violating or honoring human rights. Is it really plausible

---

[13] That states and state agencies are the primary addressees of human rights seems also to be Rawls's (1999) view, except for the odd terminological distinction he makes between "states" and "peoples." Following Rawls, human rights have the role of setting limits on a *government's* internal sovereignty and its right to self-defense (ibid. 27, 42). Outlaw *states* figure in the book as the most prominent example of human rights violators (ibid. 37, 81) and it is said that *social systems* violate or recognize human rights (ibid. 65, 68). Principle eight of Rawls's Law of Peoples requires *peoples* to honor human rights (ibid. 37). Unless we have missed something, there is no passage in *The Law of Peoples* where Rawls talks about individuals as addressees of human right claims.

to assume that no individual and no organization, party, or corporation can ever violate a human right, and that this impossibility is part of the very *concept* of a human right? Even if this were true by definition for the legal concept, as it is understood in international human rights law, it is certainly not true for human rights as moral rights. If states were the exclusive addressees, no non-state agent could ever have a human rights-based duty to intervene if a particular state violates the human rights of its citizens. In particular, the citizens of this state could never be under a duty to change the ways of their government. Note that they would not even have such a duty if they could easily do so. This strikes us as absurd.

It makes more sense to regard *all* agents (individual, collective, corporate, or institutional) who are capable of violating the human rights as being prima facie within the scope of human right claims.[14] If so, however, we are confronted with the problem of identifying the relevant duty-bearers and of specifying their duties. That is, we face the allocation problem. It does not arise with regard to the *negative* duties of non-interference derivable from human rights. For example, the right not to be tortured implies that *we all* have to abstain from torturing anyone. There is no question about who the duty-bearers are and what they have to do since these rights are at the same time universal (everybody has them) and general (they hold against everybody). The allocation problem arises for special human rights, i.e., rights that are selective in the sense that they bind only some of us. Take, for example, the rights to subsistence which are relevant to the problem of severe poverty. Even though they constitute universally valid claims of need, not everyone is obligated to provide the required means of subsistence for every other person. Nevertheless, someone (at least one of us) is under a duty to do so — and the question is who. Once more, a natural answer is: the state. While it is a mistake to think of states as the exclusive addressees of human rights, it is clear that the practical exigencies of an effective fight against severe poverty ensure that states and state-like agents play a vital role. Wherever severe poverty occurs on a large scale, its

---

[14] There are further important reasons not to start an analysis of human rights with a focus on collective and institutional agents and to begin rather at the elementary level with individuals and their rights and duties. Collectives like "peoples" or "the international community" are often not capable of coordinated rational action because of the well-known problems of collective action that derive from incomplete information among the members of a group and prisoners-dilemma like social settings. Assuming that *ought* implies *can*, a consequence of these collective action problems is that collectives as such cannot be duty-bearers and, hence cannot violate human rights either. This follows from our analysis of what it means to violate a human right in section 3. Still, governments and states as organized (corporate) agents are normally capable of rational collective action (indeed, that is what they are about) and also of protecting or violating the human rights of their citizens. But they cannot be the only agents of this kind.

eradication requires massive collective efforts and coordinated social action that only states and state-like arrangements are capable of organizing in an effective manner. States and state agencies are indeed crucial for a satisfactory solution to the allocation problem. However, we cannot just leave it there. After all, states may fail to protect the human rights of their citizens either because they are too weak or because they do not care. In both cases, valid claims of need remain unfulfilled and the question of responsibility arises again. In order to solve the allocation problem fully, we need an account of how to assign those duties that arise when primary duty-bearers fail (or can be expected to fail). At this point, it is important to recognize that the duties implied by valid claims of need are "natural" duties in the sense that their fulfillment is owed to others simply because they are human beings and not because of the existence of particular personal or institutional ties between right-holders and duty-bearers. Since they are natural duties deriving from unfulfilled urgent claims, they are not confined to the fellow citizens of those in need.

From a global perspective, the main problem for a fair allocation of duties deriving from severe poverty is this: in view of the scale of severe global poverty and given the fact that states frequently fail to provide for even the minimal needs of their citizens, at least the assignment of default duties has to transcend borders and involve international cooperation on an unprecedented scale. However, if the fulfillment of valid claims of need requires large-scale social cooperation (not to mention *worldwide* cooperation), it is not possible to allocate the corresponding duties to individual and corporate agents exclusively on the basis of those claims. As we have seen, the right not to suffer severe poverty implies merely an abstract and weak natural duty with little regulative force against an indeterminate group of people. A more complete and workable specification of these duties can only be achieved via institutionalized schemes of cooperation that assign specific duties to particular agents and thereby turn indeterminate natural duties into specific conventional ones. In comparison with the natural duties they derive from, these institutionally defined conventional duties of assistance have a much stronger regulative force. Assuming a sensible social division of labor, different agents will have different responsibilities and tasks in the collective effort of meeting the valid claims of need of severely impoverished people. This shows that whether a claim of need imposes specific duties on determinate agents is largely a question of factual and institutional context. The moral claims of a person in a car accident on a deserted highway impose rather specific duties on me *if I happen to be the only one present at the time*. In contrast, if there were other people with me, my duties would be considerably less clear. Similarly, the moral claims of orphans who are in need of a decent upbringing are by themselves not claims against any specific individual with the responsibility to take care of them. Given an appropriate scheme of social institutions like guardian courts and orphanages, however, these claims may impose rather specific (legal, and also moral) duties on judges, guardians, and others.

A satisfactory solution of the allocation problem may therefore seem to be a natural-duty-cum-fair-cooperation approach. Duties deriving from valid claims of need are natural duties of mutual assistance. We owe the fulfillment of these duties to others simply because they are human beings, irrespective of our relationship to them and independent of existing schemes of social cooperation. Given the global scope of severe poverty, however, discharging these duties requires social cooperation with an efficient and fair division of labor. Therefore, it seems natural to assume that everyone has exactly those duties and responsibilities which an efficient and fair system of cooperative help would assign to her. Since the obligations such a system would allocate depend on specific social arrangements, they would be (not natural but) *conventional* obligations, whose normative force derives, however, from the natural duties of mutual assistance they supersede.

Unfortunately, this solution works in ideal theory at best and under the assumption of full compliance, but not in the real world. First, we simply do not know what an efficient and fair system of cooperative help would require us to do. It is difficult, if not impossible, to imagine what such a global system would look like under realistic conditions. Second, in reality we may have to do more or less than the "fair share" assigned to us under an ideal scheme of cooperation. If others do less than their fair share — e.g., if they act as free-riders in a public good scenario — we may be obliged to do more. And if others, say, out of sympathy and compassion, do more than their fair share, we may not even be obliged to do ours, since the relevant claims of need have already been met. Hence, the ideal of an efficient and fair scheme of global cooperation does not give us sufficient guidance as to what specific duties and responsibilities derive from the claims of need of others.

A different approach is adopted by Leif Wenar (2003b). Wenar does not move from the top of a global scheme of cooperative help down to the bottom of specific individual duties. Rather, he proceeds from an economic principle for the piecemeal (bottom to top) establishment of an efficient scheme of cooperative help. Wenar argues for a minimal cost-provider approach towards the fulfillment of valid claims of need. Economically speaking — and economics really has a point here — this may seem very plausible indeed. Only economic efficiency will render it possible to succeed in the fight against global poverty. However, there are serious difficulties with the employment of a minimal cost-provider principle for the allocation of specific duties deriving from valid claims of need. First, there are cases in which it would be clearly unfair to assign duties of assistance consistently to agents who can provide the necessary help at minimal cost. Take, for example, parents who are old and sick and in need of help from their children, and suppose that one of their children lives close by and the other far away. Does this mean that the responsibility of caring for parents always (and perhaps exclusively) falls on the child who lives close by if she can provide assistance at minimal cost? Second, costs are not a naturally fixed quantity. They are highly sensitive to local circumstances and institutional context and vary accordingly. In any case, existing institutional arrangements will strongly affect the determination of who actually is capable of helping and who can help at minimal cost.[15] The minimal cost approach would only seem appropriate if we were already working within a comprehensive institutional framework that ensures fair results from employing a minimal cost principle. In other words, we would need something like a fair institutional background of burden sharing. This, however, brings us back to the problem connected with the natural-duty-cum-fair-cooperation approach, namely, that the idea of a fair social scheme of cooperative help provides insufficient guidance concerning the distribution of specific duties under realistic conditions.

At this point, we have to face the possibility that there may not be an ideal theoretical solution to the allocation problem. There is, however, another alternative: pragmatism. It is much less ambitious than the natural-duty-cum-fair-cooperation approach since it does not aim at a comprehensive theory for the morally adequate allocation of duties deriving from unfulfilled claims of need. It, too, is highly dependent upon factual circumstances and already existing institutional and organizational arrangements, regardless of whether they yield ideally fair and efficient distributions of specific duties of assistance. Pragmatism looks at local circumstances and established institutions and organizations that can provide at least some of the necessary help — states, multilateral institutions, corporations and NGOs. It then asks what is required in terms of individual support to fulfill one's (highly unspecific) natural duties of mutual help, given the existing circumstances and arrangements. According to this pragmatic approach, the task of moral philosophy turns into something modest and manageable. It is primarily concerned with defending the claim that we indeed have the specific moral duties of assistance assigned to us by

---

[15] Those who already have to pay high taxes to support their needy fellow citizens may not have much money left to help others in more distant places. Or, if a system of social security is already set up in one country, the citizens of this country may, because of economies of scale, be the minimal-cost providers to their neighbors. This may be so even if — from a *common sense* point of view — they would not seem to be responsible, for instance, if their neighbors could help themselves albeit at higher costs.

moral pragmatism, and with fending off the objection that there are no such things as rights to positive services, or that there are no valid claims of need deriving from global poverty at all.

7. Conclusion

In what sense and under what conditions, then, is severe poverty a human rights violation? We suggest a distinction between a weak and a strong sense of a human right not to suffer severe poverty. Severe poverty is a condition of morally unacceptable want, which gives rise to weighty claims of need against others. However, those claims qualify only as weak human rights as long as they take the highly abstract form of claims against "someone" (i.e., at least one, possibly all) with unspecified duties. Their weakness consists in the fact that they have only weak regulative force and little motivational impact and thus fail to compel specified persons to act in a determinate manner. The transformation of a weak and abstract human right not to suffer severe poverty into a strong and concrete right requires a solution of the allocation problem, namely, the actual assignment of concrete duties arising from poverty-related claims of need to specified agents. Ideally, the first step is to replace the opaque reference to "someone" in "A has a right not to suffer severe poverty against someone" with a complex disjunction that contains transparent singular terms of possible duty-bearers: "A has a right not to suffer severe poverty against B, *or* A has a right not to suffer severe poverty against C, *or* A has a right not to suffer severe poverty against D, etc." Next is the identification, through a fair procedure, of the agent or group actually bound by A's right not to suffer severe poverty as a matter of justice. We have emphasized that any plausible and workable assignment has to take into account existing networks of cooperation, social institutions, and other factual circumstances. As a result, the abstract natural duties arising from severe poverty against an anonymous group of persons will be superseded by assigned conventional and finally legal duties of determinate agents. Hence, by specifying duties towards those who live in dire poverty, we move away from a moral to a juridical understanding of human rights and human rights violations. However, it may be felt that in terms of motivational power — and also in terms of the weight of moral disapproval — a big difference still remains between saying that torture is a human rights violations and saying that failing to participate in an organized effort to eliminate global poverty (which comprises millions of people) is to violate human rights.

Chapter 18

The First UN Millennium Development Goal: A Cause for Celebration?[*]

Thomas Pogge

Philosophy, Columbia University, New York, and Oslo University; Centre for Applied Philosophy and Public Ethics, Australian National University, Canberra

In the *UN Millennium Declaration* of the year 2000, the 191 member states of the UN committed themselves to the goal "to halve, by the year 2015, the proportion of the world's people whose income is less than one dollar a day and the proportion of people who suffer from hunger." This is the first and most prominent of altogether eight UN Millennium Development Goals (MDGs) as listed on the UN website.[1]

The commitment to this goal, in such a prominent text, has been widely celebrated. The governments of the world have finally united behind the goal of eradicating extreme poverty and hunger. And they have not merely endorsed this goal in a vague and general way, but have committed themselves to a concrete plan with a quite specific intermediate target. Given the abject poverty in which so many human beings subsist today, this highly official and highly visible commitment is surely reason for celebration. — Isn't it?

I am not so sure. In any case, I want to offer four skeptical reflections that we should ponder before judging the goal our governments have set in our names.

---

[*] This essay first appeared in the *Journal of Human Development*, volume 5, number 3 (November 2004). I thank Taylor and Francis for permission to reprint it here without charge. I am also deeply grateful for the comprehensive feedback I received in Oslo and at the subsequent presentation at the Carnegie Council on Ethics and International Affairs, as well as written comments from Sanjay Reddy.

[1] See www.un.org/millenniumgoals/index.shtml. The text of the *Declaration*, as unanimously adopted without vote by the UN General Assembly on September 8 of the year 2000, had, in its Article 19, stated only six goals (www.un.org/millennium/declaration/ares552e.htm). But the difference is unimportant, reflecting merely a slight rearrangement on the website.

A. Follesdal and T. Pogge, (eds.), Real World Justice, 317-338.
© 2004 *Taylor & Francis. Printed by Springer, The Netherlands.*

1. Reflection One — on halving world poverty

The goal of halving extreme poverty worldwide by 2015 is not new. It was very prominently affirmed, for instance, four years earlier, at the World Food Summit in Rome, where the 186 participating governments declared: "We pledge our political will and our common and national commitment to achieving food security for all and to an on-going effort to eradicate hunger in all countries, with an immediate view to reducing the number of undernourished people to half their present level no later than 2015."[2]

Is the first MDG then merely a reaffirmation of a commitment made earlier? Even a slightly more ambitious commitment, seeing that the reported number of extremely poor had fallen a bit from the 1096.9 million reported for 1996 (www.worldbank.org/research/povmonitor)? Well, not exactly.

Looking closely at the two texts, we find a subtle but important shift. While the earlier *Rome Declaration* spoke of halving the *number* of undernourished by 2015, the later *Millennium Declaration* speaks of halving the *proportion* of people suffering from hunger and extreme poverty by 2015.

Substituting "proportion" for "number" makes a considerable difference. For the year 2000, some 1094 million were reported to be living below $1/day.[3] Halving the *number* of extremely poor people thus would commit us to ensuring that there are no more than 547 million such people in 2015. Halving the *proportion* of extremely poor people is less ambitious. In 2000, the total human population was 6070.6 million (http://esa.un.org/unpp/); so 18.02 percent were living in extreme poverty. Halving the proportion means reducing this percentage to 9.01 percent. Given an expected human population of 7197 million in 2015 (ibid.), the implied goal is then to reduce the number of extremely poor people to 648.5 million by 2015. The planned poverty reduction has been shrunk by 101.5 million.

What makes the difference here is the increase in the reference population. As the human population grows by 18.6 percent over the 2000–2015 period, so the number of extremely poor people deemed acceptable in 2015 also increases by 18.6 percent (from 547 to 648.5 million) and the planned poverty reduction is correspondingly diminished by 18.6 percent (from 547 to 445.5 million).

---

[2]   *Rome Declaration on World Food Security*, adopted in November 1996 at the World Food Summit in Rome, which was organized by the UN Food and Agriculture Organization (FAO). The full text is available at www.fao.org/docrep/003/w3613e/w3613e00.htm.

[3]   My rough interpolation from the World Bank's figures of 1095.1 million for 1999 and 1092.7 million for 2001 (www.worldbank.org/research/povmonitor).

The UN's interpretation of the goal cuts back the planned poverty reduction even further. The formulation of the first MDG clearly specifies the end of the plan period: the year 2015. But it says nothing about the start of this period — about the status quo ante relative to which the one-half reduction in the percentage of poor people is to be achieved. One may think that the missing baseline is obvious: it is simply the time at which the MDGs are adopted, the year 2000 — in analogy to how the *Rome Declaration* set the "present level" as the baseline. But the UN instead uses 1990 as the baseline, thereby expanding the plan period to 25 years. It interprets the goal to be that the proportion of extremely poor people should in 2015 be no more than half of what it was in 1990 (www.un.org/millenniumgoals/MDG-Page1.pdf).

The use of 1990 rather than 2000 as the baseline is significant in two ways. First, the 1990s have seen a dramatic reduction in the reported number of extremely poor people in China, the world's most populous country. By extending the plan period backwards, this reduction by nearly 150 million (www.worldbank.org/research/povmonitor) is counted toward the goal, which thus becomes much more easily achievable. Thanks to China's success, reported extreme poverty in the entire "East Asia and the Pacific" region had been halved by 1999 already — one year *before* the *Millennium Declaration* was even adopted![4]

Second, a longer plan period — 25 years instead of 15 — means a much greater population growth from the start to the end of the period. And, as we have seen already, this population growth also contributes greatly towards achieving the goal. Put precisely: the proportion of extremely poor people is a fraction that has the number of extremely poor people in the numerator and some reference population in the denominator. A fixed reduction in the value of such a fraction, here by one half, can come about through a decrease in the numerator and/or through an increase in the denominator. The greater the increase in the denominator, which occurs simply through population growth, the less of a reduction needs to be achieved in the numerator.

By lengthening the plan period, the UN nearly *doubles* the expected increase in the denominator and thus reduces substantially the required reduction in the numerator: While the human population is expected to grow by 18.6 percent in the 2000–2015 period, its growth over the longer 1990–2015 period is expected to be 36.7 percent, from 5263.6 to 7197 million (http://esa.un.org/unpp).

---

[4]   See www.un.org/millenniumgoals/MDG-Page1.pdf, showing the actual proportion of poor people in that region as 28 percent in 1990 and 14 percent in 1999, and showing the goal of 14 percent for 2015.

Let us observe the effect of lengthening the plan period by examining some actual numbers. In 1990, 1218.5 million people or 23.15 percent of humankind are reported to have lived below $1/day (www.worldbank.org/research/povmonitor). Halving this percentage, the goal would then be that in 2015 no more than 833 million human beings (11.575 percent of the expected world population of 7197 million) should be so poor. By extending the plan period backward, the UN raises the number of extremely poor people deemed acceptable in 2015 by a further 184.5 million and correspondingly shrinks the poverty reduction planned for 2000–2015 by the same number, to 261 million.

The UN makes the goal even less ambitious through regional disaggregation. It interprets the goal to be that the proportion of extremely poor people should be halved *within each region* (www.un.org/millenniumgoals/MDG-Page1.pdf). This produces a further cutback in the planned poverty reduction as regions with greater poverty incidence also tend to have faster population growth.

We can observe most of this effect by taking the developed countries, where extreme poverty is negligible or non-existent, out of the picture. The population of the remaining, developing countries grows faster than that of humankind at large. It is expected to grow by 45 percent (from 4114.7 to 5967 million) in the 1990–2015 period (http://esa.un.org/unpp). The goal of halving extreme poverty therefore becomes even less ambitious if the number of poor is put in proportion not to the growing human population, but to the faster-growing population of the developing countries. In 1990, 29.6 percent of this population were extremely poor — 1218.5 out of 4114.7 million. Thus the figure deemed acceptable for 2015 is 14.8 percent of 5967 million — 883.5 million. And so the planned poverty reduction is cut back by yet another 50.5 million: to 210.5 million. On the official UN interpretation, MDG-1 commits the world's governments to reducing the number of extremely poor persons by 19 percent — from 1094 million when the *Declaration* was adopted in 2000 to 883.5 million by 2015.

Let me sum up my first reflection. MDG-1 is meant to supersede a commitment the world's governments had made years earlier, notably at the 1996 World Food Summit in Rome. There they promised to reduce the *number* of extremely poor to half its *present* (1996) level, from 1096.9 to 548.45 million. MDG-1 departs from this earlier commitment in three important respects: first, our governments' goal is now to halve the *proportion* of extremely poor people, not their number. Second, the plan period has been extended backward in time, having it start not when the commitment was made, but in 1990. Third, the commitment is now regionally disaggregated, which further cuts back the planned poverty reduction and also detracts from the global moral responsibility of the affluent countries.

Compared to the 1996 World Food Summit commitment, MDG-1 as interpreted by the UN *raises* the number of extremely poor people deemed acceptable in 2015 by 335 million (from 548.45 to 883.5 million) and thereby *shrinks* by over 62 percent the reduction in this number which governments pledge to achieve during the 2000–2015 period. Had we stuck to the promise of Rome, our task for 2000–2015 would have been to reduce the extremely poor by 545.55 million. The *Millennium Declaration* envisages a reduction by only 210.5 million.

2. Reflection Two — on counting the poor

My first reflection may have been a little discomforting. However, there is other good news. In the words of World Bank President James Wolfensohn: "After increasing steadily over the past two centuries, since 1980 the total number of people living in poverty worldwide has fallen by an estimated 200 million — even as the world's population grew by 1.6 billion."[5] Thus, the world's politicians may not be moving as vigorously or as quickly toward the eradication of extreme poverty as we might have believed or might wish, but at least things are moving in the right direction and at a reassuring pace.

Are they really? — The numbers Wolfensohn is referring to are produced by his own organization, the World Bank, which has pioneered the dominant method for counting the income poor and also collects the most comprehensive empirical data from household surveys and other studies. These World Bank estimates — often presented precise to six digits (cf. Chen and Ravallion 2001: 290) — are widely reproduced by other UN agencies (most notably the UN Development Program) as well as by the media. And they are the numbers the UN is using to track how well the world's governments are doing in regard to the eradication of extreme poverty.

It is unfortunate, then, that the World Bank's estimates are problematic, even as rough indicators to the global poverty problem and its evolution over time. Detailed substantiation of this critique, which was elaborated in joint

---

[5] James D. Wolfensohn: "Responding to the Challenges of Globalization: Remarks to the G-20 Finance Ministers and Central Governors," Ottawa, November 17, 2001, www.worldbank.org/html/extdr/whatsnew2001.htm. These estimates appear to be drawn from World Bank 2002: 8. The World Bank's estimate of the 1980–2000 poverty reduction has since been doubled, with scant explanation (Chen and Ravallion 2004, cf. www.worldbank.org/research/povmonitor).

work with my economist colleague Sanjay Reddy, can be found elsewhere (Pogge and Reddy 2003, Reddy and Pogge 2005). Here I briefly present our main conclusions.

The World Bank's method, initially introduced around 1990, involves three steps. First, its users stipulate the level of a poverty line, defined in terms of the purchasing power that some specific country's currency had in this country in some specific base year. Until 1999, the Bank's chosen benchmark was an income of $1 per person per day in the US in 1985. More recently, the Bank has, under the same $1/day label, used an income of $32.74 per person per month in the US in 1993 (Chen and Ravallion 2001: 285) — a revision that, because US inflation was 34.3 percent in the 1985–93 period (www.bls.gov/cpi/home.htm), involved a lowering of the benchmark in the US by 19.6 percent.[6]

Second, such users undertake a spatial translation of this benchmark by calculating, for the chosen year, the equivalent amounts in the currencies of other countries, using purchasing power parity conversion factors (PPPs) of the base year. And, third, they undertake a temporal translation by converting any country's base-year amount into its equivalents for other years on the basis of that country's consumer price index (CPI). Together, these three steps yield (supposedly mutually equivalent) national-currency poverty lines for any country–year combination, which are then used to judge whether any given household in any particular country and year is poor or not.

Our first critique, concerning Step 1, is that the benchmark chosen by the Bank is too low. According to the US Department of Agriculture, the least cost of home cooking, meeting a minimal calorie constraint (varying between 1600 and 2800 calories depending on age and gender) and a set of other minimal nutrient constraints, was $5134 for a typical family of four in the US in 1999.[7] Living at the Bank's official international poverty line (IPL), such a family would have had only $1812 in 1999, and $2057 in 2004.[8] Applying the Bank's IPL in its base country — the United States — we find that it does not correspond to an income that suffices to pay even just for food alone.

---

[6] This effect is typical. Substantially lowering the international poverty line for 77 of 92 countries, containing 82 percent of their aggregate population, the revision significantly reduced the number of people counted as extremely poor (Reddy and Pogge 2005, table 5).

[7] USDA 1999b, ES-1. According to this guide for low income households and government agencies, a reference family consisting of a male and a female ages 20 to 50, and two children ages 6 to 8 and 9 to 11 needs at least $98.40 (1999) per week for food.

[8] This is $32.74 times 12 months times 4 persons, adjusted for CPI inflation since 1993 (www.bls.gov/cpi/home.htm).

Our second critique, concerning Step 2, targets the way the Bank converts its US-Dollar benchmark into foreign-currency equivalents. The Bank does so, unobjectionably, not via market exchange rates, but by examining the prices prevailing in the US and abroad.

Now price ratios between rich and poor countries vary widely across commodities. For goods easily traded across borders — "tradables," like food grains or cars — prices compared at market exchange rates differ little between rich and poor countries. For commodities not easily traded across borders ("nontradables"), especially services, prices compared at market exchange rates can be fifty times higher in rich countries than in poor ones. Labor, especially, is very much cheaper in poor countries because it is there much more abundant relative to capital and also prevented from moving freely across borders to where wages are higher.

How do PPPs reflect this great diversity of price ratios? The PPPs used by the Bank average out these price ratios in a way that, roughly speaking, weights each good or service in proportion to its share in international consumption expenditure. In this way US$1 and 13 Bangladeshi Taka are deemed equivalent in purchasing power even though the former amount buys much more tradables in the US than the latter buys in Bangladesh, while the latter amount buys much more nontradables in Bangladesh than the former buys in the US.

Now the market exchange rate of the Bangladeshi currency is 4½ times higher than its PPP, not 13, but 59 Taka to the Dollar. The PPP calculated for the Bangladeshi currency thus reflects the view that money buys 4½ times more in Bangladesh than in the US. This view may fit affluent Bangladeshi consumers whose expenditure mirrors the international pattern. But it is highly misleading in regard to very poor Bangladeshi families who spend little or nothing on nontradables, such as services, which are especially cheap in Bangladesh. These families have no choice. To survive they must concentrate their expenditures on basic necessities, especially foodstuffs. And there is ample evidence that foodstuffs and other basic necessities cost substantially more in poor countries than general-consumption PPPs would suggest (Reddy and Pogge 2005, Tables 6–11).

Given Bangladesh's PPP of 13, the World Bank assumes that a Bangladeshi family of four with annual income of 26,000 Taka is as well-off as a similar family would be in the US with $2000 per year. This is a mistake because, for such a poor Bangladeshi family, the disadvantage — that 26,000 Taka buys much less food in Bangladesh than $2000 buys in the US — is not compensated by the fact that 26,000 Taka also buys much more services in Bangladesh than $2000 buys in the US. The reason is that such a poor family does not spend money on services: on drivers, maids, or even haircuts. It simply cannot afford to do so. To survive, it must spend nearly all its income on basic foodstuffs. And it is then very much worse off with its 26,000 Taka per year in Bangladesh than a similar household with $2000 per year would be in the US. In the Bank's latest PPP base year, 1993, for example, the Bangladeshi Taka bought just over half as much (53 percent) in breads and cereals as its assessed PPP was suggesting (Reddy and Pogge 2005, Table 6B).

As the Bank periodically updates its poverty statistics by switching to a later PPP base year, this mistake tends to get larger, because foodstuffs constitute a falling, and services a rising share in international consumption expenditure. As a result, the prices of foodstuffs have a diminishing, and the prices of services a growing influence on the calculation of official PPPs. The Bank's PPPs are likely, therefore, *increasingly* to overstate the value of poor countries' currencies for fulfilling basic needs. We can expect successive poverty measurement exercises to attribute greater and greater purchasing power to the same poor family in the same country and year by assessing its income against consumption baskets containing ever more services and less food.

Summing up our second critique, if we think of the extremely poor as those who lack minimally adequate access to basic necessities, then we must conclude that, even if the World Bank's poverty line were adequate for the US, where food is cheap relative to services, the Bank, by using general-consumption PPPs for converting its IPL into national poverty lines, may still have greatly undercounted the poor in many poor countries where food is more expensive relative to services than in the US.

Our second critique reinforces the first, suggesting that the national poverty lines the Bank applies to poor countries are too low to be credible. The Bank is wrong in suggesting that a family of four could meet its basic needs on $131 per month in the US in 1993. This is the first critique. And the Bank is wrong again in using general-consumption PPPs and CPIs to translate this amount into foreign currencies and other years. The resulting national-currency amounts will have quite different (and in poor countries generally lower) purchasing power with respect to the basic necessities on which the poor do and must concentrate their spending.[9]

---

[9]   These errors are replicated by Surjit Bhalla (2002) and Xavier Sala-i-Martin (2002) who — to great media acclaim — have presented much rosier poverty statistics than the Bank's. They achieve such lower poverty headcounts by relying on national accounts data while using household survey data only to estimate the proportional distribution of each national total. This methodological divergence matters because, for most countries, national accounts data support higher estimates of aggregate private consumption than household survey data do. The discrepancy is due in part to the fact that national accounts use a broader definition of private consumption, including, for example, the consumption by non-governmental organizations, the value of housing consumed by owner-occupants,

Our first two critiques suggest that the number of people who cannot meet their basic needs may be much greater than World Bank estimates suggest. One may think that this is not so important in the context of tracking progress toward achieving the first UN MDG. If more credible, that is higher, poverty lines were used to count the poor, more people would be recognized as poor. But this would be true for all years and thus would make no difference to the upbeat trend assessment delivered by the Bank.

However, more credible poverty lines would not deliver the same trend picture. We know this from the Bank's own poverty estimates. According to its latest figures, the number of people living below its official $1/day IPL fell by 389.1 million or by over 26 percent (from 1481.8 to 1092.7 million) during 1981–2001, while the number of people living on less than twice this benchmark ("$2/day") *increased* by 285.6 million or by nearly 12 percent (from 2450.0 to 2735.6 million) over the very same period (www.worldbank.org/research/povmonitor). These figures strongly suggest that, had the Bank used more credible — higher — poverty lines, it would have reported a less rosy trend picture.

Our third critique is that the World Bank's method is internally unreliable insofar as the poverty estimates it produces depend not only on the empirical data but also, and very substantially, on the chosen PPP base year. The reason for this is that PPPs and CPIs invoke very different notions of equivalency. For example: the equivalence, in India, of 1562 rupees in 1985 with 2756 rupees in 1993 means that these two amounts had, in their respective years, the same purchasing power relative to the *Indian* pattern of consumption expenditure. The equivalence, in the US, of $293 in 1985 with $393 in 1993 means that these two amounts had, in their respective years,

---

and the consumption benefit derived from the use of credit cards and mortgages ("financial services indirectly measured" or FISM). Bhalla and Sala-i-Martin thus raise the assessed consumption of the poor by imputing to them a proportional share of such "consumption." (Focusing on GDP, Sala-i-Martin additionally imputes to poor households a proportional share of government outlays and national investment expenditures, thus counting many households as non-poor thanks to their government's spending on tanks and airports.) More generally, both authors uniformly adjust the findings of any country's household survey (mostly upward) to match its national accounts data — assuming that the latter are accurate and that the poor underreport their consumption to the same extent as their compatriots do. The authors thereby disregard other factors that are likely to contribute to the substantial and generally growing discrepancy between national-accounts and household-survey based estimates of national private consumption expenditure: that national accounts data may exaggerate aggregate consumption, and that affluent households (which often underreport their taxable incomes) are more likely to understate their consumption or to refuse to participate in household surveys. (Their nonparticipation would bias household surveys toward overestimating the poverty headcount, but generally much less so than the two authors' assumption of consumption underreporting by the poor.) For a thorough analysis of the data discrepancy, see Deaton 2003.

the same purchasing power relative to the *US* pattern of consumption expenditure. And the equivalence, in 1993, of 2756 rupees in India with $393 in the US means that these two amounts had, in their respective countries, the same purchasing power relative to the prevailing *international* pattern of consumption expenditure. Because the composition of consumption expenditure varies greatly between India, the US, and the world at large, it is a mistake to combine such equivalencies by transitivity — e.g., like this:

$293 in the US in 1985 is equivalent to $393 in the US in 1993

$393 in the US in 1993 is equivalent to 2756 rupees in India in 1993

2756 rupees in India in 1993 is equivalent to 1562 rupees in India in 1985.

Therefore:

$293 in the US in 1985 is equivalent to 1562 rupees in India in 1985.

Drawing this inference is a mistake, because the inferred equivalence would not hold up if we compared the two amounts directly, via 1985 PPPs, or in some other indirect way, via PPPs of some base year other than 1993.

Fortunately, I need not rest with the theoretical statement of the difficulty. The World Bank has delivered extensive poverty estimates based on two different PPP base years: 1985 and 1993. This switch in base year has made a huge difference to how the various currencies are valued relative to one another. For example, if 1993 rather than 1985 is used as the PPP base year, then the purchasing power of all Mauritanian incomes in all years more than triples relative to that of all Nigerian incomes in all years. The World Bank's switch in base year had the effect of raising Nigerian poverty lines for all years by 42 percent and of lowering Mauritanian poverty lines for all years by 61 percent (Reddy and Pogge 2005, Table 5). Discrepancies of this kind, of varying magnitudes, can be found across all pairs of countries.

The effect of these revisions in national poverty lines on reported national poverty rates and headcounts is even more dramatic. In 1999, applying its method with 1985 as the PPP base year, the Bank reported very similar poverty rates for Nigeria and Mauritania, of 31.1 and 31.4 percent respectively. In 2000, applying its method with 1993 as PPP base year, the Bank reported poverty rates for Nigeria and Mauritania of 70.2 and 3.8 percent respectively. Depending on which PPP base year it uses, the Bank estimates Nigeria's poverty rate to be either slightly lower or 18 time higher than Mauritania's![10]

---

[10] It is true that new survey data had become available in the interim. Still, the revision of the two countries' poverty lines clearly had a huge impact on their estimated poverty rates. And cases where the very same survey data were used tell a similar story: the Bank's

Similarly for regions: in 1999, applying its method with 1985 as PPP base year, the Bank reported that in 1993 Sub-Saharan Africa and Latin America had poverty rates of 39.1 and 23.5 percent, respectively.[11] In 2000, applying its method with 1993 as PPP base year, the Bank reported that these same regions in the same year (1993) had poverty rates of 49.68 and 15.31 percent, respectively.[12]

At any time, the classification of hundreds of millions of people as either poor or non-poor depends on the World Bank's arbitrary choice of PPP base year. And this is bound to affect the trend picture as well. In 1999, applying its method with 1985 as PPP base year, the Bank had painted a rather less reassuring portrait of world poverty than Wolfensohn was presenting two years later. Then the Bank wrote: "the absolute number of those living on $1 per day or less continues to increase. The worldwide total rose from 1.2 billion in 1987 to 1.5 billion today and, if recent trends persist, will reach 1.9 billion by 2015" (World Bank 1999: 25).[13]

Our third critique demonstrates, then, that the World Bank's method for producing poverty estimates is *unreliable*. We cannot show this by comparing the Bank's estimates to ones produced by a more reliable method — no such estimates yet exist. We show the unreliability of the Bank's method simply by comparing estimates produced with this method to one another, finding discrepancies that are much greater than is reasonably acceptable. A method must be rejected if the estimates produced with it bounce around as much as we have just observed in response to the arbitrary choice of PPP base year, which of course has nothing whatsoever to do with the actual economic circumstances of poor people.

A reliable method for monitoring how the world is doing in regard to the income poverty component of the first UN MDG must make purchasing-power comparisons not through PPPs and CPIs that invoke diverse and very broad consumption baskets (the many national patterns and the international

---

revision raised Turkmenistan's poverty rate from 4.9 percent to 20.9 percent, for example, while lowering South Africa's from 23.7 percent to 11.5 percent. Cf. Reddy and Pogge 2005, tables 2 and 3, for how the Bank's poverty rate estimates have changed for these and many other countries. Our tables are based on comparing table 4 of World Bank 1999: 236f, whose national poverty estimates are still based on the 1985 PPP base year, with table 4 of World Bank 2000: 280f, providing national poverty estimates based on the 1993 PPP base year.

[11] Cf. Reddy and Pogge 2005, table 4, based on World Bank 1999: 25, and Ravallion and Chen 1997, table 5.

[12] World Bank 2000: 23; table 2 of Chen and Ravallion, "How did the world's poorest fare in the 1990s?" (2000) at www.worldbank.org/research/povmonitor/pdfs/methodology.pdf.

[13] According to the latest World Bank figures (www.worldbank.org/research/povmonitor), the 1987–99 period saw not a 300-million *rise* in the number of people below $1/day, but a 76.1-million *drop*.

pattern of private consumption expenditure), but relative to a very much narrower consumption basket consisting of basic necessities. In addition, a reliable method must anchor its poverty lines not in some arbitrary dollar amount, but in a sound account of the basic requirements of human beings. Such a definition provides a benchmark that is both credible and uniformly applicable across all countries and years. Persons are poor if they do not have enough income to buy the basic necessities human beings generally require.

3. Reflection Three — on the speed and cost of alleviating poverty

However little may be known about income poverty trends, we certainly know that the problem of world poverty is catastrophic. According to the official statistics, about

799 million are undernourished (UNDP 2003: 87),

1000 million lack access to safe drinking water (ibid. 9),

2400 million lack basic sanitation (ibid.),

880 million have no access to basic medical care (UNDP 1999a: 22),

1000 million lack adequate shelter (UNDP 1998: 49),

2000 million have no electricity (ibid.),

876 million adults are illiterate (UNDP 2003: 6),

250 million children (aged 5 to 14) do wage work outside their family, at least 8.4 million of them in the "unconditionally worst" forms of child labor, which involve slavery, forced or bonded labor, forced recruitment for use in armed conflict, forced prostitution or pornography, or the production or trafficking of illegal drugs (ILO 2002: 9, 11, 17, 18).

"Worldwide 34,000 children under age five die daily from hunger and preventable diseases" (USDA 1999a, iii). Nearly one third of all human deaths — some 18 million per year or 50,000 daily — are due to poverty-related causes (such as starvation, diarrhea, pneumonia, tuberculosis, measles, malaria, perinatal and maternal conditions) which could be prevented or cured cheaply through food, safe drinking water, vaccinations, rehydration packs, medicines, or better sanitation and hygiene (WHO 2004, Annex Table 2). Women and girls are substantially overrepresented among those suffering these deprivations (UNDP 2003: 310–30).

At 18 million per year, the global poverty death toll over the 15 years since the end of the Cold War was around 270 million, roughly the population of the US. If the magnitude of the world poverty problem remains constant, the poverty death toll for the period from the *Millennium Declaration* to 2015 will likewise be about 270 million. Of course, this UN

Declaration is a commitment to reduce the number of extremely poor, and hence presumably also the number of poverty deaths, by 19 percent. If all goes according to plan, we may then gradually reach an annual poverty death toll of 14 million in 2015, with "only" 240 million deaths from poverty-related causes in the 2000–2015 period. Is this really a morally acceptable plan? A plan to be celebrated?

Consider some of the other catastrophes of the last century: the genocide in Rwanda, for example, when the UN and the rest of the world stood idly by while some 800,000 people were hacked to death (cf. Pogge 2005). Suppose some US politician had said, in April 1994, that the genocide in Rwanda is really terrible and that the world's governments should commit themselves to reducing the slaughter by 19 percent by the year 2009. How would this have been received? Or suppose a US politician had said, in 1942, that the German concentration camps are morally intolerable and that the world's governments should aim to achieve a 19-percent reduction in the population of these camps by the year 1957 (which goal could perhaps more appealingly have been presented as a larger reduction in the *proportion* of the world's population, or of the world's non-Aryan population, languishing in German concentration camps). People would have been absolutely horrified by such a proposal.

So why were we not similarly horrified when the world's politicians proposed, in 2000, to reduce extreme poverty so that, 15 years later, the number it affects will have declined from 1094 to 883.5 million and the annual death toll from 18 to 14 million? Why do we greet such a proposal with celebration and self-congratulations?

Some would respond that the reason is cost. We simply cannot solve the problem any faster without huge costs to the cultures and economies of the advanced industrialized countries. They will admit that fighting the Nazis was quite costly too and that decent people, even ones not themselves under threat, were nonetheless convinced that the Nazis simply had to be stopped, with all deliberate speed. But the cost of fighting world poverty, they may say, is much greater still. As Richard Rorty puts it, "the rich parts of the world may be in the position of somebody proposing to share her one loaf of bread with a hundred starving people. Even if she does share, everybody, including herself, will starve anyway" (Rorty 1996: 10). How could it be wrong to refuse such a pointless course of self-sacrifice?

This response rests on a misconception. However immense the world poverty problem is in human terms, it is amazingly tiny in economic terms. Using the World Bank's poverty estimates, we can get a very rough sense of what the aggregate income is of all the people the Bank considers extremely poor. Assessed at market exchange rates, these 1092.7 million people together live on about $100 billion annually and would need some $40 billion more per year to reach the Bank's $1/day benchmark.[14]

To be sure, the Bank's IPL is too low. So let us look at the Bank's statistics about those living on less than twice its IPL. Assessed at market exchange rates, these 2735.6 million people (nearly half of humankind) together live on about $406 billion annually and would need some $294 billion more per year to reach the $2/day benchmark.[15] How large are these amounts?

Start with the former: the collective income of the $2/day-poor. These $406 billion constitute about 1.3 percent of the annual global social product of ca. $31,500 billion. With only one-third as many people, the rich countries, by contrast, have over 60 times as much income: 81 percent of the global social product (World Bank 2003: 235).

Consider the second amount, the additional annual income of $294 billion that the presently poor would need in order to reach the $2/day benchmark. This is 1.15 percent $(1/87^{th})$ of the $25,506 billion annual aggregate national incomes of the rich countries (ibid.).

---

[14]   These figures are rough estimates derived as follows. If all people with incomes below $1/day were exactly at this benchmark, then the purchasing power of their collective annual income would be that of $430 billion in the US in 1993 ($32.74 times 12 months times 1092.7 million), which corresponds to the purchasing power of $560 billion in 2004 (www.bls.gov/cpi/home.htm). Yet, those who are extremely poor in this sense live, on average, 28.4 percent below the $1/day benchmark (Chen and Ravallion 2004, tables 3 and 6, dividing the poverty gap index by the headcount index). So they have collective annual income with aggregate purchasing power of about $400 billion and would need additional annual income with aggregate purchasing power of about $160 billion annually for all of them to reach the Bank's $1/day benchmark. I divide these two figures by 4 to adjust for the fact that the purchasing power the Bank ascribes to the incomes of very poor people is, on average, at least four times greater than their value at market exchange rates. Thus the World Bank equates India's per capita gross national income of $460 to $2,450 PPP, China's $890 to $4,260 PPP, Nigeria's $290 to $830 PPP, Pakistan's $420 to $1,920 PPP, Bangladesh's $370 to $1,680 PPP, Ethiopia's $100 to $710 PPP, Vietnam's $410 to $2,130 PPP, and so on (World Bank 2003: 234f).

[15]   These estimates are derived analogously. If all people with incomes below "2/day" were exactly at this benchmark, then the purchasing power of their collective annual income would be that of $2150 billion in the US in 1993 ($65.48 times 12 months times 2735.6 million), which corresponds to the purchasing power of $2800 billion in 2004 (www.bls.gov/cpi/home.htm). Those who are poor in this sense live, on average, 42 percent below the $2/day benchmark (Chen and Ravallion 2004, tables 3 and 6, again dividing the poverty gap index by the headcount index). So they have collective annual income with aggregate purchasing power of about $1624 billion and would need additional annual income with aggregate purchasing power of about $1176 billion annually for all of them to reach the Bank's $2/day benchmark. I again divide both figures by 4 to estimate what these amounts come to at market exchange rates.

This $294-billion amount also is only about 40 percent of what the world is spending this year just on crude oil. It is well below the military budget of the US alone. And it is far less also than the so-called peace dividend, which the rich countries reaped when they reduced their military spending after the end of the Cold War.[16] Rorty's idea that universal starvation would result from an all-out effort to eradicate world poverty completely is simply preposterous.

While the $294-billion amount is small relative to our means, it is also four times larger than what the rich countries are actually spending on official development assistance (ODA). Initially meant to reach 1, later 0.7 percent of the rich countries' GNP, actual ODA has steadily fallen throughout the prosperous 1990s, from 0.33 to 0.22 percent of the rich countries' aggregate GNP, mainly through a drop from 0.21 to 0.10 percent in the US which has nearly one-third of the entire global social product (UNDP 2002: 202). Moreover, most ODA is spent for the benefit of agents capable of reciprocation: only 23 percent goes to the 49 least developed countries. While India receives about $1.50 annually per citizen, high-income countries like the Czech Republic, Malta, Cyprus, Bahrain, and Israel receive between $40 and $132 per citizen annually (UNDP 2002: 203–5). A large part of ODA is allocated to support exporters at home or small affluent elites abroad, and only a tiny fraction, $4.31 billion, goes for "basic social services" targeted on the poor.[17]

To be sure, some affluent countries do much better than the average, and five small ones — Norway, Sweden, Denmark, Luxembourg, and the Netherlands — come close to fulfilling their obligations (UNDP 2003: 290). If the other affluent countries spent as much on ODA as these five and focused their ODA sharply on poverty eradication (notably including basic health care and education), then severe poverty worldwide could be essentially eliminated by 2015, if not before.

Many human beings live in severe poverty, lacking secure access to basic necessities. This is nothing new. What is new is that global inequality has increased to such an extent that such poverty is now completely avoidable at a cost that would barely be felt in the affluent countries.

---

[16] The developed countries were able to reduce their military expenditures from 4.1 percent of their combined GDPs in 1985 to 2.2 percent in 1998 (UNDP 1998: 197; UNDP 2000: 217). With their combined GDPs at $25,104 billion in the year 2001 (World Bank 2003: 239), their peace dividend in 2001 comes to about $477 billion (1.9 percent of $25,104 billion).

[17] Cf. http:// millenniumindicators.un.org/unsd/mi/mi_series_results.asp?rowId=592.

4. Reflection Four — on positive and negative responsibility, benefiting versus not harming

The hypothetical of US politicians proposing a planned 19-percent reduction over 15 years in response to the mass deaths in Germany or Rwanda suggested that the go-slow approach adopted and celebrated by the world's privileged today is morally no better than such a hypothetical go-slow approach would have been in 1942 or 1994.

The fact that a real effort toward eradicating severe poverty worldwide would be much less costly than the defeat of Nazi Germany suggests that the present go-slow approach against world poverty may actually be morally worse than the hypothetical go-slow approach against the Nazi concentration camps: it is for the sake of *small* gains that the world's affluent elites are refusing to undertake a much more substantial push against world poverty.

My final reflection will highlight an additional asymmetry. The US bore no significant responsibility for the existence of the Nazi death camps; and the (hypothetical) commitment to reduce them by 19 percent over 15 years was then responsive to a merely positive duty to assist innocent persons at risk. The governments and citizens of today's affluent countries conceive of their relation to world poverty analogously: we tend to believe that we bear no significant responsibility for the existence of this problem and that our only moral reason to help alleviate it is our merely positive duty to assist innocent persons caught in a life-threatening emergency. This belief, however, is highly questionable.

Our world is marked by enormous inequalities in economic starting places. Some are born into abject poverty with a 30-percent chance of dying before their fifth birthday. Others are born into the civilized luxury of the Western middle class. These huge inequalities have evolved in the course of *one* historical process that was pervaded by monumental crimes of slavery, colonialism, and genocide — crimes that have devastated the populations, cultures, and social institutions of four continents.

The privileged of today are quick to point out that they had nothing to do with these crimes and that they should not be held to account for the sins of their forefathers. And right they are! But if they cannot inherit their ancestors' sins, then why can they inherit the *fruits* of those sins, the huge economic superiority prevailing at the end of the colonial period? In 1960, when most former colonies gained their independence, the inequality in per capita income between Europe and Africa, for example, was 30 to 1. Foreign rule was removed. But the great inequality built up in the colonial period was left intact, making for a very unequal start into the post-colonial era.

One may think that the situation in 1960 is too long ago to contribute much to the explanation of severe poverty today. But consider what a 30:1

inequality means. Even if Africa had consistently achieved growth in per capita income one full percentage point higher than Europe, this inequality ratio would still be nearly 20:1 today. At that rate, Africa would be catching up with Europe at the beginning of the 24th century.

Consider also the impact such huge inequalities have in negotiations about the terms of trade. With the exception of a few giants, such as China and India, poor countries have little bargaining power in international negotiations and also cannot afford the expertise needed to represent their interests effectively. (Such expertise can be quite costly. Recall that the initial WTO Treaty weighed in at 400 lbs or 26,000 pages.) As a result, they typically end up with a lousy deal. They opened their markets widely to foreign companies, paid royalties to foreign firms for films, music, drugs, and even seeds — and still found their own exports severely hampered by rich-country quotas, tariffs, anti-dumping duties as well as subsidies and export credits to domestic producers, all of which were somehow exempted from the supposed Big Move to free and open markets. Such asymmetries in the terms of trade surely play a role in explaining why the inequality in per capita income between Europe and Africa has not declined, but has rather increased considerably since the end of the colonial period, standing today at roughly 40:1.

When they influence the design of common rules, pre-existing inequalities tend to be preserved and often aggravated. This phenomenon is evident within national societies, in which economic inequality tends to be quite stable over time. High inequality in Latin America and the US persists over time, just as low inequality does in Scandinavia and Japan. Such stable diversity suggests that inequality is path-dependent, that high inequality tends to reproduce itself because it gives the rich much greater power and also much stronger incentives to shape the common rules in their favor. Within national societies, one-person-one-vote democracy may mitigate the tendency for large inequalities to expand more and more. But there are no democratic practices the global poor might use to affect the economic rules beyond their own society. Even 85 percent of humankind, united, could not amend the WTO system.

The affluent countries and their citizens are then implicated in world poverty in two ways. We are implicated, first, because *our* great privileges and advantage as well as *their* extreme poverty and disadvantage have emerged through *one* historical process that was pervaded by unimaginable crimes. To be sure, we bear absolutely no moral responsibility for these crimes, even if we are direct descendants of people who do. Still, we are at fault for continuing to enforce the extreme inequalities that emerged in the course of that deeply unjust historical process.

Secondly and independently, we are implicated because we are using our economic, technological, and military advantages to impose a global institutional order that is manifestly and grievously unjust. How do I know this order is unjust? Simply by the fact that an alternative global order would avoid most of the suffering that foreseeably persists under the present order: half of humankind living in abject poverty and 18 million dying annually from poverty-related causes. By imposing this grievously unjust global order upon the rest of the world, the affluent countries, in collaboration with the so-called elites of the developing countries, are harming the global poor — to put it mildly. To put it less mildly, the imposition of this global order constitutes the largest (though not the gravest) crime against humanity ever committed.

Most of those who reject this view are misled by either of two thoughts, which I will briefly address in conclusion. One thought is that our global institutional order cannot possibly be harming the global poor when severe poverty worldwide is in decline. This thought is powerfully reinforced by the lively debate about globalization in which statements about the global poverty trend, about being "on track" toward the first UN MDG, have come to play a pivotal role.

As demonstrated earlier, it is by no means clear that severe poverty is in decline globally. But assume that it is. It does not follow that the existing global order is not harming the poor. After all, severe poverty may be going down not *because of*, but *despite* this order. Just as a boat may make progress even against a strong current or headwind, so the global poor may be making progress even against global rule-making processes that are slanted against them.

Moreover, even if the global institutional order were having a poverty-reducing effect, it might still be harming the global poor severely. Think of a slave-holding society, like the US in its first 90 years. Suppose its institutional order, by raising overall prosperity, was gradually improving the slaves' condition. Does it follow that this order was not harmful to those whose enslavement it authorized and enforced? Or does a gradual improvement in the condition of those condemned to serfdom or corvée labor in feudal Russia or France really show that they were not harmed by this imposition? Obviously not! Obviously, whether an institutional order is harming people in the morally relevant sense depends not on a diachronic comparison with an earlier time, but on a counterfactual comparison with its feasible institutional alternatives. Most citizens of the affluent countries take comfort in the asserted decline of global poverty, thinking of themselves as benefactors of the global poor in the belief that the global institutional order they impose kills and scars fewer people each year. They should instead take intense discomfort in the fact that a feasible alternative global order could have avoided most life-threatening poverty and its associated evils.

The other misleading thought is that severe poverty today must be traced back to causal factors that are domestic to the countries in which it persists. This seems self-evident from the fact that severe poverty has evolved very differently in different countries — rapidly melting away in Japan, the Asian tigers, and more recently China, while greatly worsening in Africa. Since all these countries were developing under the same global institutional order, this order cannot be at fault for the persistence of massive severe poverty in some of them.

Now it is true that there are great international variations in the evolution of severe poverty. And it is true that these variations must be caused by local (typically country-specific) factors. But it does not follow that these must be the only causally relevant factors, that global factors are irrelevant.

To see the fallacy, consider this parallel: there are great variations in the performance of my students. These variations must be caused by local (student-specific) factors. These factors, together, fully explain the overall performance of my class. Clearly, this parallel reasoning results in a falsehood: the overall performance of my class also crucially depends on the quality of my teaching and on various other "global" factors besides. This shows that the inference is invalid.

To see this more precisely, one must distinguish two questions about the evolution of severe poverty. One concerns the observed variation in national trajectories. In the answer to this question, local factors must play a central role. Yet, however full and correct, this answer may not suffice to answer the other question, which concerns the overall evolution of poverty worldwide: even if student-specific factors explain observed variations in the performance of my students, the quality of my teaching may still play a major role in explaining why they did not on the whole do much better or worse than they actually did. Likewise, even if country-specific factors fully explain the observed variations in the economic performance of developing countries, global factors may still play a major role in explaining why they did not on the whole do much better or worse than they did in fact.

Many aspects of the global institutional order have such causal relevance. I have already mentioned the protectionist quotas, tariffs, anti-dumping duties, subsidies and export credits that the rich countries allowed themselves under WTO rules. Likewise, the absence of a global minimum wage and minimal global constraints on working hours and working conditions fosters a "race to the bottom" where the ruling elites of poor countries, competing for foreign investment, are outbidding one another by offering ever more exploitable and mistreatable workforces.

Another important example is the global pharmaceutical regime, which rewards the inventors of new drugs by allowing them to charge monopoly prices for twenty years.[18] These rules price most existing drugs out of the reach of the global poor. And they also skew medical research toward the affluent: medical conditions accounting for 90 percent of the global disease burden receive only 10 percent of all medical research worldwide. Of the 1393 new drugs approved between 1975 and 1999, only 13 were specifically indicated for tropical diseases (MSF 2001: 10f). Millions of annual deaths could be avoided if rewards for medical research were based instead on its impact on the global disease burden. Such incentives could be funded, for instance, through a global "Polluter Pays" regime that raises funds from countries in proportion to their citizens' and corporations' contributions to transnational environmental pollution. This would replace the current rules under which the more industrialized countries can pollute the oceans and atmosphere at will, thereby imposing much of the cost of their prosperity on the rest of the world with the global poor generally benefiting least and being least able to protect themselves from the effects of pollution.

Global institutional factors also play an important role in sustaining many of the country-specific factors commonly adduced to explain the persistence of poverty. Thus, Rawls is quite right that when societies fail to thrive, "the problem is commonly the nature of the public political culture and the religious and philosophical traditions that underlie its institutions. The great social evils in poorer societies are likely to be oppressive government and corrupt elites" (Rawls 1993b: 77). But he completely fails to note that such oppression and corruption are very substantially encouraged and sustained by global factors such as the international resource and borrowing privileges (Pogge 2002a, chapters 4 and 6), the still poorly policed bribe-paying practices of multinational corporations,[19] and the international arms trade.[20]

This point also puts into perspective the popular cliché that membership in the WTO (and other international organizations) is voluntary. Yes, voluntary for a country's rulers. But not for the ruled. Nigeria's accession to the WTO was effected by its brutal dictator Sani Abacha, Myanmar's by the notorious SLORC (State Law and Order Restoration Council) junta,

---

[18] This regime was created through the Trade-Related Aspects of Intellectual Property Rights (TRIPS) Treaty, concluded in 1995. For a discussion of its content and impact, cf. UNDP 2001; Juma 1999; Watal 2000; Correa 2000; and www.cptech.org/ip.

[19] "Plenty of laws exist to ban bribery by companies. But big multinationals continue to sidestep them with ease" — so the situation is summarized in "The short arm of the law," *Economist*, March 2, 2002, 63–5, at 63.

[20] According to the (US) Congressional Research Service (2002), conventional arms transfers into developing countries were valued at $16 billion in 2001; $7 billion thereof were delivered by the US.

Indonesia's by kleptocrat Suharto, Zimbabwe's by Robert Mugabe, the Congo's (then named Zaire) by Mobutu Sese Seko, and so on.

Reflection Four supports the conclusion that the affluent countries, partly through the global institutional order they impose, bear a great causal and moral responsibility for the massive global persistence of severe poverty. Citizens of these countries thus have not merely a positive duty to assist innocent persons mired in life-threatening poverty, but also a more stringent negative duty to work politically and personally toward ceasing, or compensating for, their contribution to this ongoing catastrophe.

All four reflections I have presented challenge how people in the affluent countries tend to think about world poverty. They challenge prevailing views about the extent and trend of world poverty, about the international response to world poverty, about the causal explanation of world poverty, and about Western moral responsibility with regard to world poverty. None of these challenges is especially deep or subtle. Anyone with a basic high-school education could have examined the arithmetic of the weakening poverty targets, could have found that PPPs do not track access to basic necessities, could have worried that we may be harming the poor even if their number were in decline, could have considered institutional reforms designed to achieve much faster poverty reduction. The failure to look into these matters so closely related to the widely celebrated first MDG reveals a stunning thoughtlessness in the face of a problem that destroys vastly more lives than problems we do pay at least some attention to — the conflicts in the Middle East and the former Yugoslavia, for instance, or the massacres in Rwanda or East Timor. Our perverse priorities are all the more remarkable because we may bear a far greater responsibility for world poverty than for those local eruptions of violence and also because we can actually do something, as individuals, toward reducing severe poverty while most of us can do very little toward protecting innocent people from violence in the world's trouble spots.

In a sense, such thoughtlessness in the affluent countries is not really surprising. Of course people do not like to think too hard about harms that they themselves may share responsibility for and can do something about. Many Germans in my parents' generation avoided moral reflection under the Nazis. But were they innocent merely because they did not think? Or wasn't their very lack of thought a great moral failing? The latter judgment is widely prevalent. Germans who could truthfully say that they never thought about the fate of those whom state agents were taking from their neighborhoods and about the foreigners crushed by the Nazi war machine, those Germans were not therefore innocent. Rather, they were guilty of violating their most fundamental moral responsibility: to work out for oneself what one's moral responsibilities are in the circumstances in which one finds oneself. In this respect, we are in the same boat with those Germans: they could not possibly have found it obvious that Nazi conquests and mass arrests required no further thought from them. And we cannot possibly find it obvious that we need give no further thought to world poverty. This is perhaps an unusual claim: even if it were true that we are not required to do anything at all toward reducing world poverty, it would still be morally wrong of us thoughtlessly to do nothing. The global poor pose a morally inescapable question: What responsibilities do we have in regard to the social conditions that blight their lives? We owe them a reflective answer.

Chapter 19

Can Global Distributive Justice be Minimalist and Consensual? — Reflections on Thomas Pogge's Global Tax on Natural Resources*

Jean-Christophe Merle
Honorary Professor of Philosophy, Universität des Saarlandes, Saarbrücken, Germany

1. Twofold minimalism

There are two kinds of normative response to the problem of poverty and the considerable financial and social inequality in the world, and they are supported by two fundamentally different paradigms of justice. The *first* paradigm encompasses the theories of *just exchange* in the current sense, according to which duties between people can arise *only* through exchange. In the absence of relations of exchange, everyone is entitled to what he has earned. Thus, one can demand no more than reciprocation for what one has contributed. The *second* paradigm is that of *distributive justice*. It is based not upon individuals' contributions, but their needs. Needs justify a particular distribution.

These two paradigms contradict each other. Yet both have a certain appeal to our intuitions about justice. In fact, many institutional suggestions combine the two, namely by limiting both of them. It seems that only by combining them can the problematic cases be overcome. But the question remains to what extent each of these two principles should be reflected in concrete practice. And so a popular argumentative strategy among advocates

---

* This work supported in part by the European Community's Human Potential Program under contract HPRN-CT-2002-00231 in the Fifth Framework Program, "Applied Global Justice." I thank Thomas Pogge and Andreas Follesdal for their very precise and helpful comments, which led me to some modifications. The remaining weaknesses are mine. I thank John Michael for the translation.

A. Follesdal and T. Pogge, (eds.), Real World Justice, 339-358.

of non-mixed positions is to invoke a minimalist version of one's own position in order to win acceptance on the part of the opposition. This is especially common for theories of distributive justice, because they would demand the implementation of a different distribution from the existing one — in other words, redistribution — if the existing distribution were deemed not (fully) just. The demand for a different distribution from the existing one, it is believed, makes theories of distributive justice costlier and less "natural" than theories of just exchange, which are much closer to a laissez-faire approach. The pressure upon theorists of distributive justice to endorse minimalism is heightened by the fact that distributive justice is committed to interventionism as a means of achieving a different distribution from the existing one — state intervention in the event of domestic distributive injustice; global intervention by some international authority in the event of global distributive injustice. The principled minimalism of redistribution is therefore rounded out by a minimalism of means, according to which the implementation of a different distribution from the existing one would not require a central authority (see for instance Pogge 1994: 202, 224). Both minimalisms appear to me misleading. The first one obscures the fundamental difference between the two principles of justice: distributive justice means a distribution different from the actual one. The second minimalism is simply false in suggesting that distributive justice does not require the intervention of a national or an international legal order. Global distributive justice may be conceivable in the absence of a world government, but it cannot be implemented without one.

But here I shall focus exclusively on the example of the debate between John Rawls and some of his students, who — in opposition to Rawls's theory of justice, and also to his views in the area of international justice — advocate global distributive justice. Among the writings of these students, I shall limit myself to Thomas Pogge's proposal of a global natural resources tax, because this proposal — unlike some of Pogge's other writings, and unlike Charles Beitz (1979) — explicitly espouses a minimalist conception.

It is well known that, according to Rawls's difference principle, unequal distribution is only justified when the worst-off are no worse off than the worst-off under any alternative arrangement would be. While Pogge pleads in *Realizing Rawls* (cf. Pogge 1989, chapter 6) for the application of the difference principle at the global level in a one-stage process, Rawls — first in his paper for the Amnesty Lecture (1993b), then in *The Law of Peoples* (1999) — constructed a two-stage contract-theoretic model. First there is a contract among individuals to form a nation, then the various nations agree to a second contract, whereby every principle of distributive justice, and especially the difference principle, is decisively rejected at the global level, and at the national level applied only in democratic-liberal states. Rawls opposes any "global distributive principle" and proposes instead a mere "duty of assistance" which is intended to help "burdened societies" to "become full members of the society of peoples." In his paper "An egalitarian law of peoples" (Pogge 1994), Pogge assumes the two-stage model for the sake of his argument against Rawls's rejection of global distributive justice at the international level (Pogge 1994: 199). The first — and most important — argument Pogge formulates is aimed to confront Rawls's pragmatic arguments: "Some of the arguments Rawls advances against incorporating an egalitarian component into the law of peoples are pragmatic, mainly having to do with inadequate administrative capabilities and the dangers of a world government" (Pogge 1994: 199). Pogge wants to adapt his own argument to these pragmatic arguments. In doing so, he assumes implicitly (1) that the administrative costs of his reform proposal would be negligible, and that the proposal does not presuppose a form of "world government" (Pogge 1994: 199), and (2) that, if his reform proposal involved these implications, they would constitute a decisive argument against him. Pogge writes:

"To make it easier to address these worries, I want to put before you a reasonably clear and specific institutional proposal" (Pogge 1994: 199). As an "institutional proposal," Pogge recommends the introduction of a tax upon the use of natural resources, and global distribution of the proceeds raised by this natural resources tax.

This natural resources tax would be used to improve the conditions of those most in need. Pogge intends to resolve the difficulties of "inadequate administrative capabilities and the dangers of a world government" by a twofold institutional definition. On the one hand, he insists that his reform proposal is modest "in that it accepts the existing state system and, in particular, leaves each national government in control of the (persons and) natural resources of its territory" (Pogge 1998: 510). On the other hand, "sanctions could be decentralized: Once the agency facilitating the flow of GRD payments reported that a country has not met its obligations under the scheme, all other countries would be required to impose duties on imports from, and perhaps also similar levies on exports to, this country in order to raise funds equivalent to its GRD obligations plus the cost of these enforcement measures" (ibid. 517f). Hence, as Pogge sees it, there would be no need for a "world government" (ibid. 514).

I would like to demonstrate (1) that, despite the assumption of Rawls's two-stage model and despite the intended and emphasized modesty of the proposed tax on natural resources, Rawls's objections to global distributive justice also constitute an argument against the GRD scheme, and (2) that the GRD scheme could only be achieved by a much more substantial world government — i.e., with a much more extensive encroachment upon the sovereignty of individual states — than Pogge assumes. (This latter point is intended as a mere ascertainment; it implies neither a positive nor a negative evaluation.) In my view, this extensive encroachment upon the sovereignty of individual states would affect not only the more affluent countries — namely, through the introduction of a tax on natural resources, which would raise the price of many products — but, indeed, it would also affect poorer countries.

2. Global distributive justice as a different distribution from the existing one

The reason why Pogge does not agree with part (1) of this assessment is that he wants his GRD proposal simultaneously to serve several argumentative and justificatory purposes. In his justification of the GRD scheme, I see at least four main arguments.

1. The first is a principle quite similar to the difference principle. It maintains that the most acceptable global difference principle would be the one which would most improve the conditions of the world's neediest people.
2. The "inalienable stake in all limited natural resources" (Pogge 1998: 511), which is based upon humanity's originally common possession of the earth and its resources.
3. The principle of corrective justice, according to which developed countries should pay back some of the excessive profits they have by unfair means acquired and continue to acquire from exploiting the resources of poor countries not on a path of free and fair transactions (which would not justify any corrective justice), but on a historical path pervaded by grievous crimes and injustices and on a the current path of a "free global market, the structure of which gives to poor and powerless countries and peoples no chance to obtain a proportional share of the global economic growth" (Pogge 2002c: 229). These unfair means include not only colonization but also current international trade agreements — i.e., in the context of the WTO (cf. Pogge 2002c: 229) — and the debt conditionalities of the World Bank and IMF, etc. (cf. Pogge 2002a, chapters 4–6). Here I understand corrective justice not as a principle requiring compensation to those who have been the direct victims of these grievous crimes and injustices, but as a principle that requires alleviating the (often) extreme hardship resulting from such past or present grievous crimes and injustices. Pogge's argument applies even where past crimes and injustices have resulted in extreme hardships for descendants of those who committed those wrongs.

4. The GRD scheme ought to urge all countries to use their natural resources more parsimoniously (Pogge 1994: 223).

According to Pogge, any of these arguments (at least any of the first three), each of which rests upon a different moral value, would be sufficient to justify the GRD. Pogge writes: "a scheme like the GRD can be justified by appeal to different (and perhaps incompatible) values prominent in Western moral thought" (Pogge1994: 220).[1]

Among these four arguments, the first (which resembles the difference principle) is surely the most debatable. Although Pogge no longer accepts the difference principle (as he did in Pogge 1989, chapter 6; see Pogge 2002a, 242n223), he does accept a highly demanding principle of global distributive justice, which Rawls obviously rejects. He describes the goal of the GRD as follows: "Proceeds from the GRD are to be used toward the emancipation of the present and future global poor: toward assuring that all have access to education, health care, means of production (land) and/or jobs to a sufficient extent to be able to meet their own basic needs with dignity and to represent their rights and interests effectively against the rest of mankind: compatriots and foreigners" (Pogge 1994: 201). Although this definition does not go quite as far as a genuine difference principle, since it acknowledges a threshold beyond which no redistribution occurs, it works like a difference principle until that threshold is reached. Because Pogge adopts a two-stage model, it must be added, his quasi-difference principle would benefit not the poorest human beings in the world, but those *states* with the lowest per capita income — against the above-mentioned explicit intent of Pogge's GRD: "Proceeds from the GRD are to be used toward the emancipation of the present and future global poor." The reason for affirming this is the following. I assume as a matter of fact that there are members of the group of global poor who do not live in the "poorest societies," as defined by their "per capita income ... and population size" (Pogge 1994: 201). One may think of illegal immigrants working as forced laborers in sweat shops, of many gypsies in Europe, etc. This so-called "fourth world" living inside affluent societies would clearly not benefit from GRD funds, since they do not live within the "poorest societies." Thus, I would like to suggest that Pogge modify this criterion, in order better to fulfill his intent.

Acknowledging a threshold beyond which redistribution ceases, Pogge's definition does not go quite as far as a genuine difference principle. But it works like a difference principle until that threshold is reached. Looking at

---

[1] For reasons of consistency, I modify "GRT" (Global Resources Tax) in all quotations from Pogge 1994 into "GRD" (Global Resources Dividend), which is the expression Pogge uses after 1994.

the current state of the world, the threshold has obviously not yet been reached, nor does it appear likely that it will be in the near future. Thus, (1) given the current state of the world, the global difference principle is applicable among states ("In an ideal world of reasonably just and well-ordered societies, GRD payments could be made directly to the governments of the poorest societies, based on their per capita income (converted through purchasing power parities) and population size" (Pogge 1994: 201),[2] and (2) the proceeds from a natural resources tax would not be sufficient to satisfy this principle entirely. Pogge writes: the GRD scheme should assure that the funds, which are given to the poorest countries, serve to benefit the poorest people in the world. The rules must be such that "the entire GRD scheme has the maximum possible positive impact on the world's poorest persons — the poorest quintile, say — in the long run" (Pogge 1994: 203). Pogge emphasizes: "They must make it clear to members of the political and economic elite of GRD-eligible countries that, if they want their society to receive GRD funds, they must cooperate in making those funds effective toward enhancing the opportunities and the standard of living of the domestic poor" (Pogge 1994: 203). In my remarks, I shall make reference to Pogge's version of the global difference principle among states, bearing in mind that it differs in the aforementioned ways from a genuine global difference principle.

If you reject distributive justice with respect to goods — as Rawls does at the global level — you can under certain circumstances acknowledge an inalienable right to share in all natural resources, and a principle of corrective justice.

Nozick exemplifies this most clearly. Although he rejects all forms of "redistribution" at the international level (chapter 7), he nevertheless acknowledges the possibility of corrective justice as long as it is justified in each individual case. He also introduces a "Lockean proviso" (Nozick 1974: 178), which makes the possession of natural resources conditional upon the remaining resources being "enough and as good left in common for others" (Nozick 1974: 175).

Pogge defends global distributive justice by referring to the classic Rawlsian response to Nozick's criticism of any distributive theory of justice at the domestic level. Pogge would like to apply the same rejoinder against Rawls's rejection of global distributive justice. In his argumentation, I think Pogge fails to perceive the radical incompatibility of the two positions, and above all the consequences of this incompatibility.

---

[2]   To be sure, states receiving GRD payments are to devote them to the emancipation of poor individuals. Yet, as explained above, not all of the global poor live in poor societies that receive GRD payments.

Let us begin with the core of the rejection of the difference principle. Nozick formulates it as follows:

> If the world were just, the following inductive definition would resolve the question of justice with respect to possessions.
> 1. Whoever has acquired a possession in accordance with the principle of just acquisition has a just claim to that possession.
> 2. Whoever has acquired a possession from somebody else in accordance with the principle of just transference has a just claim to that possession.
> 3. Just claims to possessions arise exclusively through the (repeated) application of rules 1 and 2.
> The fundamental principle of a distributive theory would simply state that a distribution is just if everyone has those possessions which rightfully belong to him (Nozick 1974: 151).

The principle of just acquisition mentioned in the first point of this definition refers to the originally communal possession of natural resources, and especially to the Lockean proviso.

The second point and the concluding remark mean essentially that goods acquired in an illicit manner must be returned to their legitimate owner; it is a matter of corrective justice.

According to Nozick, the Lockean proviso for natural resources and corrective justice exhaust all just demands for the implementation of a different distribution from the existing one. Hence the implementation of a different distribution from the existing one is out of the question under any other circumstances; it would violate the result of the first distribution. Nozick regards his definition as an "historical principle," whereas he sees "redistribution theories" as "result-based principles." He looks for justice with respect to initial distribution, irrespective of the resultant distribution, whereas distribution theories define justice solely with respect to the resultant distribution. That is why distribution theories are always bound to intercede in order to bring about and maintain the desired distribution. Hence the distribution theories are redistribution theories.

Pogge presents his Rawlsian response to Nozick's criticism with respect to the domestic level — and thereby also to the international level — as follows:

> This suggests a view of the difference principle as a principle of *re*distribution, which takes from some to give to others ... . But this view of the difference principle loses an insight that is crucial to understanding Rawls's own, domestic difference principle. There is no prior distribution, no natural baseline or neutral way of arranging the economy,

relative to which the difference principle could be seen to make *re*distributive modifications. Rather, there are countless ways of designing economic institutions, none initially privileged, of which one and only one will be implemented. ... The selected economic ground rules, whatever their content, do not *re*distribute, but rather govern how economic benefits and burdens get distributed in the first place (Pogge 1994: 212).

It seems to me that Pogge's and Nozick's views both have a certain amount of truth on their side. In order to see why, it is necessary to introduce a distinction between redistribution as a *principle of justice* and as an *operative principle* (i.e., a different distribution from the existing one). Insofar as both Pogge and Nozick (as well as Rawls) assume originally communal possession of resources, there is no *natural* distribution. Whether — in an original or an ideal state — one opts for Nozick's rule of acquisition or for the difference principle, both are *original normative principles of distribution*, not principles of *re*distribution. Pogge is right about that. But if one looks at redistribution as an operative principle, the implementation of the Lockean proviso and corrective justice would, in most existing societies, require only isolated corrections, not a general encroachment upon the existing structure of property rights (though such general encroachment would be necessary in the case of communist societies, feudal societies, and societies assigning a lesser legal status to women, for example). The difference principle, on the other hand, *certainly* leads to redistribution of that sort, i.e., to an encroachment upon the existing order of ownership.[3] Pogge emphasizes that the GRD scheme would have important consequences for the poorest people in the world without costing the wealthiest people all that much. But regardless of how much it would cost, the fact remains that it would cost something for those who are not among the poorest. So, although the reform proposal does not as a principle of justice amount to a redistribution theory, it nevertheless includes redistribution as an operative principle. Indeed, Pogge himself formulates his argumentation at the operative level: "I lack the space, however, to develop and defend a complete criterion of global justice and to show what specific institutional arrangements would be favored by this criterion. I will therefore

---

[3] Here, I assume as a matter of fact that no existing society ever fully realized the difference principle. I consider neither communist nor radical egalitarian societies nor societies that have a long-standing practice of high levels of taxation to have realized the difference principle. In the first case, the reason is that the difference principle does not require equality, but the highest feasible level for the worst-off. In the second case, the high level of taxation may have ensured a welfare state that profited a majority of the population. Yet, the bottom few percent have been neglected by the welfare state, which could have done more in their favor.

employ a little shortcut. I will make an institutional proposal" (Pogge 1994: 199). The pragmatic advantage Pogge claims for his reform proposal is that it should overcome Rawls's objections to global distributive justice, which mainly have to do with "inadequate administrative capabilities and the dangers of a world government" (Pogge 1994: 199). Thus, Pogge's proposal is intended to be consensual, i.e., acceptable to Rawls. On the other hand, this reform proposal is conceived as the first step towards implementing Pogge's version of the global difference principle among states, as I defined it above. At the same operative level, then, Pogge envisions two fundamentally different, indeed mutually incompatible, *operative principles*: he is committed, on the one hand, to corrective justice and to the inalienable right to a share of natural resources, and on the other hand, to his version of the global difference principle among states.

3. Alternative diagnoses of world poverty

In the following remarks, I would like to address the concrete manifestations of this principled tension.

Both in his Amnesty International Lecture and in his book *The Law of Peoples*, Rawls applies the following argument against a global difference principle:

> The problem is often not the lack of natural resources. ... Rather, the problem is commonly the nature of the public political culture and the religious and philosophical traditions that underlie its institutions. The great social evils in poorer societies are likely to be oppressive government and corrupt elites; the subjection of women abetted by unreasonable religion, with the resulting overpopulation relative to what the economy of the society can decently sustain (Rawls 1993b: 77).

> Case (i): two liberal or decent countries are at the same level of wealth ... and have the same size population. The first decides to industrialize and to increase its rates of (real) saving, while the second does not. ... Some decades later the first country is twice as wealthy as the second. ... Should the industrializing country be taxed to give funds to the second? ... There should be no tax ... ; whereas with a global egalitarian principle without target, there would always be a flow of taxes ... . This seems unacceptable (Rawls 1999: 117).

> Case (ii) is parallel to (i) except that at the start the rate of population growth in both liberal and decent societies is rather high. Both countries

provide the elements of equal justice for women, as required by a well-ordered society; but the first happens to stress these elements, and its women flourish in the political and economic world. As a consequence, they gradually reach zero population growth that allows for an increasing level of wealth over time. The second society ... does not reduce the rate of population growth and it remains rather high. As before, some decades later, the first society is twice as wealthy as the second. ... the duty of assistance does not require taxes from the first, now wealthier society, while the global egalitarian principle ... would. Again, this latter position seems unacceptable (Rawls 1999: 117f).

While Rawls cites widespread corruption in poor countries as the cause of their poverty, Pogge emphasizes that corruption is knowingly and actively promoted even in rich countries by self-interest.

So it is true, but not the whole truth, that governments and institutions of poor countries are often corrupt: They are actively being corrupted, continually and very significantly, by private and official agents from vastly more wealthy societies (Pogge 1994: 214).

Moreover, Pogge claims, "it is entirely unrealistic to expect that such foreign-sponsored corruption can be eradicated without reducing the enormous differentials in per capita GNP" (Pogge 1994: 214).

So Pogge adds another causal relation to the one posited by Rawls. Corruption is not merely the cause of poverty; rather, a vicious cycle arises whereby poverty causes corruption. Indeed, Pogge views poverty — not corruption — as the decisive element, i.e., the two relations are of different weight.

This has the following consequences:

First, it is no longer the case that some particular actions of some individuals are the ultimate cause of poverty, but a particular set of economic institutions in which everyone participates. Poverty is deplorable in itself, independently of individuals' guilt in bringing it about.

Second, the ultimate cause is no longer local, but global. The solution must therefore also be global.

Third, Pogge takes only corruption into account, and leaves aside the other causes of poverty mentioned by Rawls: "the nature of the public political culture and the religious and philosophical traditions that underlie its institutions, ... the subjection of women abetted by unreasonable religion" (Rawls 1993b: 77). Pogge does not deny these causes, but he is not compelled to address them. I shall limit myself here to corruption. Even if poverty has many causes, he argues, it leads unavoidably to corruption, which leads unavoidably to more poverty. Strictly speaking, this is enough to demonstrate that poverty is to be combated as such. But if a condition has several causes, each of which would alone be sufficient to bring it about, then it would be futile to treat only one or some of the causes: *all* the causes have to be dealt with. Pogge, however, contests this point. He is of the opinion that modification of international privileges with respect to loans and to natural resources would help significantly in combating world poverty, even if the other factors contributing to poverty were not addressed. In Pogge's texts, though, there are numerous indications that eliminating corruption is an important part of combating poverty. For example, Pogge writes: "We live within a global economic order that is structured in accordance with the interests of the affluent high-consumption countries and coercively imposed by them. An important feature of this order ... is the international resource privilege: The privilege of any person or group exercising effective power within a country to confer internationally valid legal ownership rights in its natural resources. This privilege is of great benefit to authoritarian rulers ... this privilege is also very much in the interest of the rich consumer societies" (Pogge 2002a: 165, see also 142). Pogge himself devotes an entire chapter to the institutional means of reducing the financial advantages of seizing state power and of loan privileges. And so one might ask oneself whether corruption in poor countries would cause GRD funds to be squandered just like natural resources. If so, the GRD scheme could just wind up making wealthy countries even wealthier. Pogge is aware of this risk. He writes: "In an ideal world of reasonably just and well-ordered societies, GRD payments could be made directly to the governments of the poor societies, based on their per capita income ... and population size" (Pogge 1994: 201). Pogge goes on to write: "In a non-ideal world like ours, corrupt governments in the poorer states pose a significant problem. Such governments may be inclined, for example, to use GRD funds to underwrite indispensable services while diverting any domestic tax revenue saved to the ruler's personal use" (Pogge 1994: 202). As a means of averting this danger, Pogge makes the following suggestion: "a country might receive 60 percent of the GRD funds it is eligible for, one third of this through the government and two-thirds of it through other channels. ... These rules are to be designed, and possibly revised, by an international group of economists and international lawyers" (Pogge 1994: 202f). In these counter-measures designed for the non-ideal world, I see an acknowledgment of the necessity not only of combating or limiting corruption as a prerequisite to the GRD scheme, but also of relativizing national sovereignty, i.e., of a form of international paternalism.

4. Encroachment upon national sovereignty: Intervention in national political and social affairs

The logic of the GRD scheme leads to a more significant intervention in the "domestic" affairs of poor countries than mere payment of a natural resources tax. First, I shall draw attention to a *political* and *social* consequence, then to an *economic* one.

By suggesting that the causes he mentions are the only ones, and that poverty is not ineluctably self-causative, Rawls takes an easier — and less plausible — route than Pogge:

> Well-ordered societies can get on with very little; their wealth lies elsewhere: in their political and cultural traditions, in their human capital and knowledge, and in their capacity for political and economic organization. ... Perhaps there is no society anywhere in the world whose people, were they reasonably and rationally governed, and their numbers sensibly adjusted to their economy and resources, could not have a decent and worthwhile life (Rawls 1993b: 77).

Pogge implies no such implausible mono-causality of poverty.

If (1) poverty is be combated as such, (2) the cause of poverty is not only poverty, but also a social, political and cultural background, (3) dealing with some but not all of the causes would be futile, and (4) there is a global responsibility to deal with all of the causes of poverty, *then* more affluent countries must see to it that either (a) the social, political and cultural causes are dealt with, or (b) at least their effects are mitigated — which cannot however be a lasting solution of the problem. Option (a) demands that GRD funds be distributed not solely through local governments, but also — or even only — through "other channels," the decisions in this matter being made by the "facilitating organization" under the supervision of "an international group of economists and international lawyers," as suggested by Pogge: "Its poorer citizens may benefit through their government, they may benefit from development programs run by some other agency, or they may not benefit at all. Mixtures are, of course, also possible. ... How are these matters to be decided? And by whom? The decisions are to be made by the facilitating organization, but pursuant to clear and straightforward general rules. These rules are to be designed, and possibly revised, by an international group of economists and international lawyers" (Pogge 1994: 202f). I interpret this as the search for other channels for circumventing abusive politicians and officials in corrupt and authoritarian countries (cf. Pogge 1994: 202, for a few examples of such "other channels"). This "international group of economists and international lawyers" and these alternative channels constrain the sovereignty of the states to which these measures apply, even if only temporarily. Further restrictions may be necessary for the same reasons, although Pogge himself seems reluctant to draw this conclusion. These restrictions may be very extensive in certain cases. The need for such infringements of sovereignty calls to mind unpleasant memories of colonialism, cultural imperialism and Eurocentrism. These were also justified by "civilizing" goals, which served to cover up, however, grievous crimes, injustices and discriminations. Yet, the intervention of international institutions in matters traditionally considered as internal may also greatly benefit the populations and the countries, as is shown by international tribunals, international conventions protecting human rights, etc. In the matter I am dealing with, one certainly should pay the closest attention to the necessary measures to prevent the reiteration of these past experiences. Nevertheless, if certain social, political and cultural factors indeed cause poverty and cannot successfully be combated domestically, one should struggle against these factors, not only from within, but also from outside these countries, either by modifying or by suppressing these factors[4] by outside forces. As long as this is the intention of an intervention — and not imperialism, exploitation and cultural hegemony — there can be no talk of colonialism. Of course, it is thoroughly possible that these causes of poverty could be dealt with by impoverished countries themselves. Still, it seems implausible to expect them to succeed on their own — especially since widespread corruption is among the political and social causes, although it is surely not the only cause. Indeed, as Pogge sees it, a poor country is unable to eliminate corruption because it occurs in the service of foreign interests. But neither would the global reduction of inequalities suggested by Pogge be sufficient. Rather, these measures would have to be accompanied by modifications in the political and social system. I shall return later to the third option.

---

[4] Thomas Pogge holds that when and insofar as GRD funds cannot be effectively delivered through poor-country governments, then we should try to deliver them in other ways: perhaps by funding global public goods (for instance, medical research into currently neglected diseases, etc.) or by going through NGOs. According to Pogge, insofar as the latter options are also unviable, we may need to give up on eradicating poverty in some particular country (e.g., North Korea) rather than try to eliminate the North Korean government. On this point, I disagree with Pogge: I think that one should try to get the North Korean government to care more for the relief of hunger and poverty in its country, to reform itself to the necessary extent. And, if this cannot be achieved, this government should be removed from office, provided that such a change of regime would not bring more harm than good to the North Korean population.

5. A Principled incompatibility in dealing with poverty and inequalities

When we examine the economic dimension of Pogge's GRD scheme, we find not only clear incompatibility in principle with corrective justice and with the principle of a right to share in natural resources, but also a pragmatically incompatible interventionist consequence of global distributive justice. I shall begin with the pragmatic incompatibility.

As we have seen, Pogge posits a causal relation between poverty as cause and corruption as effect, which supposedly precedes the relation Rawls mentioned, whereby corruption causes poverty. From Rawls's perspective, the causal relation between poverty as cause and corruption as effect constitutes a legitimate ground for corrective justice — but only at the expense of corrupt politicians and officials. By proposing the inverse relation, Pogge seeks to extend corrective justice to the global sphere and its monumental inequalities. Between 1993 and 1999, though, Rawls shifted the focus of his argumentation and posited another causal relation more fundamental than the one posited by Pogge. Rawls's thesis is as follows: the considerable global differences that cause corruption in poor countries, and from which the more affluent countries profit, are essentially the result of different decisions that were made in individual countries at an earlier, egalitarian stage. In his thought experiment, Rawls assumes two countries that find themselves in the same economic situation and have comparable resources at their disposal. The development to a state of extreme inequality can be traced, according to Rawls, to decisions made in three areas: industrialization, rates of saving and birth rates. All are indispensable means to economic growth. From a Rawlsian viewpoint, if corruption arises from poverty for which a country has only itself to blame, that same country is responsible for its own corruption as well.

Pogge cannot counter this thought experiment by positing a still earlier state of inequality, because the thought experiment envisions an *original starting point*. If one searches in Pogge's 1998 paper for the building blocks of a response to this thought experiment Rawls presents in 1999, one ought not begin with the imagined *starting point* but with the *consequences*. And that is what we shall attempt to do in the following remarks.

Let us assume Rawls's starting point for a moment. Since this situation, which I shall call S1, is a state of absolute equality between two countries, the subsequent, considerably unequal situation S2 cannot be traced back to S1, but to the decisions made in both countries. The upshot is that the one country is to blame for its own poverty. Hence justice demands no adjustment, no corrective justice. This thought experiment presents us with a counterexample to the putative universal validity of the theories of global distributive justice, which plead for global redistribution. And one example is of course sufficient to refute a claim to universal validity.

But let us assume for a moment that situation S2 has come about (under just circumstances). If it leads unavoidably to corruption in the poorer country, which in turn exacerbates the poverty — I shall call this S3 — then the development from S2 to S3 cannot be traced to different decisions in the two countries. Indeed, decisions made in S2 could not possibly have influenced the development to S3. The development from S2 to S3 — i.e., the vicious cycle — cannot be blamed on the poor country. First, because the new generation cannot inherit the responsibility of earlier generations. Secondly, the new generation cannot be blamed for perpetuating the vicious cycle, since it lies in the very nature of a vicious cycle to offer no way out. Hence Pogge's thesis retains its universal normative validity.

So the choice between Rawls's and Pogge's theses depends on the diagnosis of current inequality — namely, whether they are the result of a vicious cycle or are significantly influenced by decisions made in poor countries. This diagnosis should determine whether one is for or against implementing a different distribution between wealthy and poor countries.

But it is highly debatable which diagnosis is correct.

There is one option that initially seems compatible with both diagnoses: autarchy, or protectionism, for poor countries. Presently, we are experiencing the opposite: namely, protectionism for wealthy, industrialized countries — i.e., through high agricultural subsidies. This first option is advocated by opponents of globalization. Economically, it would be disadvantageous for the world in toto, since it would sacrifice the advantages of the distribution of labor. As to whether the third world would profit, it is far from clear. But I do not want to address this debate here, since the amount of trade among countries has no impact on the GRD scheme. Even if we imagine a pure autarchy, the tax on natural resources would be collected in every country and distributed globally. And even if foreign companies were prevented from profiting from corruption in poor countries, domestic corruption and poverty would still persist in the same vicious cycle that the GRD scheme is intended to stop.

Nevertheless, the option of autarchy remains interesting, since it would admit of no situation in which *corrective justice* could be justified. Hence, not all versions of the GRD scheme are linked to corrective justice.

There is a second option, which could produce compatibility between the positions of Rawls and Pogge: namely, an appeal to the *topos* of the *originally communal possession of natural resources*. Thus Pogge attempts to justify his GRD proposal by arguing that states do not have an unrestricted right to possession of the natural resources found within their territories and therefore may be "required to share a small part of the value of any resources they decide to use or sell" (Pogge 1998: 511). He calls this payment a *dividend* to suggest that all human beings, and the now-excluded global poor in particular, "own an inalienable stake in all limited natural resources" (ibid.).

The notion of a right to share in all natural resources is accepted both by Pogge and by Rawls, but it can be interpreted differently. Pogge understands it as "a share of the economic benefits from the use of the resource in question" (ibid.). He interprets it as a right to introduce a tax upon other people's use, but it could just as easily be interpreted simply as a right to full participation. The difference is significant, since the tax on other people's use refers to a product that arises through a combination of natural resources and the work of processing them. This presents us with a difficulty, which we can understand clearly if we recall Rawls's example of a country that decides against industrialization and national saving. Such a country hardly uses any natural resources, because it does not produce much. It may be that some other countries use more natural resources than this country, and yet still not more than their share. If we assume only *a right to full participation in the use of natural resources*, there is no justification for implementing a different distribution of dividends, i.e., there is no occasion for the GRD scheme. The GRD is only justified if we follow Pogge and assume not just a right to equal use of natural resources, but a right to a share in *anyone's* use of them. So we have to distinguish, on the one hand, initial equality with respect to resources from, on the other hand, equality with respect to products. In short, since the two positions do not agree on this point, the argumentation rests on equivocation. So there remain two fundamentally distinct positions: one focusing on an original starting point, the other on the current state of affairs.

Pogge is well aware that his four arguments in favor of the GRD may not be compatible with one another: "a scheme like the GRD can be justified by appeal to different (and perhaps incompatible) values prominent in Western moral thought" (Pogge 2002a, 1994). He seems, however, to be less aware of the fact that the four different arguments lead to different measures. Pogge's version of the global difference principle among states sets goals that go beyond the GRD scheme. In short, we are dealing with four different arguments that set diverse goals. I have attempted to demonstrate this with respect to three arguments here.

6. A hybrid solution

Pogge proposes a modest tax of only 1 percent, which is in fact quite low, compared to the German added value tax of 16 percent and the

American sales tax of 5 percent on average (the sales tax rate varies from state to state, yet most of the time it is much higher than 1 percent). Full application of Pogge's version of the global difference principle among states would surely be more robust than this. But the modesty of the GRD does not change the fact that it rests upon two fundamentally different, mutually contradictory theories of justice. Pogge supports it by combining a small dose of his version of the global difference principle among states with a rather large dose of Rawls's argument.

I do not intend with this assertion to belittle Pogge's hybrid solution. I merely want to make the observation that it corresponds neither to Rawls's position, nor to Pogge's version of the global difference principle among states, which Pogge abandons for expressly pragmatic reasons. A third option would be to combine two equally justified demands, each of which corresponds partially to our moral intuitions. The following reformulation of Rawls's and Pogge's demands would allow both to coexist, albeit in a mutually constraining fashion:

1. Inequalities arising from the different decisions made voluntarily by individual states ought not to be annulled. In keeping with Rawls's demand, such inequalities should be allowed to persist.
2. Inequalities based upon states' voluntary decisions should not be allowed to prevent states from influencing their future courses. In order to prevent this, the inequalities must be held within limits, which would amount to a partial fulfillment of the difference principle. It remains highly implausible, though, that the GRD scheme, which according to Pogge would guarantee the satisfaction of "fundamental needs," "medical treatment," and "sanitary facilities for the poor," could achieve this aim. Moreover, maintaining sustenance may not be sufficient to protect a poor country form corruption.

7. Encroachment upon national sovereignty: Intervention in national economics

Would Rawls accept such a combination? Obviously not. He mentions Pogge's paper, but not the reform proposal. It seems to me that he has a good reason. Pogge seems to suspect that a pragmatic objection is at the basis of Rawls's rejection of the difference principle: "Some of the arguments Rawls advances against incorporating an egalitarian component into the law of peoples are pragmatic, mainly having to do with inadequate administrative capabilities and the dangers of a world government" (Pogge 1994: 199). Although Rawls himself objects only as a matter of principle, the pragmatic concern Pogge eludes to may be part of the reason why Rawls does not even mention the GRD proposal from 1994 in his 1999 book *The Law of Peoples*.

I would like briefly to explain why the GRD would lead to more global intervention than Pogge suggests. Pogge emphasizes: "The basic idea is that, while each people owns and fully owns and controls all resources within its national territory, it must pay a tax on any resources it chooses to extract. The Saudi people, for example, would not be required to extract crude oil or to allow others to do so. But if they chose to do so nonetheless, they would be required to pay a proportional tax on any crude extracted" (Pogge 1994: 200). Thus, although the GRD would be globally collected and distributed, the decision whether or not to tap on and utilize natural resources in the first place, as well as the ensuing economic development, would be left to the authority of individual states. This leads to the following dilemma.

First, let us imagine a case like the one sketched by Rawls himself: a country decides not to foster industrialization and national savings as means to economic growth and future prosperity. In Pogge's reform proposal, the country would pay a low tax on natural resources and, as a poor country, would receive a high GRD from other countries.

Now let us imagine a second case, in which the country decides for industrialization to stimulate economic growth and national savings and investment to assure future prosperity. In Pogge's reform proposal, the country would pay a higher tax on natural resources and, as its affluence increased, would soon receive no GRD from other countries. Hence there would be additional GRD available to fight poverty in other countries that remained poor.

I think that the difference principle demands that the poor country decide in favor of the second option, because it would improve the condition of those most in need. By saying this, I am not talking about a moral obligation for the poor states to use natural resources as much as they can so as to maximize the amount of GRD withheld for the benefit of raising the lowest socioeconomic position inside the poor countries. I am rather suggesting that the international institution(s) in charge of the GRD establishes a threshold of resource exploitation below which the state cannot refuse to open the exploitation of its resources. Of course, this minimal threshold should be determined under due and careful consideration of the protection of the environment as well as of long term sustainability, and governments should keep the right to refuse unfair offers, e.g., offers from companies proposing excessively low royalties, trying to undermine local social legislation, etc. With these conditions satisfied, the refusal to open this minimal threshold to exploitation should lead to the suspension of GRD payments to the countries refusing this threshold. The same already applies domestically. There is no legal obligation for individuals to work; yet unemployment benefits are paid only on condition that the beneficiaries cannot find a job and that they would accept a job corresponding to their qualifications, if one were offered to them. Now, in Pogge's proposal, since the decision to exploit natural resources lies within the sovereignty of the individual state, it is possible for a country to hinder the implementation of Pogge's version of the difference principle among states through its economic decisions, and in doing so to gain more from the implementation than it would if it did not hinder it. The problem, as I see it, is not so much that there would be a (rather insignificant) incentive to resist development. Rather, the problem lies in the injustice of externalizing the costs of a decision against industrialization.[5]

If Pogge's version of the difference principle among states is not to be completely abandoned, the sovereignty of individual countries — especially poor countries, but also industrialized ones, which could opt for a halt in growth and minimal consumption of goods and resources — must be brought within certain limits. This would not amount to economic colonialism or imperialism, since it would occur for the benefit of the poorest countries. Indeed, why should national sovereignty not be constrained in this fashion, when Pogge himself mentions the possibility of delegating the distribution of the GRD not to states, but to "other channels" — i.e., to "various official and unofficial international organizations like UNICEF, UNDP, WHO and Oxfam" — since they are often more efficient and less corrupt than local governments (Pogge 1994: 202; see also Pogge 1998: 515)? But if we limit the economic authority of individual states in this manner, and collect the tax on natural resources globally and without the assent of affected countries, it seems clear that we are taking a step in the direction of a "world government," wherein Rawls sees the dangers of "inadequate administrative capabilities and ... dangers." Thus, the tax on natural resources is not the most suitable means of overcoming Rawls's objections. On the contrary, it strengthens them, no matter how modest the tax on natural resources might be.

---

[5] Thomas Pogge (2000a) has raised the same objection to this point that he raises against Cohen's and Murphy's criticism of Rawls's theory of justice: he does not think that the difference principle can be applied to such decisions, which he regards as "individual decisions." I maintain, however, that the case in question here is not — like the case addressed by Cohen and Murphy — a matter concerning only the decisions of individuals, but a matter for which international institution should have competence for setting a framework. If, for instance, the realization of the difference principle requires the existence of a social minimum, a well-ordered society can justify a conditionality of this benefit (the condition being that the beneficiaries accept jobs corresponding to their qualifications, if they are offered to them) by the fact that the situation of the worst-off would be worse without such a conditionality. In this regard, conditionality plays the role of an incentive, but the argument need invoke no moral obligation on individuals to work; nor need a well-ordered society compel individuals to work by means of coercion.

Pogge's declared intention with the GRD scheme is "to make an institutional proposal that virtually any plausible egalitarian conception of global justice would judge to be at least a step in the right direction" (Pogge 1994: 199), i.e., a step in the direction of his version of the difference principle among states (cf. Pogge 1989).

The GRD does indeed achieve this step, but it does not go far enough to win over the opponents of global distributive justice. It cannot win them over, because the two conflicting conceptions are based upon fundamentally incompatible principles of justice.[6] And the opponents know full well that if they consent to take the first small step, *consistency* will force them to go the whole way. In fact, Rawls says about Pogge's egalitarian principle *itself*, five years after Pogge's proposal of the GRD, that he simply does not accept it (Rawls 1999: 166), without even discussing the proposal in any detail. Rawls even only observes that there are "largely practical matters of taxation and administration to distinguish between" his "duty of assistance" and Pogge's GRD. In other words, for opponents of global distributive justice, the cat would be out of the bag. But if the modest reform proposal fails to win over Rawls and the critics of global distributive justice, it will be necessary to consider either returning to the pure Poggean version of the global difference principle among states, or sticking with the modest reform proposal, but espousing perhaps a hybrid justification that satisfies but equally limits both demands. In my view, such a hybrid is the only way to justify minimalism. But even this would not lead to consensus, neither in principle nor through an institutional solution. So why not remain radical?

---

[6] Rawls (1999: 118) strictly limits the "duty to assistance" to assisting "burdened societies to become full members of the Society of Peoples and to be able to determine the path of their own future for themselves." This is much less than what Pogge's egalitarian principle demands.

Chapter 20

Redistributing Responsibilities — The UN Global Compact with Corporations

Andrew Kuper
Ashoka Innovators for the Public, Arlington, VA, USA

From *The Onion*:

Tanzania Loses Name To Tanning-Salon Chain

TALLAHASSEE, FL — The country formerly known as the United Republic of Tanzania has lost the use of its name to Tampa-based Tanzania Tanning Salons, the Florida Supreme Court ruled Monday.

"It was easy to establish that my client's company had a greater vested interest in the Tanzania brand name," said [the corporation's] lawyer, Ben

A. Follesdal and T. Pogge, (eds.), Real World Justice, 359-380.

Knowles. "Tanzania, the salon chain, is a rapidly growing business, adding nearly 50 locations each year. Tanzania, the African nation, is languishing under a debt of $7 billion." Tanzania Salons is also close to completing a lucrative deal that would put its moisturizing and replenishing cream on the shelves of retail stores across the nation, making the situation even more pressing, Knowles added ...

"By using the name of my client's franchise, the United Republic of Tanzania did irreparable damage to the business' sparkling reputation," Knowles said. "As far as I know, their Tanzania doesn't have tanning salons. Still, my client wouldn't want his locations associated with a location where one in six children dies before the age of 5 as a consequence of poverty-related infectious disease and inadequate health-care provisions."

The former Tanzania will hold a referendum next week to vote on a new name for the country. "We're considering a number of words in Swahili," [President] Mkapa said. "So far, the people's top choices are Karibu, Rafiki, and Triscuit."

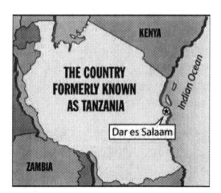

1. Theorists versus corporations: The theorists lose

Theorists of justice and development tend to exhibit a visceral loathing for corporations. We resent the appropriation and deformation of other spheres of activity by money and business. We are all too familiar with examples of insensitive and rapacious corporate practice, most notably in developing countries with weak regulatory capacity. We find it distasteful that greed is celebrated not merely as a force for good but as the prime motivating force. We react with outrage to the view (still widely held in the corporate world) that everybody and everything in this domain of human activity can be reduced to the bottom line.

But a deeper and less noble factor drives us too. We are discomfited by the messiness and polymorphous instrumentality of business, and by its insistent resistance to grand theories. The heroes of this world are "gurus" with "tips," who stress "flexibility" and "constant innovation" — such as strategist Michael Porter, investor Warren Buffet, and inventor-visionaries Bill Gates and Michael Dell. While great theorists generally seek universalist and enduring moral and legal constraints that can be widely recognized, great businesspeople and businesses are geared to respond to opportunities (preferably monopolistic) and loopholes (often short-lived, as in currency arbitrage) that no one else has recognized and few can adopt. Even if the invisible hand always ensured the best overall outcomes (it doesn't), shorter time horizons, direct and exclusionary forms of competition, pragmatic muddling-along, and narrower ultimate ends would ensure that the moral psychology of business practitioners diverges from that of the studiously abstract and systematizing thinker. It is not surprising that corporate leaders tend to respond to highly theoretical argumentation with a mixture of incomprehension and annoyance.

Yet theorists of justice and development — from political philosophers to comparativists — are hardly in a position to refute the inevitable charge of being "out of touch." Most of us have not wanted to think *about* corporations (except perhaps as agents of injustice) let alone think *like* corporations.

People on both sides believe that things have changed significantly with the burgeoning of the field of business ethics and its entry into the development discourse, accelerated by recent salutary scandals. I would caution against this conclusion. I do not mean to insult business ethics (like any new field, much of it is woolly and platitudinous) so much as to insist on its narrow philosophical scope and limited practical reach at present. In this article, I shall make a plea for boldness. I shall suggest that we need more than ethical or legal codes that can be adopted by corporations and more than guidelines for philanthropy. We need to take corporate agency and moral psychology seriously not merely as aspects of a kind of applied ethics but as a central problem of political philosophy and development theory. I shall try to say something about the shape that a political philosophy and development theory of an improved kind would have to take. And I shall do so, oddly enough, by learning some lessons from the United Nations.

2. The UN versus corporations: UN loses battle, wins insight

For its first fifty years, the UN stood with the theorists (in this one respect), keeping corporations at arm's length. After all, practitioners of peace-building and development were among the first to encounter corporate malfeasance and its consequences. Consider some major destabilizing forces in sub-Saharan Africa during this period: seeking to end the war in Angola, the UN found that unregulated markets in "conflict diamonds" and oil were fuelling the conflict and scuppering all peace accords. Corporations were actively engaged with conflicting parties on both sides, collaborating in the extraction of natural resources and appropriating a large share of the benefits. In my country of origin, South Africa, leading business interests provided aid to some opposition initiatives but overall helped sustain the Apartheid state. "White" big business had too much to gain from the systematic exclusion of 85 percent of the population from full competition in the economy (except as cheap labor). A legion of similar examples can be found in almost every region of the world and I shan't needlessly elaborate: UN suspicions as to corporate motives and behavior were often justified and often still are. Further, these suspicions (if not downright hostility) were shared by leading lights of the development community such as Oxfam and Amnesty International.

Yet by 1999, the position had changed. We find the new Secretary General of the United Nations, himself an African, proclaiming that:

> a fundamental shift has occurred in recent years in the attitude of the UN toward the private sector. Confrontation has taken a back seat to cooperation. Polemics have given way to partnerships ... Both the business community and the UN are engaged in the service of something larger than ourselves: human security in the broadest sense ... [thus] it is no surprise that the UN and the private sector are joining forces. The voice of business is heard in UN policy debates (Annan 1999).

Meanwhile, most development agencies and international non-governmental organizations had abandoned "confrontation" models for dealing with corporations (exemplified by parts of the growing anti-globalization protest movement) in favor of a variety of "engagement" models. Organizations such as Amnesty International, Greenpeace, and Human Rights Watch still use "naming and shaming" strategies, but ever larger portions of their efforts and resources are devoted to dialogue and cooperative projects with corporations (Winston 2002). Why?

To the extent that politics is about power, the answer is in the statistics. Of the 100 largest economic entities in the world, 51 are now corporations and only 49 are states (Anderson and Cavanagh 2000).[1] The combined sales of the top 200 corporations amount to 27.5 percent of global economic activity (while these corporations employ less than 1 percent of the global workforce) and are larger than the combined economies of all countries minus the largest 10 (Anderson and Cavanagh 2000).[2] While there are 191 states, the number of corporations has grown from 37,000 (with 170,000 foreign affiliates) in 1993 to over 60,000 (with 800,000 foreign affiliates) in 2002 (UNCTAD 1993).[3] Corporations grow in strength and number almost everywhere, while the decline in state power in large areas of the world continues apace — as a booming literature on "failed states," "quasi states" and "client states" attests.[4] Even in robust developed states, corporations in many cases have "begun to outflank the state externally and to gnaw away at its governance monopoly from the inside" (Ruggie 2003: 104).

If these empirical assessments are even vaguely correct, we would expect the direct and indirect impact on politics to be tremendous — and it is.[5] An outlook that ignores corporations, hopes they will have little influence, or anticipates that they can be abolished strikes most informed commentators as fiddling while Rome burns. (The appropriate response when encountering those with great power is surely not the naïve "please never use it" or "go away," but rather the eternally hopeful "this is how you should use it, and

---

[1] This statistic is based on a comparison of corporate sales with country GDP — a rough and ready, yet revealing, calculus. The United Nations Conference on Trade and Development (UNCTAD) provides the rather more conservative estimate of 29 out of 100 (*Financial Review*, August 13, 2002, "UN rates top 100 economic entities").

[2] These sales amount to 18 times the combined annual income of the poorest quarter of the world's population — roughly 1.2 billion people in conditions of severe poverty (with this poverty line estimated, some would say underestimated, at under $1 a day).

[3] The second figure is also from UNCTAD and is reported in UNDPI 2002: 19.

[4] These are precisely the areas where development capacity is most badly needed. The existence of an increasingly assertive hegemonic state, the USA, does little to remedy this absence of state capacity.

[5] There are some obvious and quantifiable intra-country effects; for instance, in the US election of 2000, the top 82 companies (included in the top 200 globally) donated $33,045,832 through political action committees (this excludes so-called soft money donations). The Center for Responsive Politics found both that "corporations in general outspent labor unions by a ratio of about 15-to-1 ... [and that] candidates for the U.S. House of Representatives who outspent their opponents were victorious in 94 percent of their races" (Anderson and Cavanagh 2000). There are also some obvious but non-quantifiable intra-country effects, such as behind-the-scenes successes by the vast lobbying industry that influences government on corporations' behalf. Almost half of the top 100 corporations have "government relations" offices within a few blocks of the Capitol Building in Washington DC (ibid.). The spill-over effects for the rest of the world are dramatic.

this is how you should avoid abusing it."[6]) Indeed, add to the figures above the massive proliferation of international NGOs, 44,000 at last count (UNDP 2000[7]), and it is no surprise to find Boutros Boutros-Ghali, the previous Secretary General, saying in 1996:

> The participation of new actors on the international scene is an acknowledged fact; providing them with agreed means of participation in the formal system, heretofore primarily the province of States, is the new task of our time (Boutros-Ghali 2000: 205).

Note the language. He was not calling for mere restraint on the part of corporations, or for mere cooperation with UN member states on the part of NGOs, but rather for something more expansive: participation in the formal system. Nobody quite knew what this meant.

Within the UN architecture itself, for instance, there was at least a place and nominal role for NGOs — in the Council of Non-Governmental Organizations (CONGO) — but there was no established place or role for corporations. Moreover, as leaders of the UN now confess, the organization's limited experience in engaging with corporations meant that such leaders had little idea about how to "convene and catalyze" and "direct" the debate on widening corporate participation in governance.[8] Thus the UN began one of its seemingly interminable rounds of dialogue with "all relevant stakeholders," including all major business associations. The concrete result was the establishment, in 2000, of an initiative called the Global Compact.

3. Enter the global compact: A melee ensues

The initiative is managed by the Global Compact Office located in UN headquarters in New York, but is a joint project of five (originally four) UN agencies. In part, the Compact is an attempt to promote and steer the "corporate social responsibility" agenda; in part, it is an ambitious attempt to

---

[6] Here I leave aside extreme cases that demand uncompromising rejection, such as fascism and Nazism. Some anti-corporate activists would like to draw an exact analogy. I shall not consider this claim here, except to say that I do not think corporate executives can be regarded as unreasonable and malevolently motivated in the same way and to the same extent as fascists and Nazis.

[7] The number of intra-state NGOs runs into the millions (India alone is estimated to have more than a million NGOs).

[8] Interview with Georg Kell, Head, Global Compact Office, May 5, 2003, New York; Interview with Michael Doyle, former United Nations Assistant Secretary General, June 23, 2003, Princeton NJ.

instigate a genuinely global public-private partnership in governance, between the UN and multinational corporations. Kofi Annan has claimed that its success or failure bears crucially on the future of the UN itself:

> I see the Compact as a chance for the UN to renew itself from within, and to gain greater relevance in the twenty-first century by showing that it can work with non-state actors, as well as states, to achieve the broader goals on which its members have agreed (Annan 2002).

Certainly, as a self-conscious and high-level initiative, led by the Secretary General of the UN, the Compact provides special lessons about the current competences, roles, responsibilities, and potentials of different agents.

At the core of the Compact are nine principles which corporations are expected to adopt (sign-up occurs via a letter from the company CEO, and often requires Board approval). The nine principles, which cover various human rights, labor rights, and environmental protections, are important but also somewhat overlapping and vague.[9] According to the main intellectual progenitor of the Compact, former UN Assistant Secretary General John Ruggie, companies who sign on are

> encouraged to move towards "good practices" as defined through multi-stakeholder dialogue and partnership, rather than relying on their often superior bargaining position vis-à-vis national authorities, especially in small and poor states, to get away with less (Ruggie 2003: 111).

The guidelines for acting upon these principles are equally vague. Adherence to the principles is strictly voluntary and there is no system of external monitoring and verification. Instead, companies self-report each year on at least one case where they have implemented one of the nine principles contained in the Compact, whether alone or in conjunction with a UN agency.[10] Moreover, the Global Compact Office has gone out of its way

---

[9] The principles are derived from the *Universal Declaration of Human Rights*, the ILO's Fundamental Principles on the Rights at Work, and the Rio Principles on Environment and Development. They are: (1) respect for the protection of internationally proclaimed human rights, (2) non-complicity in human rights abuses, (3) freedom of association and the effective recognition of the right to collective bargaining, (4) the elimination of forced and compulsory labor, (5) the abolition of child labor, (6) the elimination of discrimination in employment, (7) a precautionary approach to environmental challenges, (8) greater environmental responsibility, and (9) encouraging the development and diffusion of environmentally friendly technologies. (Note the omission of a tenth principle, on anti-corruption, long-debated and resisted, but shortly to be added to the Compact at last.)

[10] Originally, companies were required to submit a separate report to the Secretariat; then the requirement changed to a "case-study" detailing an example of acting on a principle; now companies are asked merely to include a description of their actions in their Annual

to stress that the principles are "aspirational" and not binding. The main line of reasoning behind this deeply voluntary approach is quite simple: corporations would not otherwise sign on.[11] Over 1300 multinational corporations have signed on. One of the stated priorities of Georg Kell, the Head of Office, has been to increase this number rapidly.[12]

Among the 1300 corporations are Nike, Shell, and Rio Tinto. The presence of these and other reputed human rights abusers, who were among the first and most enthusiastic to sign on, has helped provoke cynical commentary within and outside the UN. Critics insist that the absence of clear and measurable standards and of an enforcement mechanism allows corporations with poor records to "bluewash" their image by wrapping themselves in the flag of the United Nations. There is, it is claimed, an overwhelming incentive to hypocrisy — signing on for the public relations benefits and then "defecting" by carrying on with business as usual (Sethi 2002). From this skeptical perspective, the Compact affords "cover" for continued rapaciousness and represents yet another aspect of the silent takeover of governmental institutions by corporations. Typically, these critics call for the voluntary approach to be replaced by "hard law" (including codes of conduct backed up by sanctions) that reins in and regulates corporate behavior.[13]

Supporters of the Compact maintain that, on the contrary, it constitutes a first step toward holding corporations accountable. First, the Compact provides arguments, evidence and publicity that strengthen the "business case" for corporate social responsibility. That is, the Compact does seem to convince some corporations that compliance can be in their economic best interest. Second, since corporations will not sign on to "hard law" initiatives, attempting to produce "soft law" is surely better than being stuck with no law at all. The mere existence of agreed "hyper-norms" and a "learning network" provides guidance to those corporations who wish to behave well

---

Report. Some regard this change as a further watering-down of the requirements on corporations. Others argue that this change replaces isolated submissions with a system that encourages the integration of Compact principles into the main business practices and self-description of each corporation.

[11] Major US corporations that have not signed on cite fear of legal action as the primary (and often sole) reason for their reluctance. This is not entirely misguided given the recent California Supreme Court decision that Nike's promotional statements were not protected as free speech but rather constituted "commercial speech." The decision creates doubt and insecurity about the legal implications of almost all corporate public statements of commitment.

[12] Interview with Georg Kell, Head, Global Compact Office, May 5, 2003.

[13] This is a view shared even by the leaders of major NGOs affiliated with the Global Compact, who have implicitly (in writing) and explicitly (in person) threatened a walkout if no monitoring mechanism is forthcoming (see Amnesty International 2003).

(it helps potential corporate "knights"); at the same time, a corporation's public subscription to those norms provides leverage to critics (thus creating disincentives for potential corporate "knaves"). Third, the Compact's voluntary approach complements efforts to establish enforceable international legal standards rather than conflicting with such efforts. In public, supporters talk mostly about how participation in voluntary initiatives will offer learning opportunities about compliance, the result being that corporations will have less reason to fear and resist the introduction of compulsory codes. Supporters also believe that the Compact will deliver benefits such as more stable contexts for investment in developing countries. In private, many supporters envision "a creeping process of norm-creation," where an informed civil society turns adherence to so-called voluntary codes into a de facto sine qua non of participation in the global marketplace.

There are elements of truth to both sides of the controversy over the efficacy of the Compact (reality is messy; different corporations behave differently) such that it is difficult to reject predictions on either side at all emphatically. At this point, let me say only two things about this debate, so as to suggest that both sides have made similar conceptual and strategic mistakes.

3.1 Norm diffusion and enforcement

First, much of the intense disagreement over the Compact could have been avoided had the UN not committed its usual error of overinclusion. That is, the focus has been on maximizing the number of corporations signing on, not on obtaining agreement from certain corporations in certain sectors on more specific norms. As we now know from the literature inaugurated by Thomas Schelling and recently popularized by Malcolm Gladwell in *The Tipping Point*, the so-called scattergun approach does not tend to be effective in producing either norm diffusion or enforcement:

> there is something in all of us that feels that true answers to problems have to be comprehensive, that there is virtue in the dogged and indiscriminate application of effort, that slow and steady should win the race … The world — much as we want it to — does not accord with our intuition … (Gladwell 2002: 257f).[14]

In fact, norms and behaviors are spread by those with disproportionate social power and in any group — be it corporations or schoolchildren —

---

[14] See also Schelling (1978) who stresses his debt to Grodzins' (1957) use of the term "tipping point."

those powerful agents are relatively few in number. This phenomenon is explicable largely in terms of our limited capacity to access and process information, which demands that we rely heavily on cues from others, and leads us to avoid risky intra-group divergence by taking our cues from the same few agents. (These agents tend to be more knowledgeable, more skilled, more charismatic, better-located and/or in formal positions of authority.)

To produce attitudinal and behavioral change, one has to reach those key agents in particular. Moreover, the message that those key agents adopt and convey has to be "sticky" (this is the technical term): distinct, actionable, memorable and connected to the rest of the group members' daily experience.[15] The Global Compact initiative has failed to take account of either sociological lesson. In terms of agency, for example, it is an article of faith in the Compact Office that corporate "champions" will come to the fore and bring in their wake the less interested and committed corporations;[16] yet it is not clear why those self-selected champions necessarily constitute the subgroup that is effective at diffusing and encouraging enforcement of norms. Relatively late in the day, for instance, realization dawned that more signatory US corporations were badly needed to gain momentum for the Compact; but the "take what you can get" attitude often still predominates, rather than the strategy of convincing a few key US players in a few key industries. Meanwhile, the Global Compact Office's focus on securing agreements with the maximal number of corporations has helped to keep the principles vague and has watered down the Compact's message.[17]

Consider the contrast with two of the most successful development initiatives in the last decade. Global Witness, an international NGO, led an effective campaign to restrict trade in conflict diamonds. It did so not via a scattershot approach (to all diamond producers) but through targeted interventions, the most significant of which was convincing De Beers (the largest producer of diamonds in the world) that conflict diamonds were bad for business, and that a relatively simple system of tracing legitimate diamonds could do the job of stemming the flow of the illegitimate sort. De

---

[15] See Gladwell 2002 for a legion of examples across domains, and for a bibliography of more rigorous academic research on the topic.

[16] Interview with Denise O'Brien, Head of Dialogue, Global Compact Office, April 30, 2003, New York; Interview with Georg Kell, Head, Global Compact Office, May 5, 2003, New York; and Interview with Michael Doyle, former United Nations Assistant Secretary General, June 23, 2003, Princeton NJ.

[17] At meetings of the Compact, it is evident from corporate presentations that partnership projects have little in common with one another. See, for instance, the report on the Supply Chain Management/Partnerships Policy Dialogue, 2003, at www.unglobalcompact.org.

Beers then played a primary role convincing and corralling competitors, affiliates, and states to agree to a system of regulation — one that is limiting trade in conflict diamonds today and hence curbing a chief cause of political instability.[18]

The story of Transparency International is similarly revealing. TI's mission is not too far removed from that of the Compact initiative, in that the organization aims to "mobilize a global coalition to promote and strengthen international and national integrity systems" against corruption (Transparency International, 1998). TI made three crucial moves. First, the organization developed close relationships with leaders from developing countries — including Olusegun Obasanjo — who were determined that the time had come to tackle corruption in their own societies. In this initial phase, TI also focused on crystallizing its message, establishing its credibility in key societies, and creating an international support system in ways that suited the needs of leading actors in these societies. Second, TI publicized its launch and its work in pivotal media such as the *Financial Times*. Third, TI honed its methodology for measuring corruption and ranking countries;[19] it then helped convince a few major investment banks and financial information services that corruption is a source of risk. When the banks and services incorporated TI's rankings into their risk assessments and investment ratings, corruption indices immediately became a component of the international financial architecture. The result was indirect encouragement and even enforcement of corruption control among a far wider range of agents than TI could have reached, convinced and monitored on its own.

These examples are not meant to reassure; while both "soft law" victories are important and have lent impetus to a number of "hard law" initiatives (such as the OECD anti-corruption convention), there is a *very* long way to go in respect of both corruption and nefarious natural resource extraction. Rather, taken together with the tipping point literature, such case studies indicate that both sides to the Global Compact debate are mistaken in important respects. Supporters of the Compact should not be seeking to maximize the number of signatory corporations and to generate as long a list as possible of arguments for involvement (thereby diluting the Compact's "message"), but instead they should be trying to identify key corporations (with the social power to produce desired demonstration effects) and formulating arguments that persuade those primary agents. More definite

---

[18] See www.globalwitness.org for a suitably self-congratulatory account; also see the slew of citations in UN documentation leading up to *UNSCR 56/263* (2002).

[19] This methodology — while it constitutes a great improvement on having no measurement and ranking system whatsoever — still has shortcomings. But that is a separate topic.

norms and a focused message are also likely to create firmer bases for the gradual emergence of both soft and hard law.

Critics of the Compact, on the other hand, should not lament the UN refusal to propose hard law solutions (proposals that would go nowhere given the current structure of power), nor should they reject the Compact outright because it does not include a strong monitoring mechanism. Rather, they should continue to press for clear and measurable standards that could underpin hard law in the future but that provide leverage for civil society organizations at present; *then* these critics and organizations should focus resources on monitoring and publicizing the performance of the few key corporations that have tipping power. Here there are additional grounds for hope since, as Naomi Klein has demonstrated, peculiarly powerful and well-known corporations are especially vulnerable to adverse publicity: the more well-known and global the brand, the more the potential benefits of predatory behavior in one country are likely to be outweighed by the risk of damaging the overall brand (Klein 2002).[20]

3.2 Agents of governance

My second point about the Global Compact debate is that proponents on both sides have not sufficiently distinguished various aspects of the debate, and one aspect in particular has received almost no careful attention. That is, supporters and critics of the Global Compact both focus almost exclusively on

(1) how corporations might benefit from (the myth or reality of) "good corporate citizenship;"
(2) how affiliation to the Compact might encourage corporations to restrain themselves in their own operations (or discourage restraint, via "bluewash");
(3) how "outsourcing" to corporations and "partnering" with corporations has aided (or hindered) development efforts in various countries.

Unfortunately, there has been limited and platitudinous attention paid to

(4) how ongoing corporate participation in UN projects and policy-formation, and in the activities of other elements of the basic structure of global society (multilateral agencies, state and local governments, NGOs), could transform the formal system of governance.

---

[20] It is sometimes claimed that even more unsavory companies will step into a breach left by more well-known corporations that wish to avoid unethical practices. This is a real concern, but one that the logic of the tipping point does much to address, since this logic suggests that the indirect and cumulative (demonstration) effects of key players are greater than such piecemeal effects.

It seems to me that there are two main reasons for this relative silence on Boutros-Ghali's original core concern. One, most development practitioners have more immediate imperatives and time horizons in view. Their primary concerns are to encourage corporations to show restraint in existing areas of abuse and to demonstrate successes in intra-country, on-the-ground terminal projects. Two, current political theory and political science allow almost no place for corporations as part of the political authority structure:

> The place of non-state actors and movements remains poorly understood in the mainstream literature, largely because they tend to be viewed, implicitly if not explicitly, through the lenses of an "institutional substitutability" premise. That is to say, if other institutional forms at the international level do not have the potential to *replace* the territorial state they tend to be regarded as unworthy of serious consideration: interesting in practice, perhaps, but not in theory (Ruggie 2003: 104).

It is here that development theorists and practitioners should re-enter the fray — bearing in mind strategic lessons from the discussion of the Global Compact above — and can do so to unusual practical effect.

4. The theorists strike back — but need more power

There are two chief respects in which political and development theory need to adapt in the face of economic globalization and the rapid rise of non-state actors. The first change largely concerns justice, the second, democracy. Together, my suggested changes would do much to enable positive political globalization. That is, these changes would provide for the restructuring of justified political authority so as to positively contain and channel (currently runaway) economic globalization, ensuring in particular a more equitable distribution of benefits and burdens to poor and disadvantaged people. I shall discuss the two changes in turn, under the headings "redistributing responsibilities" and "reconfiguring representation."

4.1 Redistributing responsibilities: Towards justice

The current international order is formally statist, both in terms of its structure and its justification as articulated in key founding documents. The UN, for instance, is an organization constituted by states and dominated by a few states, by design. Similarly, only states may be parties to cases before the International Court of Justice. Even the great touchstone of progressive politics, the *Universal Declaration of Human Rights*, is avowedly statist in its attribution of responsibilities, with its Preamble slipping seamlessly from "the conscience of mankind" to "peoples" to "Member States."

Statism is out of kilter, of course, with the current realities of global power. But this clichéd description of the problem makes things seem better than they are: in fact, "the state" often serves as a placeholder that enables people to ignore altogether the problem of attributing responsibility. As Onora O'Neill and Thomas Pogge have pointed out, for instance, the *Declaration* — while universalist in its aspirations — almost always looks at justice from the perspective of recipients and rights to the exclusion of the perspective of actors and obligations (O'Neill 2001; Pogge 2002b). Partly for this reason, the language of rights has proliferated to the point where much of what passes for programmatic political discourse is vacuous rhetoric — enjoining somebody to do something but nobody to do anything in particular. As I and others have argued in the collaborative volume *Global Responsibilities* (Kuper 2005),[21] this vagueness damages our practical thinking about advancing human rights and relieving poverty: Unless a person or her representative can identify the agents against whom her right is held, her right may amount to little more than useless words. If, on the other hand, there is an identifiable agent or set of agents that has obligations to her — and is failing to live up to those obligations — then there is someone at fault, someone against whom she or her representative could lay a complaint or approach with a complaint, and perhaps even an effective procedure through which to ensure that her rights are enforced or violations of her rights properly remedied.

Our task, then, is to confront and answer the immense question of "who must do what for whom?" Here we can take our cue from some important work by O'Neill and Pogge, though I also want to suggest that in crucial respects neither has gone far enough. Consider first O'Neill's famous discussion of the attribution of moral responsibility within weak, predatory, or unjust states (O'Neill 2001).[22] In such contexts, she argues, non-state actors may have significant capabilities that states lack, and may have opportunities to contribute to the construction of justice precisely *because* they have greater relative powers and face fewer restrictions than they would in strong states. Moreover, it is sociologically simplistic and historically inaccurate to presume that non-state actors are necessarily ill-motivated or indifferent to justice in such underinstitutionalized environments. For these reasons, states cannot be assumed to be the "primary agents of justice" in

---

[21] The book contains seminal, revised, or new pieces by Amartya Sen, Onora O'Neill, Thomas Pogge, Susan James, David Miller, Michael Green, Christian Barry, Andrew Kuper, Peter Singer, David Held, S. Prakash Sethi, Melissa Lane, and Ngaire Woods.

[22] O'Neill provided the short and elegant formulation of the question above.

such contexts, nor can all other agents be treated as secondary agents of justice whose main contribution to justice is to conform to the just requirements of states. This argument is meant to carry normative as well as descriptive weight: with greater powers, opportunities, and freedoms come greater responsibilities — different not merely in degree but in kind.

O'Neill's argument takes us a crucial first step towards understanding the potential moral and political responsibilities of corporations. For a variety of reasons, corporations may exhibit and encourage behavior that is more ethical than that of corrupt, bellicose, or petty state autocrats in developing countries (one might think here of corporate susceptibility to some values and leverage of mass Western publics and international law, of the desire to increase stability and minimize risk, and even of the character or desire for reputation of those at the helm). Or they may not; that is, corporations may rival and surpass and amplify the misdeeds of those occupying state office. But since the empirical questions of (relative) power and motivation remain open, it is neither analytically possible nor strategically wise to identify the primary agents of justice prior to an empirical assessment of the situation.

But the argument, elaborated in this way, cuts deeper than O'Neill thinks. Recall some of the facts and figures about corporate power mentioned earlier: an empirical assessment of the current global situation may lead us to conclude that *in the vast majority of cases* the questions of relative power and motivation remain open. If corporations often outspend, outflank, corral and ultimately coerce developed as well as developing states, if corporations' power to do good or ill tends to outstrip the regulatory capacities or inclinations of state authorities in rich and powerful states, and if on some occasions corporate leaders are better (morally) motivated than rulers of developed as well as developing states, then we cannot decide by fiat that states are the primary agents of justice. In attributing global political responsibilities, we must instead begin with an empirical assessment of the capabilities, opportunities and motivations of diverse powerful actors.[23]

At this point, one can imagine corporate leaders (or the few who like to read relatively academic articles) asking why the power of corporations, enormous though it is, justifies the attribution of not only greater responsibility but also responsibility of a kind that stands at some remove from the everyday operations and preoccupations of business. There are three related tasks here: (a) establishing the grounds for allocating responsibility; (b) attributing responsibilities to diverse agents; (c) convincing those agents to fulfill their responsibilities.

---

[23] The role of motivations (current? possible? likely? ideal?) in this context is parsed interestingly by Amartya Sen, Susan James, Michael Green and others in Kuper 2005.

One way to ground corporate responsibilities, and to show that they are broader than traditionally conceived, is to follow David Miller: he insists that, where there is severe deprivation and suffering that can be alleviated, it is morally intolerable to allow it to continue and implausible to maintain that no-one has the responsibility to help (Miller 2001). That is, in principle, there is always some agent to whom responsibility can be assigned in grave cases. The question is how to pick out the exact responsible agents of justice from the multiplicity of possible agents. We might then be able to show that corporations have extensive "remedial responsibilities" not simply because they are a *cause* of or are *morally responsible* for much global poverty, nor simply because they have developed *close ties* with local communities, but because — in numerous contexts, from the local to the global — corporations are the *most capable* agents when it comes to remedying this grave situation.[24]

Considering the many tasks that corporations are best placed to perform, this argument could take us a long way. In underinstitutionalized contexts, corporations may turn out to be the only agents who are capable of providing goods traditionally supplied monopolistically by the state, such as security for local communities or enforced worker safety regulations. In densely institutionalized state contexts, corporations may still be better at core tasks of governance, such as managing some prisons, some transport networks and some kinds of political and technical education.

The familiar terms "outsourcing" and "privatization" do not capture these scenarios well (it would be a mistake and a caricature to read me as endorsing either strategy tout court).[25] Both terms suggest that there is a central agency that delegates the supply of goods and then regulates alternative suppliers; yet there may be no such strong agent (as in failed states) or that agent may refuse to delegate for pernicious reasons (as in predatory states). In less vexatious situations, most or all states still may be unable to deliver on certain global public goods even if state leaders would like to do so; here the issue is not one of delegation or monitoring but of whether corporations themselves take up the task of supplying such goods at all. Finally, at the global level, the range of tasks and systems of control may simply be too diffuse and overlapping for it to be at all plausible to identify a

---

[24] Christian Barry has suggested that, beyond the four principles identified by Miller, there are at least three other principles for allocating obligations: a beneficiary principle, a risk principle, and a contribution principle. Barry (2005, and in this volume) develops the latter to powerful effect.

[25] It is misguided and perhaps lazy to be "for" or "against" so-called outsourcing and privatization in principle rather than considering which agent (or combination of agents) can best bear which burdens and deliver on which requirements in an area of public concern.

strong central agency or to talk about governance primarily in the language of delegation. (How a global regulatory system might work under these conditions is explored below.)

An alternative route to establishing the nature and scope of political responsibilities is that of Thomas Pogge: when an institutional order avoidably fails to secure basic human rights, he argues, those of its members who significantly collaborate in its imposition are violating a negative duty of justice — they are not merely failing to help but are participating in unjustified coercion. As it stands, according to Pogge, wealthy and influential citizens and states spuriously "present themselves as the most advanced in terms of human rights and are chiefly responsible for the fact that most human beings still lack secure access to the most vital goods" (Pogge 2002b).

It is evident that this argument could apply to corporations with equal force. Indeed, given the empirical picture painted above, it is unclear why Pogge addresses himself constantly to wealthy states and does not lavish similar attention on corporations. Perhaps, as I have argued elsewhere, he and other cosmopolitan thinkers, while they rightly reject the Realist cult of unitary and unqualified state sovereignty, are still prone to understanding political authority in terms of territorially defined units (Kuper 2000, esp. 653–8). These cosmopolitan thinkers — explicitly or implicitly — are not averse to institutional substitutability as long as it involves institutions of a similar kind. In the next section, I want to suggest that overcoming this prejudice is the key to reconfiguring democratic representation in the face of globalization.

4.2 Reconfiguring representation: Towards democracy

Most democratic theories (implicitly or explicitly) are not only statist but also *electoralist*: they center primarily on election to state offices. To the extent that such theories explore positive countervailing forces to the state, they tend to focus on international civil society and multilateral institutions (established by states). Thus, although these theories may be suggestive, they have a limited amount to tell us about the role of corporations as contributors to global governance. The latter actors are neither elected nor confined to any one state; they do not enjoy the purported credibility of grassroots activists or the transitive credibility of state-signed international agreements. Yet, I have argued, these actors cannot be ignored or understood merely as secondary agents of justice. In all sorts of contexts, they can be seen to be "acting in the best interests of the public, in a manner responsive to them" (to cite Hannah Pitkin's memorable definition of "substantive representation" (Pitkin 1967: 209–40)) or at least acting *more* in the interests of various publics and in a *more* responsive manner than rulers of states.

None of this makes corporations into democratic representatives. After all, almost every government and powerful agent claims to be representative in the substantive sense — and this claim is not strictly false. (For instance, a non-democratic government might act in a representative fashion due to a leader's whimsy or a fortunate coincidence of rulers' interests with those of the public.) What is distinctive about democratic representation is that citizens are *agents* with a degree of ongoing, systematic and active control over those who act for them rather than passive beneficiaries or victims of such actions. Certainly, the current global political situation does not ensure that corporations are externally situated, internally organized, and thus made to act systematically such that they can be seen to be representative. The question that we need to ask is: could non-state actors be situated in such a fashion that they are not only contingently or occasionally "representative" but rather, in important respects, acting appropriately and under (direct or indirect) citizen control on an ongoing basis?

Initially, this seems unlikely. It is the purest fantasy to anticipate that, for instance, transnational corporations and international non-governmental organizations could be elected by a global public. But here electoralist and statist models mislead us. I would like to mention an alternative, though all too briefly.[26] This alternative is meant to indicate how corporations should be situated, organized, and made to act such that they can be considered sufficiently responsive to citizens that we can term them, in important respects, representative.

We commonly talk not only about representative *agents* but also about a *system* of representative government. The latter locution emphasizes the way in which political institutions function so as to consistently produce outcomes that take into account the interests and views of the public. This means that we have to go beyond assessing our control over individual agents of justice (or injustice). For the purposes of an overall judgment of the extent to which the public is democratically represented by its political order, we must also consider the complex division of labor between citizens and representatives and among representatives themselves. We are required, in short, not merely to tally up the quantity and quality of various representatives but in addition to examine the cumulative effects over time of institutionalized interactions.

Such a system-centric analysis can pull us in a very different direction from agent-centric analyses. For instance, adopting an agent-centric view,

---

[26] An account of democratic representation — extending to the global level — is developed at length in Kuper 2004.

we may regard the inclusion of certain actors (for example, an international NGO such as Transparency International) in formal structures of governance as unwarranted, because such actors are not appointed by citizens. But, adopting a system-centric view, we may discover that the inclusion of these actors increases the responsiveness of other representatives and of the political system overall to the views and best interests of the public. Moreover, other (elected and unelected) representatives may be able to constrain the unelected actors in turn — by providing different, sometimes countervailing information, incentives and sanctions — thereby reducing the scope of such actors for unresponsiveness. In such cases, we may have good reasons to give priority to system-centric representation: we may care more about overall control over governance and its outcomes than about whether any particular agent is elected or not.

None of this is to say that global representation can dispense with elections or states. Rather, it is to stress that the mechanisms for securing democratic representation go beyond vibrant civil society and elections (to state-created offices). This is not an entirely unfamiliar thought. Notably, a Montesquieuian separation of powers is thought to advance *democracy*, despite (or rather, because of) the fact that it introduces unelected elements into the framework of government — mechanisms that ultimately give citizens greater control over their individual and collective lives.[27] This is not intended as an exact analogy but as an indication of appropriate processes and mechanisms by which democracy should be extended. The entrenched balance of powers is no less central to defining and sustaining modern democracy (within states) than are electoral mechanisms; citizens would be no less empowered (indeed, often more so, particularly at the global level) through this mechanism than they are and would be through intra-state and electoral mechanisms; and representatives would be no less held to account (indeed, often more so, particularly at the global level) through this mechanism than through intra-state and electoral mechanisms. If such a responsive global system were created, we would be justified in calling the resulting order a form of democratic representation.[28]

I have provided a detailed account of this theory and system of democratic representation elsewhere. Here I can only recommend that we begin to develop a similar working framework at the global level — a framework that balances the power of states against that of corporations and

---

[27] When we talk of courts as representative, we mean this in a different sense from when we talk of political office-holders as such; it should be stressed that I am suggesting a *distinct* and *further* sense of "representative." Little is to be gained by collapsing senses of the term.

[28] See Kuper 2004, chapter 3, for an extensive argument to this effect. I have called the conception of an extended separation of powers developed there "a plurality of powers."

that of non-governmental organizations, such that each checks the other, and they collectively improve the responsiveness of the current global order. Clearly, our present world stands at a great remove from any such framework. But the enduring relative decline of the state seems to leave us with no more justifiable route.

Let me provide a brief illustration of the kind of plurality I have in mind in one area: international legal institutions. Currently, only states may be parties in cases before the International Court of Justice (ICJ) and states have to agree to submit their dispute to the Court.[29] (The only exception to this restriction is that UN organs and agencies may petition the Court for non-binding "advisory opinions."[30]) In practice, this means that the Court is drastically underutilized and is not a significant presence in international affairs. While the European Court of Human Rights decides about 60 cases a year, and the US Supreme Court decides about 100, the ICJ renders judgments annually on a grand total of four cases (Janis 1997: 208–12).[31]

A careful study shows one factor to be the dominant cause: states and state bureaucrats want "neither to lose political and administrative control of disputes nor to embarrass other states and organizations" (Janis 1997: 209). Meanwhile, *all* the cases before the European Court, bar one, were brought by individuals (supported by NGOs and others) and not by states (Janis 1997: 211f). As long as only one *kind* of actor is present, the situation of the ICJ is unlikely to be rectified. If, however, other actors — perhaps certain NGOs and chambers of commerce — are given standing before the international court (*locus standi in judicio* — at least as amici curiae), then more cases and more kinds of cases will be brought to the ICJ, and it may attain some of the reach and credibility of other major courts. We should be thinking about these kinds of institutional reforms, reforms that break the logic of statism, for the UN and other political organs of international society too.[32]

---

[29] *Statute of the ICJ*, Articles 34 (1) and 36 (1).

[30] *Statute of the ICJ*, Article 65 (1).

[31] The figure for the European Court is taken from 1990–94 (in the decades before that, the average annual number of cases was 17); the figure for the ICJ is taken for 1946 to 1994, during which time there was no dramatic acceleration.

[32] In Kuper 2004, chapter 4, I illustrate how the inclusion of non-state actors in formal structures and proceedings of the UN, ICJ and ICC would result in more utilization of these political organs — and utilization to better effect, enhancing global justice and democracy.

5. Balancing strategy: Corporations as friends and foes

I have suggested that the key tasks for the future of justice and democracy are (a) understanding the empirical capabilities and opportunities of non-state actors, so as to allocate obligations that states cannot meet or that these actors are better at meeting; and (b) empowering and constraining non-state actors such that they check and balance states, and are checked in turn by states as well as one another. These thoughts, I hope, go some way to deepening and addressing Boutros-Ghali's core concern that we find a way to include non-state actors as participants in the formal system of global governance.

It remains for me, in conclusion, to return to some strategic lessons of the Global Compact. First, it is futile and foolish to attempt to identify relative positions and constraints for each and every corporation or international NGO. Such dogged and indiscriminate application of effort produces neither norm diffusion nor norm enforcement mechanisms. Rather, the focus should be on identifying key agents and establishing which positions they might occupy and which constraints they might be subjected to. Second, at this point in time, the relative positioning and monitoring mechanisms of various actors are unlikely to be formally articulated, least of all in "hard law." There are, of course, some areas where hard law changes should be pursued. For instance, it might be eminently worthwhile to campaign for changes to the *Statute of the ICJ* such that non-state actors gain standing before the court; similarly, it is to be hoped that several formal regulatory authorities obtain extended mandates after the Enron debacle and other corporate scandals. But, given the current configuration of power and the limits of current international law, most balancing and monitoring processes at the global level will have to be of a "soft law" or less formalized kind. While this may be unfortunate, it is a reality that must be confronted. It is best confronted by targeting arguments, resources and efforts at holding a few socially powerful "tipping" agents to a limited class of specific norms that might one day become hard law.

In respect of both strategies, a strong start can be made by informally monitoring and evaluating a fairly small number of non-state actors who account for a large proportion of global aid, advocacy, regulation, and business: eight international NGOs, nine intergovernmental organizations, and ten transnational corporations — identified by the pilot Global Accountability Project (GAP) of the One World Trust.[33] This organization, which operates out of the British Parliament as a charity, has used a so-

---

[33] For the methodology and process of public consultation by which these actors were selected, see Charter 99, www.charter99.org.

called stakeholder analysis to measure four dimensions of internal accountability and four of external accountability relevant to the selected international governmental and non-governmental organizations and transnational corporations. Thereafter, the actors are ranked across the eight dimensions.[34] Both the identification of a limited class of actors and the attempt to provide measurable standards of accountability (in terms of which they can be consistently praised or blamed) are crucial and prescient steps.

If, one fine day, organizations such as Amnesty International, Oxfam and Human Rights Watch gain seats in important forums and contexts of governance alongside states, that will likely be cause for celebration among supporters of cosmopolitan justice and democracy. These organizations are different in kind from states and statist institutions but it is not a stretch to regard them as representative of some of our most basic interests. In this chapter, I have argued for a less intuitively appealing conclusion: if corporations or corporate bodies gain a place in governance alongside states and NGOs, that too *may* be cause for celebration. Of course, it might be the final sign of the corporate takeover of governmental institutions. Or, if the correct frameworks and strategies are developed (we have only begun to think about these frameworks and strategies for a post-statist world), it might be a sign that a new and formalized balance of powers has emerged. Corporations have enormous and potentially destructive power; but they are not necessarily the enemies of human rights and development. Indeed, it is reasonable to hope that they could occupy a more prominent place in advancing both justice and democracy.

---

[34] A number of methodological problems remain to be worked out. For instance, the term "accountability" is used too broadly in GAP, and its blueprint contains blunt, ill-advised phrases like "the term 'member' refers to member states" (Kovac and Burall 2001: 4, 15).

About the Authors

Christian Barry (1969) is Editor of *Ethics & International Affairs*. Prior to joining the Carnegie Council, he served for three years as a consultant and contributing author to the *Human Development Report* of the United Nations Development Program. His recent and forthcoming publications include Applying the Contribution Principle (in *Global Responsibilities*, Routledge 2005), Redistribution (*Stanford Encyclopedia of Philosophy* 2004), "Global Justice: Aims, Arrangements, and Responsibilities" (in *Can Institutions Have Duties?*, Palgrave 2003), and "Education and Standards of Living" (in *Blackwell Companion to the Philosophy of Education*, 2002).

Alexander W. Cappelen (1969), Dr. oecon. from the Norwegian School of Economics and Business Administration (2000), is a post-doctoral fellow at the Department of Economics at the University of Oslo and head of the Centre for Ethics and Economics at the Norwegian School of Economics and Business Administration. He works on topics in public economics, social choice and political philosophy.

Geert Demuijnck (1960), PhD in philosophy from the University of Louvain (Belgium) is professor of ethics and political philosophy at the Catholic University of Lille (France). He publishes on topics related to social justice and social policy.

Andreas Follesdal (1957), PhD in philosophy from Harvard University (1991) is Professor at the Norwegian Centre for Human Rights (Faculty of Law), and at ARENA, a Centre for European Studies, both at the University of Oslo. He publishes and consults on topics in political philosophy, focusing on developments in the European Union.

Rainer Forst (1964), Dr. phil. and Habilitation in philosophy from the Goethe University in Frankfurt, taught philosophy and political science at the Free University in Berlin, the Goethe University, the New School for Social Research in New York, and the Liebig-University in Giessen. He is now Professor of Political Theory at the Goethe University in Frankfurt. Among his publications are *Contexts of Justice. Political Philosophy beyond Liberalism and Communitarianism* (University of California Press 2002) and *Toleranz im Konflikt. Geschichte, Gehalt und Gegenwart eines umstrittenen Begriffs* (Suhrkamp 2003).

Stefan Gosepath (1959) is Privatdozent for philosophy at the Free University in Berlin and visiting professor of philosophy at the University of Potsdam. He works mainly on practical reason and on moral and political philosophy. His books include *Aufgeklärtes Eigeninteresse. Eine Theorie theoretischer und praktischer Rationalität*, (Suhrkamp 1992) and *Gleiche Gerechtigkeit. Grundlagen eines liberalen Egalitarismus* (Suhrkamp 2004).

Wilfried Hinsch (1956), Dr. phil. in philosophy from the University of Hamburg (1984). He was a Visiting Fellow at St. John's College in Cambridge in 1986 and at Harvard University in 1987 and 1988. He taught moral and political philosophy in Münster, Leipzig and Heidelberg, and is currently Professor of Practical Philosophy at the University of the Saarland in Saarbrücken. He also lectures on European Political Philosophy at the Collège d'Europe in Brugge (Belgium). His books include *Erfahrung und Selbstbewusstein* (Meiner 1986), *Zur Idee des politischen Liberalismus* (Suhrkamp 1992) und *Gerechtfertigte Ungleichheiten. Grundsätze sozialer Gerechtigkeit* (de Gruyter 2002).

Alison M. Jaggar is Professor of Philosophy and Women's Studies at the University of Colorado at Boulder. She works in moral and political philosophy, with an emphasis on feminist philosophy. At present, her main interests are in moral reasoning, especially in contexts of inequality and cultural difference, and in the gendered aspects of global justice theory.

Hilde F. Johnson (1963), Norwegian politician and social anthropologist from the University of Oslo, since 2001 Cabinet Minister of International Development. Ms. Johnson was elected Member of Parliament for the Christian Democrats in 1993 and 1997, and was Norway's Cabinet Minister of International Development and Human Rights 1997–2000.

Regina Kreide (1966), Dr. phil. in philosophy from the Goethe University in Frankfurt. She is research fellow and lecturer in the Department of Social and Political Sciences at Goethe University and currently writing a book on global justice. Among her more recent publications in this area are The Range of Social Rights (*German Law Journal* 2001) and Poverty and Responsibility in a Globalized World (*Analyse & Kritik* 2003).

Andrew Kuper (1975) was born and raised in South Africa, and holds his PhD from Cambridge University. He has been a Fellow of Trinity College, Cambridge, and a visiting scholar at Harvard and Columbia Universities. Kuper is the author of *Democracy Beyond Borders* (Oxford 2004) and editor of *Global Responsibilities* (Routledge 2005). He is now a Managing Director at Ashoka – Innovators for the Public, an organization that supports social entrepreneurs around the world.

Jean-Christophe Merle (1964), PhD in Philosophy from the Université de Fribourg, Switzerland (1993). Honorary Professor of Philosophy at the Universität des Saarlandes in Saarbrücken. He coordinates a European network on Applied Global Justice. He is the author of *Justice et Progrès* (Presses Universitaires de France 1997), editor of *Fichte: Grundlage des Naturrechts* (Akademie Verlag 2001) and *Globale Gerechtigkeit / Global Justice* (Frommann-Holzboog 2004), as well as coeditor of *Weltrepublik: Demokratie und Globalisierung* (C. H. Beck 2002), *Modelle politischer Philosophie* (Mentis 2003) and *L'amitié* (Presses Universitaires de France, forthcoming).

Thomas Mertens (1955) is Professor of the Philosophy of Law at the University of Nijmegen, the Netherlands. He has published several articles on Kant's practical philosophy and related issues, as well as on legal theory, especially in relation to Radbruch. He has also translated Kant's *Grundlegung zur Metaphysik der Sitten* and *Zum ewigen Frieden* into Dutch (Boom 1997 and 2004).

Alessandro Pinzani (1966) PhD in philosophy from the University of Tübingen (1997). He is Professor for Ethics and Political Philosophy in the Philosophy Department of the Federal University of Santa Catarina, Florianopolis, Brazil. He publishes on topics in political philosophy, focusing on the history of modern political thought and on theories of democracy.

Thomas Pogge (1953), PhD in philosophy from Harvard (1983). He teaches philosophy at Columbia and Oslo Universities, and is spending 2004–06 as a professorial research fellow at the Centre for Applied Philosophy and Public Ethics, Australian National University. His most recent book is *World Poverty and Human Rights* (Polity Press 2002).

Ser-Min Shei (1961), PhD in philosophy from Columbia University, has been teaching at National Chung Cheng University in Taiwan since 1995. He is working mainly in moral and political philosophy. Among his recent publications are Political Power, Political Authority and Political Obligation, as well as Rawls and the Site of Social Justice, both written in Chinese and published in *Societas: A Journal of Philosophical Study of Public Affairs*.

Markus Stepanians (1959) studied at Hamburg and as a Visiting Scholar at Harvard from 1991 to 1993. He received his Dr. phil. in philosophy from Hamburg University (1994) and has been teaching philosophy at the University of the Saarland in Saarbrücken since 1998. He is the author of *Frege und Husserl über Urteilen und Denken* (Mentis 1998) and *Frege – Eine Einführung* (Junius 2001, Spanish and French translations forthcoming). Currently he is preparing a collection of essays on rights (to be published by Mentis) and completing a book manuscript *Analysing Rights. A Defence of the Classical View.*

Henrik Syse (1966) PhD in philosophy from the University of Oslo (1997). He is a senior research fellow at the International Peace Research Institute in Oslo (PRIO), and a postdoctoral fellow at the Ethics Program, University of Oslo. He publishes and consults on topics of international ethics and military ethics and has also done work on professional ethics, Christian ethics and on the history of natural law and natural rights.

Leif Wenar, PhD in philosophy from Harvard University (1997), is Reader in Philosophy at the University of Sheffield. Working in moral and political theory, he has published in *Ethics, Mind, Analysis, Politics, Philosophy and Economics*, the *Columbia Law Review*, and the *Philosopher's Annual*. Wenar has held fellowships at Princeton's Center for Human Values and Tulane's Murphy Institute of Political Economy. In 2004–05, he is a fellow of the Carnegie Council on Ethics and International Affairs.

Véronique Zanetti is Professor for Ethics and Political Philosophy at the University of Bielefeld, Germany. She has published several articles on the ethics of international relations, in French, German and English. Other publications include: a monograph on Kant's concept of natural teleology (Ousia 1994), a commentary on Kant's philosophy of nature and aesthetics (with Manfred Frank, in Volume 3 of *Kants Gesammelte Schriften*, Bibliothek Deutscher Klassiker 1996) and with Steffen Wesche (eds.) *Dworkin: a Debate*, (Ousia 2000).

References

Abdullah, H., 1995, Wifeism and activism: The Nigerian women's movement, in: *The Challenge of Local Feminisms: Women's Movements in Global Perspective*, A. Basu, ed., Westview Press, Boulder CO, pp. 209–225.

Adams, M., 2001, Causation and responsibility in tort and affirmative action, *Texas Law Review* **79**(3):643–702.

Adebayo, S., 2002, N-Delta women give Shell 10-day ultimatum on demands, (November 20, 2002), www.vanguardngr.com.

Agamben, G., 1998, *Homo Sacer: Sovereign Power and Bare Life*, Stanford University Press, Stanford.

Ahmad, I., 1965, *Sovereignty Islamic and Modern: Conception of Sovereignty in Islam*, The Allies Book Corporation, Karachi.

Ahmed, L., 1982, Western ethnocentrism and perceptions of the harem, *Feminist Studies* **8**:521–534.

Aiken, W., and LaFolette, H., eds., 1996, *World Hunger and Morality*, Prentice Hall, Upper Saddle River NJ.

Alcoff, L. M., 1992, The problem of speaking for others, *Cultural Critique* **20**:5–32.

Alesina, A., and Dollar, D., 2000, Who gives foreign aid to whom and why?, *Journal of Economic Growth* **5**:33–64, also available at http://papers.nber.org/papers/w6612.

Alston, P., 1989, On the purposes of general comments and reporting by states parties: General comment, UN doc E/C.12/1989/CRP.2/Add.1.

Alston, P., 1992, The Commission on Human Rights, in: *The United Nations and Human Rights: A Critical Appraisal*, P. Alston, ed., Oxford University Press, Oxford, pp. 197–200.

Amdur, R., 1977, Rawls's theory of justice: Domestic and international perspectives, *World Politics* **29**(3):438–461.

Amnesty International, 2003, *Letter to Louise Frechette raising concerns on UN Global Compact*, April 7, 2003, http://web.amnesty.org/pages/ec_briefings_global_7April03.

Amos, V., and Parmar, P., 1984, Challenging imperial feminism, *Feminist Review* **17**:3–19.

Anderson, B., 2000, *Doing the Dirty Work? The Global Politics of Domestic Labour*, Zed Press, London.

Anderson, E. S., 1999, What is the point of equality?, *Ethics* **109**:287–337.

Anderson, S., and Cavanagh, J., 2000, *Report on the Top 200 Corporations*, Institute for Policy Studies, Washington DC.

An-Na'im, A. A., 1990a, *Toward an Islamic Reformation: Civil Liberties, Human Rights and International Law*, Syracuse University Press, Syracuse NY.

An-Na'im, A. A., 1990b, Human rights in the Muslim world: Socio-political conditions and scriptural imperatives, *Harvard Human Rights Journal* **3**:13–52.

An-Na'im, A. A., 1990c, Problems of universal cultural legitimacy for human rights, in: An-Na'im and Deng 1990, pp. 331–368.

An-Na'im, A. A., 1995, Toward an Islamic hermeneutics, in: An-Na'im, Gort, Jansen and Vroom 1995, pp. 229–242.

An-Na'im, A. A., and Deng, F. M., eds., 1990, *Human Rights in Africa. Cross-Cultural Perspectives*, The Brookings Institution, Washington DC.

An-Na'im, A. A., Gort, J. D., Jansen, H., and Vroom, H. M., eds., 1995, *Human Rights and Religious Values: An uneasy relationship?*, Editions Rodopi, Amsterdam.

Annan, K., 1999, *Address to the United States Chamber of Commerce*, June 8, 1999, Global Policy Forum, www.globalpolicy.org/socecon/tncs/annan1.htm.

Annan, K., 2002, *Address to International Business Leaders*, April 2002, Global Compact, www.unglobalcompact.org/Portal/Default.asp.

Apffel-Marglin, F., and Simon, S. L., 1994, Feminist orientalism and development, in: *Feminist Perspectives on Sustainable Development*, W. Harcourt, ed., Zed Press, London, pp. 26–45.

Appiah, K. A., 1996, Cosmopolitan Patriotism, in: Nussbaum 1996, pp. 21–29.

Arendt, H., 1970, *On Violence*, Harcourt Brace, New York.

Arendt, H., 1992, *Eichmann in Jerusalem. A Report on the Banality of Evil* [1963], Penguin Books, Harmondsworth.

Aristotle, 1996, *The Politics and the Constitution of Athens* [350 BCE], Cambridge University Press, Cambridge.

Arneson, R., 1989, Equality and equal opportunity for welfare, *Philosophical Studies* **56**:159–194.

Arrighi, G., Hopkins, T. H., and Wallerstein, I., 1989, *Antisystemic Movements*, Verso, London.

Austin, J. L., 1962, *How to Do Things with Words*, Oxford University Press, Oxford.

Bangkok Declaration, 1993, *Human Rights Law Journal* **14**(9–10):370–371.

Banjul Charter, 1984, The African Charter on Human and Peoples' Rights, in: *Human Rights and Development in Africa*, C. E. Welch Jr. and R. I. Meltzer, eds., State University of New York Press, Albany NY, pp. 152–176.

Barber, B., 1992, Jihad vs. MacWorld, *The Atlantic Monthly*, March, 53–63.

Barry, B., 1982, Humanity and justice in global perspective, in: *Ethics, Economics, and the Law*, R. Pennock and J. Chapman, eds., New York University Press, New York, pp. 219–252.

Barry, B., 1983, Self-government revisited, in: *The Nature of Political Theory*, D. Miller and L. Siedentop, eds., Clarendon Press, Oxford.

Barry, B., 1989, *Theories of Justice*, University of California Press, Berkeley.

Barry, B., and Goodin, R., eds., 1992, *Free Movement. Ethical Issues in the Transnational Migration of People and of Money*, Pennsylvania State University Press, Pennsylvania.

Barry, C., 2001, The ethical assessment of technological change: An overview of the issues, *J. Human Development* **2**(2):167–189.

Barry, C., 2003, Global justice: Aims, arrangements, and responsibilities, in: *Can Institutions Have Responsibilities? Collective Moral Agency and International Relations*, T. Erskine, ed., Palgrave, Basingstoke, pp. 218–237.

Barry, C., 2005, Applying the contribution principle, in: Kuper 2005.

Barry, C., and Raworth, K., 2002, Access to medicines and the rhetoric of responsibility, *Ethics & International Affairs* **16**(2):57–70.

Basu, A., ed., 1995, *The Challenge of Local Feminisms: Women's Movements in Global Perspective*, Westview Press, Boulder CO.

Bauer, J. R., and Bell, D. A., eds., 1999, *The East Asian Challenge for Human Rights*, Cambridge University Press, Cambridge.

Bauman, Z., 1989, *Modernity and the Holocaust*, Polity Press, Cambridge.

Bearup, G., 2004, Afghan schoolgirls poisoned, *The Guardian Weekly* May 6–12, p. 4.

Beitz, C. R., 1979, *Political Theory and International Relations*, Princeton University Press, Princeton.

Beitz, C. R., 1981a, Democracy in developing societies, in: *Boundaries: National Autonomy and Its Limits*, P. G. Brown and H. Shue, eds., Rowman and Allanhead, Totowa NJ.

Beitz, C. R., 1981b, Economic rights and distributive justice in developing societies, *World Politics* **33**(3):321–46.

Beitz, C. R., 1983, Cosmopolitan ideals and national sentiment, *Journal of Philosophy* **80**:591–600.

Beitz, C. R., 1999, *Political Theory and International Relations*, second edition, Princeton University Press, Princeton.

Beitz, C. R., 2001a, Human rights as a common concern, *American Political Science Review* **95**(2):269–281.

Beitz, C. R., 2001b, Does global inequality matter?, in: Pogge 2001a, pp. 106–122.

Beitz, C. R., 2004, Human rights and the law of peoples, in: *The Ethics of Assistance: Morality and the Distant Needy*, D. K. Chatterjee, ed., Cambridge University Press, Cambridge, pp. 193–214.

Beitz, C. R., et al., eds., 1985, *International Ethics*, Princeton University Press, Princeton.

Bell, D. A., 1996, The East Asian challenge to human rights: Reflections on an East West dialogue, *Human Rights Quarterly* **18**:641–667.

Bell, D. A., and de-Shalit, A., 2002, *Forms of Justice. Critical Perspectives on David Miller's Political Philosophy*, Rowman and Littlefield, Lanham MD.

Benhabib, S., 2002, *The Claims of Culture: Equality and Diversity in the Global Era*, Princeton University Press, Princeton and Oxford.

Bennett, J., 1995, *The Act Itself*, Oxford University Press, New York.

Bentham, J., 1987, Anarchical fallacies. Being an examination of the Declaration of Rights issued during the French Revolution, in: *Nonsense upon Stilts. Bentham, Burke and Marx on the Rights of Man*, J. Waldron, ed., Methuen, London and New York, pp. 46–77.

Berlin, I., 1969, *Four Essays on Liberty*, Oxford University Press, Oxford.

Besson, S., 2003, Human rights, institutional duties and cosmopolitan responsibilities, *Oxford Journal of Legal Studies* **23**:507–523.

Bhalla, S. S., 2002, *Imagine There's No Country: Poverty, Inequality, and Growth in the Era of Globalization*, Institute for International Economics, Washington DC.

Bielefeld, H., 1998, *Philosophie der Menschenrechte. Grundlagen eines weltweiten Freiheitsethos*, Primus-Verlag, Darmstadt.

Bird, G., 1995, *IMF Lending to Developing Countries: Issues and Policies*, Routledge, London.

Bird, G., 1996, The IMF and developing countries: A review of the evidence and policy options, *International Organization* **50**(3):477–512.

Bittner, R., 2001, Morality and world hunger, in: Pogge 2001a, pp. 24–31.

Blickle, P., Hügelin, T. O., and Wyduckel, D., eds., 2002, *Subsidiarität als rechtliches und politisches Ordnungsprinzip in Kirche, Staat und Gesellschaft: Genese, Geltungsgrundlagen und Perspektiven an der Schwelle des dritten Jahrtausends*, Duncker & Humblot, Berlin.

Bobbio, N., 1999, *Teoria generale della politica*, M. Bovero, ed., Einaudi, Torino.

Boserup, E., 1970, *Women's Role in Economic Development*, St. Martin's Press, New York.

Bossert, W., 1995, Redistribution mechanism based on individual characteristics, *Mathematical Social Sciences* **29**:1–17.

Bossert, W., and Fleurbaey, M., 1996, Redistribution and compensation, *Social Choice and Welfare* **13**:343–355.

Boutros-Ghali, B., 2000, An agenda for democratization, reprinted in: *Global Democracy: Key Debates*, B. Holden, ed., Routledge, London and New York, pp. 110–113.

Bowles, S., and Gintis, H., 2000, Reciprocity, self-interest and the welfare state, *Nordic Journal of Political Economy* **26**: 33–54.

Brandt, R., 1995, Vom Weltbürgerrecht, in: Höffe 1995a, pp. 133–148.

Briggs, C. L., and Mantini-Briggs, C., 2000, "Bad mothers" and the threat to civil society: Race, cultural reasoning and the institutionalization of social inequality in a Venezuelan infanticide trial, *Law and Social Inquiry* **25**:299–302.

Brock, D., 1991, Defending moral options, *Philosophy and Phenomenological Research* **51**(4):909–913.

Brown, D. L., 1991, Christian missionaries, Western feminists, and the Kikuyu clitoridectomy controversy, in: *The Politics of Culture*, B. Williams, ed., Smithsonian Institution Press, Washington and London, pp. 243–272.

Brunkhorst, H., 1999a, Menschenrechte und Souveränität — ein Dilemma?, in: *Recht auf Menschenrechte. Menschenrechte, Demokratie und internationale Politik*, H. Brunkhorst, W. Köhler and M. Lutz-Bachmann, eds., Suhrkamp, Frankfurt, pp. 157–175.

Brunkhorst, H., 1999b, Heterarchie und Demokratie, in: *Das Recht der Republik*, H. Brunkhorst and P. Niesen, eds., Suhrkamp, Frankfurt, pp. 373–385.

Brunkhorst, H., and Kettner, M., eds., 2000, *Globalisierung und Demokratie*, Suhrkamp, Frankfurt.

Buchanan A., 2000, Rawls's Law of Peoples: Rules for a vanished Westphalian world, *Ethics* **110**:697–721.

Buergenthal, T., 1979, Domestic jurisdiction, intervention, and human rights: The international perspective, in: *Human Rights and U.S. Foreign Policy*, P. G. Brown and D. MacLean, eds., Lexington Books, Lexington, MA, pp. 111–120.

Bull, H., 1977, *The Anarchical Society*, Columbia University Press, New York.

Bunch, C., 1987, *Passionate Politics: Feminist Theory in Action*, St. Martin's Press, New York.

Burris, B., 1973, The Fourth World Manifesto, in: *Radical Feminism*, A. Koedt, E. Levine and A. Rapone, eds., Quadrangle, New York, pp. 322–357.

Bush, G. W., 2002, The State of the Union: President Bush's State of the Union Address to Congress and the Nation, *New York Times*, Jan 20, sec. A, 22, col. 1.

Bush, L., 2002, Mrs. Bush Discusses Status of Afghan Women at U.N.: Remarks by Mrs Laura Bush, March 8, www.whitehouse.gov/news/releases/2002/03/ 20020308-2.html.

Calhoun, C., 1988, Justice, care, gender bias, *Journal of Philosophy* **85**(9).

Canetti, E., 1980, *Masse und Macht*, Fischer, Frankfurt.

Cappelen, A., and Tungodden, B., 2002a, Fiscal equalization with a balanced budget, discussion paper 24/02, Norwegian School of Economics and Business Administration.

Cappelen, A., and Tungodden, B., 2002b, Responsibility and reward, *Finanzarchiv* **59**:120–140.

Cappelen, A., and Tungodden, B., 2003, Reward and responsibility: How should we be affected when others change their effort?, *Politics, Philosophy and Economics* **2**:191–211.

Carby, H., 1982, White women listen, in: *The Empire Strikes Back: Race and Racism in 70s Britain*, Centre for Contemporary Cultural Studies, ed., Hutchinson, London, pp. 213–235.

Carens, J., 1992, Migration and morality: A liberal egalitarian perspective, in: Barry and Goodin 1992, pp. 25–47.

Carroll, J., 2003, Warring with God, *Boston Globe*, Op. Ed., October 21.

Cavallar, G., 2001, Kantian perspectives on democratic peace: Alternatives to Doyle, *Review of International Studies* **27**:229–248.

Cavallero, E., 2002, *Sovereignty and Global Justice*, doctoral dissertation, Yale University Philosophy Department.

Chan, J., 1999, A Confucian perspective on human rights for contemporary China, in: Bauer and Bell 1999, pp. 212–237.

Chan, J., 2000, Thick and thin accounts of human rights, in: Jacobsen and Bruun 2000, pp. 59–74.

Chatterjee, D. K., ed., 2003, *Moral Distance*, special issue of *The Monist* **86**(3).

Chen, M., 1995, A matter of survival: Women's right to employment in India and Bangladesh, in: Nussbaum and Glover 1995, pp. 37–57.

Chen, S., and Ravallion, M., 2001, How did the world's poorest fare in the 1990s?, *Review of Income and Wealth* **47**:283–300.

Chen, S., and Ravallion, M., 2004, How have the world's poorest fared since the early 1980s?, World Bank Policy Research Working Paper 3341, http://econ.worldbank.org/files/36297_wps3341.pdf.

Coase, R., 1960, The problem of social cost, *J. Law and Economics* **3**(1):1–44.

Code, L., 1991, Credibility: A double standard, in: *What Can She Know? Feminist Theory and the Construction of Knowledge*, Cornell University Press, Ithaca NY, pp. 222–264.

Cohen, G. A., 1989, On the currency of egalitarian justice, *Ethics* **99**:906–944.

Cohen, G. A., 1995, The Pareto-argument for inequality, *Social Philosophy and Policy* **12**:160–185.

Cohen, J., forthcoming, Taking people as they are, in *Philosophy and Public Affairs*.

Coleman, J. L., and Ripstein, A., 1995, Mischief and misfortune, *McGill Law J.* **41**(1):91–130.

Commission on Global Governance, 1995, *Our Global Neighbourhood*, Oxford University Press, Oxford.

Confucius., 1997, *Analects*, trans. and notes S. Leys, Norton, New York.

Congressional Research Service, 2002, *Conventional Arms Transfers to Developing Nations 1994–2001*, www.fas.org/asmp/resources/govern/crs-rl31529.pdf.

Connell, R. W., 1998, Masculinities and globalization, *Men and Masculinities* **1**(1):3–23.

Cornia, G. A., Jolly, R., and Stewart, F., eds., 1987. *Adjustment with a Human Face: Protecting the Vulnerable and Promoting Growth*, Oxford University Press, Oxford.

Correa, C., 2000, *Intellectual Property Rights, the WTO and Developing Countries: The TRIPs Agreement and Policy Options*, Zed Books, London.

Cranor, C. F., 1990, Some moral issues in risk assessment, *Ethics* **101**(1):123–143.

Cranor, C. F., 1993, *Regulating Toxic Substances: A Philosophy of Science and the Law*, Oxford University Press, New York.

Crocker, D. A., and Linden, T., eds., 1998, *Ethics of Consumption: The Good Life, Justice, and Global Stewardship*, Rowman and Littlefield, Lanham MD.

Daly, M., 1978, *Gyn/Ecology: the Metaethics of Radical Feminism*, Beacon Press, Boston.

Danielson, P., 1973, Theories, intuition, and the problem of world-wide distributive justice, *Philosophy and the Social Sciences* **3**:331–340.

Dasgupta, P., 1993, *An Inquiry into Well-Being and Destitution*, Oxford University Press, Oxford.

Davis, M. C., ed., 1995a *Human Rights and Chinese Values: Legal, Philosophical, and Political Perspectives*, Oxford University Press, Oxford and Hong Kong.

Davis, M. C., 1995b, Chinese perspectives on human rights, in: Davis 1995a, pp. 3–24.

Davis, M. C., 1998, Constitutionalism and political culture: the debate over human rights and Asian values, *Harvard Human Rights Journal* **11**:109–147.

Deaton, A., 2003, How to monitor poverty for the Millennium Development Goals, *Journal of Human Development* **4**:353–378.

Declaration of Human Rights in Islam, 1990, Cairo, www.humanrights.harvard.edu/documents/regionaldocs/cairo_dec.htm.

de Greiff, P., and Cronin, C., eds., 2002, *Global Justice and Transnational Politics*, MIT Press, Cambridge MA.

Demarco, J. P., 1981, International application of the theory of justice, *Pacific Philosophical Quarterly* **62**:393–402.

Derber, C., 1998, *Corporation Nation. How Corporations Are Taking Over Our Lives and What We Can Do About It*, St. Martin's Griffin, New York.

Diamond, J., 1999, *Guns, Germs, and Steel: The Fates of Human Societies*, Norton, New York.

Dixon-Mueller, R., 1991, Women in agriculture: Counting the labor force in developing countries, in: *Beyond Methodology: Feminist Scholarship as Lived Research*, M. M. Fonow and J. A. Cook, eds., Indiana University Press, Bloomington IN.

Donagan, A., 1977, *The Theory of Morality*, Chicago University Press, Chicago.

Donnelly, J., 1989, *Universal Human Rights in Theory & Practice*, Cornell University Press, Ithaca NY.

Donnelly, J., 1998, *International Human Rights*, second edition, Westview Press, Boulder CO.

Doyle, M., 1983, Kant, liberal legacies, and foreign affairs, *Philosophy and Public Affairs* **12**:205–235, 322–353.

Dworkin, R., 1981, What is equality? Part 2: Equality of resources, *Philosophy and Public Affairs* **10**:283–345.

Dworkin, R., 1986, *Law's Empire*, Harvard University Press, Cambridge MA.

Dworkin, R., 1991, Justice for Clarence Thomas, *New York Review of Books* **38**(18), www.nybooks.com/articles/article-preview?article_id=3100.

Dworkin, R., 2000, *Sovereign Virtue. The Theory and Practice of Equality*, Harvard University Press, Cambridge MA.

ECOSOC (UN Economic and Social Council), 1970, *Resolution 1503 (XLVIII): Procedure for Dealing with Communications Relating to Violations of Human Rights and Fundamental Freedoms*, www.staff.city.ac.uk/p.willetts/HR-DOCS/ERES1503.HTM.

Eide, A., 1995, Economic, social and cultural rights as human rights, in: *Economic, Social and Cultural Rights. A Textbook*, A. Eide, C. Krause and A. Rosas, eds., Kluwer, Dordrecht, Boston and London, pp. 21–40.

Elster, J., 1989, *The Cement of Society*, Cambridge University Press, Cambridge.

Elster, J., 1998, Deliberation and constitution making, in: *Deliberative Democracy*, J. Elster, ed., Cambridge University Press, Cambridge, pp. 97–123.

Epstein, R., 1980, *A Theory of Strict Liability: Toward a Reformulation of Tort Law*, National Book Network, San Francisco.

Evans, D. T., 1995, (Homo)sexual citizenship: A queer kind of justice, in: *A Simple Matter of Justice?*, A. R. Wilson, ed., Cassell, London and New York, pp. 110–145.

Ewig, C., 1999, The strengths and limits of the NGO women's movement model: Shaping Nicaragua's democratic institutions, *Latin American Research Review* **34**(3):75–102.

Eze, E. C., 1997, The color of reason: The idea of "race" in Kant's anthropology, in: *Postcolonial African Philosophy. A Critical Reader*, E. C. Eze, ed., Blackwell, Oxford, pp. 103–140.

Fajnzylber. F., Lederman, D., and Loayza, N., 1998, *What causes violent crime?*, World Bank, Office of the Chief Economist, Latin America and the Caribbean Region, Washington DC.

Falk, R., 1983, *The End of World Order*, Holmes and Meier, New York.

FAO (Food and Agriculture Organization of the United Nations), 1999, *The State of Food Insecurity in the World 1999*, www.fao.org/news/1999/img/sofi99-e.pdf.

Feinberg, J., 1970, The nature and value of rights, *Journal of Value Inquiry* **4**:243–257, reprinted in: *Rights, Justice, and the Bounds of Liberty*, Princeton University Press, Princeton 1980, pp. 130–142.

Feinberg, J., 1973, *Social Philosophy*, Prentice Hall, Englewood Cliffs, NJ.

Feinberg, J., 1984, *The Moral Limits of the Criminal Law: vol. 1, Harm to Others*, Oxford University Press, Oxford.

Feldman, H. L., 1995, Science and uncertainty in mass exposure litigation, *Texas Law Review* 74(1):1–48.

Finnis, J., 1980, *Natural Law and Natural Rights*, Clarendon Law Series, Clarendon Press, Oxford.

Fisch, J., 1984, *Die europäische Expansion und das Völkerrecht*, Reclam, Stuttgart.

Fischer-Lescano, A., 2002, Globalverfassung: Verfassung der Weltgesellschaft, *Archiv für Rechts- und Sozialphilosophie* 88(3):349–378.

Flax, J., 1995, Race/gender and the ethics of difference: A Reply to Okin's "Gender Inequality and Cultural Differences," *Political Theory* 23:500–510.

Fleurbaey, M., 1994, On fair compensation, *Theory and Decision* 36:277–307.

Fleurbaey, M., 1995a, Three solutions for the compensation problem, *Journal of Economic Theory* 6:96–106.

Fleurbaey, M., 1995b, Equality and responsibility, *European Economic Review* 39:683–689.

Fleurbaey, M., 1995c, Equal opportunity or equal social outcome, *Economics and Philosophy* 11:25–55.

Fleurbaey, M., and Maniquet, F., 1999, Cooperative production with unequal skills: The solidarity approach to compensation, *Social Choice and Welfare* 16:569–583.

Follesdal, A., 1991, *The Significance of State Borders for International Distributive Justice*, Harvard University, University Microfilms UMI No. 9211679.

Follesdal, A., 1997, Do welfare obligations end at the boundaries of the nation state?, in: *Restructuring the Welfare State*, P. Koslowski and A. Follesdal, eds., Springer, Berlin, pp. 145–163.

Follesdal, A., 1998, Subsidiarity, *J. of Political Philosophy* 6:231–259.

Follesdal, A., 1999, Global ethics, culture and development, *Forum for Development Studies* 1:5–21.

Follesdal, A., 2000a, Justice: global and European, *Global Society* 14:591–609.

Follesdal, A., 2000b, Global justice as impartiality: Whither claims to equal shares?, in: *International Justice*, T. Coates, ed., Ashgate, Aldershot, pp. 150–166.

Follesdal, A., 2001, Federal inequality among equals: A contractualist defense, in: Pogge 2001a, pp. 242–261.

Follesdal, A., Micheletti, M., and Stolle, D., eds., 2003, *Politics, Products and Markets. Exploring Political Consumerism Past and Present*, Transaction Press, New Brucswick, NJ.

Foot, P., 1994, Killing and letting die, in: *Killing and Letting Die*, 2nd ed., A. Norcross and B. Steinbock, eds., Fordham University Press, New York, pp. 280–289.

Forst, R., 1999a, The basic right to justification: Toward a constructivist conception of human rights, trans. J. M. Caver, *Constellations* 6(1):35–60.

Forst, R., 1999b, Die Rechtfertigung der Gerechtigkeit. Rawls' Politischer Liberalismus und Habermas' Diskurstheorie in der Diskussion, in: *Das Recht der Republik*, H. Brunkhorst and P. Niesen, eds., Suhrkamp, Frankfurt, pp. 105–168.

Forst, R., 1999c, Praktische Vernunft und rechtfertigende Gründe. Zur Begründung der Moral, in: *Motive, Gründe, Zwecke*, S. Gosepath, ed., Fischer, Frankfurt, pp. 168–205.

Forst, R., 2001, Towards a critical theory of transnational justice, in: Pogge 2001a, pp. 169–187.

Forst, R., 2002, *Contexts of Justice: Political Philosophy beyond Liberalism and Communitarianism*, California University Press, Berkeley and Los Angeles.

Foucault, M., 1990, *The History of Sexuality. Volume I: An Introduction*, Vintage Books, New York.

Foucault, M., 2003, *The Essential Foucault. Selections from The Essential Works of Foucault 1954–1984*, P. Rabinow and N. Rose, eds., New Press, New York.

Frankfurt, H., 1987, Equality as a moral ideal, *Ethics* **98**:21–43.

Fraser, N., 1997, From redistribution to recognition? Dilemmas of justice in a "postsocialist" age, in: *Justice Interruptus: Critical Reflections on the "Postsocialist" Condition*, Routledge, New York and London, pp. 11–39.

Frith, M., 2003, Global trade keeps a billion children in poverty, says UNICEF, *The Independent UK*, October 22.

Fuss, D., 1989, *Essentially Speaking: Feminism, Nature and Difference*, Routledge, New York.

Gabriëls, R., and Kreide, R., 2002, Demokratisches Weltbürgerrecht, in: Schomberg and Niesen 2002, pp. 337–381.

Gangjian, D., and Song G., 1995, Relating human rights to Chinese culture: The four paths of the Confucian Analects and the four principles of a new theory of benevolence, in: Davis 1995a, pp. 35–56.

Gerhardt, V., 1995, *Immanuel Kants Entwurf 'Zum ewigen Frieden'*, Wissenschaftliche Buchgesellschaft, Darmstadt.

Gewirth, A., 1978, *Reason and Morality*, Chicago University Press, Chicago.

Gewirth, A., 1982, *Human Rights: Essays on Justification and Application*, Chicago University Press, Chicago.

Gewirth, A., 1996, *The Community of Rights*, Chicago University Press, Chicago.

GFHR (Global Forum for Health Research), 2000, *10/90 Report on Health Research 2000*, Global Forum for Health Research, Geneva, also available at http://mim.nih.gov/english/news/globalforum.html.

GFHR, 2004, *10/90 Report on Health Research 2003–2004*, Global Forum for Health Research, Geneva. Also available at www.globalforumhealth.org/pages/index.asp.

Gladwell, M., 2002, *The Tipping Point*, Back Bay Books, Boston.

Glagow, M., ed., 1984, *Gesellschaftssteuerung zwischen Korporatismus und Subsidiarität*, AJZ, Bielefeld.

Gomez, M., 1995, Social economic rights and human rights commissions, *Human Rights Quarterly* **17**:155–169.

Goodin, R. E., 1979, The development-rights tradeoff: Some unwarranted economic and political assumptions, *Universal Human Rights* [now *Human Rights Quarterly*] **1**:31–42.

Goodin, R. E., 1982, *Political Theory & Public Policy*, Princeton University Press, Princeton.

Goodin, R. E., 1985, *Protecting the Vulnerable: A Re-Analysis of our Social Responsibilities*, University of Chicago Press, Chicago.

Goodin, R. E., 1988, What is so special about our fellow countrymen?, *Ethics* **98**:663–686.

Goodin, R. E., 1995, Political ideals and political practice, *British J. Political Science* **25**(1):37–56.

Gosepath, S., 1998, Zu Begründungen sozialer Menschenrechte, in: Gosepath and Lohmann 1998, pp. 146–187.

Gosepath, S., 2001, Über den Zusammenhang von Gerechtigkeit und Gleichheit, in: *Die Öffentlichkeit der Vernunft und die Vernunft der Öffentlichkeit. Festschrift für Jürgen Habermas*, L. Wingert and K. Günther, eds., Suhrkamp, Frankfurt, pp. 403–433.

Gosepath, S., 2004, *Gleiche Gerechtigkeit. Grundlagen eines liberalen Egalitarismus*, Suhrkamp, Frankfurt.

Gosepath, S., and Lohmann, G., eds., 1998, *Philosophie der Menschenrechte*, Suhrkamp, Frankfurt.

Gouges, O. de, 1995, *Mensch und Bürgerin, 'Die Rechte der Frau' (1791)*, H. Schröder, ed., Ein-Fach-Verlag, Aachen.

Green, M., 2002, Institutional responsibility for global problems, *Philosophical Topics* 30(2):79–95.

Greenhouse, L., 2003, The supreme court: advertising; Nike free speech case is unexpectedly returned to California, *New York Times*, June 27.

Grewal, I., and Kaplan, C., 1994, *Scattered Hegemonies: Postmodernity and Transnational Feminist Practices*, University of Minnesota Press, Minneapolis and London.

Griffin, K., 1978, *International Inequality and National Poverty*, Holmes Meier, London.

Grodzins, M., 1957, Metropolitan segregation, *Scientific American* 197:33–41.

Habermas, J., 1984, *The Theory of Communicative Action, Volume One*, Beacon Press, Boston.

Habermas, J., 1987, *The Theory of Communicative Action, Volume Two*, Beacon Press, Boston.

Habermas, J., 1995, Kants Idee des Ewigen Friedens — aus dem historischen Abstand von 200 Jahren, *Kritische Justiz* 28(3):293–319.

Habermas, J., 1996a, *Between Facts and Norms. Contributions to a Discourse Theory of Law and Democracy*, Polity Press, Cambridge, and MIT Press, Cambridge MA.

Habermas, J., 1996b, Reply to symposium participants, *Cardozo Law Review* 17(4–5):1477–1559.

Habermas, J., 1998, *Die postnationale Konstellation*, Suhrkamp, Frankfurt.

Habermas, J., 2002, On legitimation through human rights, in: de Greiff and Cronin 2002, pp. 197–215.

Hampshire, S., 1999, *Justice is Conflict*, Duckworth, London.

Hardin, R., 1996, Institutional morality, in: *Theories of Institutional Design*, R. E. Goodin, ed., Cambridge University Press, Cambridge, pp. 126–153.

Hardt, M., and Negri, A., 2000, *Empire*, Harvard University Press, Cambridge MA.

Hare, R. M., 1981, *Moral Thinking: Its Levels, Method, and Point*, Oxford University Press, Oxford.

Harrison, L. E., and Huntington, S. P., eds., 2001, *Culture Matters: How Values Shape Human Progress*, Basic Books, New York.

Hart, H. L. A., 1955, Are there any natural rights?, *Philosophical Review* 64:175–191.

Hart, H. L. A., 1973, Rawls on liberty and its priority, *University of Chicago Law Review* 40:534–555.

Hart, H. L. A., and Honoré, T., 1985, *Causation in the Law*, 2nd ed., Oxford University Press, Oxford.

Hartman, L. P., Arnold, D. G., and Wokutch, R. E., eds., 2003, *Rising Above Sweatshops. Innovative Approaches to Global Labor Challenges*, Praeger Publishers, Westport, CT and London.

Hay, S., ed., 1988, *Sources of Indian Tradition*. 2nd ed., Columbia University Press, New York.

Hegel, G. F. W., 1821, *Grundlinien der Philosophie des Rechts*, English translation, *Philosophy of Right*, Clarendon Press, Oxford 1965.

Heinze, R. G., ed., 1985, *Neue Subsidiarität. Leitidee für eine künftige Sozialpolitik?*, Westdeutscher Verlag, Opladen.

Held, D., 1995, *Democracy and the Global Order. From the Modern State to Cosmopolitan Governance*, Polity Press, Cambridge.

Held, D., McGrew, A., Goldblatt, D., and Perraton, J., 1999, *Global Transformations. Politics, Economics and Culture*, Stanford University Press, Stanford.

Herr, R., 2004, A Third World feminist defense of multiculturalism, *Social Theory and Practice* 30(1):73–103.

Herzog, R., 1998, Subsidiaritätsprinzip, in: *Historisches Wörterbuch der Philosophie* 10, Schwabe, Basel, pp. 482–486.

Hill, R. A., 2002, Compensatory justice: Over time and between groups, *J. of Political Philosophy* **10**(4):392–415.

Hinsch, W., 2002, *Gerechtfertigte Ungleichheiten. Grundsätze sozialer Gerechtigkeit*, De Gruyter, Berlin.

Hobbes, T., 1996, *Leviathan* [1651], R. Tuck, ed., Cambridge University Press, Cambridge.

Höffe, O., ed., 1995a, *Immanuel Kant. Zum ewigen Frieden*, Akademie Verlag, Berlin.

Höffe, O., 1995b, Ausblick: Die Vereinten Nationen im Lichte Kants, in: Höffe 1995a, pp. 245–272.

Höffe, O., 1996, *Vernunft und Recht*, Suhrkamp, Frankfurt.

Höffe, O., 1997, Subsidiarität als Gesellschafts- und Staatsprinzip, *Schweizerische Zeitschrift für Politische Wissenschaft* **3**:259–290.

Höffe, O., 1999, *Demokratie im Zeitalter der Globalisierung*, Beck Verlag, Munich.

Hoffmann, S., 1981, *Duties Beyond Borders*, Syracuse University Press, Syracuse NY.

Hoffmann, S., 1995, Dreams of a just world, *The New York Review of Books*, November 2, 52–56.

Hohfeld, W. N., 1923, *Fundamental Legal Conceptions as Applied in Judicial Reasoning*, W. W. Cook ed., Yale University Press, New Haven.

Homann K., and Kirchner, C., 1995, Das Subsidiaritätsprinzip in der Katholischen Soziallehre und in der Ökonomik, in: *Europa zwischen Ordnungswettbewerb und Harmonisierung. Europäische Ordnungspolitik im Zeichen der Subsidiarität*, L. Gerken, ed., Springer, Berlin and Heidelberg, pp. 45–69.

Honoré, T., 1999, *Responsibility and Fault*, Hart, Oxford.

Howard, R. E., 1990, Group versus individual identity in the African debate on human rights, in: An-Na'im and Deng 1990, pp. 159–184.

Huntington, S. P., 1996, *The Clash of Civilizations and the Remaking of World Order*, Simon and Shuster, New York.

ILO (International Labor Organization), 2002, *A Future Without Child Labor*, International Labor Office, Geneva, also available at www.ilo.org/public/english/standards/decl/publ/reports/report3.htm.

Imam, A., and Medar-Gould, S., 2003, Please stop the international Lawal protest letter campaigns, May 1.

International Convention on the Suppression and Punishment of the Crime of Apartheid, 1973, www.unhchr.ch/html/menu3/b/11.htm.

International Covenant on Economic, Social and Cultural Rights, 1966, available at www.unhchr.ch/html/menu3/b/a_cescr.htm.

Jacobsen, M., and Bruun, O., eds., 2000, *Differentiated Identities: The Human Rights and Asian Values Debate*, Rowman and Littlefield, Lanham MD.

Jaggar, A. M., 1983, *Feminist Politics and Human Nature*, Rowman and Littlefield, Totowa, NJ.

Jaggar, A. M., 1998, Globalizing feminist ethics, *Hypatia* **13**(2):7–31. Reprinted in: *Decentering the Center: Philosophy for a Multicultural, Postcolonial, and Feminist World*, U. Narayan and S. Harding, eds., Indiana University Press, Bloomington IN, 2000.

Jaggar, A. M., 1999, Multicultural democracy, *J. of Political Philosophy* **7**(3):308–329.

Jaggar, A. M., 2001, Is globalization good for women?, *Comparative Literature* **53**(4):298–314.

Jaggar, A. M., 2002a, A feminist critique of the alleged Southern debt, *Hypatia* **17**(4):119–142.

Jaggar, A. M., 2002b, Vulnerable women and neo-liberal globalization: Debt burdens undermine women's health in the global south, *Theoretical Medicine and Bioethics* **23**(6):425–440.

Jaggar, A. M., 2002c, Challenging women's global inequalities: Some priorities for Western philosophers, *Philosophical Topics* **30**(2):229–253.

Jaggar, A. M., 2004, Western feminism and global responsibility, in: *Feminist Interventions in Ethics and Politics*, B. S. Andrew, J. Keller and L. H. Schwarzman, eds., Rowman and Littlefield, Lanham MD.

Jaggar, A. M., forthcoming, Reasoning about Well-Being: Capabilities, Procedures and Silenced Voices.

Janis, M. W., 1997, Individuals and the International Court, in: *The International Court of Justice: Its Future Role After Fifty Years*, A. S. Muller, D. Raic and J. Thuranszky, eds., Martinus Nijhoff, The Hague.

Jones, P., 1996, International human rights: Philosophical or political?, in: *National Rights, International Obligations*, S. Caney, D. George and P. Jones, eds., Westview Press, Boulder CO, pp. 183–204.

Juma, C., 1999, Intellectual property rights and globalization. Implications for developing countries, *Science, Technology and Innovation Discussion Paper No. 4*, Harvard Center for International Development, www2.cid.harvard.edu/cidbiotech/dp/discuss4.pdf.

Kabeer, N., 1994, *Reversed Realities: Gender Hierarchies in Development Thought*, Verso, London and New York.

Kagan, S., 1991, Précis of the limits of morality, *Philosophy and Phenomenological Research* **51**(4):897–901.

Kagan, S., 1992, The structure of normative ethics, *Philosophical Perspectives* **6**(1):223–242.

Kamm, F., 1983, Killing and letting die: Methodological and substantive issues, *Pacific Philosophical Quarterly* **64**(4):297–312.

Kang, H.-R., 2004, Transnational women's collectivities as agents of global justice claims, paper read to American Philosophical Association Pacific Division Meeting, Global Justice Mini-Conference, March.

Kant, I., 1784, Idea for a universal history with a cosmopolitan purpose, in: Reiss 1970, pp. 41–53.

Kant, I., 1785, Grundlegung zur Metaphysik der Sitten, in: *Kants Werke. Akademie-Textausgabe Bd. IV*, De Gruyter, Berlin, 1968, pp. 385–464.

Kant, I., 1793, On the common saying: 'This may be true in theory, but it does not apply in practice', in: Reiss 1970, pp. 61–92.

Kant, I., 1795, Perpetual peace: A philosophical sketch, in: Reiss 1970, pp. 93–130.

Kant, I., 1797, *The Metaphysics of Morals*, excerpt, in: Reiss 1970, pp. 131–175.

Kant, I., 1798a, Anthropologie in pragmatischer Hinsicht, in: *Kants Werke. Akademie-Textausgabe Bd. VII*, De Gruyter, Berlin, 1968, pp. 117–333.

Kant, I., 1798b, The contest of faculties, in: Reiss 1970, pp. 176–190.

Kausikan, B., 1993, Asia's different standard, *Foreign Policy* **92**(24):25–48.

Keck, M. E., and Sikkink, K., 1998a, Transnational networks on violence against women, in: Keck and Sikkink 1998b, pp. 165–199.

Keck, M. E., and Sikkink, K., 1998b, *Activists Beyond Borders: Advocacy Networks in International Politics*, Cornell University Press, Ithaca NY.

Kelly, D., 1998, *A Life of One's Own. Individual Rights and the Welfare State*, Cato, Washington DC.

Kempadoo, K., and Doezema, J., 1998, *Global Sex Workers: Rights, Resistance and Redefinition*, Routledge, New York.

Kersting, W., 1996, Weltfriedensordnung und globale Verteilungsgerechtigkeit, in: *Zum ewigen Frieden*, R. Merkel and R. Wittmann, eds., Suhrkamp, Frankfurt, pp. 172–212.

Kersting, W., 1997a, Globale Rechtsordnung oder weltweite Verteilungsgerechtigkeit?, in: Kersting 1997b, pp. 243–315.

Kersting, W., 1997b, *Recht, Gerechtigkeit und demokratische Tugend*, Suhrkamp, Frankfurt.

Kersting, W., 1998, Philosophische Friedenstheorie und internationale Friedensordnung, in: *Politische Philosophie der internationalen Beziehungen*, C. Chwaszcza and W. Kersting, eds., Suhrkamp, Frankfurt, pp. 523–554.

Kersting, W., 2002, *Kritik der Gleichheit. Über die Grenzen der Gerechtigkeit und der Moral*, Velbrück Wissenschaft, Weilerswist.

Killick, T., 1995, *IMF Programmes in Developing Countries: Design and Impact*, Routledge, London.

Klare, M., and Anderson, D., 1996, *A Scourge of Guns*, Arms Sales Monitoring Project, Federation of American Scientists, Washington DC.

Klein, N., 2002, *No Logo*, Picador USA, New York.

Koller, P., 1998, Der Geltungsbereich der Menschenrechte, in: Gosepath and Lohmann 1998, pp. 96–123.

König, S., 1990, *Zur Begründung der Menschenrechte: Hobbes-Locke-Kant*, Verlag Karl Alber, Freiburg.

Kovac, H., and Burall, S., 2001, *Global Accountability Project*, One World Trust and Charter 99, London.

Kramer, M., Simmonds, N., and Steiner, H., eds., 1998, *A Debate about Rights*, Oxford University Press, Oxford.

Krasner, S. D., 1993, Westphalia and all that, in: *Ideas and Foreign Policy: Beliefs, Institutions and Political Change*, J. Goldstein and R. O. Keohane, eds., Cornell University Press, Ithaca NY, pp. 235–264.

Kratochwil, F., 1995, Sovereignty as *Dominium*: Is there a right of humanitarian intervention?, in: *Beyond Westphalia? State Sovereignty and International Intervention*, G. M. Lyons and M. Mastanduno, eds., Johns Hopkins University Press, Baltimore MD, pp. 21–42.

Krebs, A., ed., 2000, *Gleichheit oder Gerechtigkeit, Texte zur neuen Egalitarismuskritik*, Suhrkamp, Frankfurt.

Kreide, R., 2003, Review of: Giorgio Agamben, Homo Sacer. Die souveräne Macht und das nackte Leben, *Politische Vierteljahresschrift* **44**(1):104–106.

Kuper, A., 2000, Rawlsian global justice: Beyond *The Law of Peoples* to a cosmopolitan law of persons, *Political Theory* **28**(5):640–674.

Kuper, A., 2004, *Democracy Beyond Borders: Justice and Representation in Global Institutions*, Oxford University Press, Oxford.

Kuper, A., ed., 2005, *Global Responsibilities: Securing Rights By Defining Obligations*, Routledge, New York.

Kutz, C., 2000, *Complicity: Ethics and Law for a Collective Age*, Cambridge University Press, Cambridge.

Kymlicka, W., 1995, *Multicultural Citizenship: A Liberal Theory of Minority Rights*, Clarendon Press, Oxford, and Oxford University Press, New York.

Kymlicka, W., 2001, *Politics in the Vernacular: Nationalism, Multiculturalism and Citizenship*. Oxford University Press, Oxford.

Laberge, P., 1995, Von der Garantie des ewigen Friedens, in: Höffe 1995a, pp. 149–170.

LaFollette, H., 2003, Book Review of *World Hunger* (sic) *and Human Rights: Cosmopolitan Responsibilities and Reforms* by T. W. Pogge, *Ethics* **113**(4):907–911.

Lam, R., and Wantchekon, L., 1999, Dictatorships as a political Dutch disease, Yale University Economic Growth Center Discussion Paper 795, http://econpapers.hhs.se/paper/wopyalegr/.

Landes, D., 1998, *The Wealth and Poverty of Nations: Why Some Are So Rich and Some So Poor*, Norton, New York.

Lauren, P. G., 1998, *The Evolution of International Human Rights*, University of Pennsylvania Press, Philadelphia.

Le Grand, J., 1991, *Equity and Choice*, Harper Collins, London.

Lecheler, H., 1993, *Das Subsidiaritätsprinzip. Strukturprinzip einer europäischen Union*, Duncker and Humblot, Berlin.

Locke, J., 1960, *Two Treatises of Government*, P. Laslett, ed., Cambridge University Press, Cambridge.

Luhmann, N., 2000, *Die Politik der Gesellschaft*, Suhrkamp, Frankfurt.

Luhmann, N., 2003, *Macht*, Lucius und Lucius, Stuttgart.

Maasland, A., and Van der Gaag, J., 1992, World Bank supported adjustment programs and living conditions, in: *Adjustment Lending Revisited: Policies to Restore Growth*, V. Corbo, S. Fischer and S. Webb, eds., World Bank, Washington DC, pp. 40-63.

MacCormick, N., 1977, Rights in Legislation, in: *Law, Morality and Society: Essays in Honor of H. L. A. Hart*, P. M. S. Hacker and J. Raz, eds., Oxford University Press, Oxford, pp. 189–209.

Machiavelli, N., 1940, *The Prince and the Discourses*, M. Lerner, ed., The Modern Library, New York.

Machiavelli, N., 1961, *Literary Works (with Selections from the Private Correspondence)*, J. R. Hale, ed., Oxford University Press, London and New York.

MacIntyre, A., 1984, *After Virtue*, Notre Dame University Press, Notre Dame.

Mackie, J. L., 1974, *The Cement of the Universe: A Study of Causation*, Clarendon Press, Oxford.

Macpherson, C. B., 1962, *The Political Theory of Possessive Individualism*, Clarendon Press, Oxford.

Mandle, Jon., 2000, Globalization and justice, *Annals of the American Academy* **570**:126–139.

Mark-Ungericht, B., 2002, Organisationale Schließungs- und Öffnungsprozesse — Die Unternehmung und neuere zivilgesellschaftliche Anspruchsgruppen, in: *Globalisierung und Sozialstandards*, A. G. Scherer, K. H. Blicke, D. Dietzfelbinger and G. Hütter, eds., Rainer Hampp-Verlag, Munich, pp. 77–97.

Marshall, T. H., 1950, *Citizenship and Social Class*, Cambridge University Press, Cambridge.

Martin, J. R., 1994, Methodological essentialism, false difference, and other dangerous traps, *Signs: Journal of Women in Culture and Society* **19**(3):630–657.

Marx, K., 1988, Zur Judenfrage, in: *Werke, 1*, K. Marx and F. Engels, Dietz Verlag, Berlin, pp. 347–377.

Maus, I., 1992, *Zur Aufklärung der Demokratietheorie*, Suhrkamp, Frankfurt.

Maus, I., 1995, Liberties and popular sovereignty: On Jürgen Habermas's reconstruction of the system of rights, *Cardozo Law Review* **17**(4–5):825–883.

Mawdudi, A'la A., 1976, *The Islamic Law and Constitution*, Islamic Publications, Lahore.

Mayer, E., 1991, *Islam and Human Rights. Tradition and Politics*, Westview Press, Boulder CO.

McMahan, J., 1993, Killing, letting die and withdrawing aid, *Ethics* **103**(2):250–279.

McMahan, J., 1998, A challenge to common sense morality, *Ethics* **108**(2):394–418.

Merle, J.-C., 2002, Das Recht der Staaten auf Differenz, in: *Weltrepublik. Globalisierung und Demokratie*, S. Gosepath and J.-C. Merle, eds., Beck Verlag, Munich, pp. 63–73.

Merle, J.-C., ed., 2004, *Globale Gerechtigkeit / Global Justice*, Frommann-Holzboog, Stuttgart Bad-Cannstatt.

Mernissi, F., and Lakeland, M. J., 1993, *Women and Islam*, South Asia Press, Watertown MA.

Michelman, F. I., 2000, Human rights and the limits of constitutional theory, *Ratio Juris* 13(1):63–76.

Milanovic, B., 2002, True world income distribution, 1988 and 1993: First calculation based on household surveys alone, *The Economic Journal* 112:51–92, also available at www.blackwellpublishers.co.uk/specialarticles/ecoj50673.pdf.

Mill, J. S., 1978, *On Liberty* [1859], Hackett, Indianapolis.

Mill, J. S., 1998, *Utilitarianism* [1861], Oxford University Press, Oxford.

Miller, D., 1995, *On Nationality*, Clarendon Press, Oxford.

Miller, D., 1999a, *Principles of Social Justice*, Harvard University Press, Cambridge MA.

Miller, D., 1999b, Justice and global inequality, in: *Inequality, Globalisation and World Politics*, A. Hurrell and N. Woods, eds., Oxford University Press, Oxford, pp. 187–210.

Miller, D., 2000, *Citizenship and National Identity*, Polity Press, Cambridge.

Miller, D., 2001, Distributing responsibilities, *J. of Political Philosophy* 9(4):453–471.

Miller, D., 2004, National responsibility and international justice, in: *The Ethics of Assistance: Morality and the Distant Needy*, D. K. Chatterjee, ed., Cambridge University Press, Cambridge.

Millon-Delsol, C., 1992, *L'État Subsidiaire*, Presses Universitaires de France, Paris.

Moellendorf, D., 2002, *Cosmopolitan Justice*, Westview, Boulder CO.

Mohanty, C. T., 1991, Under Western eyes: Feminist scholarship and colonial discourse, in: *Third World Women and the Politics of Feminism*, C. T. Mohanty, A. Russo and L. Torres, eds., Indiana University Press, Bloomington IN, pp. 51–80.

Monbiot, G., 2003, *The Age of Consent: A Manifesto for a New World Order*, Flamingo, London.

Morgan, R., ed., 1984, *Sisterhood is Global*, Anchor Press/Doubleday, Garden City NY.

Moser, C. O. N., 1991, Gender planning in the Third World: Meeting practical and strategic needs, in: *Gender and International Relations*, R. Grant and K. Newland, eds., Indiana University Press, Bloomington IN, pp. 83–111.

MSF (Médecins Sans Frontières), 2001, *Fatal Imbalance: The Crisis in Research and Development for Drugs for Neglected Diseases*, Médecins Sans Frontières, Geneva.

Murphy, L., 1999, Institutions and the demands of justice, *Philosophy and Public Affairs* 27:251–291.

Murphy, L., 2000, *Moral Demands in Non-Ideal Theory*, Oxford University Press, Oxford.

Nagel, T., 1977, Poverty and food: Why charity is not enough, in: *Food Policy: The Responsibility of the United States in the Life and Death Choices*, P. Brown and H. Shue, eds., The Free Press, New York, pp. 54–62.

Nagel, T., 1979, *Mortal Questions*, Cambridge University Press, Cambridge.

Nagel, T., 2002, *Concealment and Exposure, and other Essays*, Oxford University Press, Oxford.

Narayan, U., 1997, *Dislocating Cultures: Identities, Traditions and Third World Feminism*, Routledge, New York.

Narayan, U., 1998, Essence of culture and a sense of history: A feminist critique of cultural essentialism, *Hypatia* 13(2), reprinted in: *Decentering the Center: Philosophy for a Multicultural, Postcolonial, and Feminist World*, U. Narayan and S. Harding, eds., Indiana University Press, Bloomington IN, 2000.

Nell-Breuning, O. von., 1962, Subsidiaritätsprinzip, in: *Staatslexikon* 7, 6th edition, Görres-Gesellschaft ed., Herder, Freiburg, pp. 826–833.

Nickel, J., 1987, *Making Sense of Human Rights*, University of California Press, Berkeley.

Nierenberg, D., 2002, What's good for women is good for the world, *World Summit Policy Briefs*, Worldwatch Institute, Washington DC.

Niesen, P., 2002, Legitimität ohne Moralität. Habermas und Maus über das Verhältnis zwischen Recht und Moral, in: Schomberg and Niesen 2002, pp. 16–61.

Nozick, R., 1974, *Anarchy, State, and Utopia*, Basic Books, New York.

Nussbaum, M. C., 1988, Nature function and capability: Aristotle on political distribution, *Oxford Studies in Ancient Philosophy*, Supplementary Volume, pp. 145–184.

Nussbaum, M. C., 1990, Aristotelian social democracy, in: *Liberalism and the Good*, R. B. Douglass, G. Mara and H. Richardson, eds., Routledge, New York, pp. 203–252. German trans. 1999 in: *Gerechtigkeit oder das gute Leben*, H. Pauer-Studer, ed., Suhrkamp, Frankfurt, pp. 24–85.

Nussbaum, M. C., 1992, Human functioning and social justice: In defense of Aristotelian essentialism, *Political Theory* 20(2):202–246.

Nussbaum, M. C., 1993, Non-relative virtues: An Aristotelian approach, in: Nussbaum and Sen 1993, pp. 242–269.

Nussbaum, M. C., 1995, Human capabilities, female human beings, in: Nussbaum and Glover 1995, pp. 61–104.

Nussbaum, M. C. (with respondents), 1996, *For Love of Country. Debating the Limits of Patriotism*, Beacon Press, Boston.

Nussbaum, M. C., 1998, Public philosophy and international feminism, *Ethics* 108:762–796.

Nussbaum, M. C., 1999, *Sex and Social Justice*, Oxford University Press, New York.

Nussbaum, M. C., 2000, *Women and Human Development: The Capabilities Approach*, Cambridge University Press, Cambridge.

Nussbaum, M. C., 2002, Sex, laws, and inequality: What India can teach the United States, *Daedalus* (Winter) 95–106.

Nussbaum, M. C., forthcoming, Response to Okin (2003), *Philosophy and Public Affairs*.

Nussbaum, M. C., and Glover, J., eds., 1995, *Women, Culture, and Development. A Study of Human Capabilities*, Clarendon Press, Oxford.

Nussbaum, M. C., and Sen, A. K., 1989, Internal criticism and Indian rationalist traditions, in: *Relativism: Interpretation and Confrontation*, M. Krausz, ed., Notre Dame University Press, Notre Dame, pp. 299–325.

Nussbaum, M. C., and Sen, A. K., eds., 1993, *The Quality of Life*, Clarendon Press, Oxford.

Obiora, L. A., 1997, Feminism, globalization and culture: After Beijing, *Ind. J. Global Legal Studies* 4:355–406.

O'Brien, R., Goetz, A. M., Scholte, J. A., and Williams, M., eds., 2000, *Contesting Global Governance. Multilateral Economic Institutions and Global Social Movements*, Cambridge University Press, Cambridge.

Okin, S. M., 1989, *Justice, Gender and the Family*, Basic Books, New York.

Okin, S. M., 1994, Gender inequality and cultural differences, *Political Theory* 22(1).

Okin, S. M., 1995, Response to Jane Flax, *Political Theory* 23(3).

Okin, S. M., 1998, Feminism and multiculturalism: Some tensions, *Ethics* 108:661–684.

Okin, S. M. (with respondents), 1999, *Is Multiculturalism Bad for Women?*, J. Cohen, M. Howard and M. C. Nussbaum, eds., Princeton University Press, Princeton.

Okin, S. M., 2002, "Mistresses of their own destiny": Group rights, gender, and realistic rights of exit, *Ethics* 112:205–230.

Okin, S. M., 2003, Poverty, well-being, and gender: What counts, who's heard? *Philosophy and Public Affairs* 31(3):280–316.

Oldenburg, V. T., 2002, *Dowry Murder: The Imperial Origins of a Cultural Crime*, Oxford University Press, New York.

Olson, M., 1993, Dictatorship, democracy, and development, *American Political Science Review* **87**:567–76.

O'Neill, O., 1974, Lifeboat earth, *Philosophy and Public Affairs* **4**:273–292.

O'Neill, O., 1986, *Faces of Hunger*, Allen and Unwin, London.

O'Neill, O., 1996, *Towards Justice and Virtue: A Constructive Account of Practical Reasoning*, Cambridge University Press, Cambridge.

O'Neill, O., 2000, *Bounds of Justice*, Cambridge University Press, Cambridge.

O'Neill, O., 2001, Agents of justice, in: Pogge 2001a, pp. 188–203.

Orwell, G., 1952, *Homage to Catalonia* [1938], Harcourt Brace, New York.

Othman, N., 1999, Grounding human rights arguments in non-Western culture: Shari'a and the citizenship rights of women in a modern Islamic state, in: Bauer and Bell 1999, pp. 169–192.

Paech, N., and Stuby, G., 2001, *Völkerrecht und Machtpolitik in den internationalen Beziehungen*, VSA, Hamburg.

Palast, G., 2003, *The Best Democracy Money Can Buy*, revised American edition, Plume, New York.

Pannikar, R., 1982, Is the notion of human rights a Western concept?, *Diogenes* **120**(75):75–102.

Parekh, B., 2000, *Rethinking Multiculturalism: Cultural Diversity and Political Theory*, Harvard University Press, Cambridge MA.

Parfit, D., 1984, *Reasons and Persons*, Oxford University Press, Oxford.

Parfit, D., 1995, *Equality or Priority?*, The Lindley Lectures, University of Kansas.

Peters, B., 1993, *Die Integration moderner Gesellschaften*, Suhrkamp, Frankfurt.

Peterson, V. S., and Runyan, A. S., 1999, *Global Gender Issues*, Westview Press, Boulder CO.

Pieper, S. U., 1994, *Subsidiarität. Ein Beitrag zur Begrenzung der Gemeinschaftskompetenzen*, Heymann, Köln.

Pierson, P., 2001, Coping with permanent austerity: Welfare state restructuring in affluent democracies, in: *The New Politics of the Welfare State*, P. Pierson (ed.), Oxford University Press, Oxford and New York, pp. 410–456.

Pilger, J., 2002, *The New Rulers of the World*, Verso, London.

Pinzani, A., 2003a, *An den Wurzeln moderner Demokratie. Bürger und Staat in der Neuzeit: Ein Blick auf vier Grundmodelle*, Habilitationsschrift presented at the Philosophical Faculty of the University of Tübingen.

Pinzani, A., 2003b, L'equivoco della governance, *Iride* **16**(39):1–12.

Pitkin, H., *The Concept of Representation*, University of California Press, Berkeley.

Plato, 1974, *The Republic*, trans. by G. M. A. Grube, Hackett, Indianapolis.

Pogge, T. W., 1983, *Kant, Rawls, and Global Justice*, University Microfilms International, Ann Arbor.

Pogge, T. W., 1988a, Rawls and global justice, *Canadian Journal of Philosophy* **18**:227–256.

Pogge, T. W., 1988b, Moral progress, in: *Problems of International Justice*, S. Luper-Foy, ed., Westview Press, Boulder CO, pp. 283–305.

Pogge, T. W., 1989, *Realizing Rawls*, Cornell University Press, Ithaca NY.

Pogge, T. W., 1990, The effects of prevalent moral conceptions, *Social Research* **57**(3):649–663.

Pogge, T. W., 1992, Cosmopolitanism and sovereignty, *Ethics* **103**(1):48–75.

Pogge, T. W., 1994, An egalitarian law of peoples, *Philosophy and Public Affairs* **23**(3):195–224.

Pogge, T. W., 1995, Three problems with contractarian-consequentialist ways of assessing social institutions, *Social Philosophy and Policy* **12**(2):241–266, and in: *The Just Society*, E. F. Paul, et al., eds., Cambridge University Press, Cambridge, pp. 241–266.

Pogge, T. W., 1998, A global resources dividend, in: *Ethics of Consumption: The Good Life, Justice, and Global Stewardship*, D. A. Crocker and T. Linden, eds., Rowman and Littlefield, Lanham MD, pp. 501–536.

Pogge, T. W., 2000a, On the site of distributive justice: Reflections on Cohen and Murphy, *Philosophy & Public Affairs* **29**(2):137–169.

Pogge, T. W., 2000b, The international significance of human rights, *The Journal of Ethics* **4**:45–69.

Pogge, T. W., ed., 2001a, *Global Justice*, Blackwell, Oxford.

Pogge, T. W., 2001b, Priorities of global justice, in: Pogge 2001a, pp. 6–23.

Pogge, T. W., 2001c, Rawls on international justice, *Philosophical Quarterly* **51**:246–253.

Pogge, T. W., 2002a, *World Poverty and Human Rights. Cosmopolitan Responsibilities and Reforms*, Polity Press, Cambridge.

Pogge, T. W., 2002b, Human rights and human responsibilities, in: de Greiff and Cronin 2002, pp. 151–195.

Pogge, T. W., 2002c, Globale Verteilungsgerechtigkeit, in: *Weltrepublik. Globalisierung und Demokratie*, S. Gosepath and J.-C. Merle, eds., Beck Verlag, Munich, pp. 220–233.

Pogge, T. W., 2002d, Responsibilities for poverty-related ill health, *Ethics & International Affairs* **16**(2):71–79.

Pogge, T. W., 2004a, "Assisting" the global poor, in: *The Ethics of Assistance: Morality and the Distant Needy*, D. K. Chatterjee, ed., Cambridge University Press, Cambridge, pp. 260–288.

Pogge, T. W., 2004b, The incoherence between Rawls's theories of justice, *Fordham Law Review* **72**(5):1739–1759.

Pogge, T. W., 2005, Moralizing Humanitarian Intervention: Why Jurying Fails and How Law Can Work.: *Humanitarian Intervention*, T. Nardin and M. Williams, eds., NOMOS volume 47, New York University Press, New York.

Pogge, T. W., and Reddy, S. G., 2003, Unknown: The extent, distribution, and trend of global income poverty, available at www.socialanalysis.org.

Pollitt, K., 2002, As Miss World turns, *The Nation*, December.

Proclamation of Teheran, 1968, www.unhchr.ch/html/menu3/b/b_tehern.htm.

Putnam, H., 1990, *Realism with a Human Face*, Harvard University Press, Cambridge MA.

Raffer, K., 2003, Some proposals to adapt international institutions to developmental needs, in: *The Role of International Institutions in Globalisation: The Challenges for Reform*, J. Chen, ed., Edward Elgar, Northampton, pp. 81–101.

Raffer, K., 2004, International financial institutions and financial accountability, *Ethics & International Affairs* **18**(2):61–78.

Ravallion, M., and Chen, S., 1997, What can new survey data tell us about recent changes in distribution and poverty?, *The World Bank Economic Review* **11**:357–382.

Rawls J., 1971, *A Theory of Justice*, Harvard University Press, Cambridge MA. (revised edition 1999).

Rawls, J., 1985 Justice as fairness: Political not metaphysical, *Philosophy and Public Affairs* **14**:223–252.

Rawls, J., 1993a, *Political Liberalism*, Columbia University Press, New York.

Rawls, J., 1993b, The law of peoples, in: *On Human Rights. The Oxford Amnesty Lectures*, S. Shute and S. Hurley, eds., Basic Books, New York, pp. 41–82, 220–230.

Rawls, J., 1999, *The Law of Peoples*, Harvard University Press, Cambridge MA.

Rawls, J., 2001, *Justice as Fairness. A Restatement*, Harvard University Press, Cambridge MA.

Raz, J., 1970, *The Concept of a Legal System*, Clarendon Press, Oxford.

Raz, J., 1975, *Practical Reason and Norms*, Oxford University Press, Oxford.

Raz, J., 1986, *The Morality of Freedom*, Clarendon Press, Oxford.

Reddy, S. G., and Pogge, T. W., 2005, How *not* to count the poor, in an anthology, S. Anand and J. Stiglitz, eds., Oxford University Press, Oxford, also available at www.socialanalysis.org.

Reid, C., 1991, The canonistic contribution to the Western rights tradition: An historical inquiry, *Boston College Law Review* **33**(1):37–92.

Reinicke, W. H., 1998, *Global Public Policy. Governing without Government?* Brookings Institution Press, Washington DC.

Reiss, H., ed., 1970, *Kant's Political Writings*, Cambridge University Press, Cambridge.

Richards, D. A. J., 1982, International distributive justice, in: *Ethics, Economics, and the Law*, R. Pennock and J. Chapman, eds., New York University Press, New York.

Riedel, M., 1993, Menschenrechtsuniversalismus und Patriotismus. Kants politisches Vermächtnis an unsere Zeit, *Allgemeine Zeitschrift für Philosophie* **18**:2–19.

Rig Veda : An Anthology : One Hundred and Eight Hymns, 1981, Trans. W. D. O'Flaherty, Penguin Books, Harmondsworth.

Ripstein, A., 1999, *Equality, Responsibility, and the Law*, Cambridge University Press, Cambridge.

Risse, T., 2000, "Let's argue!": Communicative action in world politics, *International Organization* **54**(1):1–39.

Rodney, W., 1982, *How Europe Underdeveloped Africa*, Howard University Press, Washington DC.

Roemer, J. E., 1993, A pragmatic theory of responsibility for the egalitarian planner, *Philosophy and Public Affairs* **22**:146–166.

Roemer, J. E., 1996, *Theories of Distributive Justice*, Harvard University Press, Cambridge MA.

Roemer, J. E., 1998, *Equality of Opportunity*. Harvard University Press, Cambridge MA.

Roemer, J. E., 2002, Equality of opportunity: A progress report, *Social Choice and Welfare* **19**:455–471.

Rome Declaration on World Food Security, 1996, www.fao.org/wfs.

Rorty, R., 1993, Human rights, rationality, and sentimentality, in: *On Human Rights. The Oxford Amnesty Lectures*, S. Shute and S. Hurley, eds., Basic Books, New York, pp. 111–135.

Rorty, R., 1996, Who are we? Moral universalism and economic triage, *Diogenes* **173**:5–15.

Rosenau, J., 1998, Governance and democracy in a globalizing world, in: *Re-Imagining Political Community*, D. Archibugi, D. Held and M. Köhler, eds., Stanford University Press, Stanford, pp. 28–57.

Ross, M. L., 1999, The political economy of the resource curse, *World Politics* **51**:297–322.

Ruggie, J. G., 2003, Taking embedded liberalism global: The corporate connection, in: *Taming Globalization: Frontiers of Governance*, D. Held and M. Koenig-Archibugi, eds., Polity Press, Cambridge, pp. 93–129.

Sala-i-Martin, X., 2002, The world distribution of income (estimated from individual country distributions), NBER working paper 8933, http://papers.nber.org/papers/w8933.pdf.

Saleem, F., 2003, *The News International* (Pakistan), www.jang.com.pk/thenews/jan2003-daily/12-01-2003/oped/ol.htm, January 15.

Sandel, M., 1982, *Liberalism and the Limits of Justice*, Cambridge University Press, Cambridge.

Sandler, L., 2003, Women under siege, *The Nation*, December 29.

Sansoni, S., 2003, Saving Amina, *Essence*, March, 156–159.

Santos, B. de S., 2001, *Pela Mão de Alice: O Social e o Político na Pós-Modernidade*, Cortez Editora, São Paulo.

Scanlon, T. M., 1998, *What We Owe to Each Other*, Harvard University Press, Cambridge MA.

Scanlon, T. M., 2000, Permissibility and intention, I, *Proceedings of the Aristotelian Society* Supplement, **74**:301–317.

Schachter, O., 1981, The obligation to implement the covenant in domestic law, in: *The International Bill of Rights*, L. Henkin, ed., Columbia University Press, New York.

Schachter, O., 1982, International law in theory and practice: General course in public international law, *Recueil Des Cours* **178**(9):138–149.

Schachter, O., 1984, The legality of pro-democratic invasion, *American Journal of International Law*, **78**:645-50.

Scheffler, S., 2001, *Boundaries and Allegiances*, Oxford University Press, Oxford.

Scheffler, S., 2003, What is egalitarianism? *Philosophy and Public Affairs* **31**(1):5–39.

Schelling, T., 1978, *Micromotives and Macrobehaviour*, Norton, New York.

Schiff, M., and Valdes, A., 1992, *The Plundering of Agriculture in Developing Countries*, World Bank, Washington DC.

Schomberg, R., and Niesen, P., eds., 2002, *Zwischen Recht und Moral. Neuere Ansätze der Rechts- und Demokratietheorie*, LIT Verlag, Münster.

Sen, A. K., 1980, Equality of what?, in: *The Tanner Lectures on Human Values 1*, S. McMurrin, ed., The University of Utah Press, Salt Lake City, pp. 195–220.

Sen, A. K., 1981, *Poverty and Famines: An Essay on Entitlement and Deprivation*, Clarendon Press, Oxford.

Sen, A. K., 1984, *Resources, Values and Development*, Harvard University Press, Cambridge MA.

Sen, A. K., 1985a, *Commodities and Capabilities*, Elsevier, Amsterdam.

Sen, A. K., 1985b, Well-being, agency and freedom. The Dewey lectures 1984, *Journal of Philosophy* **82**(4):169–221.

Sen, A. K., 1988, Property and hunger, *Economics and Philosophy* **4**:57–68.

Sen, A. K., 1990, Millions of women are missing, *New York Review of Books*, December 20.

Sen, A. K., 1992, *Inequality Reexamined*, Harvard University Press, Cambridge MA.

Sen, A. K., 1993, Capability and well-being, in: Nussbaum and Sen 1993, pp. 30-53.

Sen, A. K., 1995, Gender inequality and theories of justice, in: Nussbaum and Glover 1995, pp. 259–273.

Sen, A. K., 1997, Human rights and Asian values: What Lee Kuan Yew and Li Peng don't understand about Asia, *The New Republic* **217**(2–3):33–40.

Sen, A. K., 1999, *Development as Freedom*, Oxford University Press, Oxford.

Sen, A. K., 2002, How to judge globalism, *American Prospect* **13**(1):A2–A6.

Sen, A. K., and Dreze, J., 1990, *Hunger and Public Action*, Oxford University Press, Oxford.

Sen, G., and Grown, C., 1987, *Development, Crises and Alternative Visions: Third World Women's Perspectives*, Monthly Review Press, New York.

Sethi, S. P., 2002, *Setting Global Standards*, John Wiley and Sons, New York.

Shachar, A., 1999, The paradox of multicultural vulnerability: Individual rights, identity groups, and the state, in: *Multicultural Questions*, C. Joppke and S. Lukes, eds., Oxford University Press, New York.

Shachar, A., 2000a, On citizenship and multicultural vulnerability, *Political Theory* **28**:64–89.

Shachar, A., 2000b, The puzzle of interlocking power hierarchies: Sharing the pieces of jurisdictional authority, *Harvard Civil Rights–Civil Liberties Law Review* **35**(2):387–426.

Shapiro, I., and Brilmayer, L., eds., 1999, *Global Justice*, Nomos 41, New York University Press, New York.

Shklar J., 1990, *The Faces of Injustice*, Yale University Press, New Haven.

Shue, H., 1996, *Basic Rights. Subsistence, Affluence, and U.S. Foreign Policy* [1980], Princeton University Press, Princeton.

Sieghart, P., 1985, *The Lawful Rights of Mankind*, Oxford University Press, Oxford.

Silliman, J., 1999, Expanding civil society, shrinking political spaces: The case of women's nongovernmental organizations, in: *Dangerous Intersections: Feminist Perspectives on Population, Environment, and Development*, J. Silliman and Y. King, eds., South End Press, Cambridge MA.

Simon, R. L., 1983, Global justice and the authority of states, *Monist* **66**(4):557–572.

Singer, P., 1972, Famine, affluence, and morality, *Philosophy and Public Affairs* **1**(3):229–243.

Singer, P., 2002, *One World: The Ethics of Globalization*, Yale University Press, New Haven.

Sivaraksa, S., 1991, *Seeds of Peace: A Buddhist Vision for Renewing Society*, Parallax Press, Berkeley and Bangkok.

Sohn, L. B., 1982, The new international law: Protection of the rights of individuals rather than states, *American University Law Review* **32**:1–64.

Spelman, E. V., 1989, *Inessential Woman: Problems of Exclusion in Feminist Thought*, Beacon Press, Boston.

Spivak, G. C., 1988, Can the subaltern speak?, in: *Marxism and the Interpretation of Culture*, C. Nelson and L. Grossberg, eds., University of Illinois Press, Urbana, pp. 271–313.

Stapleton, J. 1988, Law, causation and common sense, *Oxford J. of Legal Studies* **8**(1):111–131.

Statute of the ICJ (*International Court of Justice*), 1945, available at www.icj-cij.org/icjwww/ibasicdocuments/Basetext/istatute.htm.

Stepanians, M., 2005, O'Neill über die Notwendigkeit einer Institutionalisierung von Wohlfahrtsrechten, in: *Gerechtigkeit. Auf der Suche nach einem Gleichgewicht*, O. Neumaier, C. Sedmak and M. Zichy, eds., Ontos-Verlag, Frankfurt.

Stiglitz, J., 2002, *Globalization and Its Discontents*, Penguin Books, Harmondsworth.

Stoppino, M., 1990, Potere, in: *Dizionario di politica*, N. Bobbio, N. Matteucci and G. Pasquino, eds., TEA, Milano, pp. 838–847.

Strauss, L., 1953, *Natural Right and History*, The University of Chicago Press, Chicago.

Striker, G., 1996, *Essays on Hellenistic Epistemology and Ethics*, Cambridge University Press, Cambridge.

Sturdevant, S., 2001, Who benefits? US military, prostitution and base conversion, in: *Frontline Feminisms: Women, War, and Resistance*, M. R. Waller and J. Rycenga, eds., Routledge, New York and London. pp. 141–157.

Summers, L., and Pritchett, L. H., 1993, The structural-adjustment debate, *The American Economic Review* **83**(2):383–389.

Swift, A., 2004, Justice, luck and the family, in: *Unequal Chances: Social Background and Economic Success*, S. Bowles, H. Gintis and M. Osborne, eds., Princeton University Press, Princeton.

Syse, H., 2002, Which nature, whose law, and what about rights? Reflections on the natural law as a tradition of universal ethics, in: *Universal Ethics — Perspectives and Proposals from Scandinavian Scholars*, G. Bexell and D.-E. Andersson, eds., Kluwer and Nijhoff, The Hague, pp. 33–43.

Syse, H., 2005, *Natural Law, Religion, and Rights*, St. Augustine's Press, South Bend IN.

Taha, M. M., 1987, *The Second Message of Islam*, Syracuse University Press, Syracuse NY.

Tan, K.-C., 2000, *Toleration, Diversity, and Global Justice*, The Pennsylvania State University Press, University Park.

Tatsuo, I., 1999, Liberal democracy and Asian orientalism, in: Bauer and Bell 1999, pp. 27–59.

Taylor, C., 1999, Conditions of an unforced consensus on human rights, in: Bauer and Bell 1999, pp. 124–144.

Teubner, G., 1996, *Global Law Without a State*, Dartmouth Publishing Group, Dartmouth.

Thomson, J., 1984, Remarks on causality and liability, *Philosophy and Public Affairs* 13(2):101–133.

Tierney, B., 1997, *The Idea of Natural Rights*, Scholars Press, Atlanta.

Tobin, J., 1978, A proposal for international monetary reform, *Eastern Economic Journal* 4:153–159.

Tomlinson, J., 1991, *Cultural Imperialism: A Critical Introduction*, Johns Hopkins University Press, Baltimore MD.

Tomuschat, C., 1985, International standards and cultural diversity, *Bulletin of Human Rights* Special Issue.

Transparency International, 1998, Mission statement, reprinted in: *Access to Information in Developing Countries*, R. Martin and E. Feldman, Commonwealth Secretariat, London.

Tugendhat, E., 1993, *Vorlesungen zur Ethik*, Suhrkamp, Frankfurt.

Tugendhat, E., 1997, Gleichheit und Universalität in der Moral, in: *Ernst Tugendhat: Moralbegründung und Gerechtigkeit*, M. Willaschek, ed., LIT Verlag, Münster, pp. 3–25.

UDHR (Universal Declaration of Human Rights), 1948, in: *Twenty-Four Human Rights Documents*, Columbia University Center for the Study of Human Rights, New York 1992.

UN Millennium Declaration, General Assembly Resolution 55/2, 2000, www.un.org/millennium/declaration/ares552e.htm.

UNCTAD (United Nations Conference on Trade and Development), 1993, *World Investment Report*, Executive Summary, UN Publications, New York.

UNCTAD, 1999, *Trade and Development Report 1999*, UN Publications, New York.

UNDP (United Nations Development Programme), 1998, *Human Development Report 1998*, Oxford University Press, New York.

UNDP, 1999a, *Human Development Report 1999*, Oxford University Press, New York.

UNDP, 1999b, Facts and Figures on Poverty, www.undp.org/teams/english/facts.htm.

UNDP, 2000, *Human Development Report 2000*, Oxford University Press, New York, also available at www.undp.org/hdr2000/english/HDR2000.html.

UNDP, 2001, *Human Development Report 2001*. Oxford University Press, New York, also available at www.undp.org/hdr2001.

UNDP, 2002, *Human Development Report 2002*, Oxford University Press, New York, also available at www.undp.org/hdr2002.

UNDP, 2003, *Human Development Report 2003*, Oxford University Press, New York, also available at www.undp.org/hdr2003.

UNDP, 2004, *Human Development Report 2004*, UNDP, New York, also available at http://hdr.undp.org/reports/global/2004/.

UNDPI (United Nations Department of Public Information), 2002, *Building Partnerships: Cooperation Between the United Nations System and the Private Sector*, United Nations, New York.

Unger, P., 1996, *Living High and Letting Die: Our Illusion of Innocence*. Oxford University Press, Oxford.

Unger, R., 1998, *Democracy Realized: The Progressive Alternative*, Verso, London.

UNICEF (United Nations Children's Fund), 2002, *The State of the World's Children 2002*, UNICEF, New York, also at www.unicef.org/sowc02/pdf/sowc2002-eng-full.pdf.

UNIFEM (United Nations Development Fund for Women), 2000: *Progress of the World's Women*, UNIFEM, New York.

Universal Islamic Declaration of Human Rights, 1981, www.alhewar.com/islamdecl.html.

UNSCR 56/263, 2002 (*United Nations Security Council Resolution on the Role of Diamonds in Fuelling Conflict*, United Nations, New York, February 6.

USDA (United States Department of Agriculture), 1999a, *U.S. Action Plan on Food Security*, USDA, Washington DC., also available at www.fas.usda.gov/icd/summit/usactplan.pdf.

USDA, 1999b, *Thrifty Food Plan, 1999: Administrative Report*, USDA Center for Nutrition Policy and Promotion, Washington DC, also available at www.usda.gov/cnpp/FoodPlans/TFP99/TFP99Report.pdf.

Utz, A. F., ed., 1953, *Das Subsidiaritätsprinzip*, Kerle, Heidelberg.

van Boven, T., 1982, The broadening and deepening of the human rights programme, in: *People Matter: Views on International Human Rights Policy*, Meulenhoff, Amsterdam, pp. 28-39.

van Bulert, V., 1995, Raja Rammohun Roy's thought and its relevance for human rights, in: An-Na'im, Gort, Jansen and Vroom 1995, pp. 93–108.

van Hoof, F., 1984, The legal nature of economic, social and cultural rights: A rebuttal of some traditional views, in: *The Right to Food*, P. Alston and K. Tomasevski, eds., M. Nijhoff, The Hague, pp. 16–29.

Van Parijs P., 1993, Rawlsians, Christians and patriots. Maximin justice and individual ethics, *European Journal of Philosophy* 1:309–342.

Van Parijs P., 1995, *Real Freedom for All. What (if Anything) can Justify Capitalism?*, Oxford University Press, Oxford.

Van Parijs P., 2002, *What's Wrong with a Free Lunch?*, Beacon Press, Boston.

Vetlesen, A. J., 1993, Why does proximity make a moral difference?, *Praxis International* 12(4):371–386.

Vincent, R. J., 1986, *Human Rights and International Relations*, Cambridge University Press, Cambridge.

Visvanathan, N., 1997, Introduction to part I, in: *The Women, Gender and Development Reader*, N. Vivvanathan (Co-Ordinator), L. Duggan, L. Nisonoff and N. Wiegersma, eds., Zed Press, London.

Volpp, L., 2000, Blaming culture for bad behavior, *Yale Journal of Law and Humanities* 12:89–116.

Volpp, L., 2001, Feminism versus multiculturalism, *Columbia Law Review* 101(5):1181–1218.

Waldron, J., 1992, Superseding historical injustice, *Ethics* 103(1):4–28.

Waldron, J., 1993, *Liberal Rights*, Cambridge University Press, Cambridge.

Waldron, J., 1995, Moments of carelessness and massive loss, in: *The Philosophical Foundations of Tort Law*, D. G. Owen, ed., Oxford University Press, Oxford, pp. 387–408.

Wallerstein, I., 1979, *The Capitalist World Economy*, Cambridge University Press, Cambridge.

Wallerstein, I., 2000, *The Essential Wallerstein*, New Press, New York.

Walzer, M., 1977, *Just and Unjust Wars*, Basic Books, New York.

Walzer, M., 1980, The moral standing of states, *Philosophy and Public Affairs* 9:209–229.

Walzer, M., 1983, *Spheres of Justice*, Basic Books, New York.

Walzer, M., 1990, The communitarian critique of liberalism, *Political Theory* 18(1):4–26.

Wantchekon, L., 1999, Why do resource dependent countries have authoritarian governments?, working paper, Yale University, December 12, www.yale.edu/leitner/pdf/1999-11.pdf.

Watal, J., 2000, Access to essential medicines in developing countries: Does the WTO TRIPS agreement hinder it?, *Science, Technology and Innovation Discussion Paper No. 8,* Harvard Center for International Development, available at www2.cid.harvard.edu/cidbiotech/dp/discussion8.pdf.

Waterfield, R., ed., and trans., 2000, *The First Philosophers: The Presocratics and the Sophists*, Oxford University Press, Oxford.

Weber, M., 1972, Politics as a vocation, in: *From Max Weber*, H. H. Gerth and C. W. Mills, eds., Oxford University Press, New York, pp. 77–128.

Weinstock, D., 2002, Miller on distributive justice, in: Bell and de-Shalit 2002, pp. 269–286.

Weiss, A., 2003, Interpreting women's rights: The dilemma over eliminating discrimination against women in Pakistan, *International Sociology* 18(3):581–601.

Wellman, C. H., 2000, Relational facts in liberal political theory: Is there magic in the pronoun 'my'?, *Ethics* 110:537–562.

Wellmer, A., 2000, Der Streit um Wahrheit. Pragmatismus ohne regulative Ideen, in: *Die Renaissance des Pragmatismus. Aktuelle Verflechtungen zwischen analytischer und kontinentaler Philosophie*, M. Sandbothe, ed., Velbrück Wissenschaft, Weilerswist, pp. 253–270.

Wenar, L., 2002, The legitimacy of peoples, in: de Greiff and Cronin 2002, pp. 53–76.

Wenar, L., 2003a, What we owe to distant others, *Politics, Philosophy and Economics* 2(3):283–304.

Wenar, L., 2003b, Human rights and responsibility, manuscript.

Wenar, L., 2004, The unity of Rawls's work, *The Journal of Moral Philosophy.* 1(3).

Wessels, A., 1995, 'Ali Shari'ati and human rights, in: A. A. An-Na'im, J. D. Gort, H. Jansen and H. M. Vroom eds., pp. 243–255.

Weston, B., 1992, Human rights, in: *New Encyclopaedia Britannica* 15th ed., 20:654–667.

White Paper on Human Rights, 1991, published by China's State Council Information Office, www.china.org.cn/e-white/7/7-I.htm

White, S., 2002, Republicanism, patriotism, and global justice, in: Bell and de-Shalit 2002, pp. 251–268.

WHO (World Health Organization), 2004, *The World Health Report 2004*, WHO Publications, Geneva, also available at www.who.int/whr/2004.

Wildt, A., 1998, Menschenrechte und moralische Rechte, in: Gosepath and Lohmann 1998, pp. 124–146.

Wilke, H., 1983, *Entzauberung des Staates. Überlegungen zu einer sozietalen Steuerungstheorie*, Athenäum, Königstein.

Williams, A., 1998, Incentives, inequality, and publicity, *Philosophy and Public Affairs* 27:225–247.

Williams, R., 1983, *Keywords: A Vocabulary of Culture and Society*, second edition, Fontana, London.

Winston, M., 2002, NGO strategies for promoting corporate responsibility, *Ethics and International Affairs* 16(1):71–88.

Wood, A., 1995, *Limits to Autocracy: From Sung Neo Confucianism to a Doctrine of Political Rights*, University of Hawaii Press, Honolulu.

Woolridge, F., 2003, Letter to the editor of the *Colorado Daily*, November 18, p. 10.

World Bank, 1999, *World Development Report 1999/2000*, Oxford University Press, New York, also available at www.worldbank.org/wdr/2000/fullreport.html.

World Bank, 2000, *World Development Report 2000/2001*, Oxford University Press, New York.

World Bank, 2002, *Globalization, Growth, and Poverty*, Oxford University Press, New York, also available at http://econ.worldbank.org/prr/globalization/text-2857.

World Bank, 2003, *World Development Report 2003*, Oxford University Press, New York.

World Bank, 2004, *World Development Report 2004*, Oxford University Press, New York.

Wright, R. W., 1985, Causation in tort law, *California Law Review* **73**:1737–1828.

Wright, R. W., 2001, Once more into the bramble bush: Duty, causal contribution and the extent of legal responsibility, *Vanderbilt Law Review* **54**(3):1071–1132.

Yasuaki, O., 1999, Towards an intercivilizational approach to human rights, in: Bauer and Bell 1999, pp. 103–123.

Young, I. M., 2003a, The logic of masculinist protection: Reflections on the current security state, *Signs: Journal of Women in Culture and Society* **29**(11):1–25.

Young, I. M., 2003b, From guilt to solidarity: Sweatshops and political responsibility, *Dissent* **3**:39–44.

Young, I. M., forthcoming, Responsibility for global labor justice, *J. of Political Philosophy*.

Yuval-Davis, N., 1997, *Gender and Nation*, Sage Publications, London.

Zolo, D., 1995, Cosmopolis. La Prospettiva del Governo Mondiale, Feltrinelli, Milan.

Printed in the United Kingdom
by Lightning Source UK Ltd.
124720UK00015B/41/A